The Man Who Invented
Rock Hudson

THE PRETTY BOYS AND DIRTY DEALS OF HENRY WILLSON

Robert Hofler

CARROLL & GRAF PUBLISHERS

NEW YORK

To agents and managers. Love them or loathe them,
movie dreams don't get made without them.

THE MAN WHO INVENTED ROCK HUDSON

Carroll & Graf Publishers
An Imprint of Avalon Publishing Group Inc.
245 West 17th Street
New York, NY 10011

AVALON
publishing group incorporated

ISBN: 0-7867-1607-X

Printed in the United States of America
Interior design by Maria E. Torres
Distributed by Publishers Group West

CONTENTS

ACKNOWLEDGMENTS

Major contributors to this biography include Carroll & Graf's Don Weise, Maria E. Torres, and John Morrone; ICM's Mitch Douglas, Buddy Thomas, and Emily Snider; Photofest's Howard Mandelbaum; and my personal line editors, Holly Millea and Marilyn Stasio. Big thanks are also due Army Archerd, James T. Ballard, Peter Bloch, Teresa Cebrian, Peter Da Fransa, Juan Davila, David Ehrenstein, Evan Fong, Val Holley, Richard Lamparsky, P. Frank Lin, E. M. McManus, William J. Mann, Eric Myers, Richard Natale, Jane Nunez, Daniel Selznick, Thomas Tapp, Leslie Van Buskirk, and the dedicated librarians at the American Film Institute, Los Angeles Public Library, Margaret Herrick Library at the Academy of Motion Pictures Arts & Sciences, New York Public Library for the Performing Arts at Lincoln Center, One Institute, Ransom Center at the University of Texas at Austin, 20th Century Fox Archives at UCLA, and Warners Archives at USC. I am especially grateful to the over two hundred people who agreed to be interviewed, either on- or off-the-record, for this book.

INTRODUCTION

HOLLYWOOD'S ADONIS FACTORY

O
n November 29, 1954, *The Hollywood Reporter's* gossip columnist Mike Connolly wrote about the proud, happiest day of Rock Hudson's life. The movie star had just been cast in George Stevens's cattle-and-oil epic *Giant,* and Connolly's one-line blurb commemorating Rock's celebration party was as cryptic as it was pumped with news ready to break: "Saturday Mo-somes: Phyllis Gates & Rock Hudson, Margaret Truman & Henry Willson."

In one of his rare acts of discretion, newshound Connolly dispensed with the ampersand that should have wedded the names Rock Hudson and Henry Willson. Fifty years into the future, "Mo-somes" could be read as slang for the two men's sexual orientation. But not in 1954. Back then, "Mo" meant something far less provocative but nearly as colorful.

"Mo" was short for the Mocambo, the Mount Olympus of Sunset Strip nightclubs. Pure tinseltown fantasy, the Mocambo was an overheated study in contrasts where oversized tin flowers and humongous velvet balls with fringe festooned flaming candy-cane columns that framed a dance floor designed to induce claustrophobia when more than two couples got up to fox-trot. The tables were equally minuscule, making it possible for the establishment to charge lots of money for not much food, which nobody could see. Overhead, rococo candelabras gave off so little illumination that revelers kept bumping into each other by mistake, and sometimes not, as they tried to check themselves out in the flecked mirrors that recast everybody's reflection in tones of warm, flattering, fake gold.

Into this hothouse of sensory overload dropped Rock Hudson and his agent, Henry Willson, the "notorious" starmaker extraordinaire who had discovered, renamed, trained, and groomed, and sometimes romanced, dozens of young men to be movie stars, if not great actors. Like everything else in his handsome protégés' lives, Henry arranged all the details of Rock Hudson's *Giant* party at Mo: the reservations to see Lillian Roth perform "Sing You Sinners," the vintage of Chateau de Rayne-Vigneau, the A-list table off the dance floor, the steep $2-a-head cover charge, and most crucial to the overall hetero tableau, his and Rock's very female dates.

Phyllis Gates was Henry's new, eager-to-please secretary; and Henry told people, only half-jokingly, that the wholesome Minnesota farm girl and Rock might one day get married. Margaret Truman was President Harry Truman's daughter, the one who fancied herself a concert singer against most critics' better judgment; and Henry told people, more than half-seriously, that America's bovine First Daughter and he were secretly engaged.

As Phyllis talked and Margaret listened politely to her date's secretary, the two men at their table proceeded to drink too much. Not that there was enough champagne to make Henry forget the clouds of scandal ready to burst three thousand miles away in the Gotham offices of *Confidential* magazine at 1697 Broadway.

Intoxicated on the alcohol and his new success, Rock was telling Margaret and Phyllis about Grace Kelly and Sterling Hayden, rumored to be his costars in *Giant*. An unusually self-deprecating celebrity, he tried not to brag, but director George Stevens had cast Rock first among the film's three leads, and it was well known around town that Clark Gable, Alan Ladd, and William Holden, fresh from his Oscar win for *Stalag 17*, had lobbied fiercely to star as *Giant*'s Bick Benedict, owner of half a million head of cattle and the most eligible bachelor in all of Texas. Rock's thank-you telegram to Stevens a few days earlier had declared the twenty-eight-year-old actor to be "walking in clouds."

And into a storm of controversy.

If Rock Hudson worried, Henry Willson worried a little more about the blackmail threats emanating from the least-respected and the most-read scandal sheet in America. At least two of Rock's ex-boyfriends had already received offers of $10,000 each to tell their story to *Confidential*. So far, no one was talking.

Emptying another bottle of the champagne, Henry couldn't help but wonder where *Confidential* was getting its information. He knew their source wasn't Ed Muhl. The Universal-International executive had a wife and kids to protect from rumors of an affair with the studio's newest, biggest star. For Ed Muhl, it was love. For Rock Hudson, it was fame. Their afternoon trysts in the VP's office had led to Rock's starring in the remake of *Magnificent Obsession* at Universal and now *Giant* at rival Warner Bros. Hopelessly smitten, Muhl had approved the deal to loan out Rock in a record seven days, making him the last person in Hollywood to squeal on the star.

Rock proposed a toast to his breakthrough success. Henry hadn't been listening to him when Lillian Roth, enshrined in more chiffon than a dozen prom queens, glided by. "Sing you sinners, sing," she sang. A recovering alcoholic, Roth was enjoying a big comeback due to her tell-all best-selling autobiography, *I'll Cry Tomorrow,* which had been ghostwritten by the *Reporter*'s Mike Connolly. "Beat your broken wings / Look up from the ashes / Of your dreams . . ." Then she disappeared up the aisle to her dressing room.

Seeing three other champagne flutes lifted, Henry played along. Congratulations! Cheers to the new year—1955 would be the best.

And as events played out, the very worst.

Giant made Rock Hudson the most popular movie star in the world for seven consecutive years, but that fame required a sacrifice of his agent/Pygmalion. Rock would be spared exposure as a homosexual on one condition: the reputations of two other Galateas from Willson's male stable had to be offered up.

Henry's first choice constituted the most difficult betrayal of his life: in its May 1955 issue, *Confidential* published "Rory Calhoun, But for the Grace of God, Still a Convict," which exposed the many armed-robbery convictions of the man Henry personally transformed into a rugged leading man.

His second choice, however, qualified as pure revenge: Four months after the Calhoun exposé, *Confidential* unleashed the September 1955 profile "The Truth About Tab Hunter's Pajama Party," which laid bare the star's police arrest in 1950 with two dozen other men. In a classic case of bad timing for the blond heartthrob, Tab Hunter had made the potentially career-crippling error of firing Henry earlier that summer.

Ink worked. So did muscle. In between *Confidential*'s reports on Rory and Tab, Henry hired Nick "PI to the Stars" Duber, with his Rolodex of off-duty LAPD goons, to take care of tabloid informers.

The locusts, however, were less easily silenced. While *Confidential* continued to snoop, respectable *Life* magazine spilled the dirt in its October 3, 1955, issue: "Fans are urging twenty-nine-year-old Hudson to get married—or explain why not."

To that end, Henry Willson gave Rock Hudson exactly one month. The groom-to-be asked only one thing: Rock wanted Phyllis Gates to wear brown to their wedding. Otherwise, it was a Henry Willson affair all the way: the November 9 date, the Trinity Lutheran Church in Santa Barbara, the bride's bouquet of carnations, roses, and gardenias. Henry thought of everything, right down to the photo-appropriate twin beds in the newlyweds' honeymoon suite at the Biltmore Hotel, where he and his client used to rendezvous in simpler, carefree, gayer days. Henry even placed phone calls to Hedda Hopper and Louella Parsons, who dutifully broke the glorious news replete with interviews from the happy threesome: Rock, Phyllis, and Henry.

For the moment, Rock Hudson's career was safe. The secret, however, was not. Hollywood and its homosexuals would never be able to hide in plain sight again.

PART ONE

Mr. and Mrs. Roy Fitzgerald: Rock and Phyllis break the news of their nuptials
from a twin-bed suite at Santa Barbara's Biltmore Hotel, November 9, 1955.

1

Rock Tab Troy

Hollywood suffered a chronic case of romantic schizo-phrenia in the 1950s. To the left side of the movie screen slouched the neurotic, tormented likes of Marlon Brando, Montgomery Clift, and James Dean, with Paul Newman the evolu-tionary link to Warren Beatty. The patently idealized males on the right, however, belonged virtually to one man: a beefy, tough-talking, chronically phobic, archconservative homosexual named Henry Willson.

The beast among his beauties, he willed to stardom those curi-ously wholesome hunks that, for convenience sake, could be lumped together as Rock Tab Troy.

Hudson, Hunter, and Donahue (not their real surnames) led a homogenized herd that came to overpopulate the Hollywood Hills in the years following World War II. Nicknamed "Henry's boys," they included Rory Calhoun, Guy Madison, Clint Walker, Clint Ritchie, Craig Stevens, Chad Everett, John Saxon, Mike "Touch" Connors, John Derek, John Smith, Nick Adams, Keith Andes, Dack Rambo, and Guy Williams—not to mention Grant Williams, Van Williams, Robert Wagner, Nick Nolte, and John Gavin, who somehow got to keep their family names (or variations thereof), as did the agent's one Gallic discovery, Alain Delon. Henry parented them all and took no less pride in—and spent no fewer dollars on—those men who brought up the rear, such long-forgotten items of overheated machismo as Cal Bolder, Rad Fulton, Rand Saxon, Race Gentry, Chance Gentry, and Chance Nesbitt.

"I use names over again," Henry said, as if he were talking about washcloths or paper clips. "I gave that Chance name to one man already, but he's not using it. He went back to Paul." Catchy, iterative, marquee-size monikers were his trademark. They were also his undoing, and like so much roadside refuse, the names eventually littered Henry's nasty slide into notoriety.

The Untouchables star Robert Stack described the *sprachgefühl* of his friend Henry Willson. "When you start out with the premise that you'll give someone a name and develop a character that fits that name, you need a sense of ironic humor," said Stack. "Willson had that ironic humor."

The names were cute. The men were sexy. Henry was neither.

In the beginning, Henry Willson took it as a compliment that people mistook him for the Hollywood royalty of Judy Garland's balding, slack-jawed, husband-director Vincente Minnelli. When the years added much poundage to his pear-shaped frame, Henry also smiled when people confused him with Commie-hunting Senator Joseph McCarthy. People said it was the eyes. And they were right: both Joe and Henry saw the world through dark eyes that appeared half asleep but were always ready for attack under the hiding place of thick, abundant eyebrows.

Henry didn't care that neither Minnelli nor McCarthy were attractive men. When it came to being drop-dead handsome, he knew it was better to behold than be.

If heterosexual men can be accused of womanizing, then Henry Willson was the ultimate *manizer*. He made the seduction of men his vocation and elevated cruising to a full-time, lucrative career. He found Robert Wagner singing in a nightclub, Clint Walker working as a Las Vegas bouncer, Tab Hunter skating at an ice rink, Race Gentry pumping gas at a filling station, Alain Delon dancing in a Cannes disco, and John Saxon staring out at him from the cover of a dime-store detective magazine. "The next thing I knew, my mom and dad were signing agreement contracts because I was still under age," said Carmen Orrico, the Brooklyn boy who found himself renamed John Saxon in Hollywood.

As Henry was fond of saying, "The acting can be added later."

Sailor boys like Rock Hudson and Guy Madison barely knew how to walk, much less emote, in front of a camera before fate brought them to Henry Willson. As a talent scout, Henry fixated on servicemen and, after much buffing and spit, he offered up these postwar icons as a new kind of hypermasculine movie hero. When audiences tired of one, he made it his business to have another, if not six or seven, primed for action in any given season. In the late 1940s, his Adonis factory arrived on the eve of Levittown, Holiday Inn, and McDonald's. If homes, hotels, and hamburgers could be mass-produced, then why not movie hunks?

The original queer eye for the straight guy, Henry Willson gave heterosexual men the necessary grace and social polish to shine in Hollywood's better executive suites, nightclubs, and Bel Air homes. He was equally effective at teaching gay men how to butch it up and pass for lovers of women on the big screen. Whichever way he cut the mold, Henry pursued the male ideal. And if the perfect *objet trouvé* occasionally failed to materialize on the beach, at the bar, or in his office, Henry produced it in bulk regardless.

When Hugh Hefner launched *Playboy* in 1953, Henry Willson had already cornered the other end of the flesh market by spawning male icons as interchangeable with one another as Bunnies—and as representative of their creator's personal sex fantasies as Hef's centerfolds were of his. There was only one fundamental difference between the two. Whereas the *Playboy* publisher made his hyper-heterosexuality the lynchpin of the magazine's marketing campaign, Henry tried to keep his sexual orientation a secret by obscuring the outré reality with a series of "engagements" that ran the gamut from pianist-actress Diana Lynn to America's First Daughter Margaret Truman.

It was a ploy that, for many years, allowed hetero Hollywood to look the other way and give Henry enough room to turn his greatest social liability into his biggest calling card. "It's like discovering that a lesbian was responsible for the *Playboy* Bunny," Troy Donahue said of his agent.

Fortunately for Henry and his stable of boys, the irony quickly evaporated somewhere over Middle America. "He smells of milk," *Look* magazine toasted Rock Hudson in 1957, when the Motion Picture Film Buyers' poll rated the star number one at the box office.

A few years later, the smell wasn't so fresh. For most of Henry Willson's career, the credo of the closet, together with his extreme political and social conservatism, kept him protected. As long as he could practice homosexuality to excess, he was content never to mention it in public. However, even that veneer of respectability began to peel away as soon as Henry arranged for his secretary Phyllis Gates to wed Rock Hudson. Designed to halt gossip about the actor's homosexuality, the marriage did quell public inquiries, but it constituted a union of such mythic inconvenience and obvious contrivance that Hollywood insiders couldn't help but laugh, leaving all three players exposed. The word soon slipped out to tarnish other reputations in the Willson bestiary. Justified or not, the catchy nomenclature that linked these men to their maker became code for the biggest, longest-running gay casting couch in Hollywood history.

Over the ensuing decades, it has not been an easy legend.

Frank Rich's obit of Troy Donahue in the *Sunday New York Times* refers to Henry Willson as "rapacious." Rock Hudson biographers Jerry Oppenheimer and Sara Davidson call him, respectively, "a disgusting person" and "a notorious homosexual" who "exuded evil."

Roddy McDowall explained the trouble with Henry: "He was like the slime that oozed out from under a rock you did not want to turn over. He sought sexual favors from many young men. I'm so glad I didn't become a Willson client," said the once child star of *Lassie Come Home*.

Some survivors give a more sympathetic nuance to the legacy.

"Anyone today who knows the name Henry Willson, knows that it has a smarmy reputation. But his life was not just that," said Robert Osborne, the host of Turner Classic Movies and, in the 1950s, a Willson client. "For anyone starting out as an actor, Henry Willson was the most powerful agent in Hollywood. And he helped a lot of people. His life is tragic, really. Henry loved Hollywood more than anyone."

"Henry Willson was much more than an agent," said Rock Hudson's longtime publicist Dale Olson. "He was Hollywood's first manager."

In addition to the many men he represented, Henry launched the careers of Lana Turner and Joan Fontaine. He got Natalie Wood her breakthrough role of Judy in *Rebel without a Cause*, and he funneled Gena Rowlands into many TV projects, which, in turn, helped to pay for husband John Cassavetes's seminal independent feature, *Faces*.

But it is the many men who made the Henry Willson legend (and ultimately unmade his reputation). For Bruce Weber's documentary *Gentle Giants*, the famed photographer chose Henry's first boy, Guy Madison, to eulogize as the prototypic post–World War II male sex symbol. How fitting that Henry should name his prototype so generically—Guy!—and that Weber would endlessly reproduce that same startlingly vacant masculine perfection, unadulterated by personality or talent, to sell everything from cologne to boxer shorts for Calvin Klein, Ralph Lauren, and Abercrombie & Fitch. A thousand testosterone-drenched ad campaigns later, the man who invented Rock Hudson still holds the patent.

"Everybody wants to be a star!" Henry Willson claimed in 1949, the year he put Roy Fitzgerald under contract at the Pretty People Studio, a.k.a. Universal-International. "But *I'm* the star!"

2

Polishing the Rock

I t was the story that launched a thousand Greyhounds to the door of Henry Willson, starmaker.

According to Rock Hudson's official Universal-International bio, the man born Roy Fitzgerald first met his mentor in 1947 on a mail delivery to the offices of David O. Selznick Productions. After a long stint as a Hollywood agent, Henry Willson was then working as head of talent for the producer of *Gone with the Wind*. Officially, his job included finding and signing new actors and directors to contracts. Unofficially, he pimped for Selznick and acted as beard for the mogul's paramour, actress Jennifer Jones. When Henry and Roy first met, it is unlikely they discussed either of these private, venereal duties—or, for that matter, the Post Office Department. After a tour in the navy as a mechanic, the twenty-one-year-old truck driver delivered peas and carrots for Budget Pack, a frozen-foods company, and hadn't worked for the postal service since he left home in Winnetka, Illinois, three years earlier.

In time, Rock Hudson chose to alter his tale of postal genesis. In this second, more likely version, he recalled going to a professional photographer and spending $25 on portraits, which he sent to every agent and talent scout in town. Only one man bothered to respond. In his hunt for actors, the industrious Henry Willson held great respect for serendipity, and when the U.S. mail failed to deliver anything of interest, Selznick had instructed him to cruise the local high schools and peruse the *Los Angeles Times'* lingerie ads to find his future stars.

For his part, Roy Fitzgerald bought a new tweed suit to meet Henry Willson. After investing in photographs, he wanted to make a good first impression and so splurged another $40 on the interview uniform. "I'd never owned a real suit. My idea of getting dressed up was to put on a sports coat and a red satin tie," he said. "The suit was so big for me that when the pants were taken in, the two hip pockets were next door to each other."

If he noticed Rock's backside, Henry saw nothing there to criticize. He liked a little shabbiness in his delivery boys, if for no other reason than to replace it with his own personal stamp of East Coast privilege and good taste. "It was September 1947," Rock recalled. "I don't think anything important ever happened to me until I walked into Willson's office that day."

Herbert Millspaugh, a retired clerk in San Francisco, told yet a third story of how Roy Fitzgerald joined forces with the Selznick talent scout. His version portrayed the callow Roy as a more seasoned operator than most truckers making their tortuous way through the Hollywood Hills. According to Millspaugh, Roy came to Los Angeles right out of the navy. It didn't matter that he had never acted professionally and, indeed, could not act. Growing up with a *Photoplay* subscription in Winnetka, Roy read between the lines and knew instinctively that some routes to stardom required no skills in the dramatic arts.

Tall enough to pass for a movie star, the six-foot-five Roy served up his other major attributes by driving his Budget Pack truck to every movie studio in town and posing near the gate in his driver's uniform, a Teamsters' badge proudly displayed over his considerable chest. When that gambit didn't attract the attention of someone on the inside, he slept with someone influential on the outside. At least, Ken Hodges told Roy that he was influential.

In the early 1940s, Hodges had produced some shows for *Lux Radio Theatre*, and since the truck driver from Illinois was already living with him, the erstwhile producer sweetened the deal by promising to return to show business as his agent.

Millspaugh insisted it was Hodges and a few of his buddies who coined the name Rock Hudson on a warm, boozy Sunday afternoon in Long Beach. Hodges kept an apartment at the Villa Riviera, which offered the twin conveniences of being near the ocean as well as the town's gay cruising area. Like most weekends, a few friends dropped by to say hello to Ken and Roy, and after several gin and tonics they did what gay men do under the circumstances and began to imagine their ultimate sex fantasy. "Ken wanted a name that suggested strength," said Millspaugh. "Someone came up with Rock. Then we looked through the Long Beach phone book to find a second name that sounded right. We came up with Hudson." Everything else written about how the name came to be was "pure malarkey," said Millspaugh. "It originated in Long Beach on that long-ago Sunday afternoon."

Millspaugh also claimed that the newly christened Rock Hudson first met Henry not at the Selznick studios but at a party hosted by Hodges in Hollywood. Given his *Lux Radio Theatre* connection, it's possible Henry and Hodges knew each other. And given Henry's knack for discovering new talent, it's also possible he wasted no time inviting Roy to his cramped, ground-floor nidus at the Selznick studios.

"And when he left," Millspaugh said, "Roy had signed a contract, something Ken had not thought to do with his protégé. Henry Willson became Roy's agent, and Ken moved back to Long Beach and proceeded to go to pieces."

At twenty-one, Roy already knew to cast his eye on older men for the quickest results. Coincidence or not, both Hodges and Henry were thirty-six years old when he met them.

Before his death in 1999, Millspaugh told his story to *E! Entertainment* for a documentary on Rock Hudson, as well as to Hudson's official biographer, Sara Davidson, who found a check dated March 19, 1948, for ten dollars, payable to Roy Fitzgerald from Vanguard Films, Inc., Culver City. It was reportedly the first check he had received for acting. It was endorsed:

> *Roy Fitzgerald*
> *Pay to the order of Rock Hudson*
> *Kenneth G. Hodges*

Did Rock Hudson, to the day he died, feel compelled to manufacture a story about his movie-star name? For sheer bland respectability, the photo-in-the-mail saga trumps being named by a bunch of Long Beach homosexuals. But the remainder of the Millspaugh/Davidson story falters on at least two counts: Rock Hudson never signed a contract with Selznick, and in early 1948 Henry was in no position to be signing his own clients. As for the ten-dollar check, the Selznick studios had no films in production during winter 1948.

Mark Miller, Rock's longtime secretary and best friend, also rejected the Millspaugh version. "Henry Willson named Rock Hudson. No doubt about it," he said. A transplanted Iowa farm boy, Miller contributed his own flourish to the famous moniker when, in 1951, he met the actor who called himself "Roc" Hudson. Outgoing and sweet-natured, Miller worked as a carhop at Jack's Drive-In on the Strip, where he delivered fries and burgers for two-bit tips. It's how he supported himself and his unemployed lover, an exceedingly well built and over-tanned actor named George Nader, who, in time, would achieve fame for refusing to shave his abundant chest hair in films like *Sins of Jezebel, Miss Robin Crusoe,* and *Robot Monster.*

Before semi-stardom engulfed Nader, he and Miller enjoyed a good laugh when their new friend Roc Hudson told them that Universal-International had jettisoned the "k" in his first name. "You can't do that!" Miller admonished. "Everyone will mix you up with *Rochelle* Hudson!" It was bad enough to be homosexual in Hollywood, but to be confused with a former ingenue whose career had peaked a decade earlier with *Babies for Sale* . . . Rock picked up the phone to call Henry, who agreed with Miller's analysis and dis-suaded Universal from making the "Roc" tweak permanent.

Miller confirmed the much-told story that Henry Willson took the name Hudson from the river and Rock from the one at Gibraltar. If indeed Henry and Roy met at Ken Hodges's gay party in Hollywood, the two men each preferred the more respectable story that a postage stamp brought them together in 1947.

It was not an easy birth, giving life to Rock Hudson. The sailor-turned-trucker came to Henry equipped with little more than a high-pitched Midwestern twang and a physique its owner could not begin to control. But Henry's natural appetency to nurture and con-trol led him to see beyond the defects and envision the beautiful klutz as the embodiment of his own perfect self. As a couple, they complemented each other: one had the brains, the other had the looks. In his usual deflected sense of lust, Henry cast his gaze as if through female eyes to describe what he saw across his desk that day at the Selznick studios. "I also saw a face that had the possi-bility of flipping a lot of women," he said.

Until then, Henry was the only person doing cartwheels to make the new kid a star. "Only twice in my life have I asked young people I was interested in to read to me," he remarked. "And both times, thank God, I didn't let what I heard influence me. And they turned out to be Lana Turner and Rock Hudson."

Other than his enormous good looks and his enormous lack of talent, there was something else that attracted Henry to Roy. "Henry liked men who were close to their mother but had no father," said Willson's assistant Gary Crutcher. "It was a temporary home life he could walk in and out of. Henry must have had hun-dreds of such 'families' over the years." Henry often slept with "his boys"—at least, in the beginning. He thought of those initial invi-tations to his bed as a paltry lagniappe for services rendered, like a waitress's tip or Green Stamps. "Sex was often an initiation for a new client," said Crutcher, "then Henry often went on to be a good, caring friend."

And a parent of sorts.

The ex-con Rory Calhoun was Henry's prototype for Rock Hudson. Rory Calhoun (born Francis Timothy McCown) lost his father when he was nine months old; at age seven, Rock Hudson (born Roy Scherer Jr.) was abandoned by Roy Sr., who migrated to California after losing his job during the Depression. Both Francis and Roy were later raised by stepfathers who gave them their respective surnames, Durgin and Fitzgerald. Henry's appetite for makeovers didn't stop with them. Arthur Gelien and Merle Johnson Jr. were two other protégés, among many, who grew up without benefit of a father, and Henry rechristened them Tab Hunter and Troy Donahue.

Roy's story was so familiar to Henry: the abusive or absent father, the desperate mother, the clutching son. The boy from Winnetka, Illinois, gleaned no comforting memories of Wallace Fitzgerald's marriage to his mother, Kay. "As soon as they were married, all my toys were taken away from me," he recalled. "My name was changed to his . . . I stayed away from home as much as possible for those nine years, and when I was home, I tried to ignore everything."

Acting *in loco parentis,* Henry rechristened his boys Rory and Rock and gave them all the care, patience, and admiration that their fathers had withheld. His obligation was prodigious. "An agent often becomes a sort of parent after discovering and grooming a personality," he explained. "I've paid to get teeth fixed, ears pinned back, and contact lenses fitted."

While Henry was more than willing to pay, the boys were simply willing. Hollywood was not without precedent for such man-made cults of personality: Mack Sennett had his bathing beauties, Howard Hawks his sultry dames, Alfred Hitchcock his cool blondes, Walt Disney his animated critters. Henry Willson was the first, and only, to maintain a stable of orphan studs.

Like any good parent or Svengali, Henry never shirked the financial responsibilities that went with the job. Rock, however, emerged as the first scion to inspire Henry to invest thousands of dollars, not only to cap the truck driver's crooked eyeteeth but to pay for his acting and vocal lessons. Henry's trucker Trilby also needed room and board and a whole new wardrobe. The forty-dollar suit did not survive the extreme makeover.

Neither did Roy's grammar. During their momentous first interview, Henry told the awkward hulk in tweed, "You don't know much, do you?"

Roy grinned so hard he exposed his bad teeth along with an inch of his upper gums. "I don't know nothing," he replied.

Henry smiled right back. "You don't know *anything*."

It was the beginning of a legendary relationship, one that inspired Hollywood insiders to speculate on its genesis. Over a hundred water coolers, it was said that the two men waited a whole day to consummate their partnership. Roy accepted Henry's dinner invitation to his Beverly Hills home, and no sooner did the soon-to-be-former trucker start his way up the driveway than the owner of the house, spying him from the front window, turned the lawn sprinklers up full. When Roy was sufficiently drenched, Henry appeared at the front door, ready with towel, apology, and an offer to help Roy out of his wet clothes.

Although repeated ad infinitum, the story ignores Roy's utter willingness from the beginning to broker sex for professional favors. Henry, too, had no appetite for anything but a quick close of the deal. This much is true: Everybody else in Hollywood took much less trouble with the boy. David O. Selznick was the first not to bother. When he refused to give Roy a contract, Henry took his new find to see Walter Wanger. In 1947, the producer of *Stagecoach* and *Queen Christina* was at the peak of his powers and still years away from the career suicide of shooting talent agent Jennings Lang in the groin for sleeping with Mrs. Wanger, actress Joan Bennett. It was a testament to Henry Willson's enormous prestige in Hollywood that he could secure an interview for the unknown Roy Fitzgerald with a powerbroker like Wanger, who was about to embark on his biggest, not to mention most turgid, production to date, *Joan of Arc*, starring Ingrid Bergman. Henry believed in Roy and expressed confidence that he could carry a spear and wear chain mail with the best of them.

To prepare for the meeting, the two men held a mock interview and Henry spent hours coaching Winnetka's Eliza Doolittle for his big Ascot moment. Henry specifically instructed him, "Be older than you are—say you're twenty-four if you're asked your age."

Wanger, unfortunately, asked the question, and sitting there in the producer's office, Roy froze, unable to recall the preprogrammed response. Finally, he turned to Henry for help. "How old am I?" he asked.

"I died," Henry said. "So did Rock's chances to get in a Wanger picture."

3

An M-G-M Rejection

Louis B. Mayer ruled from his pristine white-on-white throne room, but the real keeper of the fabled gate at Metro-Goldwyn-Mayer was a petite strawberry blonde of delicately spun steel named Lucille Ryman Carroll. As the studio's head of talent during the late 1940s and early 1950s, Carroll certified all stars-in-waiting before any of them ever saw a studio contract. Although she later regretted the decision, Carroll categorically rejected Rock Hudson when Henry Willson brought him to her offices in 1948. Tellingly, she recalled being introduced to a Roy Fitzgerald that year, not a Rock Hudson, casting even further suspicion on the Millspaugh version of the actor's name.

"I had a very large office at M-G-M with this big glass table," said Carroll. The size of that office had more to do with the function of her job than status or prestige, she claimed. "I liked to have the actors walk around my office, to see how they handled themselves."

What Carroll remembered most about Roy Fitzgerald were his enormous, oversized feet. He kept tripping over them, and she feared he would fall and smash her expensive glass table. "He stumbled and giggled, and I can't tell you what made me know that he was gay, but it was there," Carroll said. "I suspected that Henry and Rock were lovers, from the way he held Rock's hand when he stumbled. I just felt it."

While Henry and Rock's relationship was definitely sexual, it's unknown how much love had to do with it, at least on Rock's part. A Willson client named John Carlyle counted both men as his friends in the late 1940s and early 1950s. "Although he cared very much for Henry, I doubt it was love for Rock," said Carlyle. "Rock was very, very ambitious."

Carlyle was less sure about Henry's emotional attachment to Rock. "Henry totally adored and worshipped Rock," he said. "Henry could be a very generous person. But he was like a moth. He grew tired of the flame and would move on to the next man." Sometimes Henry's fickleness had less to do with his libido than the simple logistics of selling actors in a buyers' market. "If within six months an agent couldn't get you under contract at a studio," said Carlyle, "there wasn't much reason for an agent to represent the actor."

After failing to sell Roy Fitzgerald to M-G-M, Henry Willson returned to Lucille Ryman Carroll's office with many more handsome would-be actors in tow. He had a foolproof method for finding what he thought she wanted. "Henry stalked the beaches, especially Muscle Beach," Carroll said. "The first thing Monday morning Henry would call with a list of men for me to see. One day he called and told me that he had someone he was sure I would like. I assumed he was one of the beach boys."

Instead, she found herself introduced again to Roy Fitzgerald, who now called himself Rock Hudson. It was 1949, and Henry had left Selznick to be an agent with Famous Artists, one of the top tenpercenteries in town. Regardless of his client's name, Carroll remained just as unimpressed with him on second viewing. "Henry couldn't believe I wouldn't put Rock under contract," she said.

Although Willson's expeditions to Muscle Beach look primitive by today's standards, Carroll saw it differently in the context of 1940s Hollywood. World War II had depleted the leading-man ranks, and audiences were hungry for a rougher, less polished hero, one molded not on the Continental playboys of the 1930s but soldiers and sailors of World War II.

"We were always on the lookout for new, good-looking talent. Henry never wasted my time the way most agents did," said Carroll. "He knew what we were looking for. He had the best eyes in the business for young men."

Regarding Rock Hudson, Carroll had no choice but to reject him—not once but twice. "You see, the studio was very anti-gay when it came to hiring stars," she explained. "We could use them in smaller parts, as writers, and in the art department, but not in major roles. So there was no way I could have taken on someone like Rock with even the possibility of his being gay."

Carroll expressed an early, minority opinion on the sexual allure of Roy/Rock. People who knew Rock Hudson later in his life invariably described the actor as being the most masculine-acting of men, on- and offscreen. These latter impressions, however, were formed after Henry groomed and taught him how to act "like a real man," as the starmaker put it. His was a regimen repeated again and again for dozens of other homosexuals whose mannerisms spoke volumes, all of them wrong, for achieving leading-man status.

"Rock had a tendency to get nervous, which caused him to curl his upper lip when he smiled," Henry recalled. It was a cosmetic deficiency that Marilyn Monroe also suffered in her Norma Jean days. She and Rock tended to expose too much of their gums, and Henry found the habit unappetizing, not to mention "girlie," and he trained Rock to keep his lips pressed against his upper teeth whenever he smiled.

In addition to learning lip control, Rock got his wrists slapped when they went limp, his hips smacked whenever he swayed. Legs were never to be crossed or pressed together when he sat down. Henry rehearsed how to handle cigarettes, teaching Rock to use just the right amount of wrist to light it and then one quick flick of the match to put out the flame. Any trace of effeminacy was identified so it could be eradicated.

"For heaven's sake, you sound like a bird—or worse, a little girl—with that laugh of yours," Henry told one client. Together, the two men worked on a variety of other, deeper laugh tracks for when the young man needed to respond to a producer's bad joke.

In Henry's expert opinion, Rock's natural speaking voice was too nasal and high-pitched. To help lower it to a more sonorous bedroom level, he enlisted the help of the Selznick studio's vocal coach, Lester Luther. In one controversial exercise, Luther waited for Rock to become infected with a sore throat, then instructed him to scream for hours. When his vocal chords later healed, they miraculously accommodated a deeper, more seductive speaking voice. Rock could no longer carry a tune without going a half-pitch flat, as evidenced later in his career when he performed in the stage musicals *I Do! I Do!* and *Camelot*, but his speaking voice had been transformed into a new, more virile sounding instrument.

Sometimes butch was the least of it.

One evening, Henry and Rock left Los Angeles for a weekend trip up the coast to Santa Barbara's Biltmore Hotel. It was the city's finest hotel, which for someone of Henry's refined taste, made it the natural, if not the only, choice to dine and spend the night with a date. In his life as Roy Fitzgerald, Rock had never eaten in such a restaurant, and he remarked that it was "awfully expensive" for such a Mexican-looking place with its stucco walls, red tile floor, heavy oak beams, and rustic iron chandeliers. Huge, cathedral-like windows opened out to the kind of lush bluegrass lawn Roy Fitzgerald used to mow as a kid growing up in Illinois. A few yards beyond, he saw the Pacific Ocean. Henry watched as the warm, heavy breeze off the waves caused Rock's forehead to moisten. He sweated, Rock glistened. Although Henry rated the Biltmore dining room as one of the most romantic spots on the West Coast, Rock would have preferred picnic tables and a well-charred steak. Otherwise, he considered it a swell, if not intimidating, meal. And so it was only natural that he meant to help the Biltmore's many waiters when he started stacking the dishes.

Henry nearly expired into his bone-china coffee cup. Sometimes it wasn't only manners. Roy needed to embolden his self-image. "You're a movie star," Henry told him, "not a busboy!"

Plates were one thing, forks another. Henry gently but firmly scolded whenever Roy picked up the wrong one. "You don't want Hedda to see you use that fork, do you?" he warned with an understanding rap of the knuckles. Even the buttering of bread required the right panache. Henry took the time to show him how. "You don't drag the bread over your plate to butter it," he said, his voice on the verge of a singsong. "You butter it over the butter plate."

·He was demanding, but like all good teachers Henry knew when to blandish. After mastery of the silverware had been accomplished, he lavished with panegyrics worthy of a poet laureate. If Henry ever patronized, which was always, Rock mistook it for the fondest attention. "My boy," he said, "you will soon be ready for the White House!"

Roy Fitzgerald eventually made it there, thirty years later, to visit his good friends Ronnie and Nancy.

The man who invented Rock Hudson ended up broke and buried in a pauper's grave.

PART TWO

Henry Willson proudly displays a poster of "Uncle Sam," in his office at the Zeppo Marx Agency 1939.

4

A Note from Walter Winchell

Born July 31, 1911, in Lansdown, Pennsylvania, Henry Willson arrived into a prominent, if not famous, show-business family. Henry would have preferred famous, fabulously famous. He spent the next sixty-seven years elevating the more-than-humble circumstances of his birth to an appropriately exalted, if not totally inflated, level of success. As a starmaker, it was in his genes. Henry believed that a man's true history was only the crude groundwork for a more bedizened résumé—and that included the biography of Henry's own father.

When Horace L. Willson died on April 24, 1967, the obituary his son planted in the *New York Times* embellished the facts to the point of unreality. The obit read in full:

"Horace Willson, who founded the company that became Columbia Records, Inc., died Saturday. He was eighty-eight years old. Mr. Willson was credited with introducing the two-sided record. Al Jolson, Paul Whiteman, Ted Lewis, and Rosa Ponselle recorded for his Columbia Phonograph Company, which became Columbia Records, Inc. Mr. Willson leaves his wife, Margaret, and two sons."

Not much beyond that last sentence stands as the absolute truth.

Shortly after Henry's birth, Horace L. Willson became vice president of the Columbia Phonograph Company, which had been founded by then-president Edward Easton. However, he did not rise to the position of president until 1922 when the company went into receivership and was renamed the Columbia Graphophone Mfg. Co. Three years later, he resigned that position when the company, having gone belly-up, financially reorganized to become Columbia Records.

Today, the archives at Sony Music Corporation, Columbia's parent company, reveal that the primary function of H. L. Willson was to release financial statements regarding the bankrupt company's fiscal record. In his previous position there as vice president, he made "no major artist acquisitions," reported Sony's chief archivist. There also wasn't much truth to Henry's other major claim regarding his father's introduction of the two-sided record, in 1904. In that endeavor, CPC followed several other companies, including one called Berliner, which had placed a double-sided record on the market in 1900.

Surprisingly, the obituary did not include Henry's long-held, most-cherished contention regarding his father's illustrious red-white-and-blue lineage. According to his son, Horace L. Willson descended from Sam Wilson, who was none other than America's favorite war recruiter "Uncle Sam." Henry even took time to celebrate the day, in August 1961, when the United States Congress officially saluted Samuel Wilson of Troy, New York, as the long-bearded progenitor of the country's national symbol. Over cocktails at Villa Frascatti's patio on Sunset Boulevard, Henry entertained several clients with all the Smirnoff and tales of patriotism they could swallow. His great-great uncle was a veteran of the Revolutionary Army, Henry claimed, and supplied meat to the war department during the War of 1812.

"His grade-A beef was stamped U.S., which came to stand for 'Uncle Sam' among our fighting men!" Henry brayed to his coterie of boys. A hard-line rugged individualist, Henry always displayed great respect for servicemen, he made several of them celebrities, and like so many of his political bent, he never enlisted to shed any of his own blood to further the cause of liberty. Left unexplained was how Wilson came to be spelled Willson, which Henry nonetheless insisted be printed with the distinctive double consonants whenever his own name appeared in print.

"Henry Willson with two *Ls*," he told countless magazine and newspaper reporters. Henry spent his life watching journalists screw it up.

Horace L. Willson's son might have qualified as a chronic fabulist any place in the world but one, which is why Henry's decision at age twenty-one to emigrate to Hollywood, in 1933, qualified as true inspiration. His hyperactive imagination, flourish for fabrication, and dogged pursuit of those sexual fantasies that have always overpopulated the movies, made him the right person at the right place—even if it happened to be the wrong time. Henry's moxie and flair for extravagant consumption blinded him to the fact that 1933 began with FDR's bank holiday and marked the lowest ebb of the Great Depression. Let the rest of America eat in soup kitchens: he went to Los Angeles on vacation, but not as a tourist. Jazzed by the movie flimflam that suffocated most genuine talents, he took himself from lowly fan-magazine hack to vice president of Zeppo Marx's gung-ho talent agency in less than two years.

Not that being the son of Horace L. Willson came without its own privilege and position. Whether bankrupt or veering toward financial ill-repute, Willson's record company brought its well-paid president in close contact with many stars of Broadway, opera, and vaudeville, and Horace counted two of the stage's most popular performers as intimate friends. By design or happenstance, the Long Island estates of Will Rogers and Fred Stone were not far from Horace Willson's smaller but well-appointed Colonial-style manse in the Forest Hills section of Queens, New York.

The two comedians were the David Letterman and Jay Leno of their day. Fred Stone entranced audiences with his turn as the Scarecrow in an early stage production of *The Wizard of Oz*; Will Rogers did rope tricks and told political jokes in Florenz Ziegfeld's *Follies*. Corny, down-home foxes, Will and Fred were savvy businessmen who subbed for each other on stage to no great alarm from either audiences or management. To them, Henry Leroy Willson might have been perceived as just another sniveling mollycoddle who tugged at their good friend Horace's overcoat—if not for the fact that the boy shrewdly cultivated his own friends in their respective daughters Mary Rogers and Paula Stone. Hardly an attractive child, and by most accounts a truly homely adult, Henry possessed at least one extraordinary talent: He never let his own appearance prevent him from keeping the company of the world's most beautiful people. More remarkable, he forced those same exalted specimens to desire him—if not physically, then one way or another.

Take Paula Stone, Henry's classmate at St. Paul's School in Garden City. Henry and she grew so fond of each other that her father, Fred, often exclaimed, usually within earshot of a reporter, "He is my favorite son-in-law-to-be." As children, Henry and Paula enjoyed limousine rides together to school. Years later, Henry liked to give his plebian side an airing with the following piece of apocrypha regarding those memorable trips to St. Paul's: "I rode in limousines so often that I'd often look forward to taking the subway. It's the only way I had of hearing how real New Yorkers talked!"

From the way Henry and Paula talked, Queens, New York could have been Iowa, a faraway place where the glare and din of their parents' chosen business on the other side of the East River rarely intruded. "Our home was a farmhouse," said Paula Stone, who would often complete the pastoral picture by throwing in a few "cows and chickens and horses." (Unlike her friend Henry, Paula had a habit of forgetting such impressive details as the Stone farmhouse's twenty-two rooms.) In her reminiscences, she often singled out a much-beloved pet nag named Dopey. "Soon we rode well enough to have our own Wild West show," said Paula. "I got my first movie role because of things I could do on a horse."

In truth, she got her first movie role because Henry became her Hollywood agent and landed the young horsewoman a role in the 1935 Western *Hop-Along Cassidy*. Henry had even better luck with

Fred Stone, whose most memorable film appearance came that year in *Alice Adams,* in which he played Katharine Hepburn's weak but lovable old dad who lost everything in a failed glue-factory scheme. The horses, if not the chickens, had come full circle.

In its January 22, 1935, issue, *The Hollywood Reporter* reported "Paula Stone and Henry Willson will be wed here in ten days" but neglected to inform the bride-to-be, who married somebody else a few days later. Over the years, Paula and Henry were always just *this close* to getting married.

Although Fred Stone may have sincerely believed Henry and his daughter Paula would one day marry, Horace Willson must have believed it a little less.

Something about his son's tap dancing "made my father uncomfortable," said Henry. To remedy his unease, Horace pulled number-two son out of St. Paul's, and for Henry's senior year he enrolled him in the Asheville School, an all-boys boarding school in North Carolina. Neither Horace nor his older son, Arthur—or any one else in the Willson family—had ever attended Asheville, so it was no easy, predestined step when Henry found himself exiled there. Stuck away in the god-forsaken reaches of the Blue Ridge Mountains, the institution boasted all kinds of team sports in addition to splendid weekends of rock climbing and backpacking. Years later, Henry joked with friends at the irony of his father's folly. "One way or another, my dad got it into his head that the company of all those other boys would turn me into a real man," he said.

Far into the future, Henry could afford to laugh. But not in 1930 with his bags packed for what he called "my vacation in purgatory." While he learned how to dribble a basketball in an Asheville gymnasium, Broadway gaily went on without him. So did *Variety.* By the time Horace shipped his son off to North Carolina, Henry had already contributed many showbiz items to the entertainment bible. Actors, more than anyone, enjoyed reading about themselves, and Henry ingratiated himself by writing *Variety* tidbits culled from backstage visits with his newfound friends at the Professional Children's School in Manhattan.

Henry called them his "Broadway babies," because here were pals, often younger than he, who had already modeled for Madison Avenue, appeared in Broadway shows, and made films at Paramount's studios in Astoria, Queens. The little cupids included children like the Buster Brown Shoes boy Tom Brown and William Janney, whose father, Russell, produced as many as ten stage shows in a single Broadway season. These boys inspired reviewers to call them "clean" and "swell" and "wholesome" and, most impressive to Henry, "adorable" and "precious" and "cute."

No one ever used these words to describe Henry Willson at age fourteen or eight or even four. Dance instructors told him his body was all wrong—the legs too short, the hips too wide, the shoulders too sloped and narrow. As an actor, he might make it as a comic. In addition to a rather hawkish nose, his face featured a bulbous lower lip that curled down over a nonexistent chin, and Henry's dark eyes loomed so large that they made him look downright goofy. It was an inviting face: animated, open, amiable. But then, so was a clown's. And while Henry adored show people, he had no love for the smell of the circus.

Henry knew early on that he wielded a far different, more elusive talent. "I can always tell within ten minutes if the person has it or not, and with this inner sense of mine, I know if he has picture potential," he said. "I don't know how I acquired this faculty, but when I was growing up, I attended a lot of Broadway shows, and like almost everyone I was always disappointed if the stage manager announced that an understudy was taking over a leading role for that performance. But strangely enough I began to enjoy these performances the most, and after a while I'd seek out producers when the star was on vacation or ill. I supposed it was the thrill of seeing a player being given that big chance that we're always hearing about, and it does happen."

He was nothing if not a believer in showbiz mythmaking. Unfortunately, the nurturing of Henry's own myth was put on hold when

Horace Willson sent him off to that rustic North Carolina diaspora where no one had ever heard of Sigmund Romberg or Lee and J. J. Shubert. Horace took his boy away from Broadway, but no one could ever extinguish the marquee lights in Henry's heart and mind. During his one year at Asheville, Henry made a weak attempt at being a regular, normal guy when he insisted that everyone call him "Hank," not "Henry," as reported in the school yearbook. That nod to social mediocrity aside, he went about his gay way and, regardless of how distant his Broadway idols remained, Henry joined the Dramatics Club to indulge his passion. Tellingly, he knew enough about his own talents at age seventeen not to appear on stage even in the far reaches of North Carolina and instead contented himself behind the scenes by directing several plays. The yearbook made note of his favorite. It was a melodrama called *Suppressed Desires.*

After the Blue Ridge Mountains, there followed more out-of-town penance at Wesleyan University. At least Middletown, Connecticut, was close enough to New York City to allow for weekend visits so that Henry could resume his career in journalism on those blessed Saturday and Sunday retreats in Gotham. Writing for *Variety*'s "Chatter" column, he played both promoter and guardian at the gate of his parents' Forest Hills enclave of famous friends. As a gumshoe gossip, Henry protected much more than he ever revealed. Typical weekly columns featured one- and two-sentence blurbs about the two families he loved and knew best:

"Will Rogers never has and never will use makeup," Henry railed in one column.

In another issue of *Variety*, he revealed, "Walter Winchell was about three years late in his statement that the whole Fred Stone tribe have [sic] gone Christian Science."

On occasion, he also wrote about Queens-bred torch singer Libby Holman (before she was charged with murdering her husband, millionaire Zachary Smith Reynolds), and there were frequent mentions of the Hopkins sisters, Ruby and Miriam, as well as Bill Morris Jr., scion to the nation's top entertainment agency. The usual Prohibition doings sometimes surfaced to add intrigue: "Another cordial shop raided in Kew Gardens."

Henry so prized two letters from his earliest days in journalism that he kept and preserved them until he died. The first, dated July 9, 1931, came from the son of Sime Silverman, founder of *Variety*.

Will you kindly indicate on your "Chatter" copy each week whether or not you desire a by-line. I will oblige.

Very truly,
Sid Silverman

On December 12 of that year, Henry received a cherished missive from the god of gossip himself:

Dear Henry Willson:
Okay. Thanks for the news, and for your kind words about the column.

Good wishes,
Walter Winchell

Winchell wrote regularly for the *New Movie Magazine,* and by early 1933, Henry's own byline also graced the elegant fan magazine. (Its oversized pages and bold, colorful graphic design were replicated four decades later by *Andy Warhol's Interview*.) Given the economic zeitgeist, Henry's switch from theater to film coverage was brilliant even if it required no genius. Broadway was his first love, but klieg lights no longer flooded the Gotham sky over Forty-second Street when he made his weekend trips home from Wesleyan. The 1929 stock market crash dried up most investment money for legit shows, and the number of productions dipped from a high of 270 in 1927 to 180 four years later. At least half of

Broadway's ninety theaters stood empty, with worse statistics yet to come: The mighty Shuberts went into receivership. No longer able to bankroll his own shows, Flo Ziegfeld begged Waxey Gordon and Dutch Schultz, two gangsters with ghost lights in their eyes and showgirls on their arms, to finance his Bert Lahr–starrer *Hot-Cha!* And Broadway director Alexander Leftwich, a friend of the Willson family, found himself out of work despite having helmed such hits as George and Ira Gershwin's *Strike Up the Band* (1930) and *A Connecticut Yankee* (1927), an early collaboration of the new song-writing team Richard Rodgers and Lorenz Hart. What choice did Leftwich have but to follow in the wake of other stage directors like George Cukor and John Cromwell, and look for work way out west in Hollywood?

There were other casualties on the Great White Way. While Fred Stone's family continued to live off their long-running *Ripples* revue, the Depression made it impossible for producers to capitalize those lesser shows that employed so many of Henry's actor chums from the Professional Children's School. Broadway was the poorer for it, but the other coast benefited from all the giddy, youthful transmigration.

"The transition period between silent and sound was a fascinating time," wrote Irene Mayer Selznick, wife of David O. and daughter of Louis B. "A different kind of talent and more interesting minds were coming West, because words became all-important." The film community looked to theater-trained directors to guide actors through the medium's transition to sound. Even more in demand were the stage actors themselves, which could explain the cruel reversal of fortunes when Hollywood unceremoniously passed on the experienced producer-director Alexander Leftwich but signed his beautiful sixteen-year-old stepdaughter, Patricia Ellis, to a seven-year Warner Bros. contract, one that Henry renegotiated to her advantage when he followed the actress-ingenue to Los Angeles and set himself up as an agent.

The shift in talent was seismic. As early as 1930, the Broadway-to-Hollywood exodus that carried so many of Henry's friends westward had already been lampooned by George S. Kaufman and Moss Hart in their classic play *Once in a Lifetime*: "We gotta get out there, May! Before this Broadway bunch climbs on the bandwagon," one out-of-work performer warns another. "There's going to be a gold rush, May. There's going to be a trek out to Hollywood that'll make the 49'ers look sick."

Henry's close buddy Tom Brown got on the bandwagon early. By 1930, the seventeen-year-old, who epitomized the boy next door in Broadway comedies like *Is Zat So?*, lived the bachelor's life in style with his own place tucked away in the Hollywood Hills. Seduced by the heavenly scented land of orange groves, never-ending summers, and time-clock paychecks, a veritable gang of Broadway kids joined Tom Brown and included such other émigré friends as Joseph Depew, William Janney, Helen Mack, Patricia Ellis, and Trent "Junior" Durkin, who had just completed back-to-back films playing Huckleberry Finn opposite Jackie Coogan's Tom Sawyer. Soaking in the California sun, the youngsters worked sixteen-hour days, made up to a dozen films a year, and, suffering from acute exhaustion, no longer had the energy to think about their distant, cold careers back in legit on Broadway. Only slightly older than the little rascals of the *Our Gang* comedies, Henry's handpicked theater chums presented a group portrait of simple youth and uncomplicated beauty that could only be described as perfectly abnormal. It was an aesthetic Henry worshipped for the next forty years and never thought to outgrow.

Where Junior Durkin and Tom Brown had the talent and looks to go west, Henry relied on his father's largesse from the Columbia Phonograph Company to get him there. It was money that depended on a dream. "Just a few days before the stock market crash (of 1929), I had this nightmare of economic ruin," Horace told Henry's friends. "I took every dollar I had in the stock market and the bank and put it in a safety-deposit box in my home in Forest Hills. Otherwise, my family would have been wiped out."

Four years later, Horace's safety-deposit box continued to spew forth enough cash for his Wesleyan-educated son to indulge in fine dining, elegant three-piece suits, speakeasy nights, and show-biz gossip, the last of which barely covered subway fare to the Times Square offices of *Variety,* where Henry delivered his weekly "Chatter" column. More expensive than any of these pursuits was Henry's first trip to California. When Tom Brown made a generous offer of his Hollywood Hills bungalow, Horace Willson incorrectly deemed the Asheville School experiment a success and saw no reason why Henry should refuse the invitation. Broadway was grand, but the movies and their men were to be his son's life.

5

Ginger Rogers Sat Here

The year 1933 was not the most auspicious time to make a West Coast debut. After the crash of 1929, the novelty of talkies gave Hollywood the false impression it could avoid the economic slump that plagued Broadway and most other industries. But by 1933, the Great Depression finally caught up to the film capital, which barely sustained the one-two punch of FDR's bank holiday on March 4 and, one week later, an earthquake, its exact magnitude unknown but undeniably huge. (It would take Charles F. Richter another five years to invent his seismological scale.)

Compliments of Roosevelt, several financial institutions closed their cash windows temporarily, if not their doors permanently. Most studios—M-G-M the notable exception—found themselves strapped for cash and were forced to impose a 25 to 50 percent pay cut on all employees. M-G-M followed suit out of sheer patriotic empathy.

If the general economic malaise put a crimp in Henry's East Coast hauteur, he never thought to substitute wool for silk when choosing a necktie. Horace Willson even indulged his son's flair for grand consumption by letting him eschew a tiresome three-thousand-mile cross-country train trip in favor of a dust-free voyage by cruise liner from New York City to Los Angeles. "What else was the Panama Canal built for?" Henry crowed when he got to California.

While many cringed at the naked gauchery of such a remark,

others laughed along, which is how Henry Willson divided Hollywood for the next forty years. People were either repulsed or beguiled. He complemented his need to show off, however, with another compulsion that, in time, also bordered on the chronic.

"He was an extremely generous man," said Carol Lee Ladd Veitch. As the future stepdaughter of actor Alan Ladd, Carol Lee first met Henry on that circuitous trek from New York to the West Coast by way of Latin America. Being less than a year old at the time, she had to accept that fact on faith from her mother, Sue Carol.

"My mother was traveling with Dixie Lee Crosby at the time," said Veitch, her first and middle name an amalgam of the two women's names. "That's where they met Henry, and the three of them became very close friends."

Dixie Lee (born Wilma Winifred Wyatt) was a peroxide cutie credited with turning the "Varsity Drag" into one of the dance crazes of the Roaring Twenties. Her enthusiastic rendition in the 1928 musical *Good News* led to a career in the movies, which was never quite as memorable as her stage work, and after a few lackluster attempts in front of the camera, she wisely chucked the flicks to marry Bing Crosby of the Rhythm Boys. Friends had warned her about the hard-drinking, carousing band-singer, and their worst predictions turned true after twelve short months of unremarkably rocky marriage. Dixie Lee took off to Mexico to get a cheapo divorce, but not before she delivered her husband a double ultimatum: stop drinking and stop chasing women. Much to everyone's shock, the trip south yielded the desired results, and by the time she met Henry, Mr. and Mrs. Bing Crosby were already expecting their first child, Gary.

Dixie Lee and Sue Carol had been best friends ever since they costarred as flappers—one fair, the other dark as sin—in *Fox Movietone Follies of 1929*. Projecting the far racier image, Sue Carol wore skirts that tickled her kneecaps, dyed her bobbed hair jet-black and sculpted her lips into a crimson pout. No less a director than Cecil B. DeMille wanted to buy the actress's contract, and he promised to put her in four of his films. Hollywood was calling her the next Clara

Bow, the next It Girl. Fox Films even went so far as to tout Sue Carol as "the Queen of the Screen Flappers." On the eve of the big crash, *Liberty* magazine applauded Sue's newly won freedom: "Miss Carol divorced Mr. [Allan H. Keefer] just the other day, thus completing her preparations for stardom." That was 1929.

The Depression wrote another, different chapter for Sue Carol's story. The years after 1929 did not look kindly on divorced females who drank, smoked, and flapped their wings, and by 1933, life for Sue Carol was much less daringly fun with husband number two. When the aging, twice-married flapper first saw the Panama Canal and Henry Willson, she had already separated from Carol Lee's father, the actor Nick Stuart. He had it coming. Only days before Sue set sail, the rat threw a crossword-puzzle book at her. "And since I'd grown up in a family of crossword-puzzle aficionados," as she later put it to the divorce judge, the incident hurt profoundly. With a baby under her arm, Sue Carol now looked to revive her movie career when she returned to Los Angeles. As for the budding reporter on board, Henry made no secret of his *Variety* connections or that he knew Walter Winchell *personally*. If nothing else, people in Hollywood knew when they saw value in an incipient friend.

It has not been recorded whether Henry told Sue Carol how much he enjoyed her flapper classics *Slaves of Beauty* and *Girls Gone Wild*. Or if she knew that her film *Is Zat So?* had originally been done on Broadway with Tom Brown, the very friend Henry was going to shack up with when he got to Los Angeles. Or that he was practically engaged to Fred Stone's daughter Paula and that Will Rogers daughter, Mary, who now lived on her father's ranch in Santa Monica, had promised to be in their wedding party. Whatever Henry did tell Sue Carol and her friend Dixie Lee, the words charmed his way to their door when the two movie hoydens arrived back in Los Angeles.

"They were outspoken and having the time of their lives," Henry said of meeting Sue and Dixie Lee. "They were married, but they didn't act married. They knew the score."

In the years to come, Henry would gravitate to similarly liberated, free-spirited women to populate his wide circle of female friends. As for the many men in his future life, they tended to be far less opinionated, and what they lacked in conversation skills they made up for in brawn and bone structure.

Shortly after the new threesome sailed into the Long Beach port, Sue Carol and Dixie Lee Crosby gave a party to introduce their journalist friend to Hollywood's elite. Well, maybe semi-elite. If Sue and Dixie weren't exactly Norma Shearer and Joan Crawford, they had their useful connections. Dixie Lee, of course, was married to Bing, who had already achieved enough fame to play himself in several musicals at Paramount Pictures. Sue Carol may have been struggling to reassert herself in town, but as the niece of theatrical producer George W. Lederer, she came well equipped with her own notable pedigree. Lederer had staged several operettas on Broadway, including a few by Victor Herbert that starred his wife, singer Reine Davies, who was sister of William Randolph Hearst's paramour, Marion Davies. Now *that* was Hollywood royalty.

Dixie Lee had only Bing Crosby to her credit. But together, they produced Henry's best Hollywood contact when their pregnancy delivered Gary. Before he learned to crawl, Gary Crosby was the infant prop for an "as told to" article by Henry Willson, complete with photograph of adoring interviewer on his hands and knees in front of his oblivious subject.

Entitled "Baby Talk," Henry's debut article in *Photoplay* read:

> I was ushered into the spacious nursery where Gary Evans Crosby, aged 6 months, received me with all the pomp and splendor that could be expected from a young man of his age—perched in a dignified manner in the center of the floor with one toe in his mouth—the third from the left on the right foot.
>
> "What can I do for you?" inquired the starlet, in a deep baritone voice that assured me I was in the right household.
>
> "Well, Mr. Crosby . . ."

And so on. It wasn't Pulitzer Prize material, but the profile told Hollywood everything its writer wanted the town to know: Henry Willson was a friend to the stars, and the stars had a friend in Henry Willson.

Even when the truth failed to oblige, he had a gift for keeping everybody's name in the newspapers. "The Nick Stuart–Sue Carol remarrying could happen any minute," Henry wrote in a July 1934 issue of *The Hollywood Reporter*. No sooner did Sue Carol not remarry Nick Stuart than she wed another actor, Howard Wilson. (Dixie Lee and Henry played their parts; she was matron of honor, he best man.) This third marriage proved no more enduring than Sue Carol's two previous trips to the altar, and after just two years as Mrs. Wilson, she took Henry's advice and returned to show business, this time as an agent.

"It was a natural, easy, obvious thing to do," she said. "I knew everybody in the industry." That new career led to her meeting and ultimately falling in love with yet another movie thespian, Alan Ladd, who soon became her fourth, last, and shortest husband.

Henry's relationship to the stars worked both ways. He needed the bylines, they needed the publicity. Within days of his LA arrival, Henry repaid Tom Brown for his generous living arrangement by writing a defense of the twenty-year-old actor in *The New Movie Magazine*. In "Tom Brown's Buddy Looks Him Over," he pleaded with readers to see Tom as neither a "woman-hater" nor a "young Lothario."

The profile read like love pulp, but it marked an epiphany for Henry. Back on Broadway, he wrote about an actor's talent. Here in Hollywood, he wrote about sex appeal. In the theater, he shared the actor with a thousand other people in the audience. In the movies, the closeup offered him the promise, if not the reality, of intimacy with the leading man. (It was Henry's calling to achieve the reality of that promise.) He knew instinctively the movies' ultimate truth: actors either exuded sex, or they had no future in front of the camera.

One year after Henry's arrival, *The New Movie Magazine* solidified his position as chronicler of the young set by giving him a regular column. He called it "Junior Hollywood." The under-twenty-one gang included most of Henry's old Broadway friends, as well as a particularly famous-by-association new face: Patricia Ziegfeld, daughter of Flo Ziegfeld and Billie Burke, who had recently moved to Hollywood to play a series of ditzy society matrons, most notably in 1933's *Dinner at Eight*. Other new kids in town also made their way into Henry's column, youngsters few other reporters bothered to waste their ink on. From the beginning, Henry knew plenty of "swell kids," such as Ida Lupino, Robert Taylor, Fred MacMurray, Anita Louise, Betty Furness, Ginger Rogers, and her cousin Phyllis Fraser, the future Mrs. Bennett Cerf.

As a reporter, Henry wasn't big on the mechanics of their careers. He covered the B-Westerns and college romps and backstage musicals his friends churned out at an assembly-line pace as if these vehicles existed only to fill in the dull hours between the cozy beach barbecues and birthday parties and weekend romps in the desert. The "real" news wasn't the movies. It was Ida Lupino's Saturday-afternoon pool parties, tagged as "Lupy's Lousy Lot"; days at the races in Santa Anita with Bob Taylor and Anne Shirley; and Ginger Rogers's benefit fete for little Mary Blackford ("whose promising career as an actress was halted by an automobile accident"). Even more fun were the 16mm home movies shot by Ginger and cousin Phyllis, which Henry deemed "worthy of the silver screen." Also at the top of the list were weekend excursions to San Diego with the "adorable" Durkin kids, Patricia Ellis's scavenger hunt ("which sent us to Clark Gable's front door"), and dates with childhood friend Mary Rogers that featured a first-person tour of Will's ranch in Santa Monica.

Then came the Puppets. Henry took pride in the fact that he was one of the few nonthesp persons invited to join.

Four years before Richard Rodgers and Lorenz Hart wrote *Babes in Arms*, their ebullient let's-put-on-a-show-in-the-barn Broadway musical, the Puppets did exactly that in their own Hollywood Hills clubhouse. Naturally, Henry wrote about it. To be cynical, the Puppets club might have been formed expressly for him to write about such things. In his typically gushing, gee-whiz style, he filed the following valentine to the Puppets in the January 1934 issue of *The New Movie Magazine*: "Anita Louise and Tom Brown decided, one bright day, that it would be a swell idea if all the 'kids,' like themselves, who knew each other back East, could get together, form a club, rent a clubhouse, give shows and have a good time. It would keep them all together and give them a place to go in the evenings after work, and during the days when they weren't busy on a picture."

The Puppets included twenty-two of Hollywood's youngest, diligent actors . . . plus Henry Willson. According to his breathless account, a cottage in Laurel Canyon was almost rented for their clubhouse when Billie Burke and "a few other moms" scotched the idea, claiming "it was too dangerous a place to reach at night in cars." Several girls were barely sixteen, Henry noted with due concern. (In the future, Henry developed an enormous soft spot for dating underage girls with overprotective parents.) Finally, with every mother's blessing, the club settled on another address, 2107 Beechwood Drive, at the bottom of the canyon. Overhead, the Hollywoodland sign loomed, as if to show them the way home in the wilderness.

With the Puppets, Henry gave Rodgers and Hart the template for putting on a corny show. "Walking to the front door," he wrote, "we found Junior Durkin and Maurice Murphy in old corduroys, scrubbing the floor; Tex Brodus and Pat Ziegfeld, tearing off the old wallpaper in one of the back rooms; while Ben Alexander put up the new white paper, and Billy Janney and Earl Blackwell painted floors. Bob Horner was covering furniture in the front room; Patricia Ellis and Gertrude Durkin scrubbed the sink. We found Grace Durkin standing in the bathtub, washing the windows."

Henry's job as flack began and ended with his leading the cheers. "The Puppets are the grandest bunch of young people I have ever seen!" he concluded with boundless optimism.

Wherever the Puppets roamed, Henry got to costar with them in a hundred fan-magazine photographs, his face a notable standout for belonging to nobody, the sine qua non of anonymity among his celebrity pals. They were his entrée. And something more, much more. Whether he knew it or not, Henry Willson had effectively identified America's first cult of youth. It would take another ten years for the word "teenager" to be coined, but Henry led the youth pack nonetheless, chronicling and defining that peculiar interval in life between adolescence and adulthood before any wordsmith got around to naming it. His new vocation not only functioned as an entrée to Hollywood society, it filled a significant talent void during the Depression.

"Notice how many new faces are appearing on the screen these days," *Modern Screen* asked its readers. "Do you know the reason? New faces are cheaper than older ones."

The studios sought them cheap, Henry sought them willing. One of his first clients described Hollywood's social strata of the day. "If I go to parties, they are usually almost kid parties and none of the big stars ever come," said sixteen-year-old Anne Shirley, who, after doing umpteen films under the name Dawn O'Day, took Henry's advice and changed it to the name of her character in the 1934 hit *Anne of Green Gables.* "Some of the younger ones like Sue Carol, Tom Brown, Anita Louise, Helen Mack, Patricia Ellis, and Junior Durkin are in a little crowd that I am sometimes invited to join, but we are much, much too young for the great names . . ."

Because they were young, it was easier for Henry to hold the rare, if not unique, distinction of working both sides of the celebrity fence. He profiled actors for the fan magazines, and as a junior agent at the Joyce & Polimer Agency, he turned around and hawked those same actors to the studios, which were eager to buy. There was a huge market for youth movies. High-school attendance shot up from 2.2 million in 1920 to 4.3 million in 1930, giving teenagers a common experience that could now be played back to them from the screen in countless plot lines. It was as if Henry had fallen into a gold mine from which he never wanted to escape.

In the beginning, he spent more than he earned and enjoyed an extravagance that was notable even for Tinseltown. Like so many born New Yorkers, Henry resisted learning how to operate a car for years, and in the meantime, flaunted his deficiency by hiring a personal driver. So notable a gesture did not escape *The Hollywood Reporter,* which wrote (most likely at Henry's prompting), "Henry Willson's chauffeur comes to work every morning in a yellow taxicab!"

The chauffeur had the privilege of reporting for duty at the distinguished address of 1136 Tower Road. "In Beverly Hills," Henry stressed, "where the movie stars live."

It was a relatively new town. Beverly Hills had only recently replaced Whitley Heights as the most fashionable neighborhood for the motion-picture elite. Significantly, Henry's three-bedroom stone house with quaint dormer windows and shingled roof would not have looked out of place in his parents' neighborhood in Queens. Which is why they bought it for him. The Asheville School episode notwithstanding, Henry's friends commented that he always presented the most idealized relationship with his parents, and he paid Horace and Margaret Willson the ultimate compliment by replicating the décor of their Forest Hills home. Here was the house he'd known as a child, and Henry filled it with hoop rugs, early American furniture, vintage antiques, and flowered curtains. Native Californians were stunned by such dark, understated décor. "It looks like a Connecticut house," they would remark, even if few of them had ever been east of the continental divide. The bright sunlight of southern California gave everything a ripe, overstuffed look, but Henry's friends were impressed nonetheless.

Not content with copying his parents' home, Henry embellished his relationship with Horace and Margaret by telling friends that the Tower Road house was a surprise birthday gift from the two of them. "My mother and father came to visit one day and drove me to this house in Beverly Hills," he said. "I'd never set eyes on it, and here we were. They gave me the keys, and when we walked in the door, there was a fire going in the fireplace and dinner set on the dining-room table." Reportedly, the black housekeeper, Ella Mae Fuque, came along with the cranberries and dressing. (Never one to wax too poetically, Henry sometimes slipped on purpose and pronounced her name "Fuk-U.")

Whatever the truth, the exceedingly reputable Horace L. Willson never refuted the story when Henry's friends asked for corroboration. And the fact remained: no reporter-turned-agent could afford a house in Beverly Hills. Whether or not its purchase surprised Henry, the likely buyer was indeed his father. A most pampering patriarch, Horace Willson tempered his affection with a patrician countenance that many of Henry's friends said recalled the steelier aspect of their dearly departed president, Woodrow Wilson. His was a strong, unyielding love that cast him as the patron prototype, which Henry in turn replicated for dozens of Hollywood's male orphans. Even Horace's rigid conformity on the subject of homosexuality manifested itself in how Henry dealt with his future male clients: "Don't ever live with another man in this town!" Henry always instructed.

If only he had loved Horace a little less. A more rebellious son might have rejected the lessons of Asheville along with the man who sent him there. But Henry remained a devoted, obedient son. In time, his self-inflicted commitment to live alone would lead to a relentless promiscuity, a fetish for cleanliness, and a paranoia so debilitating that it reduced Henry to the psychiatric rigors of electroshock treatment.

In 1935, though, he suffered no such problems. Henry Willson was the proud owner of 1136 Tower Road, thanks to his father's love and largesse, and he immediately showed off the new Beverly Hills digs with a party in honor of his old Broadway friends Paula and Fred Stone, who now doubled as his clients. Father and daughter had migrated to Los Angeles to kick off their movie careers, and Henry commemorated the occasion with an unusually florid entry in the July 1935 issue of *The New Movie Magazine,* inexplicably written under the byline of Nemo, "the mysterious reporter no one knows":

Catching Anita [Louise] doing the town with Tommy Lee several times recently, we were afraid it might be the end of a beautiful romance between the little lady and her longtime beau, Tom Brown. But at a cocktail party in honor of Fred Stone and his charming daughter, Paula, it did this old heart good to see Anita and Tom, billing and cooing as of yore.

Premeditated or not, the party fixed up a lot of busted hearts. It might have been the very excellent punch, but whatever it was, Connie Simpson and Jack La Rue fixed up their erstwhile difficulties, deciding to carry on from where they left off several days before. And Cary Grant seemed to be finding complete solace from his Virginia Cherrill heartbreak in the delectable Ida Lupino, who looked as though she'd just stepped out of a Patou bandbox!

It was Henry Willson's first major party in Hollywood. He may not have been born a handsome man, but among his Puppet friends, no one owned a more magnificent house with more beautiful guests getting drunk on more excellent punch.

6

Bloodsuckers on the Neck

It's difficult to fathom why Henry used a pseudonym to write up his Stone party for the Junior Hollywood column. Perhaps Cary Grant, Fred Stone, and Jack La Rue qualified as too mature. Or maybe he didn't want it to sound like he was promoting his own "very excellent punch," not to mention his nascent but already expert matchmaking skills. Or, could Henry have begun to harbor qualms about representing the various clients he promoted each month in *The New Movie Magazine?* His boss at the agency, Richard K. Polimer, broke the news of Henry's employment in the February 5, 1934, issue of *The Hollywood Reporter.* The item didn't quite jibe with the truth: "Henry Willson, former fan-magazine writer, has tied in with the Joyce & Polimer office and will handle a department devoted to developing new talent. Willson will concentrate on finding and plugging new faces."

Despite the "former fan-magazine writer" assertion, Henry continued to "plug" the same Puppet actors he now repped at Joyce & Polimer—that is, until *The New Movie Magazine* went belly-up in late 1935. Richard Polimer may have felt the need to obfuscate the truth of Henry's double employ. The Hollywood establishment never thought much of agents, but when they did, they thought of them as avaricious, scheming, and dishonest. As a profession, agents comprised a thoroughly disrespected lot of double-, if not triple-dealers. Legendary gossip columnist Hedda Hopper actually topped Henry's twin gigs by holding down no fewer than three jobs simultaneously, as agent, actress, and fan writer (for *Motion Picture Magazine*), the last calling soon to occupy her full-time.

"The agent profession was still evolving," said Budd Schulberg, author of Hollywood's first powerbroker-as-Antichrist novel, *What Makes Sammy Run?*, written in 1941. "Besides the concept of flesh-peddling, what agents did, how they did it, and how much they got paid were all very much in flux in the early 1930s."

Much to Budd Schulberg's shock, his own mother joined the disreputable ranks when, in 1932, she opened her own tenpercentery, the Ad Schulberg Agency. "Agents," according to Schulberg, "were just a cut above the wantons who referred to themselves as 'actresses' when they were booked for soliciting on Hollywood Boulevard." (Upon setting up shop, Ad Schulberg hired Charles K. Feldman as her lawyer and quickly promoted him to agent, changing the name of her firm to the Schulberg-Feldman Agency, which in time became Henry Willson's future employer, the Famous Artists Agency.)

They were a relatively new force in town, these agents, even if the jokes they inspired seemed as old as the raptors trapped in the La Brea Tar Pits. If Henry had heard the one about the film actor who kicked his agent in the heart and broke his toe, he didn't let it stunt his own ambitions.

At age twenty-one, Henry was a spirited youth with a receding hairline, no chin, and only the courage of his own ignorance to show him the way. He had grown up with his eye on Broadway, where agents at the mighty William Morris Agency, founded in 1898, were treated by his father with professional respect. Horace may not have invited the Morris boys to dine at his Forest Hills manse, but he said hello in public and otherwise treated them like fellow human beings. The Columbia record label, after all, made its reputation in the world of opera and musical theater where agents functioned largely as managers. These were creative men who helped singers develop their repertoire, charted careers, and brokered contracts for individual stage properties that ran for months, sometimes a full year, on the Great White Way. Gotham's agents functioned as the masterminds behind world-class talents.

On the West Coast, their counterparts took 10 percent. Period.

In Hollywood, Henry confronted a power structure of performer versus employer entirely different from what his father knew back east. The Broadway theater never called itself an industry, but the movies did, and for good reason. Despite its recent boomtown beginnings, Hollywood in the 1930s avoided the creative, chaotic laissez-faire ethic of the theater in favor of a hard-line factory mentality that favored efficiency and mass production over talent and individuality. Performers here received long-term contracts that gave them fixed weekly salaries and a constant stream of screen projects. In other words, movie execs like Paramount's B. P. Schulberg and M-G-M's Louis B. Mayer had a point when they insisted that there was no more need for agents in Hollywood than on Ford's assembly line in Detroit. It wasn't a pretty job, being an agent, and as far as the movie studios were concerned, somebody *didn't* have to do it.

Lack of pride was a professional prerequisite: Henry, along with 150 other penny-ante West Hollywood agents, found himself routinely banned from the motion-picture lots.

A *Hollywood Reporter* article of the period summed up the general disdain: "In order to combat the growing habit on the part of agents to stop by his window on the M-G-M lot and sell him talent over the sill, Ben Piazza, studio's casting chief, is having the building remodeled with the windows raised to eight feet. Piazza claims the agents will have to learn how to walk on stilts before they'll catch him again."

Other studios were fed up as well. In its November 26, 1935, edition, the *Reporter* ran the edict: "Paramount cancelled all agent passes granting general access to the lot yesterday and replaced the free roaming privileges with a 'by appointment only' system designating various executives whom agents must see in the future on talent deals."

Billy Wilkerson, the *Reporter*'s raffish publisher, had founded the town's first trade newspaper only five years earlier, in 1930, and from the beginning, he knew which side of the business buttered his editorial pages. Besides, he didn't like agents accosting studio execs at his new nightclub, the Trocadero, and he nearly hit the red tile roof when one agent, posing as a waiter, made a pitch over pea soup to a hungry producer!

"There are more agents here than Heinz has beans and not one of them working for the interest of the picture business, his client, or the producer," Wilkerson wrote in his weekly column. "They are only after their 10 percent and 20 percent grab, and their activities are agitating the whole business."

Wilkerson's major competition, *Variety*, seconded his opinion with a memorable headline, "Fade-Out for Agents."

In time, Henry would brag that agents ruled the business. But not yet. In 1934, his quick segue from fan-magazine writer to agent was seen as a step down to the last rung of the Hollywood professional ladder. When the movies learned to talk, only Myron Selznick had stopped crawling long enough to command any real power as an agent. He didn't have much competition: The William Morris Agency had waited until 1927 to open a Los Angeles branch, an outpost that didn't see the arrival of top lieutenant Abe Lastfogel until 1933. Another giant, the Music Corporation of America (MCA), carried no clout until Lew Wasserman landed on the West Coast in 1939. Before Lastfogel and Wasserman came to town, Myron Selznick, brother of David O., cornered an astonishing 95 percent of the agency business in Hollywood.

Wiped clean from Selznick's bargaining table were the other 5 percent who found themselves divvied up among the town's 150 boutique agencies. It was at one of these human-scrap joints, the Joyce & Polimer Agency, that Henry began his career. Back then, most of these operations were pop-and-son concerns that occupied the second-floor office above a florist or dress shop on Sunset Boulevard in the unincorporated part of the city known as West

Hollywood. It was there, among the orange groves and two-bedroom bungalows and front yards with picket fences, that Hollywood's lesser agents could escape the annual $100 licensing fee that the city of Los Angeles levied on such businesses.

Whatever the liabilities of being a West Hollywood agent, the clubs and former speakeasies of Sunset Boulevard more than compensated, especially for a young man of Henry Willson's gregarious, outgoing disposition. When his commissions failed him, he told friends, "My father sent money from home." The extra cash, in turn, let him perfect the art of late-night agenting in all its glory of fine wine, good food, and abundant sex.

It was part of the game then, especially the sex, and Henry was hardly the only agent vulnerable to the sins of the trade. "When I became a talent agent for MCA, the word 'agent' was synonymous with 'pimp,' " said Lew Wasserman. "Talent agents wore green suits and hung around street corners with big cigars in their mouths. The badge of a talent agent was a Charvet tie."

Henry took care of the sartorial part by dressing like his much-admired father. Where most East Coast émigrés quickly graduated to sweaters and slacks in sunny California, he showed up in the middle of the day wearing a natty striped suit complete with vest and a silk tie dimpled to perfection.

The pimp part was another matter. Considering the prevailing mores of the time, sex should have been the last sin to get a man crucified in Hollywood. It was a truism Henry Willson lived to disprove. He hardly invented the gay casting couch, but in the blatantly heterosexual world of Hollywood, where sex appeal trumped talent, it was not completely unheard of for handsome male actors to keep their virtue relatively intact on their climb to stardom. With few homosexuals and virtually no women in any positions of real power, male sexuality wasn't a readily exchanged commodity. Henry's niche in the business—"developing new talent," as Richard K. Polimer put it to *The Hollywood Reporter*—may have placed him low on Hollywood's power ladder, but it gave him high visibility among those willing and eager to enter the business by whatever route possible.

If Henry had homosexual mentors, he never spoke of them. But he was nothing if not clever, and following the example of Hollywood's established powerbrokers, Henry quickly made the necessary sexual adjustment. Granted, Myron Selznick looked and acted like an ogre. But Frank and Vincent Orsatti were enticing examples for any eager cormorant looking to make his way in the movieland forest.

In the 1930s, the glamorous Orsatti brothers topped the list of agents who peddled flesh, literally. Raffishly debonair and handsome enough to work both sides of the camera, the brothers defined the term "lady-killer." Rivaling their famous clients for photo exposure in the party sections of *Photoplay* and *Modern Screen*, they luxuriated in the glow of being photographed at all the best clubs and premieres. For arm decoration, the blonde of the moment sufficed, and the Orsattis were known to rep, marry, and divorce a few of them. Many more were offered the privilege of having sex with a studio executive, all in exchange for a studio contract at $75 a week.

"It was well known that Orsatti had special connections to Louis B. Mayer because he supplied him with his women," said Budd Schulberg. It was a myth proved true in 1962 when a Justice Department memo started that "Frank Orsatti had a special in with M-G-M."

The Orsattis were more the rule than the exception. It was the starlet's lament: "Who do I have to screw to get out of this movie?"

"A lot of these producers had stables of girls," said Bette Davis. "They gave them $75 a week and gave them a bit part now and then to keep them happy. And they also had other services." (Two decades later, nothing much had changed. When the Justice Department investigated the monopolistic practices of Lew Wasserman's MCA, FBI agents discovered that the agency worked its starlets as prostitutes to curry favor with TV network executives.)

Columbia Pictures's Harry Cohn was so notorious a womanizer that he built a passageway from his office to the dressing rooms of his contract actresses. Darryl F. Zanuck of 20th Century–Fox improved on Cohn's sexual efficiency by installing a boudoir off his office, and it was well reported that his routine there brought the workday to a halt at 4 P.M. sharp every day while an actress serviced him.

The adjective "notorious" rarely tarnished the reputations of such men. For a homosexual like Henry Willson, the word would stick like feathers to tar.

Before he earned that opprobrium, Henry's "personal touch" meant that he was more friend than reporter. And when he became an agent, he took that intimacy several steps further to be friend, father, confidante, protector, bed partner, and, when his sexual interest waned, friend and father all over again. From the moment he stepped off the boat from Gotham, Henry merged his business and private life. One look at Sunset Boulevard and its many haunts and Henry knew he had found a playground that was more his home than any house he ever owned.

Also known as the Strip, the boulevard possessed a third, now-forgotten nickname. Henry and his generation of late-night gadflies called it "The Neck." A winding thoroughfare that undulated half-way up the Hollywood Hills, The Neck connected the movie studios located in the Hollywood flats with the new, palatial homes being built in Beverly Hills. In filmland's ever-changing conurbation, it supplanted Whitley Heights near the Cahuenga Pass as the preferred place to live. "When I got to Los Angeles, I had to live in Beverly Hills," Henry told friends. He need only ask, and Horace provided.

The move westward meant trading convenience in the Heights for prestige and space in the Hills. It also required a long drive down Sunset Boulevard to get to Paramount, RKO, Columbia, and, over in the Valley, Universal, and Warners. In their migration westward, Henry and his Beverly Hills neighbors traveled the Strip day and night and worked there in second-floor agencies. Below them, the ground-floor stores and eateries turned the street into an early version of one long shopping mall. Still, Sunset Boulevard remained a rustic country street. Occasionally, a car blew out a tire and there would be a traffic jam. Otherwise, the groves of orange trees, poppies, and poinsettia were just the throw of a cocktail glass beyond those colorfully flimsy two-story storefronts that made up a Potemkin village of the Far West.

Native Californians found it all terribly cosmopolitan. In 1933, *Photoplay* described the West Hollywood thoroughfare as the only place in Los Angeles where "you can eat in any language under the sun."

For transplanted New Yorkers like Henry, the Strip's contrived international ambiance came off like so many sideshow tents strung together and put up overnight at the circus. Many sneered. In his classic Hollywood novel *Day of the Locust,* Nathaniel West lambastes the Los Angeles architecture, which ruthlessly threw ersatz Rhine castles against ersatz palaces out of the *Arabian Nights.* "Both houses were comic, but he didn't laugh," West wrote of his protagonist, Tod Hackett.

Henry never stopped laughing. He reveled in this new city's chaotic sense of exaggerated fun. Only in Los Angeles could he walk into the Coconut Grove, and admiring the fake palm trees out of Rudolph Valentino's *The Sheik,* feel like a movie star before his job ever took him to a soundstage. Henry loved the clubs, hated the office. Restaurants and bars were a better place to ply the young with wit, good humor, food, and liquor—all charged to his neverending tab and paid for by Horace Willson. Henry said it's how he liked to interview prospective clients. "They can relax and I can get a real feel if they are a good bet," he explained.

Henry chose a restaurant according to its theme and his mood. High-drama negotiations meant borscht and vodka at the Bubliccki. For something more playful, he went for fruit drinks at the Bali. And as a galloping Anglophile with ancestors traced back to the Revolutionary War (he never forgot to remind people of his Uncle Sam) he made the Cock 'n' Bull with its roast-beef buffet a favorite early-evening hangout. Business interviews began there, then progressed to the Café Trocadero where Henry could order either Larded Tenderloin of Beef Forestière or Vol-au-vent of Sweet-breads Toulousaine. The more French-sounding the better. Henry said he spoke the language flawlessly, not that anyone in Los Angeles would know the difference. After emptying a bottle of the Troc's Chateau de Rayne-Vigneau, the young agent switched to his signature white crème de menthe to give his breath a peppermint glow at night's end.

In between the Cock 'n' Bull and the Troc, Henry's daily pere-grinations on The Neck took him by Darrin's automobile show-room and the Forget Me Not flower shop. Those two establishments cast light both strong and dim onto his own future among the orange trees and rattlesnake nests: Darrin's, a redo of an old bottling works off Cole Drive, was where everyone from Clark Gable to Charlie Chaplin bought their custom-built cars. Twenty years later, Henry would tweak the name over the showroom door and rechristen one of his boys James Darren. Farther east, the Forget Me Not was owned and operated by one of the town's most famous mothers, Mrs. Lewis J. Selznick, her bankrupt husband an early Hollywood casualty of hubris and ill connections. Flossie Selznick ran the store with her third, now-forgotten son, a brain-damaged youth named Howard who would live and die in the Benzedrine-driven, vodka-soused shadows of his famous siblings, Myron and David O. Although Henry didn't know it when he bought his first boutonniere from Flossie, her son David would soon be his most illustrious boss and, for better and worse, his most profligate mentor.

More significant to Henry's immediate future, Perry's Brass Rail café made a big comeback on the Strip in 1933. A failed eatery, Perry's underwent a successful revamp in the hands of the fourth Marx brother, Zeppo, who invested $10,000 and installed a flock of singing waiters with rouged noses and fake handle-bar mous-taches. "Now it's a handout for the picture mob who find the place a laugh resort," declared *Variety*. Henry wandered in one night with best friend Tom Brown, and spotting Perry's new owner doing duty behind the bar, he worked Zeppo Marx like he worked Sue Carol and Dixie Lee Crosby on their way through the Panama Canal.

"If Zeppo had been an agent then, he would have hired me on the spot," said Henry, never guilty of self-underestimation. Unfortunately, the transplanted New Yorker had to wait a whole two years for Zeppo to open his own agency and ensconce him there, in June 1936, as a vice president. Like the Brass Rail, the new Zeppo Marx Agency took off from the get-go and soon developed a rep for handling star couples, including Clark Gable and Carole Lombard, Robert Taylor and Barbara Stanwyck. Zeppo was born to the biz. "It's not right," he once cracked. "Just think of it, all those actors, writers, and directors getting 90 percent of their salaries."

Henry facilitated his move from dowdy Joyce & Polimer to Zeppo's swanky outfit by signing the distaff side of the Marx Brothers team. He knew her from his cub reporter days at *Variety* when she starred on Broadway. In a most unlikely twist of fate, the great Margaret Dumont would be Henry's meal ticket to the Hollywood big time.

7

Junior Hollywood

Before he left Joyce & Polimer, Henry delivered on his reputation for spotting talent barely out of the womb. In this case, it was a seventeen-year-old boy he'd been watching on the Broadway stage for nearly a decade. A May 1934 item in *The Hollywood Reporter* revealed that Henry Willson "set the deal" for Junior Durkin to play the son of Aline MacMahon in *Big-Hearted Herbert* for Warners. After the double success of *Tom Sawyer* and *Huckleberry Finn*, Durkin had been one of the most sought-after juveniles in the film business. But unlike other stage actors who'd gotten a taste of picture-making, Junior kept his theater career active. He'd grown up on the stage, having made his debut at age two in the musical *Some Night*, followed by playing W. C. Fields's kiddie foil in the 1923 play *Poppy*. Despite his movie hits opposite Jackie Coogan, Junior refused to sign a long-term studio contract, which quickly forced Henry to show his agent mettle by setting up a series of individual projects at Hollywood's better studios.

The Hollywood Reporter ran a blurb that Durkin was handled under the "personal supervision" of Henry Willson, who recommended that everyone immediately stop calling him Junior. His real name, Trent, sounded more mature, and Henry liked the rhythm, as he put it, "of one syllable followed by two syllables or vice versa." After placing Durkin in *Little Men*, based on the sequel to the Louisa May Alcott classic, Henry signed his client to play the lead in the film adaptation of Eugene O'Neill's *Ah, Wilderness,* to be produced by M-G-M. Even though he had not yet turned eighteen, the actor would be billed for the first time as Trent Durkin, a proper adult name worthy of mention alongside those of his illustrious costars, Wallace Beery and Lionel Barrymore.

Henry welcomed Trent into his new Beverly Hills home as what he came to tell friends was "my first and last roommate." More often, he called him "my client." Even among homosexual acquaintances, Henry tended to speak in a kind of sexual code. Despite the notoriety that would eventually devour him, his actions spoke more truthfully than any words he ever uttered. Henry never referred to himself as a homosexual nor did he ever call anyone his "lover," "partner," or "mate." The preferred titles were "friend," or better yet, "client." He did describe himself as a "late-bloomer" sexually.

As one close associate put it, "Probably sex *was* love for Henry. Big cocks were love. Success was love. The one thing he could not tolerate was loneliness. He had to have someone in his life always." Henry preferred crowd scenes over intimacy; he called many people his best friend, but no one ever became a life partner for so much as a year or two. Even in his correspondence, Henry signed off with the word "fondly," never "love." Of the thousands of men who traveled in and out of his life, Durkin may have been the only one to live in his home for more than a weekend. Whatever the true nature of that relationship—Willson was twenty-three to Durkin's seventeen in 1935—it turned out to be tragically short.

On May 4, the two men were on holiday at the desert ranch of Jackie Coogan's parents, located just outside San Diego. Jackie and Junior had made an effective oil-and-water portrait on screen, and they got along privately as well. Together with Coogan's father, John, and two ranch hands, the boys had spent the day dove hunting in the desert. Never the sportsman or athlete, Henry begged off the hunt to stay behind with the women, in this case, his friend Paula Stone and Durkin's two sisters, Gertrude and Grace. Henry's client Patricia Ellis had planned to make the trip but remained back in Los Angeles.

She cut her lip the day before in a fall on the set of *Freshman Love,* just one of the seven films she would make that year, playing yet another singing coed. A visit to the doctor forced Patricia to postpone any San Diego plans for at least a day.

On return from their hunt, John Coogan drove Jackie's new coupe, his twentieth-birthday present to his son. They were on the San Diego–Imperial Valley Highway when a car swerved in front of them, forcing the older Coogan off the road and down a steep ravine that sent the vehicle into a spin.

"It came fast around the turn, way over on our side of the road," Jackie said of the other car. "Dad swerved out toward the edge and I felt the car skid off the soft shoulder. Then it went over the side."

Jackie was thrown clear of the vehicle the first time it turned over, and he escaped with only two broken ribs and numerous bruises. The other four men, including Trent, were all killed.

Three hours later, an airplane from Los Angeles carrying Coogan's mother, the former vaudeville star Lillian Toliver, arrived in San Diego, accompanied by Patricia Ellis and her unemployed step-father, Alexander Leftwich. Mrs. Coogan grieved exuberantly but soon remarried, and in record time she and her second husband, Arthur Bernstein, spent her son's vast fortune of $6 million, leaving him only $1,000. (The lawsuit he brought against them resulted in the Jackie Coogan Law, which protects the earnings of minors.)

Henry Willson referred to the tragedy with unusual discretion in his *New Movie Magazine* column. He momentarily interrupted his breathlessly upbeat reporting to print a small photo of Durkin with the caption: "Death always seems the more cruel when it takes the young. Junior Durkin had a splendid future. We shall miss him."

Ah, Wilderness was only days away from starting production. The world would never get to know Henry's newly renamed Trent Durkin. Either to avoid confusion or out of respect to the seventeen-year-old, the magazine changed the title of Henry's column for that one issue. Instead of "Junior Hollywood," Henry slugged it "Young Hollywood."

PART THREE

A Paramount publicity photo captures Cary Grant and Randolph Scott at home, 1223 North Sweetzer Avenue, West Hollywood, early 1930s.

8

Cary Grant's Roommate

In the early 1930s, it was not unusual in Hollywood for bisexuals and homosexuals to live together "with discretion." In some cases, it wasn't so discreet, as evidenced in Paramount Pictures' "at-home" photo shoots with Cary Grant and Randolph Scott. In one such photo-driven interview, preedited and distributed free-of-charge to the fan magazines, Grant revealed, "Here we are, living as we want to as bachelors with a nice home at a comparatively low cost." The two men first moved in together in 1932, rooming in a small courtyard building at 1223 North Sweetzer Avenue in West Hollywood. They later upgraded to a house on the Santa Monica beach. Showing no need for girlfriends, the two men were a frequent couple at William Randolph Hearst's castle up the coast at San Simeon, and they delighted other guests with their quaint habit of wearing identical outfits to the publisher's costume parties. It was a romance that flourished back in Los Angeles's speakeasy world when lavender was the rage that held the stage, and drag entertainers like Rae Bourbon and Jean Malin headlined LA's "panze joints." It was well known among the nance crowd on both coasts: Speakeasies had a bad-good rep for looking the other way at the sight of women in trousers and men dancing with men. Henry loved such hang-outs in Harlem and Greenwich Village and anticipated going to Hollywood's equally liberated counterparts on the Strip.

But it was not to be. The laissez-faire mores of the speakeasies were officially outlawed in 1933 with the repeal of Prohibition.

Although alcohol was legal again, Prohibition's end led to the implementation of vice laws that essentially prohibited its sale to homosexuals (or, at least, people who engaged in homosexual acts). It was a case of political horse-trading: In exchange for legalizing alcohol, conservative politicians demanded that deviant sexual behavior—that is, homosexuality—be made illegal in the newly legitimate bars and clubs. When the Barn, at 6426 Sunset Boulevard, with its "floor show in which men masquerade as women, and women pose as men," suffered its first police raid, several female impersonators got slapped with six-month jail sentences, all *after* Prohibition had been repealed.

And the problem wasn't just transvestites. In the best Hollywood society, Cary Grant and Randolph Scott found it advantageous to stop showing up at premieres as each other's date and to start looking for wives. Into this repressive climate arrived the resilient, adaptable, ultimately cunning Henry Willson. As a journalist, and later as a press-savvy agent, he made his reputation by executing the art of the romantic cover-up. It was a talent that the motion-picture industry gave Henry ample opportunity to test and hone in post-Prohibition Hollywood.

The new vice laws regarding sexual deviants and the sale of alcohol were reflected in other conservative measures of the day. On July 1, 1934, a former postmaster general named William H. Hays discovered eponymous fame when the Production Code Administration adopted his proposal of self-censorship for the industry, and effectively outlawed the depiction of overt sexual behavior and language, not to mention "sexual deviancy," on the screen. They called it the Hays Code.

Publicity photos of Cary and Randy at home, camping it up like an old married couple, may have gone unnoticed in the speakeasy era. But not in late 1933. *The Hollywood Reporter* went into homophobic overdrive with reports of this "long-haired town for males" and a reprimand that "Cary and Randy were carrying the buddy business a bit too far." There was also an item that "Cary Grant,

Randy Scott, Betty Furness, and Cesar Romero and some more took a serious (but not too serious!) pledge not to marry for five years." The juxtaposition of the three male homosexuals and Furness, a frequent beard for Grant and Romero, was no editorial accident. While the fan rags made a practice of serving up romantic illusion, they also found a way to deliver the truth. A *Photoplay* profile of Romero, included in an article called "Bachelors by Choice," raved about his Latin good looks but cautioned: "Still he seems slated for bachelorhood."

By 1934, Grant followed the *Reporter's* advice and took actress Virginia Cherrill for his wife. Despite the camouflage, *Photoplay* managed to give the real score in its article, "Still Pals": "Not even a wife could separate Randy and Cary—but then Virginia wouldn't want to." Regardless, she wasn't given much opportunity. Thirteen months after they tied the knot, Mrs. and Mrs. Cary Grant untied it with a divorce after he attempted suicide.

The historian George Chauncey observed the demarcation between the liberated Prohibition era and the conservative years that followed: "The revulsion against gay life in the early 1930s was part of a larger reaction to the perceived 'excesses' of the Prohibition years and the blurring of the boundaries between acceptable and unacceptable public sociability." In the late 1940s and early 1950s, it would be different but the same. In the red-baiting political climate of postwar years the House Un-American Activities Committee succeeded in linking Communists and homosexuals. In HUAC's eyes, subversives were subversives, whether political or social, and therefore worthy of expulsion from America.

As a homosexual, Henry Willson made the necessary adjustments at all times, and with no interest in being a victim or rebel, he put on the hetero mantle to turn adversity and fear to his professional advantage. Horace Willson's son learned at least one lesson of survival and self-discipline from his studies at the Asheville School: After Junior Durkin's death, Henry never repeated risking career suicide by living with another man.

Although he rarely spent the night alone, his housemates were invariably one-night or weekend guests. It was a self-inflicted rule that he followed for the rest of his life and imposed on all his gay male clients. To disobey meant virtual banishment from his representation, as several clients were later to learn.

Homosexuality may have been forbidden, but Henry never let any social liability get in the way of seeing his own name and face in print. In essence, he became Hollywood's first Zelig—seen everywhere with everybody before people knew who he was or what he did. Let other agents bask in the reflected light of their clients' glory. From the minute he arrived in Hollywood, the Henry Willson moniker found its way into the gossip and news columns of *Variety* and the *Hollywood Reporter* with astounding regularity, especially for one so new to the business. He worked the press like no other agent. Whether he was promoting a client ("Margaret Dumont got a hundred cans of Campbell's soup along with her salary for appearing on the *Hollywood Hotel* hour, and tried to pay off her agent, Henry Willson, with 'em!") or his own faux-romantic life (a series of "girlfriends" like Paula Stone and Patricia Ellis were forever on the verge of walking down the aisle with him but invariably married someone else at the last minute), Henry never failed to conjure up news even if what he reported wasn't new. Only Myron Selznick received more coverage for the major deals he brokered; only the Orsattis nabbed more trade-paper items for the women they dated, wed, and divorced. "Vic Orsatti's idea of the perfect girl must be a blonde who thinks like a brunette and acts like a redhead," opined *The Hollywood Reporter*.

Regarding the flamboyant Orsattis, reporters wrote what they saw (and suppressed much that was unprintable). With Henry, his colleagues in the press dutifully translated into print the sexual chimera he fabricated for them to see. Night after night, he showed up in a tux at Billy Wilkerson's Trocadero with yet another woman, usually a client, his datebook a virtual replication of the Puppets club's female roster.

"He was safe in every way," said actress Joan Fontaine, an early client. "Evidently Henry was simply attracted to his own sex." When Henry started squiring Fontaine around town, she was better known as her sibling's go-fer than a formidable actress in her own right. "Her sister, Olivia de Havilland, was the star," said Henry, "and Joan was sort of acting as her chauffeur and maid, and quite unhappy doing little more than bits." If success has many fathers, then he could claim to be Fontaine's first Hollywood daddy. He negotiated her contract with Jesse L. Lasky, which led to an RKO contract, which led to a deal with David O. Selznick, which led to her winning an Academy Award for *Suspicion* in 1941.

Before Joan Fontaine found a husband, an Academy Award, and another agent, Henry was already in pursuit of other photographer bait. Marge Belcher, for one, remembered elegant parties at Henry's new Tower Road house and their nights together line-dancing at the Trocadero. Belcher was a mature sixteen years old.

"I didn't get one of his fancy names, he changed my name from Marjorie Belcher to Margery Bell," said the actress-dancer. (A few years later, director-choreographer Gower Champion would do Henry one better and permanently change her name to Marge Champion, his dancing partner and wife of many years.) A true child of Hollywood, Marge learned how to dance from her father, Ernest Belcher, who worked as a dance instructor on silent films for Charlie Chaplin, Cecil B. DeMille, and Mack Sennett. By the time she signed with Henry at the Zeppo Marx Agency in 1937, the teenaged Marge had already achieved anonymous but enduring fame among the movie-going public as Walt Disney's prototype for the princess lead in his animated *Snow White and the Seven Dwarfs*. (Later, she would also be the model for Disney's Tinkerbelle in *Peter Pan*.)

A proper English gentleman, Ernest Belcher harbored few illusions about the men of Hollywood, which is why he forbade his underage daughter to go out on dates with them. Yet he saw no impropriety with her line-dancing the night away with Henry at the

Troc. "Henry was a very good ballroom dancer, he loved to dance, and it was just the beginning of swing and the jitterbug," Marge recalled. The transplanted New Yorker beguiled the native California girl. "Henry was so much more sophisticated than the guys I grew up with in Los Angeles," she said. "He had all the graces, was very cultured, he dressed well, knew all about the theater and good wine and restaurants. He wasn't handsome, but he was slender and very presentable." He was also as outgoing as he was attentive, a rare combo anywhere but a genuine novelty in Hollywood. Henry talked to excess but he also knew how to give the impression he could listen. He asked questions and managed to be aggressive without being pushy. "I wouldn't have known what to do with arrogant," said Marge Champion. "And he had that Eastern flair. We had a word for them: 'eggheads.' They looked down at us poor westerners."

It never occurred to such a proper, young LA lady that Henry's many good graces, style, and taste had anything to do with his being homosexual. "In 1937, I didn't know what that was," said Marge Champion. "It wasn't talked about. It was a different time."

Sixteen-year-old girls weren't the only ones to plead ignorance on the subject. The future father of the gay-rights movement, Harry Hay, didn't always know one when he saw one in the 1930s. After graduating from Los Angeles High School in 1930, Hay went on to write screenplays, join the Communist Party, and, by the end of the decade, get married—to a woman. "There wasn't really even a word for it," Hay said of homosexuality. "Either you were considered a total moral degenerate, and there were very few of those, or you were a married man with children who had this peculiar vice of sleeping with other men on occasion. It was like saying someone drank too much or they gambled."

Marge Champion likened her agent's sexual orientation to such other outré subjects of the period as life-threatening diseases and exotic religions. "Growing up in Hollywood, I always thought you had to whisper words like 'cancer' and 'Jewish,'" she said. Ironically, her own mother informed Margery, then seventeen, that she was, in fact, half Jewish. Some topics required hushed tones, others weren't mentioned at all. "Nobody came out of the closet then," she said. "That must have been very worrisome to Henry."

Anxious or not, her agent delivered. Henry secured three films for Margery Bell in as many weeks, all of them Westerns starring an Iowa farm boy named Bob Baker. Each movie was shot in six days and carried the virtually interchangeable titles *Singing Outlaw*, *Courage of the West*, and *Honor of the West*. When Margery finished those three gigs in as many weeks, Henry booked her on a vaude-ville tour with a new comedy trio that just couldn't miss, he insisted. When the show closed on the road three weeks later, Margery Bell didn't blame Henry for stranding her in snowbound Buffalo, New York. Sixty years later, she continued to believe she owed him everything. "From *Snow White and the Seven Dwarfs* to the Three Stooges," the actress-dancer recalled, "I traveled east and decided to stay here."

9

Lana Turner at the Troc

I f it was no romantic treat, a night out on the town with Henry Willson qualified as a safe harbor for starlets used to fighting off the advances of Harry Cohn, Darryl F. Zanuck, or the Orsatti brothers.

Or Billy Wilkerson.

To inaugurate the repeal of Prohibition in 1933, the *Hollywood Reporter*'s publisher converted the old La Boheme speakeasy at 8610 Sunset into a swank new dinner club. He named it the Café Trocadero. Everyone else called it the Trocadero or, for short, the Troc. A dashing, inveterate gambler, Wilkerson knew much less about newspapers than he did nightclubs, having run a few speakeasies in New York before moving west in 1930 to start *The Hollywood Reporter*. With his new publication, he took on *Variety*, which focused its editorial content more on vaudeville, and gave Hollywood its first locally based trade paper. Movie people didn't think they needed a trade paper, and fortunately for them Wilkerson was not above being bought. His novel approach to journalism included taking loans from studio heads and putting them on the books as prepaid advertising in the *Reporter*, which in turn gave Wilkerson the money to open the Trocadero, followed in quick succession by Ciro's, LaRue, and L'Aiglon.

Stars and powerbrokers who frequented the Troc got to see their names in the *Reporter*. It was a cozy deal for everybody—

and one Henry knew well, thanks to his *Variety* credentials. Although Wilkerson made a habit of trashing agents in his weekly column, people said Wilkerson liked Henry. Or at least, that's what Henry said people said. If the two men didn't share an interest in the opposite sex, they developed a common obsession with the Trocadero.

Wilkerson plugged his club in every issue of the *Reporter,* and as a journalist and later an agent, Henry curried favor at the newspaper by taking up late-night residence there. The two men had an unofficial agreement: Henry bought Wilkerson's expensive champagne, Wilkerson put Henry's name in print. Henry brought starlets to the Trocadero, Wilkerson put their names in print. What other journalist-turned-agent could pay the steep $7.50-a-plate for dinner plus an additional $9.00 for a bottle of Chateau de Rayne-Vigneau 1901? Larded with cash from home, Henry ordered both night after night, and he treated the bartenders and hatcheck girls to extravagant tips, and doubled the going rate to a full 10 percent with the club's waiters. Even more to Wilkerson's liking, Henry never complained when the publisher–club owner walked off with one of his dates at midnight. There were also Henry's precious notes to the Troc's most physically imposing customers: "If you are interested in getting into the movies, I can help you. Henry Willson. Agent."

On Sunset Boulevard, everyone was interested. And Henry's pick-up notes soon became a cherished Trocadero ritual. For such an extravagant youth, they emerged as his one lesson in simplicity: First, he sent the missives, and if that didn't send the beauties running to his table, Henry's blooming ego rarely prevented him from his beelining it right to theirs. As a rule, the notes did what they were intended to do. Henry stayed put at his table near the great south wall, which Wilkerson had replaced with one enormous window, its view a spectacular carpet of lights downhill to Santa Monica Boulevard and beyond to the LA flats. Henry loved it there, against the glass and lights and dark reflections, and he turned his table into his veritable living room.

Like most of his sex, he had little time for subtlety late at night. Many were called, and when they paid homage at his table, he let the eager ones know, "This can all be yours." Then Henry raised a glass of white crème de menthe to the window and whatever lay beyond. He was rarely wrong. Most people he toasted ended up living in the flats.

There were two very notable exceptions, and both came to Henry through his Wilkerson connection.

The night Henry met Bill Orr could have been any other night at the Trocadero. Newly installed at the Zeppo Marx Agency, Henry arrived at the nightclub in his chauffeur-driven car, which, guaranteed an impressive entrance. He avoided taking the stairs to the Bar and Grill in the cellar, where folksy copper pots dangled overhead from a low ceiling and thick red-and-black plaid wall coverings muffled the din to make for soft, intimate conversations. Henry preferred being seen, if not heard, which made the upstairs dining room more his scene. Shaking sweaty hands, kissing powdered cheeks, he brushed past the crowded tables and dancing couples on the main floor to take up his usual perch near the south window. From there, he could gaze at two cities of light: the real Los Angeles, spread out like a thousand votive candles, and the fake Paris on the opposite wall, rendered in paint and bordered with a cream-and-gold frame. That panoramic mural was wide enough to feature both the Eiffel Tower and nearly a mile's worth of the Seine. Having been to Paris, Henry preferred looking at the lovely boy across the room.

Out on a date with his mother, Bill Orr had arrived in Los Angeles that very morning. It would be quite a day for him. No sooner did he put on his tux and follow his mom to the Troc than he received a hand-delivered note from Henry Willson. Like a hundred others, it read: "If you're interested . . ."

As notes go, the one Henry sent Orr was worth its weight in a ton or two of gold. Every Warner Bros. TV show from 1955 to 1965 ended its credits with "Wm. T. Orr, executive producer," and it was through Orr that Henry would place dozens of his clients in such long-running TV series as *77 Sunset Strip, Cheyenne, F Troop, Surfside Six,* and *Maverick,* among others. However, before television took up residence in every American home, it was through Henry that Bill Orr launched his own career in show business.

Orr was celebrating his eighteenth birthday the night he received Henry's note. "He was from a very socially connected family back east, and Bill had just graduated from Philips Exeter when he met Henry," said Nan Morris Robinson, a close friend to both men. Exceedingly self-possessed for a high-school grad, Orr had also been blessed with a chiseled face that, in Henry's opinion, recalled the masculine grace of Clark Gable.

"It is made for the closeup," Henry told him.

"And what is a closeup?" asked Orr.

Henry could only smile at such a combination of beauty, youth, and ignorance. What more could a man want in another man? Henry quickly impressed with the promise of a screen test. "I think my friend George Sidney would like to direct it," he told Mrs. Orr. A Broadway actor-turned-director, George Sidney was a charter member of the Puppets club, and Henry had written about him glowingly in a few of his "Junior Hollywood" columns.

The M-G-M screen test was scheduled, but Sidney's attack of appendicitis derailed the project. Undaunted, Henry regrouped by having Orr cast in the revue *Meet the People,* which led to his being chosen to play Mickey Rooney's best friend in *The Hardys Ride High* and a few other films. The Exeter grad had set foot on stage only once or twice at school, but Henry knew star potential when he spotted it. Orr delivered on that promise when he played his greatest part a few years later as husband of Joy Page, stepdaughter of Jack Warner.

At least she called herself Joy Page. Her face, if not her voice, had already been immortalized as a Bulgarian refugee in one of the crowd scenes in the 1942 classic *Casablanca.* Her fortune as an actress didn't change much when she adjusted her name to Joy Ann

Page for *Kismet,* in 1944, and to Joanne Page for *Man-Eater of Kumaon,* in 1948. Sometime between the infrequent movie projects, Joy found time to convince her powerful stepfather to buy Bill Orr's contract from M-G-M and give him one at Warner Bros., where his rapid climb within the company, to head of production at the studio's TV division in the 1950s, inspired many "the son-in-law also rises" jokes. It didn't hurt Bill's ego any less that the line had already been used on David O. Selznick, who bolted up the Hollywood ladder when he married Irene Mayer, the daughter of Louis B.

Put-down or not, the joke was no laughing matter to the future clients of Henry Willson who became stars in Warner's many TV series: Van Williams, Guy Williams, Clint Walker, L. Q. Jones, Robert Fuller, John Smith, and Nick Adams all secured employment through Orr in his heyday. (In time, Orr would pay his old agent friend the ultimate compliment of creating the most priapic name ever to grace a Hollywood leading man. His act of *hommage* was jumpstarted by Henry's client Clint Walker, who walked off the set of the Western series *Cheyenne* in 1957 in a snit over money. Orr tried to replace him with a virtual unknown whose parents had saddled him with the impossible name Orton Whipple Hungerford III. When one Warner executive suggested they rename Orton with something more manly—"It's got to be as sexy as an erection" he reportedly instructed—it was Orr who thought of his old friend Henry and blurted out, "How about Ty Hardin?"

Billy Wilkerson was more directly responsible for another one of Henry Willson's early discoveries. Like most powerful Catholics in Hollywood, the thirty-seven-year-old publisher–club owner was a man of many contradictions: he went to Mass every Sunday, and during the week, gambled away thousands of dollars and slept with nearly as many women not named Mrs. Billy Wilkerson. One of those women was a delicious-looking sixteen-year-old whom Billy had spotted one day at the Top Hat Malt Shop, near the *Hollywood Reporter* offices and kitty-cornered from her school, the legendary

Hollywood High on Sunset Boulevard and Highland. Billy thought she was so special that it struck him one day that the girl could be a movie star. Tellingly, he did not inform such power agents as Myron Selznick, Bill Morris Jr., or Ad Schulberg of his momentous discovery. Billy knew they would laugh in his face if he sent them someone like Judy Turner. Henry, on the other hand, had quickly emerged in Hollywood as the agent of first-resort for the amateur performer with undeniable good-looks and questionable talent.

On Wilkerson's recommendation, Mildred Turner accompanied her underage daughter to meet Henry. Henry liked mothers, but not this one. "She brought her daughter in and dressed her like a middle-aged hooker with this cheap fur stole, paste jewelry, a few coats of makeup and her hair piled on top of her head," he recalled.

Henry told the girl to come back tomorrow. "Only this time, wash your face, no makeup, and wear whatever it is you wear to Hollywood High," he instructed.

The second meeting left him enchanted, and Henry then saw what Wilkerson had seen in the girl: a rare, if not unprecedented, combo of schoolgirl innocence and raw sex. Judy and Henry talked. She asked about the poster of Uncle Sam on his office wall. He told her the whole story. Henry was always good at getting youngsters to "open up." It was then, "and only then," that he saw what the camera captured in closeups. Judy smiled and Henry smiled, too. Hollywood was such a small world. Judy Turner turned out to be the classmate of another recently signed client, and while she possessed not a jot of Margery Bell's talent as a dancer or actress, Henry knew he was looking at the real thing across his desk. Sex appeal meant more than talent. Maybe sex *was* talent. Let Margery Bell make oaters with Bob Baker and do the vaudeville circuit with the Three Stooges. He could make *this* girl a star.

It took no effort on his part to squeeze her into a bit in David O. Selznick's production of *A Star Is Born,* starring Janet Gaynor and Fredric March. Judy's role wasn't large. She wasn't even credited. "I think she was in a scene set around a swimming pool," said Henry.

"She had no lines. She got $25 for it, but Selznick turned her down for a contract."

More small appearances followed in *The Great Garrick, Topper,* and *The Adventures of Marco Polo*, but no studio came forth with a contract. Somebody at Fox told Henry why nobody was buying: "She can't act."

"I didn't say she could act. I said she could be a movie star!" Henry shot back. Over the next thirty years, his ethos of star-making would never be better expressed.

When studio execs failed to cooperate, Henry fell back on his journalistic instincts and trotted Judy over to the Trocadero; he knew the photographers would take notice and do their magic. He even made it a double date, and to ensure newspaper coverage he brought along his more famous clients Anne Shirley and James Ellison, who were having an especially good year. Shirley had just appeared as Barbara Stanwyck's rather clueless daughter, Laurel, in the year's top weeper, *Stella Dallas*. And Ellison starred as Buffalo Bill in DeMille's *The Plainsman* opposite Gary Cooper's Wild Bill Hickcok.

The double-date ploy worked. More interested in shooting Anne and Jimmy, a photographer obliged Henry and took a picture of Judy hanging on his arm. The *Los Angeles Times* reprinted it; Mervyn LeRoy saw it and he bit.

The director was making a film with Claude Rains about a girl's murder and how it sets off a racial war in a small Southern town. There was a small but key female role he hadn't yet cast in *They Won't Forget:* Mary Clay doesn't get much screen time, and she ends up dead. LeRoy saw the newspaper photograph of Henry at the Troc with the inviting brunette. He called to ask, "Who's that girl?"

Henry sent his assistant Solly Baiano to introduce Judy to the director. "I was looking for a very sexy but very clean, wholesome, young girl," said LeRoy. He took one look at Judy Turner. "The minute she walked through the door, I knew she was the girl for the part," LeRoy said.

LeRoy didn't care for her name or her brown hair. And he never confused her with an actress. But LeRoy did like the way she jiggled in a tight sweater, so he signed her to a personal contract at $50 a week and made sure the jiggle *and* the sweater stayed in the final film. He even scored the music to keep beat with the rhythm of her breasts as they bounced in Judy's seventy-five-foot tracking shot. Then, as promised, he promptly had her character shot to death.

In June 1937, Henry performed his second favorite task as agent: He took Judy to a screening of her first credited film. It wasn't always an easy initiation. After she got a glimpse of herself in *They Won't Forget,* Judy told Henry, "I hope I don't look like that."

"Fortunately, you do," he replied. It didn't matter that Henry had no desire to sleep with her, since he knew every other man in America would pay good money—or the price of a movie ticket (then 25 cents)—to take his place.

She was quite a girl, and after Judy Turner graduated from the left arm of Henry Willson, he sent her on dates with movie tough-guy George Raft, twenty-six years her senior. "It's all right," Judy said. "George always waits until I get my school homework done before we leave the house."

Judy's new name was Henry's idea—unless he stole it. Sometimes Henry's best ideas weren't his own. Over the years, he, Mervyn LeRoy, and the girl herself took turns claiming full credit for coming up with that special name: Lana Turner.

Whoever created it, Marge Champion knew the person most responsible for making her old Hollywood High classmate a star. "I was just cute and Henry didn't quite know what to do with me," she said. "But Lana, she was so sexy and Henry knew exactly what to do with her."

So did Billy Wilkerson. With Henry dishing him the gossip and the girls, the publisher saw to it that the now-blonde nobody got the full star treatment at *The Hollywood Reporter* long before she headlined a movie. The Hollywood High coed couldn't doodle without *The Reporter* fawning over her art: "Lana Turner's sketches have become so popular she's thinking seriously of a two-way career," Wilkerson's newspaper announced. Even a minor publicity stunt inspired *Reporter* ink: "Lana Turner is going to stage a hayride to the Trocadero's Big Apple Barn Dance next Tuesday."

Until his death, Henry trumpeted his discovery of the bombshell despite her undue speed in switching to the William Morris Agency. Intriguingly, Henry's ultimate success as a starmaker rested with an actor he rarely mentioned. Born in Fresno, Jon Hall (*né* Charles Lochner) never let the technicality of his California birthplace distract him from his claim that he descended from Tahitian royalty. Equal parts of destiny, chutzpah, and Henry, the actor found his greatest success playing an island native opposite the sarong-wearing Dorothy Lamour in *Hurricane*. A South Seas epic with lots of palm trees and even more grass skirts, the movie made Hall a star, and over the course of his career, he also bared his sun-roasted abs in *South of Pago Pago, Aloma of the South Seas,* and *On the Isle of Samoa.* The 1930s was the decade of swim champions-turned-movie stars like Johnny Weissmuller and Larry "Buster" Crabbe, and while Jon Hall never played Tarzan, he cut a mean backstroke with a trunk full of medals to prove it.

None of which would have significantly enhanced the rise of Henry Willson if Hall's appearance in *Hurricane* had not juiced the imagination of a twelve-year-old boy in Winnetka, Illinois. In 1937, Roy Fitzgerald bought a movie ticket to see *Hurricane* at the Teatro del Lago in his hometown, and gazing up from his popcorn, he took one look at the near-naked Jon Hall and knew he had to see himself on the big screen. It would be Henry's calling to take that star-struck homosexual boy and turn him into Rock Hudson.

PART FOUR

Casting *Since You Went Away*, David O. Selznick and Henry Willson find their sailor in Robert Moseley, a.k.a. Guy Madison.

10

Memos from David O. Selznick

*G*one *with the Wind* opened in December 1939, and along with everybody else in Hollywood, Henry made like a sheep to the altar of the film's producer. Henry's offering to David O. Selznick was humble. On May 18, 1940, he sent a typewritten missive to the president of Selznick International Pictures, Daniel T. O'Shea:

Dear Mr. O'Shea,

I hope you won't mind my sending you this short note, as I know you are tremendously busy in New York, but I understand there is a strong possibility of a major move being made in the Selznick organization and I would like at this time to ask you to keep me in mind, as you have so kindly done to date, for a possible position in the organization.

In the event you are thinking of a talent man, I am enclosing a recently compiled list of my "protégés" for the last six years. [Anne Shirley, Lana Turner, Jon Hall, Joy Hodges, Joan Fontaine, Alan Curtis, Marie Wilson, Dick Hogan, Russell Hayden, David Bruce, Wm. T. Orr, Alan Baldwin, Barbara Pepper]

Courteous as it was cruel, O'Shea's speedy reply took only two days to reach Henry. The response was even more to the point than the initial inquiry: "There is absolutely no foundation whatsoever to the rumor which you mention."

Period.

O'Shea's reply must have been hurtful in its bluntness, but then, the truth often is. In 1940, the producer of *Gone with the Wind* dissolved Selznick International Pictures to create David O. Selznick Productions, followed by Vanguard Pictures two years later. Selznick ballyhooed the latter division as his outlet to increase production with more modest-budgeted films. In reality, it was little more than a business stratagem designed to avoid paying taxes. With Henry's usual gung-ho optimism, he misinterpreted the move as a call to action when, in fact, the arduous task of bringing *Gone with the Wind* to the screen had forced its egomaniacal filmmaker into an emotional tailspin that left him incapable of putting another film into production for three years. Irene Mayer Selznick explained her husband's apparent paralysis. "What movie can you make after *GWTW*?" she asked. "Well, you can't make something piddling."

While Selznick waited for his creative juices to replenish themselves, he didn't have to worry about his immediate cash flow. In addition to the enormous profits from *Gone with the Wind*, Selznick loaned actors he had under contract to other studios and then pocketed the significant difference between what he paid Ingrid Bergman, Joseph Cotten, and Joan Fontaine and what M-G-M, Paramount, and Fox paid Selznick in return for their services. The producer made only one film, *Rebecca*, between the years 1940 and 1943, but he did make a lot of money.

"Selznick was a flesh-peddler," said Henry. Which meant something, coming from an agent.

In one important respect, Selznick's development of post-*GWTW* projects initiated the so-called "package deal" that would soon define the Hollywood way of making movies. "They were valuable projects and he sold them as packages [to other studios], using the actors he had under contract," wrote Irene Selznick, referring to such films as *Suspicion* and *Jane Eyre*, both starring Joan Fontaine.

It was a novel way to make movies, but more than a little dishonest to the actors who had contracted to work for Selznick. "I thought I'd signed on to work for the greatest film producer in the world. I could not have been more thrilled," said Shirley Temple. Neither could her superprotective mother, Gertrude, who summed up the arrangement: "We're leaving [Shirley's] career entirely up to Mr. Selznick," said Mrs. Temple. "Whatever he says, goes."

Unfortunately, so went her daughter's career. Shirley Temple looked to shed her moppet status under the producer's aegis, but in the end the child star made only two Selznick pictures, *Since You Went Away* and *I'll Be Seeing You*. "I was loaned out for the rest," said Shirley Temple. "They did nothing for my career, and Selznick made a lot of money."

The flesh-peddling also upset Irene Selznick. "I couldn't understand what there was to be proud of in getting a sum many times these people's salaries and not sharing it with them. It was not nice money, not our kind," she scoffed.

Pride, if not moral qualms, sent Selznick back to the storyboards in 1943. For his grand return to moviemaking, he hired Henry Willson as his first (and only) head of talent at Vanguard Pictures, and together they set out to cast the screen version of Margaret Buell Wilder's recent bestseller. It's title, *Together,* hardly exemplified Selznick's monomaniacal way of making movies, and so he called it *Since You Went Away*. Like the Margaret Mitchell adaptation, Selznick's follow-up project told the story of war through the eyes of well-groomed women who kept the home fires burning in uncommonly expensive abodes. And like *Gone with the Wind,* it offered the moral solace and gratis servitude of a black housekeeper, again played by Hattie McDaniel. A major difference in the two treatments was Selznick's increased participation on the second one: he adapted *Since You Went Away* himself and took full credit for his efforts, that is, after Wilder sued him and lost in court.

Henry's tenure at Vanguard began with the film's casting in July 1943, and he had no doubt that *Since You Went Away* was his big moment. After knocking about in Hollywood as an agent for ten years, Henry finally got to play on the inside of the studio's feudal walls—and with the *seigneur* himself! In the Selznick oligarchy, it was a case of the willful leading the willing. Nine years Selznick's junior, the thirty-two-year-old agent effectively entered a six-year apprenticeship in financial, artistic, and sexual profligacy, as well as severe substance abuse, from which Henry would emerge, if not a radically changed man, then the fully formed person of his own Hollywood legend.

First, the drugs. According to Irene Selznick, her husband indulged in the 4 A.M. habit of writing peculiar notes to their help, in which he instructed the maids to wake him only three hours later. "Regardless of what I may say," he wrote night after night. Severely addicted to Benzedrine, Selznick introduced the amphetamine to Henry, who improved on its effectiveness by mixing it with opium pills. ("For the pain," Henry said, referring to his colitis.) Henry, in turn, proffered the potent concoction to under-the-weather friends. "It sure took care of any hangover," said one Willson assistant.

The drugs only drew Henry closer to Selznick in temperament. Hyper, mercurial, prone to violent mood swings, each man possessed an ebullient, if not careless, generosity that masked a nearly debilitating compulsion to control others. Although they ultimately morphed into prodigal twins, they sprang from entirely different fathers.

Horace Willson loved show people, Lewis Selznick never stopped hating them. "Less brains are necessary in the motion picture business than in any other," the latter once observed. The hearts of David Selznick and Henry Willson flew in the other direction, like Icarus to the sun.

Whereas Horace Willson offered the very portrait of New England conservatism, Lewis Selznick was a prodigious film distributor who gambled heavily and lost everything. Before destitution arrived, he coached his sons Myron and David in financial licentiousness by giving them weekly allowances of $750. The money was the adolescent boys' exercise in carpe diem: "Spend it all. Give it away. Throw it away," ordered their father. "But get rid of it. Live expensively. If you have confidence in yourself, live beyond your means. Then you'll have to work hard to catch up. That's the only fun there is: hard work. Never try to save money. If you do, then you have two things to worry about: Making it and keeping it. Just concern yourself with making it. The rest will take care of itself."

Of course, it didn't.

David Selznick reveled in repeating his father's words on the transience of money, and Henry followed them like a lamb ready to be fleeced. In good times and bad, Henry spent every dime he ever made and much more, lavishing his cash on clients and friends, both of which never came cheaply in Hollywood. Like Selznick, Henry concerned himself only with the making and the spending of money, although not necessarily in that order. And like Selznick, Henry ended up bankrupt, oblivious to the fact that money is one thing that never takes care of itself.

His lack of fiduciary expertise aside, Henry brought to the job many qualities, most of which belonged to some of the screen's greatest talents. During his career at Vanguard, Henry tried to get Selznick to sign Montgomery Clift, then Broadway's brightest new actor, as well as the directors James Whale, responsible for Hollywood's most iconoclastic horror films, *The Old Dark House* and *Frankenstein*, among them, and Roberto Rossellini, who had already directed such masterpieces of Italian neorealism as *Open City* and *Paisan*. None of these major artists, however, ever contracted with Selznick, who personally saw to it that each deal unraveled over details both large and petty. In Hollywood, the archetypal triumph of surface over substance ended as it was destined: yet another willing victim, Henry cast an appreciative eye on not only real talent but the glamorous, coruscating sheen of the movie business. The glare ultimately blinded both Selznick and Henry, but in the beginning it was a hard, steady beam that showed them the way: "I didn't say she could act. I said she could become a star," said Henry. It was the mantra he repeated like the cry of a bird happy to be lost in paradise.

Selznick believed that what you called a body had the power to make it smell sweeter to the moviegoing public. A penchant bordering on an obsession, nomenclature also came to beguile Henry.

As Selznick the mentor once told Henry the protégé, "Veronica Lake is the best synthetic name in the business!" Selznick worshipped celebrity, display, glitter, and all the nonsensical fantasies that represented Hollywood at its most intoxicatingly ephemeral. Henry took one whiff and thought he saw eternity. It all lasted only thirty years, which in Hollywood is often confused with forever.

Although Selznick always took credit for the concept of *A Star Is Born,* his working credo came closer to "a star is made." Selznick and Henry shared that need to be the maker, not the midwife. In their opinion, an intriguing new name required a physical makeover, as well as the personal touch of a sexual initiation. Those carnal duties figured into Henry's services at Vanguard, and his being homosexual only made him a better fit for the job. Unofficially, he operated as both Selznick's beard for his married paramour Jennifer Jones (*née* Phyllis Isley) and his pimp. The latter calling had him procuring would-be starlets selected from photos of anonymous females that Selznick personally clipped from magazines and the morning newspapers. One page from the *Los Angeles Times* came attached to the DOS note that "the girl standing against the surfboard might be worth getting in." Another, among dozens others like it, read, "Find her. I think she has potential." When Hedda Hopper remarked in her gossip column that a certain young woman was "the greatest beauty that has come to town in years," Selznick gave Henry the order: "Please look her up immediately so that if she is this sensational I can see her before I leave town." He didn't remember her name. He didn't care if she was an actress or, as Hedda pointed out, that "she was married to an agent."

Selznick and Henry spent hours perusing the latest issues of *Vogue* and *Life,* careful not to overlook a potential female conquest

among the printed columns. One such trip through the pages of
Life inspired the boss to write that "the bathing girls at the cove . . .
there are three or four girls featured who look extremely interesting." In addition to the clippings, Henry filed detailed reports on
his trips to local beauty contests and photo shoots for underwear
catalogues ("There is no expense," he wrote of one model, "as she
is coming to Los Angeles in two weeks to visit her brother").

Two weeks into Henry's job at Vanguard, Selznick gave him the
assignment to go "out into the field," as he put it, to cast *Since You
Went Away*. He wanted his new talent scout to search beyond the
usual Hollywood haunts and find "real people," albeit ones who
looked good enough to be movie stars. Selznick expanded on
Henry's repertoire of note tricks at the Troc and gave him very specific out-of-office, after-hours marching orders. In casting the film's
smaller roles, the producer wanted verisimilitude: "I suggest you try
to find the time as soon as possible to look over the girls at Hollywood High and other high schools around town," he ordered.

Henry fancied late nights at Ciro's, Billy Wilkerson's new place
on the Strip, and the Mocambo, which had replaced the Trocadero
as his favorite haunt. But if Selznick wanted him to spend afternoons on Santa Monica Boulevard in front of Hollywood High,
Henry did as he was told. Not that Selznick was without scruples
on the subject of trolling the local campuses for camera-ready
nymphs and maenads. "Quite seriously," he cautioned, "I suggest
that you make arrangements in advance with the school authorities
or with the police so that you don't find yourself in jail!"

Selznick also recommended visits to unusual live-entertainment
venues, ones Henry never frequented as a cub reporter back in
Manhattan, where Broadway and the speakeasies of Greenwich Village were his scene. "I suggest you cover the Ice Follies," Selznick
offered, "being sure to see the whole show and to cover in particular the men who are in it."

It was like ordering the cow to mow the grass.

If Henry's penchant for sleeping with his clients preceded his tenure with Selznick, he could not have found a better teacher to help him polish his technique of casting from between the sheets. "David was, to me, a voluptuary of the most revolting sort," remarked Joan Fontaine. "You know, he'd try to rip your clothes off."

"If you walked into David's office and he had his shoes off, watch out!" warned Shirley Temple.

"Selznick was a real womanizer, no doubt about that," said Rhonda Fleming. The producer cast the twenty-two-year-old actress as a sexually disturbed woman in Alfred Hitchcock's *Spellbound*. It was her first major role for the studio, and the actress claimed she had to look up the word "nymphomaniac" in the dictionary before essaying the role.

The producer, however, had ways other than *Webster's* to educate her on the subject.

"He called me to his office and immediately put his arms around me," the actress recalled. "Selznick was a great big man and he squeezed me." Terrified, she broke away to run down the one flight of stairs to Henry's office on the ground floor. "I was in tears, and Henry barreled out to talk to Selznick. I don't know what he said behind those closed doors, but Selznick never tried it again."

What Henry told Selznick in the actress's defense remains open to speculation, especially in light of what another actor reported. According to Craig Hill, Henry proved far less gallant when the producer publicly accosted Shirley Temple. Shortly before Henry landed Hill his first screen role, in *All About Eve* (playing Anne Baxter's leading man in the play-within-the-movie *Footsteps on the Ceiling*), he took the opportunity to show off his latest blond discovery by making the rounds of the Sunset Strip clubs. One evening, Henry's tour included a stop at a party hosted by Selznick, who had taken over a fancy eatery for the occasion. Henry did his usual survey of the scene from a banquette when Hill, seated at his side, noticed a linebacker-size guy putting the moves on little Shirley. No sooner did she start to struggle than Hill, a very boyish-looking twenty-one year old, rose to her defense. "I'll punch that jerk out if he doesn't leave her alone," he told Henry.

"Calm down," whispered Henry, making sure his fledgling would not fly the coop. "That jerk is David O. Selznick."

Being homosexual did not make Henry immune to the old double standard. If the weaker sex needed to be protected from producers, men could take care of themselves when it came to men like Henry Willson. In years to come, they called him "notorious." And yet, despite all the accusations of sexual comeuppance, coercion, and conquest that were to embellish Henry's reputation, no injured party ever accused him of ripping his clothes or giving unsolicited bear hugs. Henry's seduction technique required much less aggression. "Some guys just threw themselves at him," said Troy Donahue.

That onslaught of too-willing flesh came later in Henry's career. In the 1940s, talent still counted for something. Of all his duties at the Selznick studios, Henry took the most pride in his much-lauded training program for actors. The instructors he hired for Selznick went on to teach the craft at the top studios, notably Helen Sorrell at 20th Century–Fox and vocal-teacher Lester Luther at Warner Bros. (As an agent, he could always rely on Sorrell and Luther to send their most promising students his way.)

And there were other duties in his early days at the Selznick studios. Henry negotiated with the legendary Abe Lastfogel of William Morris Agency for Ingrid Bergman's troop tour in Alaska, as well as Shirley Temple's tour of Europe. There were her breasts, too. "My pride and joy," said Shirley Temple. "David wanted them strapped down, but I refused." Henry also recommended "possible surgery on Gregory Peck's ears."

More time consuming were the endless queries from Selznick's office. He wanted to know about the availability of directors Billy Wilder and Michael Curtiz. The latter, according to the producer, "had less than a year to go" at Warner Bros., which had released *Casablanca* the year before. Selznick also had it on good information that Wilder, ready to embark on the film noir classic *Double Indemnity,* "is not too happy at Paramount."

Barely a month on the job, Henry heard from Selznick on a

matter of utmost importance: "What is happening with Frank Sinatra?" the boss had to know.

A year earlier, the singer had performed with Tommy Dorsey's orchestra at the Paramount Theatre on Times Square, a month-long engagement that marked the first time teenage girls screamed en masse at a singing idol. People called them "bobbysoxers," named after the heavy white stockings that girls rolled at the ankles. Little did it matter that a few of the so-called bobbysoxers got paid to shred their vocal cords at the Paramount. The caterwauling phenomenon jump-started Sinatra's career, and the singer was already a huge star by the time Henry Willson started work at Vanguard in July 1943.

Selznick, however, was never one to let reason muddy his thinking, and he expected the miracle of a Sinatra-signed contract delivered to him overnight. In the producer's belated estimation, there had been only two great "sex-appeal favorites among male entertainers to appear on the horizon since Clark Gable." They were Sinatra and Alan Ladd, who the year before had married Henry's old shipboard buddy Sue Carol.

Henry knew all about the men who got away. Back at the Zeppo Marx Agency, he had received head shots from a new radio actor. Very handsome, very blond. And when Henry listened to him perform on the radio, he found the actor's voice equally impressive in its depth and versatility. But when they met, Henry gazed down at a near midget in lifts.

"I didn't think Alan Ladd had any future in the business," he recalled. "He was simply too short. Of course, I didn't tell him that." Instead, he recommended Ladd to another agent, Sue Carol, who in turn made the five-foot-five actor a star (and her husband).

Henry kept that major miscalculation to himself during his first days with Selznick. The boss adored Sue Carol's latest husband and would have given anything to put him under contract. "Although Ladd is probably the biggest star in motion pictures at this moment, I have very little doubt that a good picture on the market today with Sinatra would outgross it," Selznick pontificated. His good friend William Paley over at the Columbia Broadcasting System had told him "many, many months ago" that Sinatra was fast exceeding Bing Crosby in popularity.

Not so many, many days into his job at the Selznick studios, Henry got the order to "pick up the threads" and hop on the Sinatra bandwagon. Selznick memoed him, "Every evidence points to the truth of the assertion of *Time* magazine that not since Valentino has anything been seen to compare with the astonishing effect Sinatra seems to have on his female audiences." If Henry could not deliver Sinatra's signature on a contract, Selznick threatened, it was "worse in some ways than losing out on Clark Gable!"

Selznick could argue, belittle, rant. When Henry checked into the Sinatra situation at the William Morris Agency, Abe Lastfogel informed him that RKO had already signed the singer. At Paramount Pictures, Sinatra had played himself in brief big-band sequences in *Ship Ahoy* and *Las Vegas Nights*. RKO, of course, had grander designs. The execs there planned to build him up big with the back-to-back assignments of *Higher and Higher* and *Step Lively*, in which Sinatra would star as a playwright who sings!

Selznick never acquired a taste for bad news. He had absolutely no problem blaming Henry for RKO's victory and tersely termed it his studio's "greatest miss."

11

Monty Clift Escapes

In Henry's first month on the job, more trouble arrived in the person of James Whale. *Since You Went Away* still had no director, though the first day of filming was only two months away. Selznick himself posed a real producer problem, and one of which Hollywood's best directors were acutely aware. On *Gone with the Wind*, Selznick went through no fewer than three (George Cukor, Victor Fleming, Sam Wood). The autocratic, micromanaging producer could only function in tandem with a director capable of withstanding his meddling, incessant demands. In so many other words, he admitted as much when he queried Henry to find "some young director or an old-time director who at the moment is not on top" for *Since You Went Away*.

Henry thought he found the latter candidate in James Whale. Although his horror classics *Frankenstein* and *The Old Dark House* would appear to have made him a peculiar choice for the high-gloss pictures of David O. Selznick, Whale had also directed *Show Boat* and *The Man in the Iron Mask*, the kind of prestige pictures with scope that had been Selznick's stock in trade a decade earlier when he produced *A Tale of Two Cities* and *Anna Karenina* for M-G-M. Regarding the "not on top" commendation, Whale fit that bill, too. A few years earlier, the director had experienced a debilitating failure with *The Road Back*, a film that he intended to be his personal indictment of Europe after World War I—until Universal unceremoniously fired him from the project.

Whale was not the most malleable director to pair with Hollywood's least accommodating producer. Henry must have reasoned that Whale, now age fifty, had acquired the requisite humility after more than two years of unemployment. Having made no new films, Whale now occupied his time gardening and directing plays at his little theater company, the Brentwood Players.

There was another minus that qualified as a plus: Whale's homosexuality linked him to one of Selznick's most loyal directors, George Cukor, who helmed four films for the producer, including a personal favorite, *Little Women* with Katharine Hepburn. Cukor was a genuine talent, but as a homosexual bachelor he held tenuous power in the heterosexual milieu of Hollywood where the wives of studio chiefs, and not the chieftains themselves, were his closest friends. Selznick was the exception. A true liberal, Selznick was also savvy enough to know how to work a social liability like Cukor's sexual orientation to his own professional advantage.

One month on the job, Henry delivered, if not the ultimate coup of Frank Sinatra, a very formidable talent in the person of James Whale. Henry drew up the contract, but when he submitted it for Whale's signature, Selznick dictated one of his last-minute queries. It was paramount, in the producer's opinion, that Whale initial the note before signing the contract. As Selznick explained it to Henry, "I frankly want to protect us against any future misunderstanding."

An informal addendum to the contract, Selznick's brief note laid out in excruciating detail how much Whale's "market value" would escalate upon his signing with Vanguard. The producer wanted it made clear in "advance of signing" that he demanded total and absolute obedience from any employee. "If Jimmy signs," wrote Selznick, "there must be a promise of no complaints, no matter how much we might subsequently make on him. No complaints about forty weeks or about assignments or about interference from me."

Selznick's flesh-peddler reputation had grown murkier since the release of *Gone with the Wind*, and people now called him an employment trap. Despite her Best Actress Oscar for *Suspicion*,

Joan Fontaine was anything but grateful for his ownership of her services, especially when she was still being paid a pre–Academy Award fee. She increasingly groused about Selznick's tendency to loan his actors out to other studios, paying them their contractual salary while he pocketed the enormous overages. In Fontaine's opinion, Selznick was much worse than any agent. "You take 90 percent and leave the actors 10 percent," she balked. Significantly, Fontaine continued to be loaned out on a regular basis, and made only one film for the Selznick studios, *Rebecca* in 1940.

Selznick saw similar loan-out potential with Whale. "I am in hope that Jimmy's first picture will be for us," he said. "If it is not, it will nevertheless be carefully chosen to further his career and his value to both himself and to us. The same will be true of later pictures." His comment left wide open the possibility that Whale would direct not *Since You Went Away* but some lesser project.

Contracts have a way of turning into coffins, and Selznick found a final nail to hammer into the Whale agreement: He effectively reneged on his early promise to give the director's theater company, the Brentwood Players, use of the studio's telegram service. The producer wondered if there weren't a "more advantageous" arrangement that would give the studio "more control" over the situation.

Whale, as expected, failed to initial the note. Nor did he care to sign the contract. He gave the matter a day's deliberation before he contacted Henry with his refusal to work for the studio. Selznick single-handedly ruined the deal, and he gave Henry full credit for its failure. First Sinatra, now Whale. Selznick felt he been left standing "at the altar" twice now. "I am pretty annoyed about the whole thing!" he raged at Henry.

Shortly before production began on *Since You Went Away,* Selznick fell back on an old standby, director John Cromwell, who had caused the producer no problems years earlier on *The Prisoner of Zenda*. The ever-reliable Cromwell was perfect for the job, said Selznick, who raved about his "innate dignity . . . and the calmness and the integrity to give me what I want" for *Since You Went Away.*

Shirley Temple summed up the general opinion of the last-minute hire. "Cromwell was not the most inspiring director," she said.

On a losing streak, Henry made it zero-for-three during his first year with Selznick when he strongly recommended that Montgomery Clift be put under contract. The twenty-three-year-old Broadway star had recently appeared in Thornton Wilder's *The Skin of Our Teeth,* and a starring role in Lillian Hellman's *The Searching Wind* was projected for 1944.

Henry was hardly ahead of the Hollywood pack on Clift, and he admitted as much to Selznick when he warned, "Every studio in town is offering deals to Montgomery Clift." Indeed, when the actor toured in *There Shall Be No Night,* the show's 1941 engagement in Los Angeles generated much movie interest in Clift. Louis B. Mayer, for one, offered him no less a role for his screen debut than that of Greer Garson's son in *Mrs. Miniver.* Clift liked the script but thought less of Mayer's seven-year contract, which he called "slavery," and returned to work on Broadway as soon as the *Night* tour ended. "Monty wasn't arrogant, he just knew what he wanted," said his friend Roddy McDowall, who recalled Clift considering several scripts in the mid-1940s. "He rejected them all."

Fearing that Clift would not be an easy sell, Henry attempted a rare but ultimately foolhardy compromise with Selznick. Instead of the usual seven-year contract, Henry believed that Clift might agree to a mere five years if given the option to make two films, not three, during the fourth and fifth years of the agreement. After several meetings with Clift in New York, Henry sent telegrams of encouragement back to Selznick and bragged that all their business talks had been conducted in private "without his agent present," he added. Genuinely excited, Henry thought he had prevailed where other Hollywood hotshots, such as Mayer, had not. "I think Clift is ready," he wrote Selznick. "Hal Wallis seems to be our principal contender." Optimistic to a fault, Henry predicted that Montgomery Clift's name would grace the marquee of a Selznick picture.

But it was not to be. The actor got offered Selznick's standard contract for three pictures a year over seven years, which he rejected. If Selznick regretted losing Clift, he never said so in a memo. He saved that rebuke for Henry's failure to sign the aspiring actress Pat Kirkland, whose mother, Pat Carroll, had been one of Hollywood's biggest musical-comedy stars of the 1930s. The daughter would turn out to be something less in the 1940s.

Myron Selznick had been touting Pat Kirkland for months, and he made his brother acutely aware that Columbia Pictures had "enormous enthusiasm" for Kirkland to star in the studio's sure-fire hit *Kiss and Tell*. Myron's raves pushed his brother to tell Henry, "I hope that we have not lost ourselves in an important new star by this indifference to a girl who made a very definite impression in Chicago, and about whom our New York and Hollywood offices should have been on their toes even without any prompting from me."

Henry's first full year with the Selznick studios ended disastrously in the opinion of the only person who mattered. "It has been the poorest year in our history as far as new personalities of importance go," Selznick lashed out.

Henry's failure with Clift was the movies' loss as well. Hollywood would have to wait until 1948 and his first film performances in *The Search* and *Red River* to see how Clift's gift for understatement would revolutionize the art of screen acting. Pat Kirkland, on the other hand, created the kind of impression in Hollywood that prevented her from ever appearing on-screen. Shirley Temple, under contract to Selznick, got loaned out to make the forgettable *Kiss and Tell* at Columbia, while Kirkland scrounged for guest spots on such late-1940s drama anthologies as *NBC Presents* and *Kraft Television Theatre*. Her inevitable, premature end came in a clear case of nepotism with the one-season TV series *The Egg and I*, in 1951. The show starred Pat Carroll, and as if not to tax her talent, Pat Kirkland played the star's daughter.

12

The Face and the Beard

H enry did make good on one of his boss's early demands. He hired The Face.

"I wish you would get hold of Anita Colby," Selznick instructed. "I think she would be a wonderful adjunct to the publicity department in line with my desire to smarten up this department."

In the previous decade, The Face had graced more magazine covers than any other model and became the first to earn $100 an hour in Depression-era dollars. Henry offered Anita Colby somewhat less to be Selznick's "feminine director," and he paid the tall, ashen-haired beauty a salary commensurate with his own: $250 a week.

The producer's son Daniel Selznick saw Anita Colby and Henry Willson as virtual equals at his father's studio, the ying-yang twins of style, promotion, and packaging. "It is a fascinating parallel between Anita Colby and Henry Willson," said Daniel Selznick. "Colby was in charge of the women, Willson was in charge of the men."

His is a telling comment. In 1944, *Time* magazine reported on the Selznick star factory ("Colby is his one-woman finishing school") and put the former model on its cover. Not mentioned in the article were any of the men in the Selznick stable or their keeper, Henry Willson. If the analysis of male beauty remained a taboo, the distaff sex was more than enough to fill the editorial void.

Anita Colby's friend, the radio personality Jinx Falkenburg of *Tex and Jinx* fame, described the job of "feminine director" at the Selznick studios. "She was in charge of coordinating all of these [female] stars of the Selznick stable, on screen and off," said Falkenburg, who first met Colby during an interview for the *Herald Tribune*. "She decided how they should be photographed, how they would dress, how public they should become, what interviews they should do. She was the den mother for the top beauties in America."

Anita Colby focused exclusively on making Selznick's actresses presentable to the public, and in the process she created a panoply of techniques for grooming and styling women as varied as Ingrid Bergman ("You cannot overpower Ingrid with clothes") and Jennifer Jones ("Her clothes need the dressmaker, rather than the tailored look"). It was a cosmetic template that Henry reinterpreted for Selznick's male actors, and one he returned to repeatedly in his subsequent career as keeper of Hollywood's Adonis factory.

Anita Colby and Henry Willson, however, operated from vastly different human canvasses. Due to her flawless face, the former model performed her tasks with much ballyhoo that included her very public rejections of marriage proposals from Clark Gable and Jimmy Stewart.

No less a self-promoter, Henry had to content himself with the distinct disadvantage of his humble physical appearance. Equally significant, *Time* magazine was not about to champion the exploits of Selznick's "masculine director," a title that would have been looked at askance, as much then as now. While female beauty has always fascinated the public, male good looks weren't so readily contemplated, or even acknowledged, in the 1940s. During World War II, masculinity became synonymous with heroic violent action, and to draw attention to physical attributes was thought to soften the subject, trivialize it, make it feminine. All of which left the field wide open for exploitation by someone eager to learn and adept at ingenious subterfuge. Henry's sexual orientation only helped to make him the ideal, if not natural, pupil.

"Henry would have learned all those grooming techniques from Selznick and Anita Colby," said Robert Osborne. "Colby even taught the stars how to light a cigarette, how to sit and cross their legs. If Henry saw some guy who didn't have any social background, he had to teach him how to behave at a producer's Sunday brunch, so he could fit in. Otherwise, it could be the end of your social advancement in Hollywood."

In their first year with Selznick, Henry and Anita devoted most of their time to Jennifer Jones, set to star in *Since You Went Away*. Their duties with the actress rarely crossed: Colby was the actress's fashion mentor, Henry was her beard. Finally, work began on Selznick's two most cherished projects: the making of *Since You Went Away* and the romancing of Jennifer Jones.

Selznick had loaned the actress to 20th Century–Fox the year before to make her film debut in *The Song of Bernadette*. At least Selznick claimed it was her film debut. For a week or two, The Face deflected Hollywood's attention away from Jennifer Jones, and she led insiders to speculate that it was the studio's new feminine director, and not the saintly but, in fact, married ingenue, who occupied the affections of the equally married Selznick. Likewise, Henry's unofficial job was one of obfuscation. Jennifer needed an escort to Hollywood's various social events, and Henry eagerly obliged to be her official date.

"My father certainly wasn't going to let Jennifer loose with a straight man," said Daniel Selznick.

It helped that his father was gay-friendly, having achieved some of his best work with George Cukor. "He certainly couldn't have been homophobic if he hired Henry Willson," Daniel Selznick surmised. "My father was an extremely tolerant human being. I'm surprised he didn't sign more black actors. He was tolerant of minorities and misfits and people with psychiatric problems." (David O. Selznick's own sessions with a female psychiatrist, Dr. May Romm, led him to make one of the first films on the subject of psychoanalysis, Alfred Hitchcock's 1945 *Spellbound*, with Ingrid Bergman and Gregory Peck.)

In his employment of minorities, Selznick may have actually

preferred working with male homosexuals for one important reason: the eunuchs in his court offered no competition when it came to seducing the actresses. As an escort for Jennifer Jones, Henry made an inspired choice. Not only was he sexually non-threatening, he could dance and carry on a conversation with a mute, and as he knew everyone in town, Henry relished introducing the shy Jennifer to Hollywood's elite while keeping her away from the riffraff. Still, their frequent dating created its own spectacle:

In what universe other than Hollywood could a woman, unofficially estranged from her husband (Robert Walker), date a well-known homosexual (Henry Willson) to cover up her affair with a married man (David O. Selznick)? Incredible as it may seem, it was a farce that had been preceded by a charade of even greater transparency.

In his pre-Selznick years as an agent, Henry indulged in minor adjustments to the truth to embolden a career. With Selznick's promotion of Jennifer Jones, he learned the art of wholesale fabrication, which required the total recasting of an actor's profile from her birth to the present. In a series of press releases, the Selznick studios fictionalized the Jennifer Jones biography, eradicating not only her marriage to Robert Walker but the couple's sons, Robert Jr. and Michael, and two potboilers she had cranked out for Republic Pictures, *Dick Tracy's G-Men* and the John Wayne western *New Frontier*, both made in 1939 using the actress's real name, Phyllis Isley.

Selznick preferred a less complicated story for his new protégée and paramour, one Fox dutifully disseminated in its studio bio for Jones upon the release of *The Song of Bernadette*: "Jennifer Jones arrived at the Selznick office one day straight from Oklahoma, and read a scene from a stage play, *Claudia*, that the producer had plans for as a movie. David O. Selznick was so overcome with her beauty and talent that he signed her on the spot."

Louella Parsons, either chronically drunk or just plain lazy, ran the story verbatim. Other reporters weren't so easily duped and dug up the truth about the husband, the two kids and the two really, really bad movies. Jennifer Jones somehow survived the failed cover-up, but what never got written about, until many years later, was Hollywood's open secret that Jones, playing a fifteen-year-old virgin in *The Song of Bernadette,* had committed adultery with one of the most important powerbrokers in Hollywood.

Selznick "would ask her to come see him at ten, eleven o'clock at night," recalled the producer's secretary Frances Inglis. "I would hear the scuffling going on in his office, and Jennifer running around the desk and David chasing her, and Jennifer running out with her face as red as a beet, and getting into her car and rushing off . . . It was a sudden fusion of supply and demand. She needed his help, he desperately needed to give it to her."

If the powers at 20th Century–Fox were worried that Selznick might sully their saint in residence, studio head Zanuck could hardly start throwing stones through the citadel windows. He had already created a Hollywood laugh riot by casting his mistress, Linda Darnell, in the role of the Virgin Mary in *The Song of Bernadette.*

For Selznick, it was lust at first sight for Jennifer Jones, not to mention the two other actresses he cast in *Since You Went Away.* The film's credit roll informed moviegoers: "This is the story of the unconquerable fortress, the American family." But most Selznick employees knew better. Their boss tried to bed all three headliners of his home-and-hearth epic, and that included not only Jennifer Jones but Claudette Colbert, the mother of the "unconquerable fortress," and her other on-screen daughter, Shirley Temple. One attempt to seduce the matriarch of the group resulted in a letter of apology to the actress's husband, Dr. Joel Pressman. Which did not exempt Colbert from Selznick's derision. When Selznick failed to bed her, he duly complained about Claudette's taking off three whole days every time she got her period.

"I would really appreciate it if Claudette would try to get by on one [day] for the duration. Tell her there's a war on. We all have to make sacrifices," Selznick fumed, to no avail.

Shirley Temple was an easier but no more willing prey. Since Selznick held her under contract, he didn't have to resort to withholding privileges when she resisted his advances. "If you hold out," Selznick insisted, "you could get loaned out!"

She did and he did.

Hollywood's most famous child star recalled the 127 endless days it took to shoot *Since You Went Away*. "David kept expanding Jennifer's role, and every afternoon she would disappear for an hour or two with him," said Shirley Temple. "No wonder the movie took forever."

Although Selznick's biographer David Thomson made a case for such rapacious behavior—"He might have argued that actresses needed to be loved, that they could hardly shine without it," Thomson wrote—it can only be imagined what lessons of sex and power Henry learned from working in such an openly libidinous environment. If actresses begrudgingly accepted a producer's droit du seigneur, they did their duty in silence, as the rest of the Hollywood fiefdom looked the other way. Like the cast of *Since You Went Away*, film crews knew to wait patiently until the master had finished before they returned to work.

As a talent scout and agent, Henry Willson confronted the same marketplace, but he entered it from the opposite, less populated corner. In some respects, his was more the buyer's market: so many men, and so few in any position of real power to help them in exchange for favors, sexual and otherwise.

13

Guy (Madison) Worship

When he wasn't squiring Jennifer Jones around town, Henry worked at finding the many servicemen and women needed to populate *Since You Went Away.* Selznick wanted "really attractive girls for any of the close shots," he specified, and for the movie's big dance sequence, he insisted the jitterbuggers must be "the best that could be obtained, as if this were an out-and-out musical."

Henry's first few months at the Selznick studios were a disaster, and if he failed to discern his imperiled status there, the closing sentence on the memo of October 18, 1943, could not have outlined his future more clearly: "I shall watch with interest how you carry out these assignments, Mr. Willson!" wrote Selznick. It was a withering condescension that only grew over time, a demeaning attitude that the producer parceled out to no other employee, arguably, with quite the same relish.

Henry cast the film's smaller roles, and in that capacity, he delivered relative unknowns who soon developed star cache. These novice thespians included Guy Madison, an actor who kickstarted the TV western craze in the early 1950s with *The Adventures of Wild Bill Hickok*; Rhonda Fleming, well-known as the movies' Queen of Technicolor for her red hair and exquisite coloring; John Derek (future husband of Bo Derek, Linda Evans, and Ursula Andress), whom Henry named Dare Harris for his roles in *Since You Went*

Away and *I'll Be Seeing You*; and good friend Craig Stevens, a Warner Bros. contract player who eventually headlined TV's *Peter Gunn*. Stevens and Henry knew each other from their Zeppo Marx days together, and the actor named Gail Shikles walked away from the experience with a less sexually dubious moniker. More hetero enhancement came when Henry recommended that Stevens marry Alexis Smith. Their wedding neatly coincided with the release of *Since You Went Away* in spring 1944.

Henry loved the Selznick gang. He even took a page from the Puppets' get-togethers a decade earlier and replicated those Beachwood Canyon days at the clubhouse by inviting the *SYWA* kids to his Beverly Hills home for backyard barbecues and pool parties. Henry now clocked in at thirty-two, but looked well over forty, and continued to hang out with actors too young to vote. Though he saw himself as an older brother, he came off more like a doting father. Parents especially trusted him.

"Some of us were still teenagers, and Henry kind of acted as our chaperone," said Shirley Temple. "He always encouraged us to play charades at these parties. He thought it was good training for young actors. But he never played. Henry just watched."

Fruit punch, soda, and hot dogs were served, and when Henry decided to really cut loose, he would turn off the lights, burn a few candles, and then call everyone into the dining room. "Let's have a séance!" he cried with excitement. There were such squeals of nervous delight that Henry had to hold the girls' hands to calm them down. He held the boys' hands, too. Shirley Temple remembered the spooky happenings with vivid fondness. "We were able to raise the table just by concentrating," she said of the séance.

On leave from the navy, Guy Madison made the occasional guest appearance at Henry's parties. Among the *SYWA* actors, he easily qualified as the freshest, if not the most gifted, talent. Selznick had wanted the war's reality embodied in the bit part of Seaman Harold Smith. Always the consummate showman, he noted, "With a real sailor in the role, we can promote him, get some publicity."

For Henry, his edict was providential. At Selznick's insistence, he expanded his talent searches to include not only the Hollywood Canteen but army camps, the Los Angeles waterfront, and various other ports of call. Henry was nothing if not an optimist to pursue such a hit-and-miss approach to spotting talent. As chance would have it, he found his Harold Smith, not washed up in the surf but seated in the audience at a *Lux Radio Theatre* broadcast.

Henry incorrectly remembered meeting the sailor at a *Lux* performance of *A Star Is Born,* with Janet Gaynor, who did not appear in any broadcast during the 1943–44 season. The first version of the story, about a Hollywood ingenue on the rise and her dissolute star lover on the way down, had been produced by Selznick in 1937, and Henry recalled going to the radio version as his boss's emissary. More likely, he went to represent the Selznick studios and hand-hold Claudette Colbert on November 1, 1943. *Since You Went Away* was well into production, and Colbert was performing in a patriotic piece, a radio adaptation of the movie *So Proudly We Hail* for *Lux*'s audience. Regardless of the play or the actress, it is doubtful Henry ever made it backstage, and if so, that he spent much time there chatting up any actress. (For the record, Judy Garland performed the *Lux Radio Theatre* version of *A Star Is Born* on December 28, 1942.)

Lean, his hair sunbleached, and a perfect fit in his navy whites, Robert Moseley took the train up from San Diego on a forty-eight-hour leave, which was about forty-seven hours more than Henry needed to spot him in the theater, tap him on the shoulder, and say, "My name is Willson. I'd like you to meet David O. Selznick and Dan O'Shea. If they think as I do, you're in the movies."

Years later, Henry offered a more succinct description of what he saw that day. "Guy was Tom of Finland come to life!" Henry exclaimed, invoking the name of the famous illustrator whose pornographic drawings turned muscle-laden cops, sailors, soldiers, and cowboys into gay icons.

Henry planned to take Moseley to meet Selznick the very next day, but some time between that appointment and their leaving the theater, he squired his Ganymede over to the Mocambo. Often described as a nightclub's nightclub, the swank joint at 8588 Sunset Boulevard couldn't fail to impress a young sailor who'd never stepped in a bar classier than the local Tap-a-Keg. Then again, a former telephone linesman like Moseley might have felt the Mocambo's fabric motif of suede on satin on velvet more akin to being buried alive in a coffin than a night out on the town.

Pure Hollywood fantasy, the club's décor inspired one reporter to call the Mocambo "a place in Hollywood which looks like Hollywood—magnificent, luxurious, exotic and unique."

He left out "overripe." The club's sensory overload unsettled men of Moseley's simple, untried tastes. On the other hand, it allowed Henry to play cicerone of the Hollywood night. As always, he pointed out the celebrities, took charge of ordering the food, picked out the right bottle of wine, and told semiwicked tales about the bartenders and hatcheck girls. It was Henry's game to decode the protean flickers of expression on his male date's face: which inspired the bigger reaction, he wondered, the boy stories or the girl stories? Along the way, Henry made sure to instill comfort and confidence. "You could be a star," he told his dates. "You're better looking than any movie actor here." And then he would lean in: "You are a star. Now it's up to me to let Hollywood know."

It was only natural that Moseley might mistake the sexual heat wafting across the table for sheer professional passion. At such moments, Henry was a man's most enthusiastic best friend on earth. His attention was focused, and if his eye ever wandered, it never traveled far. "Any of your buddies over there?" he liked to ask, nodding to the less fortunate servicemen stranded at the bar.

Since men in uniform couldn't afford the tiny tables clustered around the dance floor, they gathered at the bar where well-heeled patrons indulged their patriotism by getting the boys dead drunk. Servicemen never paid for what they imbibed, and by closing time they posed the easiest target for anyone willing to take aim. At such an hour, Henry felt it his duty to take a tour of the troops and offer them his line, "Have you ever thought of being in the movies?" When that failed to get their attention, he gave out his card in case they had second thoughts about an early-morning tour of 1136 Tower Road. "In Beverly Hills," he added. "Where the movie stars all live."

Henry ushered Moseley past the cramped tables and the long line of sailors at the bar. Henry's old client Anne Shirley was waiting at one of the plush banquettes in the back. Moseley recognized her from the tear-jerker *Stella Dallas*. Her performance nabbed the actress an Oscar nomination, but who remembered? That was six years ago—a lifetime for an actor, an eternity for an ingenue like Anne Shirley, who had once been Henry's photographer bait for Lana Turner. By 1943, she had not more than a half dozen roles left under her dirndl, but photographers were fond of the actress. Always the chaperone, Henry made sure to sandwich Anne between himself and his real date for the night.

Henry introduced Anne to Moseley. When she went to powder her nose, Henry gave the sailor an order, "Ask her to dance. Anne loves to dance."

Moseley wanted to know why Henry didn't ask her himself. He rolled his eyes. "I hurt my foot," said Henry. Moseley hadn't noticed a limp, but did as he was told when Anne returned from the ladies' room.

Watching the two youngsters together on the dance floor, Henry made a mental note: get Moseley into dance classes at Arthur Murray's. The boy couldn't dance, he couldn't carry on a conversation, he couldn't figure out which fork to use, and it was assumed he could not act. Beyond that, Henry told Moseley not to worry about his meeting tomorrow with Selznick.

"If you've got the kind of natural attractiveness that registers on screen," he told him, "the rest will come later."

Indeed, Selznick agreed with Henry. Moseley looked perfect for the role of Harold Smith, a sailor who enjoys a brief conversation with Jennifer Jones and Robert Walker in a bowling alley. In fact, the real sailor so embodied the ersatz one that Selznick dispensed with a screen test, and immediately expanded the part from one to two scenes. No, Moseley couldn't act, not an inch. His beauty came undiluted by talent, which is why Henry gave Moseley a piece of acting advice for his scene in the bowling alley.

"Chew gum," he told him. "It will give you something to do."

The war instilled in Hollywood a new sense of efficiency, and seven days later Robert Moseley was back on duty in the South Pacific. It is not known if Henry—or anyone else, for that matter—consulted with Moseley about changing his name to Guy Madison. As with Lana Turner, Henry had to compete for credit with at least two other people: Selznick and Madison's future agent, Helen Ainsworth, a portly lesbian who was equally well-known in Hollywood for being a Christian Scientist, advocating health food, and calling her clients "my children."

At first, Henry called Moseley "Guy Dunhill" but soon had a better second thought.

"There was the bakery, the Dolly Madison Bakery, across the street from the Selznick studios in Culver City," he said. "We were looking for something really all-American, and what was more American than Dolly Madison?" Of course, the Dolly had to go. "So I thought up the name Guy."

Henry's guy worship had begun.

14

Saint Jennifer Jones

Selznick sent Henry to the 1944 Academy Awards with Jennifer Jones, nominated that year for her performance in *The Song of Bernadette*. A few weeks earlier Henry had also been her date for the first-ever Golden Globe Awards. Not one of the town's ritzier fetes, it was held on a weekday afternoon in the commissary at 20th Century–Fox, and the stale scent of the lunch menu lingered in the air as Jennifer received a one-sheet scroll proclaiming her the year's top actress.

The Academy Awards were far more illustrious.

With Jennifer nervously clutching his arm, Henry never looked more the Hollywood insider than on the night of March 2, 1944, when the *Los Angeles Herald* immortalized his date by publishing a photograph of the smiling couple. Henry sent one copy home to Horace and Margaret and dutifully clipped a few more for posterity, adding them to his already voluminous collection of scrapbooks. No refugee from the Puppets gang, Jennifer Jones on Oscar night qualified as the big time. Henry had arrived.

Unfortunately, his many beautiful tuxedos had to stay home in the closet that evening. He and Jennifer obeyed the "no formalwear" rule recommended by Bette Davis, who, after creating the Hollywood Canteen with actor John Garfield, had turned her attention to remaking the Oscars ceremony into a new, democratized awards show.

Since its inception in 1927–1928, the ceremony took place in the Roosevelt Hotel's intimate (some said "cramped") ballroom. In one of many sweeping reforms, Bette Davis suggested moving the whole affair across Hollywood Boulevard to the 2,258–seat Grauman's Chinese Theater. Once a private industry party, the awards became a national event in 1944 as radio covered the festivities for the first time and no fewer than two hundred servicemen received free passes to attend.

The autocratic membership of the Academy thought so much of the new open-door policy that they did not nominate Davis for the first time in six years, and epithets of "screw that bitch" could be heard in the traffic jam outside the theater. Unlike the Roosevelt, the Chinese Theater failed to provide parking attendants, which meant that Henry, Jennifer, and the 2,256 other arrivals had to make a cumbersome three-block trek to the theater's fabled courtyard, where photographers roamed around unfettered to attack all unsuspecting celebrities. Henry held Jennifer for a number of shots, but he soon got the heave-ho when photographers ordered him to step aside and "get out of the picture" so she could be photographed with her good friend and fellow nominee Ingrid Bergman.

Of the nominated actresses that year, Selznick claimed an amazing three whom he had under contract: Jennifer Jones, Ingrid Bergman (*For Whom the Bell Tolls*), and Joan Fontaine (*The Constant Nymph*). Jean Arthur (*The More the Merrier*) and Greer Garson (*Madame Curie*) completed the slate of five nominees.

The new streamlined, media-friendly Academy Awards was, in part, Garson's contribution to posterity. The previous year, her Oscar acceptance speech for *Mrs. Miniver* clocked in at several minutes, making her the butt of countless jokes over the past twelve months. If she planned to repeat her prolix feat, the academy had no intention of giving Garson the chance.

Jennifer took her seat between Ingrid Bergman and Henry. A few seats away, Shirley Temple sat beside David O. Selznick and his wife, Irene, who could barely contain her rage. In all the pandemonium of

Oscar night, Selznick had jumped into one limo with friends, leaving poor Irene to find her way to Grauman's in another car.

Mrs. Selznick wasn't the only distraught female in attendance.

Henry noted a distinct change in Jennifer whenever her Hollywood mentor-lover hovered nearby. "I always thought Selznick made Jennifer nervous in public," he commented. "He was such a perfectionist. Her clothes, her hair, even her attitude concerned him. He was always criticizing how she looked, how she spoke. It would have driven most other women crazy."

When the curtain at the Chinese Theater finally rose that momentous night, there were audible gasps and then a delayed round of bright, nervous applause. In all its magnificent nakedness, a twelve-foot-high replica of the Oscar statuette stood center stage. The golden icon had not yet embedded itself in the Hollywood consciousness, and the statue's sheer size on the stage of the Chinese Theater proved overwhelming, if not downright shocking, in its priapic grandeur.

"The biggest Oscar you ever saw—twelve feet if it was an inch," reported the *Los Angeles Times*. "It gave everybody an awful start."

Everybody except Henry. The oversized statue activated his imagination, as Hollywood hokum always did. Dazzled by the glistening nude, Henry concocted a promotional frippery that required only one thing: somebody foolhardy or desperate or ambitious or dumb enough to carry it off. "I knew then that one day I'd have one of my actors painted gold to represent Oscar on Academy Award night," he told friends. Five years later, Henry convinced a former truck driver that impersonating an Oscar would help make him a star. Creative, audacious, and genuinely awful, Henry was never more prescient. Dipped in gold body paint and wearing matching skin-tight trunks, Rock Hudson would launch a thousand photographs, as well his career, on Halloween night 1949.

Until then, Henry had to put his dream of a twelve-foot phallus into mental storage, and content himself with carrying out the hetero fantasy of squiring his boss's paramour to the awards. The Academy had not yet established the tradition of opposite-sex presenters in the actors' categories, which left ripe the potential for Greer Garson, last year's recipient, to gauchely name herself the winner. Fortunately, lightning did not strike the actress twice, and Garson announced Jennifer Jones's name to tumultuous applause. Anita Loos commented on the newest Oscar winner, "Look at Jennifer's face, fresh as a cherub. This year's Cinderella story, but with the real drama yet to unfold."

Allowing Henry to wet her cheek with his congratulations, Jennifer continued to play the saint, a role that her pathological shyness put well within her acting range. She accepted the Oscar and managed to be as simple and self-effacing as Garson had been longwinded and self-aggrandizing the year before. "I apologize, Ingrid. You should have won," a shaken Jennifer Jones announced, holding on to the microphone for much-needed support. She then did what so many winners, as well as losers, must do. She cried.

Backstage, Bergman emerged equally gracious in front of a battery of reporters. "No, Jennifer, your Bernadette was better than my Maria," she told her friend as Henry looked on, holding Jennifer's purse and fur coat.

The following day, there was no time to celebrate. Henry worked on an important release from the Selznick studios: "Jennifer Jones has filed for a divorce from Robert Walker."

While Selznick busied himself on all fronts with his newest leading lady, Henry waited patiently for the next furlough that brought Guy Madison back to Tower Road. He came home a star. Selznick's publicity instincts hit the intended target with his casting of a real-life sailor in *Since You Went Away*. Inspired by the movies' mirror, fans wrote thousands of letters to the Selznick studios, wanting to know more about the blond, gum-chewing sailor whose telamon physique had been so well served by his country's uniform and a few thousand push-ups.

To the girls back home, Guy Madison's pecs symbolized what Betty Grable's legs did to the guys overseas, and Henry had little difficulty turning the twenty-one-year-old sailor into the fan magazines' World War II poster boy. Unbridled in his enthusiasm, he gave *Photoplay, Modern Screen,* and other fanzines unlimited access to his taciturn protégé in press maneuvers that had Guy spending more time with still photographers than cinematographers. Over the next decade, these photo-driven publicity campaigns became a Henry Willson specialty, one he perfected with dozens of other young men. Talent, much less emotion, rarely interfered with the rotating visual displays of the perfect male specimen. A raw, essentially incompetent performer, Guy Madison presented a tabula rasa that made him the consummate model, especially if photographed in his navy uniform or, as Henry suggested, in equally rugged attire, whether it be white T-shirt and jeans or shirtless, his chest covered with hair in some shots, as smooth and glabrous as a baby's behind in others.

Formal portraits of bare-chested male stars were a rarity before the war. The most notable exceptions were Johnny Weissmuller and Buster Crabbe who had the good excuse of working the vines as Tarzan. There was also Henry's early client Jon Hall, who put on nothing more than a miniskirt in his South Seas epics. Blame it on the rain forest. If the actor's habitat was steamy enough, the moviegoing public could relax and enjoy the blatant exploitation of the male form. Ogling a Tarzan or a Terangi (Hall's character in *Hurricane*), audiences knew these medal-winning swimmers had good cause to be half-naked in and out of the water. Whoever thought to impugn their masculinity with intimations of narcissistic exhibitionism?

Otherwise, Gary Cooper, Cary Grant, Clark Gable, and Tyrone Power left much to the imagination in the 1930s and kept their top button buttoned and their neckties tied. Not that America wasn't ready for more. When Gable took off his shirt in *It Happened One Night*, exposing a bare torso, undershirt sales in 1934 plummeted. It would take another eight years and nothing less than a world war to institutionalize such exposure.

World War II introduced a more body-conscious man and, just

as significantly, a new documentary approach to portrait photography. The glossy, highly dramatic lighting, popularized by photographer George Hurrell in the 1930s, looked grossly artificial during the war years. Overt stylization reeked of foreign exoticism, which could be construed as not only unpatriotic but downright sexually suspect. Newsreels and *Life* magazine inundated a xenophobic America with candid, unretouched shots of bare-chested sailors and soldiers, their lean but bigger physiques having been developed by digging trenches and swimming in the Pacific. Henry Willson stood first in line on the home front to mass-produce the new masculinity, and, seizing it as his patriotic duty, he exposed his boy's pecs and washboard abs to any photographer brave enough to document them. It was in Guy Madison's honor that Hollywood columnist Sidney Skolsky, operating from his "office" at Schwab's drugstore, coined the word "beefcake." In one memorable *Photoplay* shoot, Henry instructed the sailor to sprawl out shirtless on the grass in his Beverly Hills backyard. Later that afternoon, when the photographer went off to develop his acetate, Henry brought out his own camera and talked Guy into removing his trousers as well.

It was a more naive era. For Guy's shirtless spread in *Photoplay*, the magazine duly reported, "Nowadays, when Guy's in town, he's Henry Willson's house guest. His only complaint on this score is that 'the bed is too big and too soft.'"

A decade later, a celebrity could sue for having such homo stuff printed about him. In the more naive clime of 1944, however, Guy and Henry came off as nothing more than best buddies, with the older of the two simply doing his bit for the war effort. Even Selznick played along and distributed publicity photos of Guy enjoying an intimate breakfast of waffles and eggs at Henry's home.

When the war ended, Selznick decided it should continue for Guy Madison. Wasting no time, he loaned the actor to RKO to play yet another serviceman in *They Dream of Home*, which the studio retitled *Till the End of Time* to take advantage of Perry Como's hit song.

The film exposed Guy to Henry's paternal side. Ready to protect his beefcake cub at all costs, Selznick and his talent scout nearly came to blows over the monumental task of cutting and coloring Guy's locks. Henry recommended a shorter, less flamboyant look that prevented the hair from "cascading like shimmering water over chiseled rock," as one fan put it in a letter to the Selznick studios. Paranoid over the possibility of any effeminate attribute, Henry also convinced Guy to try a rinse that banished some of his hair's more charming highlights, courtesy of the Pacific salt water and sun. Too charming, in Henry's opinion. Whenever one of his boys questioned his grooming tips, Henry explained, "You don't want to look like a sissy, do you?" No sissy did.

On his assembly-line route to masculine perfection, Guy was the first of many men Henry sent to Comb 'n' Shears, where he kept a running tab. Henry entrusted the cutters there to give every head the right flair. Sideburns were kept short so as not to appear "low class." And the barbers knew to "lay off the grease."

In interviews, a well-rehearsed Guy Madison never forgot to genuflect. "I can't even begin to thank him," he said of Henry. "He arranged this and that, picked people for me to take lessons under, taught me how to dress, what to buy, showed me what the score was. We're more or less buddies, you could call it."

Selznick, however, hated the new, masculinized Guy. He ordered Henry: "I hope you will watch his photographs and see to it that his hair looks like it did in *SYWA* as to color and cut and not the way you improved it."

Despite his pro-sissy stance over Guy's hair, Selznick had grown suspicious of Henry's relationship with the actor, not that he cared whether the two men were lovers. He felt Henry had neglected his duties at Selznick studios and promptly canceled plans for him to accompany Guy on a publicity tour in the east to promote *Till the End of Time*. Money concerns were cited: the film starred a Selznick player, but it was not a Selznick picture.

Insensitive to Selznick's rebuke or too smitten to care, Henry paid his own way to New York City to be with his Galatea of the

South Pacific. Guy had never been to Gotham, much less a Broadway show, and Henry reveled in taking him to the Copacabana, Radio City Music Hall, the Empire State Building—in short, the works. Henry could not contain himself. Despite Selznick's expressed suspicions, he risked even further injury to his professional reputation by sending rapturous reports back to the boss. Guy Madison was a major star in the making, Henry insisted, and in one transparent attempt to disguise his own infatuation, he noted that the girls absolutely adored Guy.

"The reaction has been tremendous and almost unbelievable," Henry gushed in one letter. "Crowds follow him in the street and last evening hordes of bobbysoxers followed the car through the crowded theater section for ten blocks." The two men had gone to see Broadway's newest star, Judy Holliday, in *Born Yesterday*. The tale of a beautiful but vulgar young woman who undergoes an intellectual transformation appealed to Henry's paternalistic side. He liked controlling the middle ground offered by Guy, who was both more attractive and less aware than he.

After the theater, Guy became unsettled when the limousine angled its way through screaming "corridors" of female fans. Henry locked the doors, held his hand, and told Guy, "Enjoy yourself! You're a star!"

In one letter, Henry begged Selznick to put Guy into a new movie as soon as possible. "This would be a good time to announce it," he insisted.

Three thousand miles away, Selznick did not share his adjutant's boundless enthusiasm. The producer may have had no compunction about bedding the talent, but at least the actresses he slept with had talent, despite what Bosley Crowther of the *New York Times* kept writing about Jennifer Jones's excessively mannered performances. Selznick branded the aseptic Guy Madison as little more than a figment of his own marketing campaign. (The actor redeemed himself in the decade that followed by making an effectively lock-jawed Wild Bill Hickok in his 1951–1958 TV series. Guy went on to make thirty-four more films, a standout being 1960's *La Schiava di Roma* in which he played a turn-of-the-millennium mercenary.)

As starmaker, Selznick took full credit for any success and deflected any blame for all failures. On the delicate subject of Guy Madison, Selznick informed Henry, "His success in *Since You Went Away* was attributable in very large part to the fact that I let him do very little and wrote a part exactly to what he was in life, without the slightest demand for any acting ability. The same thing was true of *Till the End of Time,* which I demanded that he play only because it was written for him and written from his own inexperience and natural limitations as an actor."

Instead of a putting Guy in a major production, per Henry's request, Selznick considered throwing the actor into an adaptation of the comic strip *Steve Canyon.* The decision horrified Henry. "I know that Ann Sothern is having a miserable time losing the identity of Maisie," he cautioned, referring to another cartoon-turned-movie mishap.

Henry cared deeply about Guy. Selznick could not have cared less. Suddenly, the reprimands turned personal, and Selznick let Henry know: "I have a feeling that you stopped looking where you should for the leading men of the future—in the armed forces—when you fell under the fascination of one Guy Madison!"

15

Faux Fiancées

Henry continued to handhold his sailor-boy despite rebukes from Selznick. It was a matter of principle. Let Selznick fume and dictate another ream of complaint memos. Henry felt compelled to enter a game of emotional one-upmanship. Never the passive-aggressive type, he put it on the line. "It will be necessary for me to work at home," Henry declared.

Blame it on his Uncle Sam lineage, Henry always veered toward the imperious. His Vanguard job only burnished his self-image, and in time he came to think of himself *as* David O. Selznick. Shirley Temple recalled a particularly frigid coast-to-coast train ride on the Twentieth Century when the temperature dropped so precipitously that her mother, Gertrude, had no choice but to complain to the porter. "My daughter is going to catch a cold if you don't turn on some heat in this car," she ordered.

Gertrude Temple was a commanding woman, but she had more than met her match. The porter shuddered along with the two Temples, but not from the chill in the air or his fear of the formidable Gertrude. He pointed to a man on the far side of the dining car. "That gentleman told us to turn off the heat," he replied, refusing to confront the amphibian in pinstripes. The man, of course, was Henry Willson.

Porters on luxury trains did as Henry said. Henry did as Selznick said. But the Guy Madison rebuke went to the core of Henry's pride, his love for another man, and he could take no more.

More came in another DOS memo. Curiously, the latest reprimand concerned not Guy Madison but an actor at the other end of the talent spectrum. Selznick flew into a rage when *The Hollywood Reporter* ran a story that Ethel Barrymore had signed a multipicture deal with his studio. The facts were all there in black-and-white, and Selznick saw red: according to the trade paper, the theater's dowager queen would be lent to RKO to make *None But the Lonely Heart* with Cary Grant and *The Spiral Staircase* with such other Selznick actresses on loan-out as Dorothy McGuire and Rhonda Fleming. In Selznick's opinion, Ethel Barrymore didn't mean much at the box office but she was a big deal nonetheless. Not since *Rasputin and the Empress,* made thirteen years earlier, had the sister of John and Lionel Barrymore gone Hollywood. During that time, she had remained loyal to Broadway, where she already had one theater named in her honor.

Henry scored Ethel for Selznick, but even that signing won him no immunity from his boss's unyielding need to find fault. It enraged Selznick that a trade publication could make such a momentous announcement without his imprimatur, and he demanded to have the transgression explained. Henry could not defend himself. The leak, after all, came from his cramped office at 9336 West Washington Boulevard. It was there that agents, actors, casting directors, and other hangers-on gathered to look over the shoulder of his secretary, Ruth Burch, and read whatever spilled from her Smith-Corona.

Expert at playing the sycophant, Henry knew when to switch into major dramatic mode. Like the time he got into work at 10 A.M., and Selznick sniffed, "Bankers' hours."

"Bankers go home at three o'clock," Henry replied, angry that his late-night approach to talent-scouting had gone unappreciated.

Or the time he screwed up with the Barrymore release. Never one to apologize, he barked back, "I have to work from my home . . . for the complete fulfillment of my duties, and incidentally, in order to keep my nerves from being completely shot."

The showdown over office space took place in the summer of 1946. Selznick called the missive with Henry's ultimatum "a rather frightening communiqué from the office of Field Marshall Willson" and promptly rejected any thought of an office move to the Tower Road residence in Beverly Hills. Selznick was a bully, but one who knew how to finesse when the situation demanded. He asked his president, Daniel O'Shea, "Maybe we can get Diana Lynn to intercede and help us here."

It made sense on one level. Henry and Diana had recently announced their engagement.

On another level, it made total nonsense. "Henry's engagement? That's an oxymoron!" laughed Keith Andes, a Broadway actor whom Henry signed to a Selznick contract in the mid-1940s. Neither Andes nor Shirley Temple remembered seeing Diana Lynn at any of Henry's parties. In a 1970 interview, Diana Lynn recalled a "UCLA beau" she dated in 1946 but made no mention of her reported fiancé of that year. According to Lynn, there wasn't much romantic action for a teenage actress in Hollywood. "It was like going to a convent in a remote section of France," she said. "Boys saw me as an oddity."

Henry saw her as his ticket to hetero respectability, and the announcement of their engagement made all the papers long before everyone in town stopped laughing. Born Dolly Loehr, daughter of an oil-company executive, Diana Lynn followed Paula Stone as Henry's official fiancée. Once again, the romance would derail somewhere between the much-publicized engagement ring and the final walk to the altar with another man. From his Broadway buddies to the Puppets set, Henry loved showbiz babies and Diana got her start even younger than Paula. He envied their childhood success, they envied his having had a childhood. It wasn't sex, but it was something.

Baby Dolly, as Diana Lynn was billed early in her professional career, learned to play the piano before her feet could touch the pedals, and so delighted audiences with her derring-do on the keys that

Paramount Pictures featured her at age twelve in its 1939 musical *There's Magic in Music.* A long-term contract followed and Diana soon graduated from baby grands to postbaby roles in two entries in the studio's long-running Henry Aldrich series, *Henry Aldrich Plays Cupid* and *Henry Aldrich Gets Glamour,* among other films.

Pert, dainty, and laced together with a stinging wit, Diana Lynn resembled a porcelain doll whose tongue could puncture asphalt. The actress didn't think much of her stage name. "It sounds like a Chinese laundry," she once cracked. "Patently made up."

She thought even less of life in Hollywood. "I missed a normal childhood," Diana said. "If someone told me they were interested in a career in the movies, I'd say, Become a manicurist."

Diana and Henry were destined to meet if for no other reason than the movie capital suffered from an exceedingly shallow dating pool during the last days of World War II. Despite his I-A draft status, Henry Willson managed to avoid the armed services and was officially "rejected" for military duty on August 15, 1942. By then, at age thirty-one, he was slightly beyond the cusp of duty, and if that didn't protect him, there were two well-timed hernia operations. Although friends say he truly suffered from the ailment, colitis is not mentioned in Henry's draft file. Neither is his homosexuality, which would have slapped him with a IV-F ("rejected for military service; physical, mental or moral reasons"). (The scarlet category IV-F had only recently been expanded to include homosexuals. Prior to 1940, a man had to be caught practicing sodomy to be expelled from the service.)

With so many men still stationed overseas, the dateable ones left behind in Hollywood, like Henry Willson and his friend Craig Stevens, kept bumping into each other in the town's better tearooms. Paramount Pictures set up a few dates between Diana Lynn and Jennifer Jones's new ex, Robert Walker. The former Dolly also did duty in the Hollywood formicary with the newly discharged Guy Madison, who met his future first wife, actress Gail Russell, through Diana, which led to Diana's meeting Henry who, at age thirty-six, had begun to feel the pressure to acquire a female appendage, as did the twenty-five-year-old sailor.

"Di is my best friend, Henry is his," Gail Russell told *Modern Screen* in the article "Hollywood's Strangest Love," an account which strongly criticized Guy for not marrying his girlfriend of so many, many weeks. In a pattern Henry would see repeated with other matinee idols, the Hollywood press corps touted a man's bachelorhood for all of six or seven issues before the editors turned testy and required an immediate exchange of wedding rings by year's end. As *Modern Screen* reported, "Guy talks about a flagstone walk, a barn, four kids; but he refuses to mention the little item called a wife!" The magazine put it on the line, "There ought to be a wife!"

In 1949, Guy married Gail, whose success five years earlier playing an ingenue haunted by a ghost in *The Uninvited* preceeded her descent into alcoholism, which led to few other significant film roles. Rumors of her lesbianism were upgraded to bisexuality in 1953, when she was named as a correspondent in John Wayne's divorce trial by the actor's estranged wife, Esperanza. Guy followed suit the following year and divorced Gail.

Henry and Diana took longer *not* to tie the knot. Her being nearly twenty years his junior made the actress ideal to play the role of fiancée in a year-long round of publicity photos and stories. While Henry liked men with strong emotional ties to their mothers (and none to their fathers), he preferred dating women young enough to live with parents who expected their daughters to be brought home before 10 P.M.

To that end, *Photoplay* played along, and in October 1946 published an article entitled "Diamond on Her Finger," in which the magazine's readers learned that "Diana Lynn tried it on for size 'just in case . . . ' Then she thought over its engaging effect . . . and put it on again." To accompany the twosome's engagement profile, *Photoplay* published a photo of Diana and Henry at the Mocambo, the duo safely ensconced in his favorite banquette.

Henry loved the coverage, but even the most slavish of fan-magazine writers sometimes stumbled upon the occasional *mots justes*. According to *Photoplay*, Henry had suggested Bermuda as a honeymoon spot, to which Diana replied, "But I'm afraid we shouldn't find anyone there we knew. Don't laugh at me, darling . . . I know you well enough by now to know that you aren't happy unless there are people around . . . at least near enough to telephone you. I want you to enjoy our honeymoon!"

The writer concluded, "There speaks an understanding heart."

To promote his faux engagement, Henry looked beyond the fan magazines. When his diamond ring for Diana turned out to be a few sizes too large for her pianist's finger, he returned it to the jewelers (Black, Starr & Gorham), who at his insistence informed Hedda Hopper and Edith Gwynne at *The Hollywood Reporter* of the snafu. When the two gossips reported that the couple had broken up, Henry seized the opportunity to demand a correction. Always a big thinker, Lynn's fiancé had something more expansive in mind than a mere two-sentence retraction.

"If you have room on one of your back-page ads someday, perhaps you could correct the impression that I got my ring back," Henry wrote. He politely complained that he and his fiancée had not yet officially announced their engagement (despite having already been interviewed on the subject by *Photoplay*), that Diana had simply tried on the diamond ring for size and, having found it too large, returned it to the jeweler for one with a snugger fit.

Henry wanted to know, "Do you suppose you could work a picture of Diana and me on the back page . . . and an explanation." Killing two birds with one article, he recommended that "the story" be illustrated with his and Diana's faces pasted over those of Gregory Peck and Jennifer Jones. To help facilitate such a bizarre visual, he included a poster of the two actors' newest film, *Duel in the Sun*, which Selznick had readied for imminent release. In conclusion, Henry assured *The Hollywood Reporter*, "Everything is just fine." He signed the letter, "The Rambling Romeo," a pointed takeoff on the newspaper's gossip column, "The Rambling Reporter."

His joyous engagement aside, the year ended on a discouragingly minor note for Selznick's head of talent. Henry had been touting a new director from Italy, Roberto Rossellini. But as with Montgomery Clift and James Whale, the deal failed to materialize. Once again, Selznick chafed at the terms, which were bigger dollarwise than what the producer had offered Alfred Hitchcock in the late 1930s. Or so Selznick said. "The figures are much too high for the last four years to warrant our breaking in a new director," the producer wrote in his terse dismissal of the Italian neorealist.

PART FIVE

Henry Willson, the matchmaker: Rory Calhoun takes Lana Turner to the Los Angeles premiere of *Spellbound* at the Carthay Circle Theater, 1945.

16

Ex-con Rory Calhoun

First, Guy Madison. Then this new guy, Rory Calhoun. One was as blond and clean-cut as the other was dark and feral. Whatever the physical stimuli, Selznick felt compelled once again to put the brakes on Henry's hormonal overdrive. "You simply must restrain your exuberance and behave in a more conservative and grown-up fashion about these things," Selznick chastised.

Henry had committed the mortal sin of flackery by telling Louella Parsons that Rory was the "new Clark Gable."

Selznick went into orbit when he read the item in Parson's *Los Angeles Examiner* gossip column. He let Henry know, "I went to the greatest pains to stop anyone from referring to Ingrid Bergman, when she was unknown here, as 'a second Garbo.'"

Henry tried to defend himself. He made the usual bow to Selznick's "vast experience" in these matters but insisted that boozy Louella had gotten it wrong. He argued that, in her usual stupor, she misinterpreted his innocuous comment that "Rory's success would be on a par with Gable's," not to mention Robert Taylor's.

This much was clear. In his painless, infatuated segue from Guy to Rory, Henry established a pattern that would repeat itself with a long succession of male clients. The rush of sexual excitement that followed any new discovery led to a truncated honeymoon as the career reality of their professional marriage surfaced in *Variety*'s Monday-morning grosses. Four years after his debut in *Since You*

Went Away, Guy Madison never ceased to take his shirt off with expert aplomb. But Henry wasn't blind: Guy had significant problems walking and talking in front of the camera, and his laborious effort to mimic a living, breathing person offscreen also depended heavily on one's imagination. Every morning, regardless of the movie set, Guy Madison greeted his female costar with the same remark: "You're good-looking . . . for a girl!"

Guy thought he was making a joke.

Girls thought he was being a jerk.

Whether Henry's romantic interest fell victim to the actor's numbing predictability is not known. He may have taken his cue from Selznick, who characterized Guy's limited appeal as "strictly one to youthful audiences, especially bobbysoxers." Although he didn't dismiss Madison completely, Selznick pointed out his obvious limitations with the succinct critique: "He will never be a Mansfield or a Booth."

The producer found much more potential in Henry's newer discovery, Rory Calhoun (born Francis Durgin), whom he thought possessed the "broader appeal" to play the "heavy," as well as "the leading man." Henry was more to the point in his praise and described Rory as "the most exciting man" he had ever met. Their initial meeting must have prefigured the first time Stella laid eyes on her Stanley Kowalski, who, in the future and immortal words of Tennessee Williams, explained the attraction of time-honored gentility to brute force: "I was common as dirt," Stanley tells Stella. "You showed me the snapshot of the place with the columns. I pulled you down off them columns, and how you loved it . . ." Henry, the Wesleyan-educated WASP homosexual, met his ultimate sex fantasy in the shape of an Irish ex-con who skipped high school in favor of the federal penitentiary. Whether it was love or lust, Henry never could tell the difference. Rory arrived in his life at a moment of acute emotional vulnerability. On the verge of a nervous breakdown, Henry informed Selznick president Daniel O'Shea of his problem in a letter dated January 2, 1947. He would have to take off a few weeks to visit his cabin retreat in the San Gabriel Mountains. "This is not a vacation," Henry wrote. "I need rest."

Henry also needed Rory, and he invited him to be his companion for those winter days in the mountains. As a couple, they made a shadowy study in contrasts.

Francis Durgin's hard-core criminal past started in his childhood when he made a career out of stealing from newsstands and grocery stores. It was his theft of a nickel-plated revolver at age thirteen in 1935, however, that landed him in the Pacific Lodge reformatory. He might have remained there, for an indeterminate stay, but the lack of metal bars on his cell window gave him immediate access to another round of stealing. When he graduated from jewelry to cars, the federal government took over his rehabilitation. "We went into the hot-car racket," Francis Durgin said of a fellow escaped inmate. "He knew a used-car dealer in Salt Lake City, Utah, who paid $100 for every brand-new late model sedan we delivered."

Durgin made the major mistake of driving a stolen car across state lines, a federal offense that sent him to the penitentiary in Springfield, Missouri, for three years. And when he finished serving that sentence, there was a longer term waiting for him back in California at "the big house," San Quentin. Francis Durgin had not yet turned eighteen.

Maximum security prevented him from any future jail breaks and led to his parole shortly before his twenty-first birthday. Durgin had spent his entire teenage years in one form of incarceration or another. Employment-wise, he wasn't suited for much—mining, lumberjacking, cow-handling, hustling. Then, one day in 1943, he rode a horse through the Hollywood Hills and there, among the chaparral and cacti, he ran smack dab into a five-foot-five matinee idol, who conveniently had an agent for a wife, who knew this well-positioned head of talent over at the Selznick studios . . .

Sue Carol Ladd's first order of business for Durgin was to recycle his stepfather's surname, McCown and cast Durgin, now Frank McCown, into a Laurel and Hardy comedy called *The Bullfighters*. The role came with one line: "If that guy's a bullfighter, I'm Mickey Mouse." It was a beginning, she said.

And nearly the end—until Sue Carol threw a party at her Holmby Hills home for all her unemployed clients. Hoping to snag a Selznick contract, Mrs. Ladd invited her good friend Henry. Publicly, he couched his enthusiasm for another man the way homosexuals often did, by refracting his desire through the eyes of the opposite sex. As Henry told the story, one of the Ladds' dogs started yapping in the other room and, naturally, he went to investigate. The cur led Henry to a six-foot-three tree of a man.

"I was deciding that I really didn't blame the pooch, when I discovered that the girl with me was gazing at this same young man with that look that girls sometimes get," said Henry. "You know, I thought, if girls get that expression when they don't even know his name . . . and when he's wearing that sweater . . . maybe he has what it takes."

Francis Durgin had committed the mortal sin of a sartorial faux pas. There he stood in the home of Hollywood royalty, Henry noted, and, in the august presence of Mr. and Mrs. Alan Ladd, he wore neither coat nor tie but rather a plain black turtleneck sweater. And it was after 7 P.M.! "You don't even think about going into Beverly Hills without a jacket on!" Henry used to admonish his clients.

If it is true what people in Hollywood say about good agents—they must be starving or madly in love with a client—it is no wonder Durgin languished under Sue Carol's care. Never in need of a good meal, Henry persuaded Selznick to sign the actor to a seven-year contract without so much as a screen test. He banished the failed movie name, Frank McCown, and replaced it with something equally Irish but a tad more stylish.

Henry called him "Troy Donahue."

Durgin wore the name for a week or two before trying on another.

Going back to his inventory of names, Henry retrieved "Calhoun." And skipping right over the young man's major career as a hoodlum, Henry played up his brief stint as a firefighter to coin the name Rory, as in "roaring blazes."

Henry had other names for his new boy. "I call him Smokey," he told Hedda and Louella. And despite the story he fed Selznick, Henry did compare Rory Calhoun to Clark Gable. He went even so far as to recommend a Gable-style moustache to balance Rory's thick eyebrows, making sure to trim the latter and pluck the hair above the nose so that the actor bore no resemblance to the excessively hirsute, slightly Cro-Magnon specimen of his prison mug shots. For a few weeks of blissful infatuation, Henry played Rory's twin and grew a moustache of his own. In one *Modern Screen* photograph, taken in a studio screening room, the two men sport identical "cookie dusters," as the magazine noted. Unlike Gable's handlers, who left well enough alone, Henry made sure to pin back Rory's big ears.

Henry had once shown Guy Madison the benefit of Combs 'n' Shears and Carroll's Men's Store. Now it was Rory's chance to witness how such small touches of cloth and scissors could turn a man from thug to movie idol. "It's finding the right mix," said Henry. Plaid shirts during the day, a black tuxedo at night; Pabst Blue Ribbon chased with Dom Perignon; or bowling followed by ballroom dancing.

Ever mindful of Rory's turtleneck faux pas at the Ladds, Henry insisted on sculpted, padded jackets. More than good fashion, they were camouflage for Calhoun's narrow shoulders. Henry assured him, "Don't worry. Cary Grant has the same problem."

The trick was never to obliterate the thin, taut thread of sexual frisson that linked bad boy to leading man. Underlying all of Rory's adoptive good manners and fine clothes, Henry kept his sights on what made his newest pumpkin a Cinderella in his eyes. "He is moody and unpredictable and . . . he has a temper which flares like lightning and disappears almost as quickly," gushed Henry. For a brief moment, he lost himself and forgot to invoke the female perspective.

"Henry was well bred and educated, Rory was this unformed tough guy with a dark past," said Henry's assistant Gary Crutcher. "Henry usually went in for more wholesome types, all-American. But Rory was different, and Henry knew he had to give Rory some polish if he was going to be accepted in Hollywood."

The makeover had only begun.

17

Never a Groom

I n the beginning, Henry's interest in actors had been grounded in
his first love, the theater. But after a few years in Hollywood, the
former stage-door johnny became a connoisseur of something far
more elusive, intangible, maybe even bogus. They call it star quality.

"Rory Calhoun had little acting experience when I met him,
either," said Henry, comparing him to his first great screen discovery, Lana Turner. "But that doesn't matter too much," he added
as a distant afterthought.

Henry's first role for Rory required no acting ability whatsoever.
All Rory had to do was walk. Lana Turner would do the rest.

Shortly after her sweater-jiggle walk in *They Won't Forget*, Lana
Turner did forget and dropped Henry to sign with the William
Morris Agency. She and her first agent, however, remained good
acquaintances, if not friends. (As late as 1958, he was known to set
her up with afternoon sex dates, a service he rendered with
increasing frequency for other friends and business associates.)
Henry and Lana shared an appreciation for well-endowed men, and
he could wholeheartedly recommend Rory. Momentarily between
husbands in 1945, Lana needed an escort for the premiere of Alfred
Hitchcock's *Spellbound,* and seeing a brief window of opportunity,
Henry used the event to showcase Rory Calhoun. He suggested a
white fox wrap for the platinum-blonde star and, of course, a black
tuxedo for his dark knight.

"Those photographs of Rory Calhoun and Lana Turner were seen everywhere," said the publicist Frank Liberman. "Rory was unknown in Hollywood. Of course, Lana was already a huge star. And there they were together at this premiere."

Inside the Carthay Circle Theater, Lana glistened in white, Rory simmered in black. "They were a study in contrasts, and the photographers went wild," said Liberman. "Henry was a genius at this kind of publicity, which back then could work to launch a very successful career."

Selznick showed faith in Rory by selling the actor's services to other studios. Henry made sure to take good care of him. After languishing under the management of Sue Carol Ladd, Rory now ran the gamut from high romance (*Adventure Island* with Rhonda Fleming) and Freudian film noir (*The Red House* with Edward G. Robinson) to kitchen-sink drama (*That Hagen Girl* with Ronald Reagan and Shirley Temple).

Acting was only half of it, if even that. In the beginning, Henry kept his Argus-eyed watch over Rory by taking him to Ciro's and the Mocambo. When Diana Lynn had finished her piano practice, she sometimes tagged along, and as an accoutrement for Rory's right arm, there was the ever-reliable Vera-Ellen, an ex-Rockette, who, like most dancers, did as she was told. Ex-cons are another story, and Rory soon opted to be seen with his new bedmate, the French actress Corinne Calvet.

As date material, Vera-Ellen possessed the better credentials, in Henry's opinion: She had starred opposite Dick Haymes and Danny Kaye in a few Sam Goldwyn comedies. Calvet had yet to land a Hollywood screen credit—except as Rita Hayworth's replacement in the arms of Orson Welles, who, if he looked at her and squinted, thought Corinne looked something like his former wife. And there were other problems: Corinne had studied at the Sorbonne and her scientist father had invented Pyrex, which meant that she wasn't about to take marching orders from any talent scout or agent.

Worst of all, the actress single-handedly ruined Rory's chances over at Columbia Pictures, where she made the fatal error of resisting the sexual advances of Harry Cohn. The studio head had invited Corinne, Rory, and a few other partygoers for a weekend cruise on his yacht when, dangling a long-term contract in front of the actress, Cohn did what he usually did during career negotiations with an actress—he tried to rape her. Or so she claimed.

Rory gallantly came to Corinne's defense. Or so she said.

"You're finished," Cohn yelled at Corinne. And by association, that meant Rory, too.

Henry enjoyed his friendships with fiery, opinionated women, and he showed that appreciation by occasionally turning them into clients. But when it came to dates for his boys, he preferred more malleable women, which did not include the headstrong Corinne Calvet.

The actress proved more gracious in her opinion of Henry. She remembered him as "a brilliant talent scout who recruited material for Selznick's school for young film hopefuls." She and Rory double-dated with Henry and Diana Lynn. "When they broke their engagement, our foursome slid easily into a threesome," she reported with apt disappointment.

Unfortunately for the French actress, Rory committed the major offense of asking her to marry him without first seeking the approval of his mentor, who often took more time choosing his boys' wives than their next movie. Whatever allegiance Rory owed Henry, it eclipsed his love for Corinne, who had every reason to feel her fiancée status had been compromised. The couple had planned a press conference to announce their wedding. Corinne fixed her hair, of which there was a lot, and even bought a new dress. But when the big hour arrived, no Rory. Unbeknownst to Corinne, Henry had given his protégé an ultimatum: "Break up with Corinne or I'll take the young man that delivers her mail and make him a big star," he said, referring to Rock Hudson.

With her fiancé not to be found, Corinne made the rounds of Hollywood nightclubs, which after ten minutes led her to Ciro's.

"Rory and Henry sat next to each other in interesting proximity.

A bottle of iced champagne rested between them," she recalled, insinuating a relationship more than professional. "The smile on Henry's face gripped my heart with fingers as cold as the bed of ice surrounding the bottle. I was overcome with a feeling of love mixed with a sense of death."

But not so overcome that Corinne couldn't find her way to their table.

Henry spoke first. "Tell me about your weekend, Corinne. Did you have fun?" It was a nasty remark, not worthy of Henry's usual clever subterfuge. He knew the weekend in Catalina had ended with King Cohn's attack and Rory's brave, foolhardy defense. The conversation at Ciro's devolved from there.

When the two men left the nightclub, Corinne jumped into her car and followed them to Henry's new home. Henry had recently made the big move westward to the very posh Bel Air, and his house was just a mile up the canyon from the exclusive Hotel Bel-Air. Arriving at 1536 Stone Canyon Drive, Corinne made a point to park her car in Henry's driveway, effectively blocking Rory's escape route. No sooner did Henry stop Corinne at the front door than Rory made his dramatic entrance brandishing an automatic pistol, which he fired into an unsuspecting eucalyptus grove across the street. It was just a warning, but the shot duly alerted neighbors who took it upon themselves to inform the police. When sirens disrupted the night air, Rory ordered Corinne to get in her car, drive up the canyon road, and then duck under her steering wheel until the police left.

An hour later, Corinne drove back to Henry's place and learned the truth. "Rory's car was still parked in Willson's driveway," she said. "The entire house was dark."

Henry put up no roadblocks when Rory soon found another potential fiancée. Lita Baron sang at the Mocambo under the stage name Isabelita, and, like any good Catholic, she claimed to be a bona-fide virgin, much to the amusement of Rory's ex. "A virgin!" Corinne chortled. Less judgmental, Henry played wedding arranger with back-to-back nuptials: Guy Madison married Gail Russell, and when he was finished with them, Henry took Rory and Lita up to Santa Barbara to register for a quiet ceremony there. For some reason, Lita had forgotten to pack and needed a ride back to Los Angeles, courtesy of her brother, Pete. Henry stayed behind in Santa Barbara with Rory. They made arrangements and otherwise enjoyed themselves as only two bachelors can.

It may have been Lita's big day but Henry wanted to celebrate too, and he made sure to furnish his version to *Photoplay* as an exclusive. "Henry gave Rory a 'bachelor's dinner' that evening," the magazine reported. "There were just the two of them but they had champagne and all the trimmings. A bit of hustle and bustle wasn't to be allowed to interfere with a single tradition!"

Two day's later, at Trinity Episcopal Church, Lita's sister Mary was the lovely maid of honor, and Henry got to play his favorite role when Rory cast him as best man.

Never a groom, Henry was happy to watch. No sooner did Diana Lynn turn twenty than she gave Henry the heave-ho. Their engagement had lasted a few months and provided a ton of copy. Faster than she could say "I don't," she married the noted architect John C. Lindsay in 1948. Fellow former child star Jane Withers was her maid of honor. She vaguely remembered seeing Henry and Diana together sometime before the wedding. "They went out on three or four dates," said Withers.

As it was time to go fiancée-shopping, Henry saw no reason to look very far.

"I was on the list," said Rhonda Fleming. "He was determined to get engaged to somebody. I guess he needed to cover that he was gay."

Born Marilyn Louis, the red-haired beauty first met Henry on her way to Beverly Hills High one autumn day in 1942. His black Cadillac kept circling the block and she kept walking faster. It was, after all, Beverly Hills. Henry finally got out of his car to give her his standard, "Have you ever thought of being in the movies?" It worked for men at the Mocambo, it worked for Marilyn Louis on her way to algebra.

Henry named her Ronda Fleming. Selznick added the letter "h" for no better reason than his inserting an "O" between his first and last names. It just looked right.

Shortly after the Diana Lynn break-up, Henry invited Rhonda to a dinner party at his home. There were several other guests, but at some point in the evening the host asked the most ravishingly beautiful woman present if she would stay a little later than the others. He wanted to be alone with her so they could talk.

"I thought he wanted to discuss a new part or film for me," said Fleming.

With his housekeeper Ella Mae Fuque doing dishes in the kitchen, Henry finally found himself alone with his protégée, who only five short years earlier had been running barefoot, dodging his black Cadillac, on her way to Beverly Hills High. Now she was a star. Rhonda always said she owed Henry everything. He was about to find out if she meant it.

From his suit pocket, Henry produced a small black velvet box and opened it. Rhonda immediately recognized the diamond ring that Diana had been wearing only two weeks earlier. Henry chose his words carefully and made sure to keep the formalities to a minimum. He asked, "Will you accept this ring?"

The former Marilyn Louis almost passed out. "Henry tried to put it on my finger," she recalled. "He tried to do that."

Rhonda Fleming declined his proposal as discreetly as circumstances allowed. She told Henry she was "flattered." Dumbfounded was more like it. Three years earlier, the word "nymphomaniac" had not yet entered her vocabulary, but standing there in the foyer of Henry Willson's home, saying goodnight to her amiable, rejected suitor, she did know the meaning of "homosexual."

After her refusal to marry him, Rhonda and Henry remained good friends and made a frequent twosome on the Hollywood party circle. According to the actress, he never broached the subject of marriage again.

18

Jaguar in the Rain

Before he married off his two best boys, Henry enjoyed squiring Rory and Guy about town. They made attractive, contrasting bookends as they rode through Beverly Hills in Henry's black Cadillac. Most people didn't know enough to gossip. Other people, namely homosexual people, knew more than enough to talk among themselves about Selznick's overly nurturing head of talent.

"It was very unusual to see a man like Henry Willson with two of his stars," said Ed Colbert, a photographer. "Maybe an agent or manager would go to lunch or dinner with one star, but never two." As an avid chronicler of the Hollywood scene, Colbert kept a vigil at restaurants like Chasen's and Romanoff's where he waited to nab the candid shot of a celebrity. On occasion, Henry showed up with Rory and Guy. He liked to dress them in pin-stripe suits that matched his own. "Henry would drive around with Rory and Guy," said Colbert. "They made this eye-catching portrait—the one so dark, the other so blond. And there was Henry behind the wheel. It was talked about." At least, in certain circles.

In the late 1940s, there was a continental divide in sexual awareness between homosexuals, who knew, and heterosexuals, who preferred not to. For Henry, it was the best of both worlds. He provided the smoke and mirrors of fiancées for the straight majority. Regarding his brethren in the minority, few of them held any real power in Hollywood, and in his opinion it made little difference what they gossiped about. Besides, Henry couldn't help himself. Whether playing a hand of bridge together or helping Guy and Rory to mend their leather chaps, Henry enjoyed being kingmaker, and he commemorated that status in a series of publicity shots. In a few of them, Rory and Guy showed up wearing Henry's sweaters and ties.

More often, he paired his boys on dates with the opposite sex. Sometimes females weren't enough, and as it was a professional given that a male actor's masculine attributes were suspect, Henry gilded the macho lily by introducing his boys to suitably violent sports. An August 1946 profile in *Photoplay* made the following observation on the blossoming friendship between Rory Calhoun and Guy Madison: "The first time they made an engagement to go hunting together Rory appeared with the usual rifle and a few rounds of ammunition. All that Guy tossed into the car was that famous bow of his and a quiver of arrows." Guy Madison explained: "I never could see hunting strictly as slaughter. This way it's more of a game—the animal has a little chance anyhow."

Killing was tough, acting was soft. Which is why a male actor needed a sport, and Henry never failed to provide one to burnish his boys' public image. Privately, he offered a slightly more involved, if not complicated, exploration of Guy and Rory's personal dynamic.

"Henry was very hush-hush," said his male assistant Pat Colby. "He didn't tell stories out of school."

"He much preferred stories of Hollywood glamour, not sex stories," agreed Gary Crutcher, another yeoman of longstanding.

But Henry did tell ribald stories on occasion. Like the one about Rory and Guy in the rain in the parked car.

The two men became best friends who lived out their lives as married men, fathers, and neighbors in the Palm Springs area. In hindsight, Henry's tale may reveal more about the psychosexual makeup of its teller than any physical relationship his two protégés actually enjoyed together. Then again, Rory and Guy were young, sinfully good-looking, and it was Hollywood.

(TOP) Henry Willson watches over clients Lana Turner and Paula Stone at a Beverly Hills cocktail party, 1937. (BOTTOM) *Hurricane* lovers Jon Hall and Dorothy Lamour impress the young Roy Fitzgerald, 1937. *Photos courtesy of Photofest.*

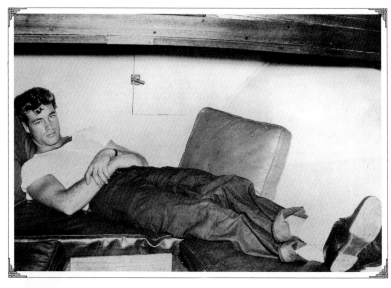

(TOP) A little R&R: World War II sailor Guy Madison poses out of uniform, 1944. (BOTTOM LEFT) Rhonda Fleming dazzles the eye in Hitchcock's *Spellbound*, 1945. *Photo courtesy of Photofest.* (BOTTOM RIGHT) Getting macho, Rory Calhoun takes aim with bow and arrow, 1947. *Photos courtesy of Academy of Motion Picture Arts & Sciences.*

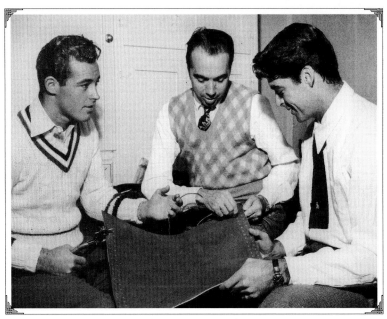

(TOP LEFT) Columnist Sidney Skolsky interviews Guy Madison and coins a new word, "beefcake," 1944. Photo courtesy of *Academy of Motion Picture Arts & Sciences.* (TOP RIGHT) Henry escorts Jennifer Jones to the Oscars, and she wins, 1944. (BOTTOM) Henry helps Guy Madison and Rory Calhoun sew their archer's arm guard, 1947. *Photos courtesy of Photofest.*

(TOP LEFT) Henry dances with the president's daughter, Margaret Truman. (TOP RIGHT) Rhonda Fleming and Henry dress up as Mr. and Mrs. Bo Beep, Ciro's, 1948. (BOTTOM) Robert Wagner dines with Henry and 20th Century Fox's acting coach Helen Sorrell. *All photos courtesy of Photofest.*

(TOP) Vera-Ellen and Rock paint themselves gold to be twin Oscars at the Hollywood Press Photographers Ball, Ciro's, 1949. *Photo courtesy of Bison Archives.* (BOTTOM) Rock does blackface, as the Wild Man of Borneo, while **Piper Laurie** plays Circe and an antebellum **Elizabeth Taylor** tickles a pig, Ciro's, 1950. *Photo courtesy of Photofest.*

Before and after: Sailor Roy Fitzgerald smiles with his old teeth 1946 *(courtesy of Photofest)*, and the new ones Henry buys for him, 1950 *(courtesy of Academy of Motion Picture Arts & Sciences)*.

(TOP FROM LEFT TO RIGHT) John Saxon a.k.a. Carmen Errico; Mike "Touch" Connors in *Sudden Fear*. **(BOTTOM FROM LEFT TO RIGHT)** TV cowboy Robert Fuller; "Gentle Giant," Clint Walker. *All Photos courtesy of Photofest.*

(TOP) The son of a wealthy Beverly Hills businessman, Robert Wagner avoids the Henry Willson name-change. *Photo courtesy of Photofest.* (BOTTOM) Due to forces beyond their control, George Nader and Rock are never profiled in *Confidential. Photo courtesy of Academy of Motion Picture Arts & Sciences.*

As Henry told his tale, he was driving through the Hollywood Hills one night, making the rounds. (At some point in his Hollywood tenure, he learned to operate an automobile and dispensed with his chauffeur.) Henry believed that maintaining a star's image never stopped, it went on twenty-four hours a day, and he put it upon himself to be his clients' caretaker, guardian, and, if necessary, shadow. These self-appointed duties required him to keep an ever-watchful eye, to make sure his various charges toed the Hollywood line and maintained only the most appropriate friendships.

On this particular April night, the city of Los Angeles was experiencing one of its rare electrical storms. Not only did the rain come down in heavy sheets as Henry's car approached Rory's house, but lightning joined the symphony of water and wind, its repeated flashes illuminating a vehicle parked in the driveway. Henry recognized it as Guy's Jaguar coupe. Whether he feared the worst or the best, Henry knew enough to turn off his headlights, put his own car into low drive, and approach the house in relative quiet and darkness. It was then that he saw someone in Guy's car, and despite the torrential rain, Henry's sense of paternal duty forced him to make a closer inspection. "Could it be?" he wondered. "The Jaguar was rocking from side to side." As if struck by an earthquake.

There in the rain, as the thunder and lighting provided ample special effects, Henry Willson realized his sweetest humiliation. "Rory was fucking Guy!" he said. "And they had always told me they didn't like to do it with men."

Henry said he felt betrayed but somehow mentioned nothing about feeling incredibly excited. He confronted Guy, who insisted that his storm-tossed dalliance with Rory was a momentary lapse, the first and only time. "But I knew that couldn't be true," said Henry. "Rory was so big, and Guy was taking him with no problem." According to Henry, Guy always maintained his relative innocence: "It was the first time!"

Rory, however, later confessed that, yes, their affair had been going on for months.

Guy and Rory. They constituted the original poles of Henry Willson's sexual template: the dark thug with the criminal past on one end, the blond, wholesome sailor on the other. Literally. What better sexual apotheosis to witness for an unattractive outsider? In his rejection, Henry found himself literally left out in the rain to watch as the reportedly heterosexual ex-con ravished the all-American defender of the nation's freedom.

Over the years, Henry recast Guy and Rory in the movie that never stopped unspooling in his mind. The bodies and faces of a thousand other young men took their places, and it was Henry's calling to put them on the big screen for the whole world to see and enjoy. It was his ultimate fantasy: Rory and Guy in the rain making love. Like most fantasies, it was almost too good to be true.

Sometime in the 1950s, Henry told this story to an actor named Paul Nesbitt, who believed every word of it. Nesbitt was something of a fantasy himself. Among other Broadway credits, Nesbitt played the role of Adonis, no less, in Noel Coward's comedy *Look After Lulu* in 1959, and according to several observers, he fit the role to perfection. Earlier in Paul's career, Henry had suggested he call himself Chance Nesbitt. It was a good stage name, and the actor used it. No one else was calling himself Chance, but Nesbitt knew to drop the name when his swimming buddy at the YMCA took special notice of it.

"Tennessee Williams ruined the name Chance when he used it in his *Sweet Bird of Youth*," said Nesbitt, referring to the play's hustler character, Chance Wayne.

Sweet Bird of Youth and *Look After Lulu* opened within a week of each other on Broadway in March 1959. By then, Nesbitt had switched to using a name so bland that no playwright would want to mess with it. He called himself Paul Smith. Today, his professional name is Paul Nesbitt, which is also his real name.

Henry never agreed that Nesbitt should drop the catchier moniker, but the actor knew better, and according to him, Tennessee Williams duly apologized for the career infraction.

19

Farewell to Tara

In December 1947, Selznick threatened to fire Henry if he didn't come through with major loan-outs for Alida Valli, Louis Jourdan, Rhonda Fleming, and Alan Marshall. Never contrite, always unsatisfied, Selznick held Henry responsible for his cash-flow problem. To his credit, Henry produced the needed financial miracle on demand and found work for the unemployed in Selznick's acting stable. He even sent Selznick a Christmas note replete with confidence in face of the obvious emotional strain: "It is urgent that I get away completely from Hollywood, phones, etc., for a couple of weeks. This is not a vacation—but a rest. I eat, sleep, dream about the studio and my work. The only escape is a complete change of scenery for a couple of weeks."

Despite tantrums and ultimatums on both sides, the two men maintained a working relationship that resembled a troubled yet devoted marriage. In one typical missive, Henry wrote Selznick, who was away on business in New York. "I think it's about time you came home. All is forgiven!" That was April 21, 1948.

Henry kept his job with Selznick for one simple reason: he knew the whereabouts of every A-list script in town—and for good reason. Out of his own pocket, he lavished birthday, holiday, and wedding gifts on secretaries, readers, typists, mailroom boys, anyone who had early access to screenplays or novels under option. Thanks to Henry, Selznick was often in a position to phone Harry

Cohn or Darryl F. Zanuck about a script within hours of its delivery to their studio. Then came the pitch: Ingrid Bergman, Gregory Peck, or Joseph Cotten would be perfect for the lead.

It was essential information. In early 1948, Selznick needed money more than amphetamines. He had only one film in the can, *Portrait of Jennie,* starring Jennifer Jones, and it had been a troubled production from the beginning. After playing a sultry siren in *Duel in the Sun,* Jones was cast more to type, as a somewhat elusive ghost, in *Jennie.* "David concentrated exclusively on Jennifer and let everything else fall apart," said Shirley Temple. Selznick's paramour, however, could not be blamed for the many rewrites, reshoots, and long shutdowns on *Jennie.*

In Hollywood, genius is forever—until it's over. Selznick had made *Gone with the Wind,* but that was ten years ago. Once upon a time, he also signed Gregory Peck and Ingrid Bergman. But in 1948, he passed on Peggy Lee in favor of lesser talents. The blonde jazz singer was a notable find for Henry. She had enjoyed a huge success with the release of the single "Manana," and Henry found her extremely photogenic, "unlike Jo Stafford," he informed Selznick, referring to Lee's major singing competition of the day. Peggy Lee looked to make well over $300,000 in 1948 for her recording and club dates.

Selznick, however, let Henry's deal with the singer evaporate somewhere over Culver City, and instead he signed Tod Andrews, an actor who had previously been credited as Michael Ames in the horror films *Voodoo Man* and *Return of the Ape Man.*

Impending bankruptcy can have an especially dulling effect on a man's genius. Instead of obsessing over his own movies, Selznick began to focus on the money lost by not putting his actors into somebody else's film. William Wyler's adaptation of *The Heiress* became a singular obsession; it was the kind of drenched-in-prestige screen adaptation he had specialized in in the 1930s. And Selznick, better than anyone, knew how it should be cast.

Because it was Wyler, and not Selznick, directing *The Heiress,* the director saw fit to put Olivia de Havilland in the lead, and he toyed with costarring Joseph Cotten. Selznick hated the idea and claimed the actor was "too old" to play the charming but near-destitute suitor Morris Townsend. Selznick instead suggested Tod Andrews for the role. Or Rory Calhoun. Or Guy Madison, who, unlike Cotten, was not gainfully unemployed. Better yet, Selznick enthused, "I think [William Wyler] would be very foolish indeed to pass up [Louis] Jourdan."

Selznick didn't care that Morris Townsend had been conceived as an American by playwrights Ruth and Augustus Goetz. Or that Henry James, who wrote the original source material, the novella *Washington Square,* had a similar take on the character. Selznick knew better, and he told Henry to tell Wyler, "The picture itself would be greatly improved if the fortune hunter were a foreigner, perhaps even with a title, since this would fit the picture perfectly and also would be in exact keeping with the nature of the Henry James stories."

Henry did as ordered. He invited Wyler to a preview screening of *Letter from an Unknown Woman,* starring Joan Fontaine and Louis Jourdan. He did his best to sell the director on Jourdan, but it made no difference. Wyler wasn't buying. As Henry reported back to his boss, "After giving it a great deal of thought, [Wyler] says that he actually has to have an American in this role."

The rejection prompted one of Selznick's more withering reprimands: "I am candidly most discouraged and disappointed by our lack of success, in this connection, and would like to ask for some immediate and more successful action."

Henry could take small satisfaction when Wyler cast the Morris Townsend role with the one who got away, Montgomery Clift. Adding even more insult to the producer's self-perceived injury, Wyler's work on *The Heiress* pushed back the production dates on his other film, *Sister Carrie,* based on the Theodore Dreiser novel, which was to star Jennifer Jones and Laurence Olivier. When Selznick realized that *The Heiress* delay would leave his foremost actress and paramour unemployed, he felt compelled to take revenge somehow, somewhere. Even the smallest challenge to his authority sent him into emotional overdrive.

"I am informed that Rory Calhoun is driving around town in a 'super hot rod,' whatever that might be," he complained to Henry. "Can't you talk sense to Rory about the dangers and unattractiveness of such juvenile behavior, if it be true?"

That demand came in September 1948, and it was naked in its pettiness, especially in light of Henry's devotion to the nascent race-car driver. But by then, Selznick's words carried little sting.

Anita Colby had recently departed the Selznick studios, to take a vice president's position with Paramount Pictures. Irene Selznick, now a successful Broadway producer with Tennessee Williams's *A Streetcar Named Desire,* finally divorced her cheating husband, who soon married the long-languishing Jennifer Jones. It was also time for Henry to leave. Otherwise, he would have been fired. Selznick no longer required a talent scout or a beard, for that matter. As Henry explained the split, "Selznick always needed money after 1949. He always lived in the most extravagant manner, and his gambling debts were high. He spent most of his time on the phone arranging deals for his contract people, and he became an unofficial flesh-peddler."

Henry could have been talking about his future self. But at the moment of his escape from Selznick's Tara in Culver City, he was guilty of nothing more than a mild case of hubris and a sincere need never to read another memo signed DOS Despite the long, arduous servitude, it had been prestigious while it lasted. When Henry returned to agenting, he was the only one in his profession who could ever claim, "I worked for the man who made *Gone with the Wind.*"

Meanwhile, when Selznick least needed bad news, he got it with *Portrait of Jennie.* Released in early 1949, the $4-million project turned into an immediate financial disaster that quickly netted less than $2 million in rentals. On April 4, 1949, the cover of *The Hollywood Reporter* said it all: "Selznick Studio Goes on the Block: Two-Day Auction Sale of All Production Equipment Set; Valued at $500,000." There was nothing else to be done.

PART SIX

At age twenty-five, contract-player Rock Hudson poses for his first round of publicity photos at Universal-International, 1950.

20

Self-reinvention

enry Willson read *The Reporter*'s historic headline from the safe vantage point of his new desk at the Famous Artists Agency. Henry had relished working on the inside of the industry, but since there were no films to be cast for Selznick, it made sense to segue back to agenting. "Coming from the Selznick studio, Henry Willson enjoyed enormous respect in Hollywood, and Charlie Feldman's Famous Artists was strictly top-drawer," said Roddy McDowall, who had considered signing with Henry Willson in 1949. Instead, McDowall gave up his languishing post-*Lassie* film career to move to New York and act on stage.

Jack Larson agreed. "Henry didn't wait for the studios to phone him with a role for his clients, the way most agents would," said the actor, who admired Henry's ability to scoop other agents and secure his clients an early look at the best scripts. "Only Lew Wasserman and Leland Hayward had that kind of know-how and expertise," Larson said. "I'd say that Henry Willson was one of the top three agents in Hollywood for an actor."

Henry had a talent for making career changes at the least opportune moments. His first entry into the tenpercentery world, in 1934, coincided with the worst days of the Depression. Fifteen years later, thanks to the unlikely but critical coupling of TV and the U.S. Supreme Court, the outlook for the motion-picture industry wasn't much cheerier when he left his post with Selznick. The court had ruled that Hollywood maintained a monopoly on movie production and distribution, and ordered the studios to divest themselves of their theater chains. In his majority opinion, Supreme Court Justice William O. Douglas wrote, "It is clear, so far as the five majors are concerned, that the aim of the conspiracy was exclusionary, i.e., [sic] that it was designed to strengthen their hold on the exhibition field. In other words, the conspiracy had monopoly in exhibition for one of its goals."

While the court's one-to-seven decision sent the box office into convulsions, the new medium of television almost put the movies out of business. Being a chronic optimist, Henry either made a habit of ignoring pessimistic reports or he had a knack for working bad news to his advantage. Dire reports for the studios meant that agents, in time, would control Hollywood. Years later, Henry's client Van Williams (of *Green Hornet* fame) put it best, "Henry had a one-track mind, but within that one track he could work miracles." (Williams should know. For an ex-college football star like him, who had virtually no acting experience, the famed Willson legerdemain delivered back-to-back gigs on *Bourbon Street Beat* and *Surfside 6,* which led to his greater fame portraying the Hornet opposite Bruce Lee's Cato.)

Henry's miracle could be spelled in one word: "teenagers." He was pushing forty when he returned to agenting in 1949, but his eye for talent continued to fixate on the narrow parameters of the original Puppets crowd of juveniles and young adults. It remained a relatively new market, but one that had already redefined the American economy.

Teenager. It was a new word, one that had been minted, anonymously, during World War II: In 1942, a clothing manufacturer put out its special line of apparel called Teentimers. Two years later, *Seventeen* magazine began publication. (In 1957, the magazine's owner, Walter Annenberg, introduced Dick Clark's *American Bandstand* on his Philadelphia TV station.) In the postwar economy, while television kept most people at home to watch the *Philco TV*

Playhouse and *The Milton Berle Show,* there grew an interim group, caught between adolescence and adulthood, that couldn't wait to get out of the house, eat pizza, neck and pet, and spend their new dollars. One collective, raging mass of hormones, the newly monikered "teenagers" were no longer a romance waiting to happen with the movies. From its inception, the dark-room medium had been the perfect date forum—a fact not lost on Washington, D.C., politicians who railed against the movies' inherent immorality from the get-go. It was only a matter of time: by the late 1940s, movies reached their popular concupiscent zenith with the introduction of drive-in theaters, otherwise known as "passion pits."

"It was the time of all those bobbysoxer movies," said Turner Classic Movies's Robert Osborne. "Studios were still developing young talent, and there was an enormous demand for the kind of young performers that Henry discovered and represented better than anyone else in Hollywood."

Henry's earliest clients could not have asked for a more financially supportive or emotionally committed starmaker. Henry Willson shared the former, if not latter, trait with his new boss at the Famous Artists Agency, Charlie Feldman, who spent up to $100,000 a year on the development of new talent. There was, however, one major difference. Whereas Feldman drew upon the largesse of his sizable agency, doling out up to $400 a week in expenses until some young thing won the lottery with a studio contract, Henry paid the tab out of his own pocket. His supporters called him a father figure. Detractors thought of him as a control freak. Never one for self-analysis, Henry sided with the former group.

"I'm what you might call a Salvation Army worker at heart," he said, "and the kids in this business know it."

Henry's return to agenting was inspired by an actor who had never acted. Like Guy Madison, Roy Fitzgerald served in the navy, as a mechanic, and even though Selznick wasn't in the market for any more boys in bell-bottoms, Henry saw something unique in the extra-tall kid with lousy teeth and even worse grammar. In other words, Henry had become professionally involved, which meant Henry was personally involved.

"Rock Hudson was a cross between Superman *and* Clark Kent!" Henry gushed.

If it wasn't love, then it was a deeply expensive appetite. Henry kept Rock Hudson fed, housed, and clothed for one full year before he found another patron to help share the bills. After turn-downs from Selznick, M-G-M, and Walter Wanger, Henry forged a most unlikely partnership to turn Rock Hudson into a star. Or at least get him his first job in front of the cameras.

Raoul Walsh defined the word "macho," which is why Henry told Rock to butch it up for his first interview with the veteran film director. Blue jeans, a plaid shirt, and cowboy boots were the pre-ferred interview costume, even if the heels pushed his six-foot-five frame up even higher. (Back at the Selznick studios, Anita Colby had advised Joan Fontaine to keep it "smart, feminine, and refined." For Rock, Henry turned that sartorial edict into quiet, manly, and plaid—with the emphasis on "quiet" after the Wanger debacle.)

Walsh liked a man who knew how to fill a pair of boots. On movie sets, the director always wore them and had ever since he rounded up horses for D. W. Griffith on such early one-reelers as *In Old California* and *The Gold Seekers*. Back then, Walsh did a little bit of everything. He even played John Wilkes Booth in Griffith's 1915 *The Birth of a Nation*. In addition to the boots, Walsh's trade-mark was a black patch he wore over his right eye long before Arrow shirts turned it into a fashion statement. He was one tough guy, and in the fantasyland of Hollywood no one cared that he lost his eye not in battle or a barroom brawl but when a jackrabbit smashed through the windshield of his jeep.

"Raoul was tough as a fucking boot," said L. Q. Jones, one of Walsh's most frequently hired actors. Few in the business ever played in more movie and TV Westerns than Jones. He had been a client of Henry's in the 1950s and appeared in a number of movies directed by Walsh, who gave him his first job, in the World War II film *Battle Cry*. Forever the heavy, Jones had the face of a rattlesnake, and so it meant something when he compared his favorite one-eyed director to a leather boot. "Walsh gave kudos to nobody who didn't deserve them, and he thought Henry was a helluva agent," said Jones. "He may not have liked him as a person, which might come off as anti-gay today, but he respected Henry as an agent."

A so-called "real" man, Walsh directed nothing but so-called "real" men, and acting "real" in a Raoul Walsh film sometimes meant not showing undue skill as an actor. The display of too much dramatic range compromised the tough, taciturn image, if a man wasn't careful. Fortunately for Rock, Walsh did not come equipped with the gaydar of M-G-M's Lucille Ryman Carroll. When he asked Rock to read, Henry feared the worst—and Rock did not disappoint. Walsh pronounced him, "Green but ripe. At the very least, he'll be good scenery."

Henry and Walsh put Rock under personal contract, jointly investing $9,000 in his living expenses, acting lessons, and whatever else it took to keep a twenty-four-year-old ex-truck driver happy in Hollywood. The celluloid accouchement, however, could not take place without a film role. Walsh's 1949 war movie *Fighter Squadron* had a peculiar genesis, even for Hollywood. "Jack Warner had all this war footage left over from a documentary he made," said actor Jack Larson, who, as did Rock, earned his first screen credit with the film. "The War Department had given him some bogus honorary lieutenant-colonel title, and Warner wanted it immortalized." (Even though Warner rarely left Los Angeles during the war, the studio chief insisted that visitors to his Burbank command post address him as "Colonel.")

Larson's assignment to play Lt. Shortly Kirk in *Fighter Squadron* scored the seventeen-year-old actor several scenes, including one with the newly named Rock Hudson. For his debut role, Rock got to recite only two lines, his first: "You've got to buy a bigger blackboard."

But after thirty-eight takes, it kept coming out "bligger backboard." Or variations thereof.

Curiously, the option to replace Rock with another actor who could talk in front of a camera never materialized. "Walsh had him under personal contract," explained Larson. "Otherwise, I doubt if Rock would have survived."

Those thirty-eight takes aside, Walsh cracked a nasty whip. Robert Stack, the film's star, recalled one scene in which Rock managed to screw it up without uttering one word. "He just stood there," Stack said.

Even then, Walsh found him incompetent. "Jesus Christ!" he yelled at Rock. "You're standing there like a goddamn tree—get out of the middle of the shot, for Chrissakes, or stand sideways so you don't block everybody."

According to Stack and Larson, Henry somehow missed Rock's embarrassing screen debut, even though he had been a frequent visitor to the Walsh set. Earlier in the film's production, Henry arrived on the back lot to hand-hold his other anxious client. "I did a screen test with Rory Calhoun for *Fighter Squadron*," said Larson. Again, there were many takes, too many for a mere test. "It was obvious that Henry Willson had a great interest in Rory Calhoun. In fact, the cameraman Sid Hickox, who worked on many Raoul Walsh films, noticed the extra care they took on this screen test. It was talked about. Willson had real clout on the set and he also had great, great interest in Rory Calhoun."

Perhaps one Henry Willson acolyte was enough for any director to wet-nurse. For whatever reason, Walsh didn't bite twice, and despite the attention lavished on Rory's screen test, he wasn't cast in *Fighter Squadron*.

Against all odds, Universal-International eventually signed Rock to a $75-a-week contract, which reimbursed Walsh and Henry their initial $9,000. The signing in 1949 represented a small accomplishment for Famous Artist's newest agent, but one that led to the creation of an enduring Hollywood icon.

To his credit, Rock was always something more than an urchin stud on Henry Willson's leash. Although he followed his "bligger blackboard" blunders with equal incompetence on the set of *Shakedown*—

Rock played a doorman in the film noir and director Joseph Pevney had to show him "about eight times how to open the door!"—he had the guts to demand star treatment right from the beginning.

"One day, Rock was very upset," Pevney recalled. "He came to my office at Universal and I told him to tell me about it." Rock thought he wasn't getting enough work at the studio and complained that Henry wasn't doing anything for him there. Pevney told him, "That's Henry's job, to get what you need. Tell him what you want and if he doesn't give it to you, get rid of him."

According to the director, "That's what Rock did." And in 1950, Rock Hudson clocked in no fewer than six movies for the studio.

The following year, Pevney's taunt came back to haunt him when the studio cast the actor in the more sizable role of a prizefighter in a remake of *Iron Man,* starring Jeff Chandler. Pevney, whose major talent as a director was his ability to stay on schedule, objected. The role of "Speed" O'Keefe was a southpaw and Rock was right-handed. "Rock had to be taught how to box left-handed, it was nuts," said Pevney.

Aaron Rosenberg, the film's producer, told his director to stop fuming. "Rock Hudson will be a big star someday," he said.

"Aaron, I'll wait," Pevney replied.

21

Big Fish, Big Pond

I n 1949, Rock Hudson didn't figure much into Charlie Feldman's big profits at Famous Artists. Nor did this other kid Henry was touting. Over the next four years, Natalie Wood and Rock remained minor figures at the agency. Feldman called them "no-name no-talents," and he used to boss Henry, "Get out and sell our real stars, like Irene Dunne and Charles Boyer!" But getting the biggest 10 percent was never Henry's calling. More intrigued with fantasy than reality, he saw great potential in Rock and Natalie, and made sure to take both with him when he opened his own firm, Henry Willson Management, in 1953.

Before that day arrived, Henry and Charlie were nearly a perfect fit. One did the deals, the other delivered the dreams. With his overweening ego, Henry could never have worked for any mere mortal in the business. Feldman had all of David O. Selznick's class and none of his micromanaging insanity. And unlike Zeppo Marx, who placed a moratorium on Henry's self-serving scoops to *The Hollywood Reporter*, Feldman expected his agents to be high-profile and gave them plenty of room to expose or hang themselves. His own eye fixed on the spotlight, Henry took a running leap whether it be trapeze or noose at the other end.

There was something else that drew him to the head of Famous Artists. Unlike Marx or Selznick, Charles K. Feldman looked like a star. "His handsome features never grace a movie screen, but

Charlie Feldman earns $500,000 a year," one reporter gushed in print. There was a time in Hollywood, if a man grew a moustache to dress his undersized upper lip, he got compared to Clark Gable. Feldman was one of the few who could withstand the competition.

By the time Henry joined Famous Artists in 1949, it was one of the most powerful agencies in Hollywood, with over three hundred clients and an annual gross business of more than $10 million. Only William Morris and MCA were mentioned in the same nervous exhale as Famous Artists. Known as the Big Three, they maintained a talent monopoly, much as Myron Selznick had two decades earlier. Luckily for the Big Three, David O. Selznick's brother no longer reigned, having died of much booze and even more bile in 1944.

And there was another, greater vacuum waiting to be filled: in the late 1940s, the film companies were divested of their theater chains at the very moment TV sets entered American homes en masse. Those were the first two nails in the coffin of the fabled studio system. The increasing power of the agencies would be the third and final.

Early in his talent enterprise, Feldman dared to come up with an original idea in a town that could tolerate only so much creative thinking. If David O. Selznick introduced it, Feldman perfected it. Known as "the package deal," Feldman's concept provided work for his clients whenever the studios deigned not to employ them. It was Henry's good fortune to work for two men—Selznick and Feldman—who arrived at the same production stratagem from opposite corners of the marketplace.

As Feldman explained it, "I didn't go into competition with the studios. I just bought what they didn't want or had passed up. I would wrap a story up and then stick an important name on the label, usually the name of a star or top director. The rest was easy. No producer in his right mind would turn down a deal like that."

In a master stroke that no other agent swung, Feldman secured a special arrangement with the Screen Actors Guild (SAG) that allowed him to be an agent, as well as produce such films as *The Lady Is Willing* and *Red River*. (Lew Wasserman, Henry Willson, and a few other agents would later follow suit to obtain similar waivers. Wasserman's MCA had the advantage of repping Ronald Reagan, president of SAG, whose cooperation with the waivers led to MCA becoming the most active producer in Hollywood.) In a clear conflict of interest, Feldman essentially worked both sides of the industry, which explained why SAG had to approve each and every picture he produced. His competition felt slighted, and rightfully so. According to *The Hollywood Reporter*, "Other 10 percenters are beefing that Feldman is using his employer cap to woo clients away from their current flesh-peddlers." For a time, the producing arm of his firm looked formidable. In 1949, the year Henry Willson joined, Feldman prepped no less than $20 million worth of properties, having spent $2 million to purchase the film rights to Tennessee Williams's *A Streetcar Named Desire* and George Orwell's *1984*.

Henry landed in this hotbed of film activity as part of a deal Feldman brokered between David O. Selznick and Jack Warner. Valued at $1,800,000, the arrangement gave Warner Bros. the services of Selznick's stable of stars, which included (among others) Jennifer Jones, Gregory Peck, Joseph Cotten, Shirley Temple, Alida Valli, Keith Andes, Rhonda Fleming, and Louis Jourdan. No one knew the Selznick stable better than Henry, which made him the perfect link to all parties. *Collier's* magazine explained the significance of the deal: "Warner Bros. needed new names. They were in a bad way. Audiences apparently were tired of seeing the same Warner faces in the same type of stories. Along came Charlie. He analyzed the problem, and Jack Warner was smart enough to see it. Selznick had the stars that Warners could use and wasn't doing anything with them at the moment. Charlie simply packaged the deal."

Besides brokering the Selznick talent, Henry Willson displayed other qualities that impressed a man of Feldman's humble background. As the great-great-nephew of Uncle Sam, Henry flaunted an East Coast lineage of respectability and old money to which Feldman, having grown up in Bayonne, New Jersey, and been orphaned along with six other siblings, could never lay claim.

Henry's natural polish and hauteur added a veneer of authenticity to Feldman's acquired patrician taste, which embraced English-style paneled offices, Van Gogh on the walls, and a much-publicized penchant for reading Henry James before breakfast. If Charlie Feldman was self-made, then Henry was a reinvented man who quickly adopted all of Feldman's grander, more ostentatious traits: midday arrivals at the office, long business lunches at Romanoff's and Chasen's, and, of course, a big black Cadillac. When it came to the showman's flair for truly grand gaucheries, however, it was Henry Willson who taught his new boss some very old tricks of the trade.

22

Dazzling at Ciro's

Shortly after putting Rock under contract at Universal-International, Henry concocted a publicity stunt so brazen that it would either win his client much-needed publicity or land him a gig wrestling Gorgeous George on TV. Rock's film work had won him little attention at the studio, and in less than six months, his contract would be up for renewal. Universal liked to throw novice actors into a few movies, blow them out into theaters, then wait to see if anyone's face stuck in the public consciousness. Not content to wait, Henry set out to manufacture the kind of excitement on the outside that Rock's performances weren't generating on the inside.

Even at the Selznick studios, with its first-rate "exploitation" department, talent scout Henry Willson proved himself adept at promoting an actor. Sometimes it didn't take much in the local, small-town atmosphere of Hollywood. In the days before saturation bookings of movie releases unspooled thousands of prints in a single weekend, one or two marquees made a difference, especially if they were as strategically located as Grauman's Chinese Theater on Hollywood Boulevard. One morning, Henry drove his Cadillac by the town's most fabled venue, its cement footpath laid down by a veritable herd of stars. Unlike everyone else on the street that day, he had not come to Grauman's to take snapshots or measure his shoe size alongside a bunch of farmers from Iowa. Rory Calhoun's latest picture, *Sand,* was playing in the theater, and Henry wanted to see Smokey's name up in lights. But when he rolled down his car window, Henry, to his exaggerated sense of horror, could not find the name Rory Calhoun on the town's most famous marquee. Like so many citizens of Hollywood, he took an existential view of filmmaking and saw every project as a life-defining success or loss. As much as he considered Rory's performance in *Sand* a triumph, the marquee oversight qualified as a catastrophe, in his opinion.

Henry never thought to consider that *Sand* starred Mark Stevens and Coleen Gray, not Rory Calhoun. A reasonable person might expect the third-billed actor to have his name bumped from the signage. But Henry Willson had no time for reason when it came to Rory Calhoun.

On such occasions, Henry knew to carry his bluster and outrage like a badge of honor. "We gave personal service in those days, beyond the call of duty," he used to brag. Henry confronted the theater's manager. His adamant, take-charge tone had been honed to cut through any flunky's orders, and he soon taught how to squeeze on a third name. He even wrote it down on a piece of paper: "*Sand* starring M. Stevens, C. Gray and R. Calhoun." Never a trusting man, Henry waited on the Hollywood Boulevard sidewalk until his instructions were carried out to the letter, literally.

Marquee-massage for Rory was one thing. Rock Hudson's shakier fortunes at Universal required more audacious maneuvers. On the evening of October 31, 1949, Henry took his endangered contract player by the hand and, using a bucket of gold paint, showed all of movieland his mettle as the real master of the meretricious.

The world itself may have been on the verge of falling apart: in the coming months, North Korea would invade South Korea, the USSR developed an atomic bomb, Harry S. Truman toyed with a hydrogen version, and Senator Joe McCarthy claimed 205 Communists worked in the State Department. Thousands of miles away in Hollywood, Henry Willson had more important nonsense on his mind. His plans were to slather Rock Hudson from head to foot in gold body paint and send him to the Press Photographers Ball as a living, breathing six-foot-five Oscar statue. Rock stood a few feet shy of the gold monster Henry saw at the Pantages Theater on Academy Award night 1944, but unlike that hunk of plaster, his boy knew how to both walk and talk. Sometimes at the same time.

The Press Photographers Ball was a Hollywood ritual that had all the sophistication of a high school prom, only famous. In 1949, the local cadre of photographers had not yet turned into a pack of multi-eyed wolves, and the stars counted many of them as good guys whom they knew by name as Hymie and Scotty and let into their homes to photograph their children's birthday parties. The Ball was the stars' way of saying thank-you to the little people with the cameras who, in turn, could make an extra buck selling photos of the stars making fools of themselves in crazy costumes. Henry did his bit for the cause: the previous year, he and Rhonda Fleming dressed up as Mr. and Mrs. Bo Peep and carried two adorable lambs.

As Henry saw it, the Ball would mark Rock Hudson's debut to the press corps. The event posed only one minor obstacle: Friendly as they were, the photographers wouldn't waste good film shooting a nobody like Rock, which meant Henry needed to find a famous female to escort him there. To that end, he dusted off Vera-Ellen. Still flash-bulb blind from her back-to-back photo-driven romances with Rory Calhoun and Guy Madison, the ever-reliable dancer had no problem attracting the photographers, who knew her fondly as Miss Turnstiles in the hit M-G-M musical *On the Town*.

Which ever of his boys needed his picture taken, Henry could count on Vera-Ellen to provide the romantic disguise. So what if she was anorectic? She occasionally missed a meal but never a date. Plus, she was no dummy: Vera-Ellen had been wise and ungracious enough to call Rory "that convict," and regarding Rock, she was known to whisper sotto voce, "He's queeeeeeeeeer." Although her many dates with Henry's boys were strictly business, even Vera-Ellen's overexposure could not have prepared her for Henry's latest stunt. It was one that had been goosed by even more recent inspiration than the Pantages Oscar five years earlier. In 1948, the good

Catholic friends Loretta Young and Rosalind Russell went to the Press Photographers Ball dressed as the Toni Twins, their respective wigs all in a frightful frizz. Loretta and Roz's visual parody of the famous Toni ad campaign—"Can you tell which twin had the home permanent?"—got Henry to thinking: Toni Twins, Oscar Twins. Roz and Loretta, Rock and Vera-Ellen.

"Henry was brilliant at getting publicity for his clients," said Frank Liberman, a personal publicist for Bob Hope and other stars. "Like the time he had Rock Hudson and Vera-Ellen dress up like a pair of Oscars."

If Rory Calhoun or Guy Madison had too much dignity to play along, Rock and Vera-Ellen possessed the requisite amount of shameless ambition to fulfill Henry's phallic fantasy. Rock put on gold trunks and skullcap, Vera-Ellen slid into an ensemble of gold bikini and wig, and Henry painted their skin to match. The picture would not have been complete without their matching metal swords, ready to skewer an imaginary roll of film at their equally metallic feet. As usual, Ciro's hosted the ball, and the crowd there went berserk the moment Henry's duo stepped off the red carpet and into the nightclub's comfy porch. Despite the kleig-light glare outside, every camera inside had no problem finding its next target.

"Those photographs were seen everywhere," said Liberman. "Before that, few people in Hollywood knew who Rock Hudson was." It may not have been as classy as sending Rory Calhoun to the *Spellbound* premiere with Lana Turner, but sometimes class has nothing to do with it in Hollywood.

The golden spectacle of Vera-Ellen and Rock Hudson stunned many Hollywood insiders. "I couldn't believe it," said newscaster Nick Clooney, father of actor George Clooney. "This shy, sweet, young thing showed up dressed like that. It was really something."

In addition to Rock and Vera's Oscar routine, the photographers' fete in 1949 featured Red Skelton's Confederate soldier, Roddy McDowall's walking mailbag, Betty Hutton's bearded cowpoke, and Ann Blyth's rotating helicopter. Like a bunch of eight-year-old Halloween tricksters, they all posed on Ciro's porch before sitting down to dinner at the club's famed red-and-white chequered tables. Despite the formidable competition, Rock and Vera-Ellen stole the show.

Louella Parsons, in fact, took one look at them and couldn't help but be shocked or aroused or something. When she called the auriferous actress over for a radio interview, Vera-Ellen remembered Henry's instructions, and taking Rock in hand she introduced him to the empress of gossip. Louella gave Rock his first major interview.

Who cared that he could only grin and gush? The next day, the *Los Angeles Examiner* billed him as "Vera-Ellen's date," and Henry could not have been happier despite his male ingenue ending up sick in bed after the *Goldfinger*-like paint job nearly caused him to asphyxiate. Henry learned his lesson. The next year he sent Rock to the Photographers Ball in black face as the Wild Man of Borneo, his body equally bare but the paint job kept to a minimum.

The Oscar stunt also stuck in Vera-Ellen's memory, whether she wanted it to or not. "For years after that night, people came up to her and said they remembered seeing those photographs of her with Rock, dressed as Oscars," said the actress's close friend, Paramount producer A. C. Lyles. And years later, Vera-Ellen remembered her Oscar cohort: "The best thing about Rock was that his mother was a wonderful cook," said the actress.

Henry's inspired flimflam effectively launched and defined other careers in the age of Eisenhower and Howdy Doody. Henry added Lili St. Cyr to his client list shortly after he caught her Ciro's stripper act, a 1951 engagement that brought her a few days in court and much press. Lili couldn't sing, dance, or play the banjo, but she did slip in and out of a bubble bath to great effect. "Sex is currency," Lili said, famously. "What's the use of being beautiful if you can't profit from it?" Henry made sure Lili did by putting her in several lucrative B-films before her attempted suicide in 1958.

From the earliest days of his agenting career, Henry's boys tended to be far less controversial. They did and said as they were told. If not, Henry made it clear from whence they came and where he could find another just like them. "You're the tops!" Henry sang. "You're the pants on a Roxy usher."

In one of his more preposterous ploys, Henry took the malleable Robert Earl Van Orden and renamed him John Smith. He touted him as a "Gary Cooper type," but when the actor languished in a few B-films, Henry insisted the name switch be made legal—two days before Thanksgiving in 1957.

As a man of the law, Superior Judge Bayard Rhone of the Los Angeles Court lived in the film capital but didn't always understand the fuss generated by Hollywood people. "You mean you've got a good name like Robert Earl Van Orden, and you want to take a common name like John Smith?" he asked.

"Yes, just plain John Smith," replied Henry's charge. "I'm the only one in the business. I think it's a wonderful idea." Henry couldn't have said it better. In fact, it's exactly as he told it to the former Robert Earl Van Orden: according to Henry, show business had a glut of Vans—Van Johnson, Van Heflin, Mamie Van Doren, Bobbie Van—but few named Smith.

Judge Rhone could only shake his head. "I also have a note here that says something about Pocahontas," he added.

"Oh, she's here. Pocahontas Crowfoot," Smith testified, nodding to the Native American woman sitting next to his agent in the courtroom. Henry had advised his Pocahontas to rent a deerskin outfit from one of the studios. Instead, the retired nightclub entertainer arrived wearing a full-length mink coat. Henry could only roll his eyes.

"Well, what about her?" asked the judge.

"That's her real name," said Smith.

"Oh, and you're John Smith—I see," he said. "The petition is granted."

It may have been John Smith's big day, but outside the LA court-house, it was all Henry's. On a first-name basis with each reporter, he celebrated by carving up a roast turkey and serving it piping hot to the Hollywood press corps, who knew a good buffet when they saw one. If only he could have served liquor as well. Henry knew the way to a good newspaper story: free food, free booze, free press. Smith was not the most articulate actor on the planet, but between Pocahontas and the turkey, Henry delivered his reporter friends a good story for tomorrow's paper.

"God, I love this town!" Henry said. Then he cut another slice of turkey.

When the reporters left to file their stories, Henry shook John Smith's hand and kissed Pocahontas good-bye. An hour later, Henry's Native American was back typing away at her desk job on the 20th Century–Fox lot.

Whether making his movie name legal actually helped John Smith, he achieved his greatest fame a few months later when Henry took him off the feature-film treadmill and signed him to the long-running TV western *Laramie*, which starred yet another Henry Willson discovery, Robert Fuller. During the peak of the TV oater craze, past-and-present Willson discoveries nearly dominated the genre, a veritable parade of Marlboro men: Guy Madison in *Wild Bill Hickok*, Rory Calhoun in *The Texan*, Guy Williams in *Zorro*, Don Durant in *Johnny Ringo*, Nick Adams in *The Rebel*, and L. Q. Jones in practically every TV Western ever made.

Henry's biggest success in the TV oaters was also the biggest physically. The size of Clint Walker's lats, in fact, figured into his 1959 contract dispute when Warners had him working twelve-hour days on *Cheyenne*, the first hour-long TV Western. "I need my work-outs," demanded Walker, who ultimately secured a two-hour morning time slot at the studio gym.

At the height of the Western craze, 114 of the three networks' 160 shows were Westerns. "That's our business," said L. Q. Jones. "It is cannibalistic and not very bright or creative. We tend to do what the guy next to us is doing."

Henry Willson had a genius for recycling, but even he eventually forgot about all the Vans who overpopulated Hollywood. When asked to justify the impulse that made him call an actor John Smith, he could only sigh, "I just got tired."

23

From Race to Touch

Effective as they were shameless, Henry's tactics at promoting clients also extended to his methods for acquiring them. In 1952, his last full year with Famous Artists, Henry launched the careers of Mike "Touch" Connors and Race Gentry on nothing more than a dare and a hunch, respectively.

It astounded Henry that some people, lucky enough to grow up in the shadow of the studios, held no interest in being a movie star. John Pipero was that LA anomaly. Henry first spotted the dark, brooding seventeen-year-old at a Texaco filling station on the corner of Overland and Pico, which was little more than an evening's stroll to the fabled studios of M-G-M in Culver City. Across the Hollywood Hills at Universal, Rock had begun filming one of his first starring roles, the outlaw John Wesley Hardin in Raoul Walsh's Western *The Lawless Breed*. The assignment required Rock to sire a son and age twenty years on-screen. Henry thought the Texaco gas-jockey looked enough like Rock to play his teenage son. He mentioned to Pipero that they were filming a Western at Universal.

"Henry came into the gas station on a regular basis," said Pipero. "I wasn't interested in acting. But finally, I told my mom and dad about it." He liked the movie money, and Henry liked the boy: strong, cocky, sure of himself.

Walsh shared Henry's enthusiasm. "I was underage, so my mom and dad had to sign everything," said Pipero.

But there was one problem. "People won't know how to pronounce your name," Henry told Pipero. Italian-American actors would have to wait a few more years before Hollywood executives learned how to pronounce names like Tony Franciosa and Ben Gazzara. If ethnic concerns bothered Henry, he never mentioned them. "Maybe he didn't want to hurt my feelings," said Pipero. "Henry was a very considerate man." And besides, Henry had a catchier, simpler name in mind, one that would brand the actor to the agent.

"Race Gentry was the name of this novel," said Pipero. "No, I never read it. I hated that name. Henry told me I could change it to John Gentry later, if I wanted."

During test screenings for *The Lawless Breed*, a Universal marketing person rifled through the evening's preview cards and noticed several raves for Race Gentry. "Hmmm," he wondered. "Must be the name of Rock's new horse."

The actor renamed Race Gentry dropped out of the acting profession when a film producer sexually propositioned him. According to Pipero, Henry was aghast and assured him that such untoward behavior was a total aberration in the movie business. "I told Henry if that's what Hollywood was all about, I wanted nothing to do with it," he said. After a stint in the navy, the actor quit the movies despite a long-term Universal contract, which he bought out with his own savings. He later moved to San Diego, where he became a general contractor and raised a family. As Pipero explained, "I never had any interest in Hollywood."

Henry had better luck with Mike Connors, if not much more longevity in terms of representation. Connors had come to the attention of Famous Artists during his UCLA stint as a star basketball player, and college fans knew him as "Touch" Connors. An agent at Famous Artists, Marc Newman, thought the six-foot-one guard might have a career in films. After a few months of representation, the agent had second thoughts.

"Newman told someone that I was a useless cause," Connors recalled. "He said I'd never make it as an actor." Connors took the hint, but rather than be dismissed by his agent, he decided to pull the plug himself and fire Newman personally. In a rare display of decency, Connors wanted to tell the agent face to face what he thought of him. Not so decent, Newman had little interest in being confronted and left Connors waiting for hours outside his office at Famous Artists.

When Henry Willson walked by, he saw Connors sitting in the hallway. "What are you doing here?" he asked.

Connors mentioned how he had been badmouthed around town by his own agent. "Now no one will hire me," Connors said.

"Wait here," said Henry, who, ignoring Newman's secretary, walked straight into his colleague's office. A few moments later, Henry emerged with the weight of Connors's career on his well-padded shoulders, and gave him the news. "I made a bet with Newman, and I'm going to handle you here at the agency," Henry told his newest client.

"So what's the bet?" asked Connors.

"That I can get you a job in six weeks," replied Henry.

Connors never flattered himself with thoughts that Henry considered him a great actor. "He just wanted to prove that this other agent was an asshole," said Connors. "Henry was hyperkinetic, a go-getter, and when he was riding high, he thought he could do anything." In a way he could, as Connors told the story. "Henry was one of the few hard-working agents in Hollywood," he said. "He made people stars who under normal circumstances wouldn't have been."

It was Henry's secret weapon as a starmaker: Henry believed in his boys more than they did in themselves. For an actor with no income and even fewer credits, such confidence was uniquely comforting. And when he believed, Henry delivered. Seated in Henry's office, Connors could feel it: here was a man who could gift-wrap a young man his dreams.

Henry's pitch was standard.

"I've worked on the inside, at the Selznick studio," he said. "These other agents don't know the first thing about how movies get made, how they're cast." He threw back his arms to cradle his head, and while he was too much the New England gentleman ever to put his feet up on the desk, he did allow the considerable heft of his body to settle into the office chair. He might have been chatting up the neighborhood boy who mowed his lawn or washed his car. Connors relaxed too, and they talked. Henry asked the routine questions, but showed special concern when Connors mentioned that his father had passed away. Henry expressed his condolences, then offered a smile that was the first warm comfort the former college basketball player ever knew in Hollywood.

It was natural enough for Henry to treat Connors's agent, Marc Newman, like an inferior. Henry treated most agents not named Charlie Feldman like subservient jerks. But when it came to the real underlings—the secretaries, the mailroom boys, the stenographers, the messengers—Henry never barked or threw a low blow. "They're the ones who do the real work," he claimed. In his Selznick days, Henry spent his own money to ply dozens of office assistants with expensive gifts of silver from David Orgell's on Rodeo Drive, huge birthday cakes from Freda Schroeder's bakery, and long-stem roses from David Jones florists.

Greased with Henry's gifts, the studios' secretaries and mailroom boys came to constitute a vast network of moles who fed him tips, gossip, and, most important, film scripts fresh off their bosses' mimeograph machines, which is how Henry knew of a role in Joan Crawford's new film. It would be perfect for Connors's film debut. As he said, "It's a good bet."

On the subject of Henry Willson, heterosexual men seldom failed to raise a certain subject, often without being asked. "Henry never made a pass at me," said Connors. Which isn't to say he escaped the Willson touch.

Born to Armenian immigrant parents, Connors's real name was Kreker Ohanian, but friends called him Mike and at UCLA he earned the nickname Touch for his finesse with the basketball. If he wasn't a war hero, he was the next best thing: an athlete. "Henry asked me if I had any nicknames," Connors said. He made the mistake of mentioning his UCLA moniker, Touch.

Henry sat up. "That's what we'll call you! Touch Connors."

"I got rid of that as soon as I could," Connors insisted.

Long before Connors jettisoned Touch—it took him six years and fifteen films—Henry set out to win his bet with the doubting Marc Newman. His office moles served him well: *Sudden Fear* did indeed feature the supporting role of a lawyer, and even though Connors had never acted in a film, he had a real affinity for the role, as he was studying law at UCLA. Henry always preferred typecasting over acting. "You are that character," Henry told Connors. Not expressed was the agent's knowledge that Crawford had taken to casting her male costars on the proverbial couch, and the tall and dark Connors fit her current bill of men to perfection.

Henry set up a meeting for Connors with the producer Joseph Kaufman, who delivered his assessment: "Are you kidding? He's got no experience."

Not ready to lose his bet, Henry then arranged for a "chance" encounter between Connors and the film's director, David Miller, by instructing his new client to wait outside the RKO gate at precisely 5 P.M. Connors did as he was told, and while Miller proved only slightly more receptive than Kaufman, their meeting led to a screen test. Connors read for the part, Crawford saw the screen test and, as Henry predicted, she liked what she saw. Crawford approved him with a pat on the shoulder and the kind words, "You're the young attorney we need."

Her benediction left Kaufman exasperated. He couldn't believe it and told Connors, "Against my better judgment, Crawford thinks you'll be fine for the part."

Connors enjoyed the best of both worlds. Not only did Henry Willson not make a pass, neither did Joan Crawford, who was too busy fighting with her *Sudden Fear* costar Jack Palance. The forty-eight-year-old actress was going through one of her many screen transitions. Warners was offering her nothing but crap, so she bought out her contract, for $800,000, and made *Sudden Fear,* an independent feature released by RKO, for $200,000. She received her third and last Oscar nomination for the effort. It wasn't easy.

"There were days Joan looked so angry that I was afraid she was going to chuck something at Jack," said Connors. "She put all this intensity into her performance instead. I just hid to stay out of her way."

According to Connors, Hollywood's dragon lady thought enough of his abilities on the set to introduce him to her agent, Lew Wasserman. Other reports have said that Mike Connors's departure from the representation of Henry Willson took a circuitous route over many years before the tentacles of Wasserman's octopus, otherwise known as MCA, finally welcomed the actor into its grasp. As printed in *The Academy Players Directory,* Henry represented the actor named Touch Connors in 1953, the first year of his eponymous firm Henry Willson Management. The studio biography of Touch Conners (sic) for the film *Sudden Fear* also makes the connection: "It was Henry Willson, his agent, who thought he should be known as Touch Conners (sic) for purposes of his career."

During their short tenure together, Henry went to unusual lengths to promote the unknown actor, including mocking his own queer sexual orientation. In one publicity ploy, Henry got his journalist crony Mike Connolly to print the following item in *The Hollywood Reporter*: "That Touch Connors is a he-man who'll put all of Hollywood's sissy lovers to shame."

It constituted an unfortunately typical spectacle. The Hollywood cognoscenti put Connolly and most of Henry Willson's other pretty-boy clients in that category of "sissy lovers."

24

Up the Ladder with Tony Curtis

Occasionally, it happened. One of the biggest teen idols escaped Henry Willson's grasp. For Tony Curtis, the omission was entirely deliberate.

In 1954, the former Bernie Schwartz climbed a ladder to have his photograph taken alongside Robert Wagner and Rock Hudson. *Life* magazine had come to the Universal Pictures lot to document the movies' top three "bobbysoxers" for its March 1 issue. The stockings' thick, white, popcornlike texture was known for widening the feminine ankle into a perverse inversion of Chinese footbinding. But guys wore bobbysocks too, and it was "the bobbysoxers," as *Life* called Curtis, Wagner, and Hudson, who attracted the girls who wore most of the bobbysocks.

For the *Life* shoot, the three men put on their cleanest white socks and loafers. Tony wore khakis; Rock and R.J. butched it up in jeans. At least male sex symbols got to wear clothes. A few months before *Life* published its piece, fledgling publisher Hugh Hefner put out the first issue of *Playboy*, which featured Marilyn Monroe in a black halter top on the cover and on the inside, as the actress famously remarked, "I had nothing on but the radio."

Tony Curtis remembered being king of the *Life* shoot. "Henry had represented Rock and R. J., and according to *Life*, I was the No. 1 bobbysoxer," he said. But if ladders are any forecast of coming success, Rock occupied the highest rung at the famed photo session. Nevertheless, in its official survey of female moviegoers under the age of twenty-one, *Life* reported that Tony, indeed, came in first, followed by R. J., and with Rock in a near third. Never fearful of a monopoly on pretty boys, Henry wanted to rep Number One as well. Tony Curtis made certain he never got the chance.

In 1948, Curtis had opened in a revival of Clifford Odets's *Golden Boy* at Greenwich Village's Cherry Lane Theater, which brought him to the attention of Joyce Selznick, an agent who counted David O. Selznick as her cousin. She quickly secured the actor with the dark curls and even longer eyelashes a six-month option at Universal, worth $50 a week, as well as an interview with her producer-cousin on the West Coast. "David asked if I had any representation in Hollywood, which I did not," said Curtis. Selznick recommended to Curtis his former head of talent, and Henry in turn pursued him. He sent Curtis a note: "Would you be interested in meeting at my office?"

"But I didn't hurry or bother with it, I was under contract," said Curtis.

At Universal, Tony and Rock took acting classes together. Sophie Rosenstein taught, as did Henry's friend Estelle Harmon, and their students included Barbara Rush, Piper Laurie, Dennis Weaver, Jeff Chandler, and Hugh O'Brian (who eventually found his greatest fame not in the movies but on television playing the title role in *Wyatt Earp*). It was a chummy group. Rock and Hugh had attended Winnetka's New Trier High School together, and when they reunited 2,500 miles away on the Universal back lot, they traded stories about Paramount's new star Charlton Heston.

"Rock and I were freshmen together. Heston was a senior at New Trier, and he was in this production of *The Pirates of Penzance*," said O'Brian. "Back then, we couldn't imagine doing such a thing—and in tights."

A few years later, they both did it in and out of tights on the Universal back lot. O'Brian appeared with Rock in *The Lawless Breed* and *Back to God's Country*, Tony performed with him in *I Was a*

Shoplifter and *Winchester '73*, which featured the taller of the two in the first of his assignments playing Native Americans. Sometime before that Young Bull indignity, Rock introduced Curtis to his agent. Theirs was an awkward meeting in the Universal commissary. Tony hadn't bothered to respond to Henry's original query about representation, and suddenly they were face to face.

"When I came to California, I met a lot of people who were agents. They came on very heavy. I just didn't respond," said Curtis. "With Henry, I was probably more interested than I was in most of the others. But there was something about the way he behaved, not that he danced around—nothing radically homosexual in his behavior. But I felt a little frightened. He was very friendly, but there was something unread in his behavior. I felt uneasy. Rock, by that time, was very associated with Henry, and the rumors had already started to spread."

And already there were those names—Rock, Guy, Rory, Touch—that branded the men to their owner, and for good reason. "Hollywood forgets who discovered and nurtured the star in the first place," Henry explained. "With me, it was different, because everyone knew that I had named them."

In the beginning, it was good business, as much for Henry as his boys. "These kids who start out without the benefit of a Broadway or TV reputation need a name that'll draw attention right away," he said, "something that will help identity them until they really learn their trade and can get by on their own." The catchy nomenclature became Henry's calling card to thousands of star-struck boys and girls who read about him in *The Hollywood Reporter* and *Photoplay* and thought it took nothing more than their own good looks, delusions of grandeur, and a Henry Willson monosyllable to make it in Hollywood. Even a classy rag like *Look* trumpeted Henry's status as the fairy godfather of Hollywood. As early as 1952, the photo magazine published the article "How to Create a Movie Star," which identified "Harry Willson" as the man behind the man. After giving due credit to Rock Hudson's height and bone structure, *Look* reported, "The rest of his success can fairly be laid to the incubation machine of his personal sponsors and Universal-International, the studio which owns him."

Look published one quote from Rock that forever established him as culturally challenged. "We used to do whole scenes from plays and scripts," he said, "and especially something called *Hedda Gabler*—you know, like Hedda Hopper—by a guy named Ibsen. It was the dullest stuff you ever heard." It was no contest: Henry came off the more intelligent force in the magazine profile. No backseat starmaker, he took full credit for Rock's name, his grammar, his clothes, and everything else that took Roy Fitzgerald from truck-driver to "bobby-sox idol."

Robert Aiken was just one of thousands who believed every page of the Cinderella story, and inspired by its words, left his home in St. Peterburg, Florida, to hitchhike his way to the other coast. Friends had told the six-foot, dark-haired twenty-two-year-old that he looked a lot like Rock Hudson. On his long cross-country trip, Aiken made an alphabetical list of all the movie studios, which led him to Columbia Pictures on his first day in Los Angeles. He assumed that any agent important enough to be interviewed by *Life, Look,* and the *Saturday Evening Post* had to maintain an office at a movie studio.

The guard at the Columbia Pictures gate laughed when Aiken asked to see Henry Willson. "But Henry was famous enough, they did know his office address," said Aiken, who made the trip to Carol Drive in West Hollywood. His would be a momentous baptism. After an impromptu lunch, Henry invited Aiken to his home for a small party of friends. They had dinner; and there was a special cake for dessert. No one ever said anything about a birthday, but when Henry lit the candles, he told Aiken to take his place near the pool where Rory Calhoun and Guy Madison once swam. Then everybody sang "Happy Birthday."

"Look at the cake," said Henry, pointing to the name embossed in thick frosting. "Happy birthday, Ford Dunhill!" It did not matter that Robert Aiken had never made a movie or that his next birthday was months away. He had a star's agent, Henry Willson, and a star's name.

Ford Dunhill sounded a lot like the name Humphrey Bogart once coined as an appropriate Willson moniker: Dungg Heep. All of Hollywood was playing the game. Whenever news flagged, Henry's friend Mike Connolly filled his *Hollywood Reporter* column with a few parodies of his own: "Henry Willson, we're told, is signing a Southern boy named Wyatt Trash."

Tony Curtis had his own personal favorite. "I liked Ben Dover," he said. "They all had that Willson touch." And with that touch came problems. "The whole town knew what Henry Willson represented," said Curtis. "Everybody who went with him had to sexually express himself to Henry, I'm putting it nicely. With Henry, it was almost mandatory."

Although Jack Larson proclaimed Henry "one of the three best agents" of the early 1950s, he chose never to sign with him. "He had an aura," said Larson. "You know what I mean?"

Other homosexual actors of the period also found reasons to avoid the go-getter agent. "I often think what would have happened if I'd signed with him," said Roddy McDowall, who visibly shuddered at the thought. In fact, the most critical portraits of Henry Willson often came from Hollywood's most famous homosexuals, as if association certified their own sexual orientation to the greater film community. When Jack Larson came out in a 2003 *National Enquirer* profile, he alluded to his long friendship with Rock Hudson but said he continued to keep his distance from Henry Willson, whom he called "lecherous."

Elaine Stritch, who performed with Rock Hudson in *A Farewell to Arms*, loved the actor, loathed the agent. "I met Henry Willson on the set, and I didn't trust him. He was a very, very dangerous man. He controlled all those guys—Rock, Rip, Rap, Tab and Troy."

Farley Granger agreed: "It was awful what he made his clients do, men like Rock." Granger had been represented by Charlie Feldman when Henry worked at Famous Artists in the early 1950s. When asked if Henry's treatment of those male actors was any more rapacious than Feldman's sexual liaisons with several of his female clients, Granger stepped back. "Well, if you want to look at it *that* way!" he exclaimed.

Hollywood tended to look at it that other way. And the town still does. In *Vanity Fair*'s 2003 Hollywood issue, writer Peter Biskind linked Feldman's prowess as a dealmaker with his success at seducing women. "Feldman was the last of the playboy producers, the men-about-town with the voracious appetite for life," Biskind wrote admiringly, naming sisters Joan Fontaine and Olivia de Havilland as just two of Feldman's girlfriends.

If Henry Willson ever went so far as to bed two brothers, consecutively or in one fell swoop, he kept it a secret. According to many reports, however, he did not always feel compelled to hide his sexuality in homophobic Hollywood. "Henry made no bones about being gay," said Joseph Pevney. The director claimed to have been "shocked" when he learned of Rock Hudson's homosexuality but was less than surprised when it came to guessing the sexual orientation of his agent.

"At a time when most were in the closet, Henry was not," said Universal's acting teacher Estelle Harmon.

"Henry was obvious," said James DeCloss, an actor who Willson represented in the early 1950s. "I remember seeing him walk around with Rory Calhoun over at Universal. He was clearly very attracted to Rory. Everybody could see."

Dennis Hopper acted with Willson clients Rock Hudson in *Giant* and Natalie Wood in *Rebel without a Cause*. "Henry would come on to you verbally in front of people," said Hopper. "He would practically grab you by your nuts!"

These first-person observations from heterosexuals present a conundrum often found with "obvious" or reportedly out-of-the-closet homosexuals in the 1950s. Henry's unbridled displays of attraction to other men made him notorious. But somehow, Henry

didn't know that everyone knew. The same was true of his friend
Roy Cohn, who worked for Senator Joseph McCarthy in America's
other most homophobic town, Washington, D.C. Like Cohn, Henry
was a political and social conservative, and his office assistants
remembered placing several telephone calls between him and Cohn.
The two men were also alike in the extent of their self-delusion. In
his book *The Gay Metropolis*, Charles Kaiser reveals that
McCarthy's aide "always denied that he was gay, even after he
began to surround himself with a coterie of young men in public."
Kaiser believed that Cohn's tough-guy pose "may have been partly
motivated by his desire to disguise his sexuality from others—and
perhaps, on some level, even from himself."

The respective cognoscenti of Hollywood and Washington, D.C.,
were aware of each man's sexual orientation; yet Henry Willson,
like Roy Cohn, believed that he successfully projected a heterosexual façade. "Anybody who knows me, and knows anything
about me . . . would have an awfully hard time reconciling that with
any kind of homosexuality," Cohn told the journalist Ken Auletta.

Entertainment reporters tend to be less probing in their questions. If any of them ever asked Henry Willson about his sexual orientation, the response never made its way into print. Even in the
company of close friends, Henry rarely spoke of his physical relationships with men. Women were a more open, if not dishonest,
book. "Henry did speak of his former fiancées as if these women
constituted genuine romantic relationships," said his assistant Gary
Crutcher. He would then shift the gears of conversation and entertain dinner guests by taking a breadstick, breaking it in half, and
holding it high. "Hey, Guy Madison!" Henry joked, making fun of
the actor's less-than-spectacular endowment.

In the end, the secretaries and assistants who worked for Henry
Willson present the clearest portrait of the man as a very closeted
homosexual. "Henry Willson had no idea that I knew he was homosexual," said Betty Butler. His longtime secretary had heard the boy
stories before she started work at the Henry Willson Agency in

1960. "I had no interest in working for him or Rock Hudson. I hated those *Pillow Talk* movies, but I fell under Henry's spell. He was the most generous, caring man."

"Henry had no idea he was notorious in Hollywood," said Richard Segel, an agent who worked at the Henry Willson Agency in the 1960s.

Henry's longtime assistant Pat Colby agreed. "Henry was not campy or flamboyant," he said. "And he didn't like men who were. If you had remarked on one of his all-boy parties being very gay, Henry would have been outraged."

Never an effeminate man, Henry gave off the paternal yet threatening aura of a Mafioso, especially after he shed the gaminlike exuberance that led people in the 1940s to compare him to the epicene Vincente Minnelli. "He came off tough, like a hood," said John Gilmore, a client who later befriended Henry's bête noire, James Dean. "He bulldozed his way into those studios, and he didn't care what they thought of him. No one messed with Henry Willson."

It was as if the power added the pounds. The more Henry weighed, the less he looked like Judy Garland's one-time husband and the more he resembled another director. "He had the silhouette of Alfred Hitchcock," said John Pipero/Race Gentry.

Beauty is in the eye of the beholder, and Henry was happy to leave the dieting and exercise to his clients. After the age of forty, his formerly slim profile fell victim to a gourmand's taste for rich foods and a stupefying amount of alcohol, tastes acquired from long, late nights at the Mocambo and Ciro's. Befitting his growing status as pasha of the pretty boys, Henry took pride in his newly acquired weight, as if excessive heft symbolized his new influence as a Hollywood powerbroker. While his body and speech slowed down, he took on a new gravitas that challenged everyone never to cross him.

Henry's profile wasn't the only thing that had changed since his days at the Selznick studios. Back then, Henry liked nothing better than to open up his office or his home in Beverly Hills and have the photographers from *Photoplay* and *Modern Screen* shoot him with Rory or Guy. His maid, Ella Mae Fuque, was a frequent bit player in these at-home photo sessions. She smiled for the photographer as Henry and his weekend guest enjoyed her hearty breakfast of waffles and eggs at a beautifully appointed dining-room table.

But that was in 1943. Near the end of the decade, attitudes were already beginning to shift, and not to the left. "It all begins in 1947/48/49 when we had the feeling that the country was moving toward a police state," said gay-rights pioneer Harry Hay. "We had loyalty oaths; all the teachers had to take loyalty oaths. And I thought at the time that the scapegoat wouldn't be Jews or blacks . . . it will be us."

Hay, the commie outsider and self-proclaimed "radical fairy," could not have been more different from Willson, the conservative Republican insider. But in his own sub rosa way, Henry also noted a sea change in the public's regard for displays of male affection. Henry came to learn that, unlike his many "fiancée" press releases, the publicizing of his friendships with male starlets—now ten to fifteen years younger than he—no longer constituted smart business in the 1950s. Not only had he become a middle-aged "bachelor"— that euphemism for persons of his sexual orientation—but the sexual climate had grown several degrees more knowledgeable and less tolerant during the witch-hunt hysteria of the HUAC era.

Right-wingers believed the American culture to be under siege not only by Communists but sexual subversives. It outraged them: Homosexual writers dared to write about homosexuals. In the late 1940s, Tennessee Williams's *A Streetcar Named Desire* stunned audiences with its revelation of a young wife, Blanche du Bois, married to a homosexual young man; and Gore Vidal delivered his first gay-themed novel, *The City and the Pillar*.

Facts caught up with fiction, in 1947, when the LAPD arrested tennis great William "Big Bill" Tilden on charges of contributing to the delinquency of a fourteen-year-old boy. Tilden got slapped with five years' probation, and that was only the beginning. A three-time winner at Wimbledon, Tilden subsequently went to jail for seven and a half months when police caught him with a seventeen-year-old boy. Pedophilia itself was not the real shocker: for the first time, America was stunned into the realization that sports and homosexuality were not mutually exclusive.

Other myths were also exploded. After nearly a decade of research, Dr. Alfred Charles Kinsey delivered his book *Sexual Behavior in the Human Male*. Published in 1948, the 804-page tome reported that "at least 37 percent of the male population has some homosexual experience between the beginning of adolescence and old age." Rock Hudson and his friends George Nader and Mark Miller devoured the book, excited by its revelations regarding men of their orientation. Others were appalled and angry, and they threw the book down in disbelief.

While such exposure should have heralded greater tolerance, its immediate impact produced the opposite effect. It exposed homosexuals to a public that heretofore did not know they existed—or, at least, never gave them much thought. The subject was now fearsome. Kinsey himself could not bring himself to write the word "homosexual"; he instead kept those interviews under a file marked "H-histories."

Henry also knew to take care. After publicizing his friendships with Guy and Rory at the Selznick studios, he became more circumspect in his dealings with Famous Artists clients in the early 1950s, and that included Rock Hudson as well as Robert Wagner and Keith Andes.

In private, Henry was honest enough to follow his own sexual inclinations. Professionally, he never stopped deploying his uncanny knack for knowing exactly what excited women romantically, which, in an industry with few female executives, had its buyers. The all-male club of Jack Warner, Darryl F. Zanuck, and Harry Cohn had no idea what women wanted in a man. They listened to Henry, and in turn, he dazzled his boys with these hard-won connections, both social and business in nature. In the course of a week, Henry often delivered a dozen studio interviews. And they were "quality" interviews, as he never failed to point out.

A trip to Culver City to meet David O. Selznick ranked first on the list. Even though insolvency had reduced Selznick to operating from a one-room office at his old Washington Boulevard studio, the legendary producer never failed to meet with Henry's clients. Who among these high-school jocks and army privates was not in awe of the man who made *Gone with the Wind*? Regardless of how many times he repeated himself, it meant a lot when Selznick told each and every one of them, "I would put you under contract immediately, but I have nothing to offer you right now." Then he would turn to their agent to add, "And Henry, don't let me forget about this young man. I think he's a good bet."

Selznick's rancor, expressed in a thousand memos to Henry, no longer disturbed the office air off Washington Boulevard. It was now Henry's choice to defer to his old, feisty boss, and in the presence of his nervous clients, he and Selznick traded war stories about the making of *Since You Went Away, Spellbound,* and *Duel in the Sun*. Henry wowed his young wards as he stroked the semi-retired master with memories that he and Selznick could not help but revel in for an hour or so. "The two men obviously had enormous affection and respect for each other," said Henry's client John Carlyle.

Henry followed the impressive but futile Selznick ritual with more productive business interviews. After playing the raconteur for his old boss, Henry trotted his boys to the studios, where he now turned into the seasoned salesman and knew the upcoming slate of productions better than any VP.

"Henry had tremendous leverage at studios like Universal, Warners, and Fox," said his client L. Q. Jones. "Men like Jack Warner and Darryl Zanuck relied on Henry to come up with their new stars. They knew he had better instincts in spotting talent than they did. As a result, Henry's clients at those studios were treated very well."

Sometimes, there existed an enormous gap between Henry's business connections and what he had to sell. "Henry aimed too high," said Robert Fuller, who went on to achieve cowboy fame in the longrunning TV series *Laramie*. Before that success engulfed him, the tall and craggy actor's only performing experience came from a few acting classes taught by the equally tall and craggy Richard Boone in his pre–*Have Gun, Will Travel* days. Henry could not have cared less when Fuller told him that Boone had studied at the famed Actors Studio in New York. "All that Method stuff," Henry scoffed, his arms waiving away any notions of art and craft. "Hollywood wants good-looking people, charm, personality!"

On that score, Henry thought Fuller had enough handsome armor to meet the terror of Columbia Pictures. "I'd never appeared in a movie or TV show, and yet here I was meeting Harry Cohn!" exclaimed Fuller. "He was the meanest man in Hollywood, and one of the most powerful. Henry had those kinds of connections."

Henry also sent Fuller for an interview with Burt Lancaster, who was casting his circus film *Trapeze*. After a pep talk from Henry, the actor-producer thought he might have found his costar in the agent's newest client. "I spent an hour talking to Burt in his office. It was ridiculous," said Fuller. "The role Lancaster auditioned me for was the one that eventually went to Tony Curtis, who was already a big star at Universal."

Other impossibly optimistic* interviews followed. Fuller finally told Henry, "Can you get me a one- or two-line part?"

Henry reared back. "I don't represent one or two-line actors!" he said.

But, of course, he did. Universal's Ed Muhl and Warners' Bill Orr were the most regular buyers. Henry's assistant at the Marx Agency, Solly Baiano, headed up talent at Warners. And further down on the food chain was his Selznick secretary, Ruth Burch, who, during the 1950s, cast up to fifteen TV shows a season. Ruth could always be counted on to find room for one of Henry's boys.

If such long-held business friendships produced few instant thrills of recognition in Henry's boys, any rube from Kansas knew the names Alan Ladd and Darryl F. Zanuck. All Henry needed was two nickels to arrange a double date with their daughters, Carol Lee Ladd and Susie Zanuck. Before the big night arrived, Henry never forgot to advise, "Whatever you do, when you say hello to Alan Ladd, sit right back down. You'll tower over him and he doesn't like that!"

Henry sometimes played the fifth-wheel on these group missions. When Susie and Carol Lee retreated to the powder room, Henry told the photographers to hold off on the flash until a suitable female decoy could be located. They always did. Terry Moore often wedged herself between Henry and a boy. (Fifty years later, the starlet with the painfully broad smile could still recite the line in Mike Connolly's *Hollywood Reporter* column that made her immortal for a week or two: "Natalie Wood could well become the next Terry Moore.")

A real pro at the arranged Hollywood date, Terry added lessons of her own to Henry's curriculum. She even advised her escorts that they need not tire themselves with making conversation, because it was enough to move their lips and go, "Blablablablablabla." Photographers mistook it for actual speech.

The automatic pilot of dates, Terry Moore carried out her duties with professional aplomb. Henry depended on the actress to wear a sexy but nonthreatening outfit, to say the cute but innocuous thing, and because the actress was carrying on a secret romance with billionaire kook Howard Hughes with whom she couldn't be seen in public, it worked both ways: Terry needed a steady supply of male escorts to go to movie premieres, and Henry's boys needed the romantic contrast of the opposite sex. "I went out with Rory and Guy and Rock—to make them look more macho," Terry Moore surmised.

Sometimes a bit of romantic interest on their part might have been appreciated. "Oh, not another one!" the starlet complained when Henry proposed a date with his new hunk John Smith.

"Oh no, this guy is a real man," Henry assured her.

Looking back on her trumped up dates, Terry explained the prevailing psychology of the time. "It didn't matter what the truth was," she said. "In Hollywood, they only cared about the public's perception. As long as the public didn't know someone was gay, it didn't really matter."

Henry put it with only slightly more finesse. "There's nothing like a love affair, phony or real, to keep the fan pepped up," he said.

When Terry Moore wasn't lurking within camera range, Henry searched to find another suitable female, even if that meant enlisting the presence of 20th Century–Fox's menopausal acting coach. Helen Sorrell may have been pushing sixty, but she knew how to slide in between Henry and the toothsome Robert Wagner with the best of them. Photographed on the Strip, the threesome made an intriguing portrait. While Sorrell looked borrowed and scrunched sitting between the two men, Henry wore the benevolent look of a godfather, proud and possessive. R. J., on the other hand, did what all young men do when they find themselves in such situations among their elders: he giggled, he blushed, and he otherwise failed to look anything but completely embarrassed.

PART SEVEN

Early in their careers, Robert Wagner and Natalie Wood share the same starmaker-agent, Henry Willson.

25

And Natalie Wood Makes Three

For Robert Wagner it happened one night, as these Henry Willson sightings invariably did. A singer named Lou Spence was performing at a cocktail lounge called the Gourmet, located on Canon Drive in Beverly Hills, when Henry wandered in to waste the hours between greeting and dining at the Cock 'n' Bull and greeting and dancing at the Mocambo.

"Lou loved the way I did a couple of numbers and he asked me to sing with him," Robert Wagner recalled. "Henry came in and saw me and sent me his card."

Like a thousand others before it, the note read: "If you want to get into films, I can help you."

It was 1949. "I was knocking around as an actor then, trying to get started," Wagner said. "So I went to see Henry Willson."

Always ready for another roll of the human dice, Henry thought he saw a potential star behind the Gourmet's baby grand. "The changing expressions on his face," he said of the nineteen-year-old Wagner. "I watched his face mirror every thought and word—that, together with his look and bright, clean-cut personality. I saw a sincerity and a relaxed quality that would come right across the screen. Given the opportunity, I was sure he couldn't miss."

Helen Sorrell, Fox's dramatic coach, wasn't so sure. "At first [Wagner] used his voice so poorly that I had to pretend to be hard of hearing to get him to speak up," she said.

Card in hand, Wagner went to see Henry at Famous Artists after their impromptu meeting at the Gourmet. But as the actor tells his remarkable version of the story, he was already signed to the agency at the time of their introduction—and he had signed a contract at 20th Century–Fox, too. "Each agent at Famous Artists handled a specific studio," Wagner insisted, "and Henry did not cover 20th Century–Fox."

In fact, the trifecta of Fox, Universal, and Warner formed Henry's most fertile feeding ground for talent. And Wagner's studio bio from the 1950s makes clear which agent signed his original contract with Fox:

"Willson took him to 20th Century–Fox, where he made a screen test with actress Patricia Knox. The studio liked it and took a ninety-day option on his services. Meanwhile, Willson had arranged another test—for the top male role in M-G-M's *Teresa*. Director Fred Zinnemann guided Bob through the test, but before he could snag him to a contract, 20th picked up its option and inked Wagner to a seven-year contract."

Tony Curtis, Jack Larson, John Carlyle, and other actors remember Wagner being a Willson client at Famous Artists. There is also the proof of several studio contracts: according to Fox documents held at the studio's UCLA archives, Henry Willson negotiated Wagner's first contract at the studio, which was accompanied by a missive to him from Fox's legal counsel George Wasson: "Mr. Henry Willson: We are enclosing herewith an executed copy of the contract, dated April 12, 1950, between this corporation and Robert J. Wagner, a minor, actor." The $150-a-week salary was for six months. There were also letters from Fox to Willson on March 26, 1952, and March 23, 1953, both of which exercised options on Wagner's contract. After the success of *Beneath the 12 Mile Reef*, which grossed an impressive $4 million in 1953, Henry negotiated a new contract for Wagner, starting at $1,250 a week.

Wagner offers a different scenario of his movie genesis: "I was represented by Jack Gordean at Famous Artists," he claimed, naming one of Feldman's partners in the firm.

Erasing the name Henry Willson from one's résumé became a favorite pastime for many 1950s stars, not that Wagner was ever the prototypical Willson protégé. Except for the fresh-scrubbed looks and ample lips, which brought a blush of sensuality to his otherwise prep-school mien, Robert Wagner had little in common with Henry's growing gaggle of male orphans. None of them had spent his teenage years in a house overlooking the golf course of the Bel-Air Country Club, where the young R. J. caddied for Clark Gable, Cary Grant, and Bing Crosby. None had a successful businessman-father who supported his son when he eschewed the steel mills to pursue an acting career. Robert Wagner Sr. cosigned his son's contracts, nixed a Willson name-change, and did not object when another gay mentor, Clifton Webb, chose to lead R. J. through the Hollywood wilderness. But unlike Rock Hudson and a few others, Robert Wagner refused to make the segue from Famous Artists to Henry Willson Management in 1953. R. J. left managerial loyalty up to his future wife.

Natalie Wood's legend has contributed its own share of Hollywood apocrypha to the name Henry Willson. According to one recent biography of the actress, Natalie Wood signed with Henry Willson of Famous Artists with hopes that he would introduce her to his client Robert Wagner.

Nice story, but it never happened.

Even at age thirteen, Natalie Wood was not the kind of girl to require a date service, especially the kind operated by Henry Willson. More significant, she signed with Famous Artists in 1946, three years before either Henry or R. J. came aboard. Feldman's flock took good care of her from the very beginning. One year after Natalie's mother, Mud, signed with Famous Artists, the child actress landed her first big role, in *The Miracle on 34th Street*.

Mud. That's what little Natalie called her mother.

The archetypal stage mother, Mrs. Marisa "Mud" Gurdin added a new page to the mommy-as-monster book when she tore the wings off live butterflies to force her nature-loving six-year-old daughter to cry on cue. It worked. The little actress bawled her eyes out and nearly stole the show from headliner Claudette Colbert in the sudser *Tomorrow Is Forever*.

Natalie was quite the girl. Mud was quite the mom.

"Natalie's mother went through agents the way boiling water goes through coffee grounds," said Robert Wagner. In truth, the adolescent actress had very consistent representation while being trotted around Hollywood by her mother, and most of it was with Henry Willson. "Natalie adored Henry, and so did Mom," said Lana Wood, the actress's sister. "They both thought he was the be all and end all."

Charlie Feldman hired Henry expressly to handle young talent, and it made perfect sense that the ten-year-old Natalie, fresh from such cornpone classics as *Chicken Every Sunday* and *Scudda Hoo! Scudda Hay!*, would be assigned to the care of Selznick's former head of talent. Henry may have been nearly forty, but he never stopped keeping pace to the quicker beat of starlet hearts.

Although other agents also worked on the Natalie Wood account at Famous Artists, it was Henry who won the actress's loyalty (or more likely Mud's approval) when he left Feldman's agency to open his own firm, in 1953. He knew it was time to leave when the boss reprimanded him, "Why are you wasting all your time with this Rock Hudson and Natalie Wood?"

Henry's response to Feldman's question was Henry Willson Management. His first clients at the firm were Rock and Natalie, and the child actress was duly repaid for her loyalty when, two years later, Henry delivered Natalie the role that took her from pigtails to Trojans, playing Judy in *Rebel without a Cause*.

In the meantime, Henry set out to make her a star. "The fan magazines could sustain or build a career until the studio gave them the right role," said Henry. He worked the rags like no other agent. He often manufactured such a rush of cover profiles that fan mail inundated the studios, encouraging producers to hire an actor who had done little more than pose for still photographers.

Stroking the press, Henry hit his stride with Natalie as soon as she turned thirteen and could be photographed in a constant rotation of dates with his many male clients. Henry played the chaperone while

Tab Hunter, Nick Adams, John Carlyle, John Gilmore, and Tom Irish took turns offering their arm, and not much else, to Natalie. Considering her youth, the heat had to be kept to a minimum, which, considering the Willson clientele, rarely presented a problem.

For example, Tom Irish. The blond actor played Elizabeth Taylor's brother in *Father of the Bride* but was better known throughout America as the boy-half of the Paper Mate Sweethearts. Beginning in 1953, Tom Irish and Trudy Wroe puckered up to hit the tube no fewer than five thousand times a year, their interlocked faces recognizable to forty million viewers as the golden avatars of the nation's most popular brand of ballpoint pens. They were an ad agency's dream: despite all the above-the-neck action, the two-some's lambent youth never suggested any kind of movement elsewhere. Irish's relationship with Natalie Wood was equally chaste: not many twenty-one-year-old males could date a girl seven years their junior and fail to raise suspicions. Only Irish wondered why Mud neither noticed nor cared about the age difference.

"She could have objected, but she never did," he said.

At age twenty-three, Nick Adams (born Nicholas Aloysius Adamschock) presented an even older date for Natalie. Over-reaching even by Hollywood standards, the actor attracted attention when he gamely put his own name on the marquee of a Beverly Hills theater, where he worked as an usher. The management fired him, but cruising by in his black Cadillac, Henry Willson saw the name and immediately identified with the Jersey boy's relentless show-manship and careful attention to marquee detail. Blond, cute, and as squirrelly as a leprechaun, Nick Adams was more character actor than the leading-man type Henry usually represented. Regardless, a Warners contract led to the role of Chick in *Rebel without a Cause*. The film's director was never overly fond of Adams, "The most ambitious actor I've ever known," said Nicholas Ray. In the Henry Willson date pool, Nick Adams was one client, among many, who glommed on to Natalie Wood to get his picture taken.

Tab Hunter was another. Looking back at his dates with the teenage actress, he commented, "Once the machine got rolling, it was quite powerful, and the press carries it one step beyond. They reported it every way: 'Natalie is in love,' 'Natalie has lots of boyfriends, and Tab is number one.' All that nonsense. She really loved R.J. Wagner."

Louella Parsons commented on a peculiar proclivity in the young actress's lineup of dates when she reported that Natalie was "cheapening herself with all this romance activity with Nick Adams, Tab Hunter, Raymond Burr, and heaven knows who else." Her linking of the three homosexuals recalled Edith Gwynne's earlier *Hollywood Reporter* column that mentioned Cary Grant, Cesar Romero, and Randolph Scott in as many words. In both eras, the general readership interpreted the editorial combos one way; insiders understood the more tantalizing, not to mention valid, connection.

Natalie Wood's sister, Lana, speculated about Mud's choice of other nonthreatening men for her older sister. "Tab Hunter . . . was also around, courting Natalie, and he was the one my mother liked," she reported. "The others she tolerated."

Under the careful watch of a Warners publicist, Natalie made the following observation: "I can always depend on my mother to prevent some overzealous young actor from mixing pleasure with business."

She might have been talking about Tom Irish. In her Natalie Wood biography, *Natasha,* author Suzanne Finstad writes that "it was pure luck that Irish, at twenty-one, was a gentleman."

More likely, it was purely Henry's protection.

Irish claimed to have enjoyed the dates his agent arranged with the thirteen-year-old Natalie. He picked her up in the family car, an old Cadillac hearse, and together they went to semitony restaurants like the Captain's Table and whatever semi-important premiere Henry Willson happened to be on the docket for the week. "Our encounters seemed to just—gosh, they went so fast," gushed Irish. "We were sitting there, mixing, at your little premiere, and you're in and you're out, and then you go off to some other spot and looking and talking to other people. There wasn't too much of being all by ourselves or up on the hill or something," said Irish, obliquely referring to—gosh—sex. "We just didn't do any of that in those days."

While Irish displayed a good memory for his Henry

Willson–arranged dates with Natalie Wood, his total recall did not extend to time spent after hours with Willson himself. "I hardly knew the man, and I was never represented by him," said Irish. "He was never my agent."

Other Willson clients remember a different relationship, and snapshots of the period show Henry and Irish posed together on cruise ships, rowboats, and tarmacs, complete with leis strung gaily around their necks. In addition, *The Academy Players Directory* lists Tom Irish as a Willson client from 1953 to 1955. (When the actor-model later switched careers to become a respected painter, a press release from the Wally Findlay Galleries in Beverly Hills listed several proud collectors of Tom Irish's art. They included Henry Willson, Rock Hudson, and Phyllis Gates.)

In 1955, the year Henry secured Natalie her career-defining role in *Rebel without a Cause,* Warners wasn't particularly interested in the juvenile actress and saw her not as a leading lady but as a freckle-faced kid in gingham. For the James Dean picture, they wanted someone with more gravitas, someone whose name could help sell tickets, someone named "Debby [sic] Reynolds," according to Warners' casting files. (Likewise, for James Dean's role of Jim, the casting file suggests Tab Hunter, John Kerr, or Robert Wagner.)

"The big problem was that up to that point I had really only played children," Natalie said. "Although I was fifteen, I was finding it difficult . . . to convince the studio that I was out of pigtails."

If Lee Strasberg is the father of Method acting, then Henry Willson gave birth to Method casting. Just as Henry coached Touch Connors how to approach the director of *Sudden Fear,* Natalie's solicitation of *Rebel* director Nicholas Ray had all the hallmarks of a Henry Willson setup. "I actually was in a bad car accident with Dennis Hopper," said Natalie. "I was in hospital, sort of semiconscious, the police were asking me my parents' phone number, and I kept saying, 'Nick Ray, call Nick Ray, the number is . . .'"

When Ray finally came to the hospital, Natalie taunted him, "Nick, they called me a goddam juvenile delinquent, now do I get the part?"

Hopper corroborated the story. "It was a head-on collision in Laurel Canyon," he said. "Natalie and I were thrown from the car, and she was knocked unconscious."

At the time, Hopper was under contract to Warners; Natalie was not. "Henry Willson got her in there and opened the door, and he had the wherewithal to think of her for the role in *Rebel*," said Hopper. "Natalie was put under contract to Warners during the filming of *Rebel*. Henry wasn't a good agent; he was a great agent."

For her audition, Hopper read with Natalie. "I played Jimmy's part. I also tested with Jayne Mansfield," he said. "In fact, Nick tested me with every starlet in this city for the [Judy] role."

The Warners publicists made much of the fact that the role included a five-minute crying scene, which according to their tabulations "equaled the mark set by Betty [sic] Davis at Warners in 1948 in *Winter Meeting*." Natalie was jazzed. "I also get slapped around by my father, am picked up by police for wandering around the streets after 1 A.M., and have a wonderful love scene with James Dean," she said. "I've played daughter to about every top star in Hollywood. I've had enough. I can be a femme fatale, too," added the actress, now seventeen years old.

For all Natalie's efforts to titillate, the *Rebel* role she played wasn't exactly the one she read with Hopper. In their zeal to make the film less controversial, the powers at Warners expunged any suggestion in the original script that the teenage Judy was anything but a virgin. The words may have been changed or deleted, but it is to Natalie's credit that her Judy is clearly a very sexually experienced young woman.

So was Natalie Wood. Behind the scenes of *Rebel*, the actress made up for whatever it was she didn't do with Tab Hunter or Tom Irish or Nick Adams, who played Chick to Dennis Hopper's Goon in the film. Hopper had different designs on the actress, none of which had anything to do with publicity. He recalled his competition with Nicholas Ray. "Nick was having an affair with Natalie," Hopper said. "I was also having an affair with her, which didn't make for a very happy movie."

26

Wholesome, but Never Fresh

I f Mud saw nothing untoward in her adolescent daughter's going out with a twenty-one-year-old man, Debbie Reynolds's mom, Maxene, also had an open mind when it came to entrusting her daughter to the male clients of Henry Willson. Crowned Miss Burbank in 1948, the sixteen-year-old Mary Frances Reynolds won the beauty contest with her dead-on impersonation of Betty Hutton. It was a performance that also impressed Henry's former Zeppo Marx assistant, Solly Baiano, now working at Warners in its talent department. He knew that Mary Frances's outgoing personality and measurements (33-23-34) would impress many men, including Jack Warner.

But first they had to deal with Maxene. "My mother was very protective, and she was very careful who I went out with on those studio dates," said Debbie Reynolds. As painfully polite as they were awfully good-looking, Henry's boys projected an aura that said they would stop if a girl said no. The thing was, girls didn't want to say no. Debbie was a notable exception.

"Oh sure, I dated all the boys who were homosexual, because I liked them better," she said of Henry's clients. "They weren't fresh. They were fun. They were sweet. They didn't come on to me. All the straight guys were coming on to me. And I couldn't stand that. I was seventeen. I was a virgin. I didn't want hands all over me. And the gay boys were so nice to me. We became great friends."

In his 1950s novel of Hollywood dreamers, *The Slide Area,* Gavin Lambert described the kind of boy-man groomed by Henry Willson: "He seemed to have that impeccable American sexuality and body structure, factory packed and returnable to makers if not in perfect condition." Those words summed up Craig Hill, the same Willson client who once came to Shirley Temple's defense (before Henry prevented him from interfering with David O. Selznick's designs on the moppet) and later dated Debbie Reynolds (before she married the man of her Coca-Cola dreams, Eddie Fisher). A contract player at 20th Century–Fox, Hill played one of James Cagney's lieutenants in the 1952 remake of *What Price Glory,* and, later, would be Debbie Reynolds's costar in the swamp classic *Tammy and the Bachelor.* (Now living in Barcelona, Spain, Hill acts in Spanish-language films.)

Henry played chaperone on their dates. If his boys were tame with the girls, Henry took up the slack. One night when Debbie sat next to Craig in the backseat of Henry's black Cadillac as its owner drove them from one publicity event to the next, she started to worry about what their chauffeur for the evening had imbibed. "It was raining and it was obvious to me that Henry was on something," Reynolds said. Henry was more than drunk. "He was hyper. Not that that was unusual for Henry, but much more so than usual. He was driving crazy, we were up on Mulholland Drive, and I asked to get out of the car even though it was raining." (Fifty years later, Craig Hill did not recall the incident.)

Natalie Wood proved the more willing ingenue. Even in their adolescence, she and her friend Margaret O'Brien knew that Henry took them out "as a front" for his boys. At the time, O'Brien was the bigger star, having won an honorary Oscar the previous decade for playing Judy Garland's kid sister in *Meet Me in St. Louis.* Unlike Natalie Wood, she would be forced into premature retirement when the pigtails started to compete with the crowsfeet. Before that calamity struck, the two girls took turns coaxing each other into double-dating with Henry's boys.

"It's a free dinner with Henry, we might as well go out," said Natalie, who made the rounds of clubs and premieres with her friend. As Margaret O'Brien remembered it, "Henry would have the boys sitting with us, escorting us—and they were really good-looking young actors—and then Henry would bring us home, or he'd have the boys bring us home early, and then they'd go out."

John Carlyle costarred with Natalie Wood in *General Electric Theater*'s 1954 *Feathertop,* and dated her several times under Henry's less-than-careful eye. "Natalie was a child on the verge of becoming an adult star. She was gorgeous and very melancholy and horny, with 'horny' being the operative word," said Carlyle. The same could be said of their chaperone. "Henry would start drinking, and after he sent Natalie home, he would pick up sailors at the Mocambo," he said.

Sometimes Henry didn't send her home soon enough. "It was not unusual for Natalie to be at some party and go off into the bedroom and make out with some guy. You would walk into a dark room and there was Natalie making it with the guy," said Carlyle.

When his boys didn't put out, Natalie and Margaret contented themselves with the inevitable game of trying to figure out which of their dates had slept with Henry. It was no secret that when Henry's card trick didn't work with the sailors at the bar, he took out cruise insurance by traveling with an attractive client like John Carlyle, whom Henry was promoting as the "next Montgomery Clift."

Sometimes Natalie herself was the bait. Henry arranged for her and a teenager named John Gilmore to take some publicity photos on the Santa Monica Pier (a local landmark Natalie would revisit a decade later for the opening carnie sequences of *Inside Daisy Clover*). He put them through the usual setups: eating cotton candy together, trying their luck at a shooting gallery, walking hand in hand on the beach. Henry was "very paternal" with Natalie, Gilmore said. He was less so with Gilmore.

When the photos were developed, Henry invited Gilmore to his Bel Air home for a private viewing. The nineteen-year-old actor expected to find his model partner there as well, but Henry surprised him by not inviting Natalie to see the photos or take a dip in the pool or smell the jasmine in his front yard. Instead, Henry gave Gilmore a tour of his many photo albums, which included not only the Santa Monica Pier shots but several others taken over the years. There were photographs of Henry with the Puppets; Henry with Jennifer Jones on her big Oscar night; Henry dressed like a shepherd with his Little Bo Peep, Rhonda Fleming; and Henry playing photographer for a naked Guy Madison, sprawled out on his manicured back lawn.

Gilmore got the hint. As he explained it, "The obvious inference was, 'See what I did for Guy. You take your clothes off and I can do the same for you.'"

When Gilmore resisted the chance to follow Guy's clothes trail, Henry gave him the hard sell. "Tab and Rock and Guy have cared for me personally, you understand?" said Henry. "You see where it's led them."

A few days earlier, Henry had been telling Gilmore that he could be "the next Robert Taylor or a young Gary Cooper." Now, sprawled out on his bed and stroking himself with baby oil, Henry wasn't so sure about the teenager's chances in Hollywood. It could be that Gilmore's teeth were too small for the movie screen. Henry had certain prerequisites for stardom, and the size of a person's teeth was a paramount consideration.

Sometime between the dental analysis and zipping up his fly, Henry came down with an unusual case of parsimony and decided against paying his dentist, Dr. Phillip J. Tennis, to have anything in Gilmore's mouth replaced or capped.

Unceremoniously dumped by his first agent, Gilmore sought other representation and eventually moved to New York City, where he met a fellow Hollywood émigré, James Dean, who at that time had also failed to make it in the movies. "Jimmy Dean developed this rebel image, but it was all pose," said Roddy McDowall, who knew the actor in New York and earlier in Los Angeles, when he took uncredited roles in *Sailor Beware, Fixed Bayonets,* and *Has Anybody Seen My Gal?,* which starred Piper Laurie and Rock Hudson. "It was the early 1950s, and Jimmy Dean would have given anything to be a movie star in the vein of Rock Hudson," said McDowall. The posing never stopped. Considering Dean's anti-Hollywood image and the shortness of his career, McDowall wondered, "Who posed for more photographs than Jimmy Dean?"

Rock had his own, more subtle, put-down of the rebel actor. Referring to *Has Anybody My Gal?,* he liked to point out, "James Dean was in that film, too, in a very small role, with slicked-back wavy hair, very neatly combed."

Together, Dean and Gilmore harbored a love-hate relationship with homosexuals, a minority group, which, according to their mutual accounts, held a virtual lock on the studio gates. Gilmore repeated his famous dead friend's sexual jeremiad. "I wanted more than anything to just get some little part, something to do," Dean said, "and they'd invite me for fancy dinners overlooking the blue Pacific, and we'd have a few drinks, and how long could it go on? That's what I wanted to know. The answer was it could go on until there was nothing left, until they had what they wanted and there was nothing left."

Powerbrokers like Zanuck and Cohn could pillage their stable of starlets, and rarely did any of the women cry that their lives were destroyed. Young men, on the other hand, tended to see any gay agent or casting director as a modern-day Procrustes, ready to cut off their legs to make them fit into his bed. According to Gilmore, Henry Willson was just one of several agents who formed an unofficial club that treated hopeful young actors as mere "postcards" to be passed around among them. In addition to Henry, the small network included Warner Toub, Dick Clayton, John Darrow, and Robert Raison, who represented Dennis Hopper, among others.

"Raison and Willson procured boys for each other," Hopper confirmed. "They were sharing sexual favor, and the guys—gay or straight—were going along with it." For teenagers like Gilmore,

Dean, and Hopper, the town gave off nothing but queer vibrations. "One agent would promise some young guy that he'd make him a star in exchange for sex," said Gilmore. "But somehow the big break never came, and the agent would pass him to one of the other agents, who'd sleep with him and then pass him on. Nothing ever happened for the boy. And the agents would move on to some other boy."

When it came to picking representation, male starlets had the choice of 150 other Hollywood agents, the vast majority heterosexual, who would not hold their hands on the long road to success or failure. While James Dean, for one, was especially fond of directing his macho disgust at homosexuals, he nonetheless managed to seek out several of them to be, if not major powerbrokers, his effective career doormen. Radio producer Rogers Brackett not only housed and fed Dean, he provided the right connections for the actor's first radio series, CBS's *Alias Jane Doe,* in 1951. The following year, he provided the entree for Dean's first Broadway play, *See the Jaguar.* No sooner did Dean dump Brackett than he hooked up with Dick Clayton, who brokered the deal that led to his three Warners films: *East of Eden, Giant,* and *Rebel without a Cause.*

For all the legendary tales about the powerful, dirty old men who preyed on the innocent, many Hollywood observers found the playing field more than level, if not tilted in the male ingenue's favor. In the 1950s, Lawrence Quirk wrote for *Modern Screen* and *Photoplay,* which his uncle James R. Quirk had founded forty years earlier. No issue of *Photoplay* went to press that Henry didn't phone Larry Quirk to pitch a new boy, who couldn't possibly miss with the girls. "I've got a good angle on this guy," Henry would begin. "Maybe you'd like to do this story . . ."

Quirk respected the agent. "Willson wasn't just some old guy who sucked dick, it isn't that simple," he said. "Henry was actually very fatherly. He promoted and nurtured these young clients and didn't expect much from them. The implication was, these agents picked them up for sex, but many of these young men hung around and got a lot out of these agents. Henry, and other agents like Dick Clayton, carried some of these guys until they could connect with a studio. The agent would get emotionally involved. The handsome young men would see the older man was interested and take advantage."

As a reporter, Quirk listened to many actors complain about their agents. Few, however, ever spoke ill of Henry. "Why would they?" he asked. "He supplemented their income until they got work."

Despite his success, Henry never grew immune to ingratitude, as if anyone ever does. "To succeed, an actor has to be narcissistic and driven," said Quirk. "The actors are worse than the agents when it comes to dropping people. Tennessee Williams put it best when he wrote, 'The beautiful make their own laws.'"

Others agreed with Quirk. "It was amazing what some heterosexual men would do to get a career in Hollywood," said Henry's friend Fred Winston. "Many thought nothing of sleeping with another man, if it got them a job." (Winston became one of TV's top set decorators, "dressing" the interiors for such longrunning series as *Taxi* and *Murder, She Wrote*.)

"These young guys would do anything to further their careers," said another friend, Nan Morris, who dated Troy Donahue. "It's astounding the number of Willson clients who denied having been repped by Henry. It makes you wonder what they had to hide."

"Gay men, straight men, they threw themselves at him," said Henry's assistant Pat Colby. "I saw it happen again and again, countless times."

For all the queer-conspiracy talk of his youth, Gilmore harbored no ill will toward Henry Willson fifty years later. "He gave a number of people their first shot at stardom," said Gilmore, who now lives in Los Angeles with his wife and family. "It was then up to us if we made it or not."

Male actors who sought out Henry Willson could rarely claim they were starving, but many were hungry for more than food. They needed to both escape and ascend, to be made bigger than life and immortal on the movie screen. Henry's desire to control extended far beyond the addition of another name to his catalogue of sexual conquests. According to those who knew him, he delighted in the arrangement of other people's lives, and this included all the extravagant trappings of a big wedding ceremony, as well as the hasty orchestrations of a one-night stand.

"He would fix up guys with guys, and guys with girls, and girls with girls," said his client Van Williams, who remembered Henry's "thing" to get him together with the ubiquitous Terry Moore. "But she wasn't my type, and Henry was upset that didn't work out." Instead, the future *Green Hornet* star married Vicky Richards. "Henry always wanted to OK whoever you were dating or going to marry."

Henry had his reasons. "Your career could depend on it!" he insisted. It didn't matter if his boys were gay or straight; they usually followed his advice. Henry's edicts on romance were born of care, experience, and cold professionalism. Naked fear also played its part.

27

Tabloid Mole

A staunch conservative who sprang from a long line of Republicans, Henry would nod in agreement when his friend Roy Cohn succeeded in convicting Julius and Ethel Rosenberg, who were executed on June 19, 1953, at Sing Sing prison. And the following year he would watch the Army-McCarthy hearings on television and shake his head at the Senate's censure of Senator Joseph McCarthy.

The conservative homosexual is, and never has been, an anomaly. Or a rarity. From Roy Cohn to journalist Whittaker Chambers, prominent gay men found it professionally advantageous in the era of HUAC to position themselves to the right of California's senator-turned-vice president, Richard M. Nixon. It was a time when the epithets "pinko" and "fag" were often interchangeable.

In 1950, Republican National Chairman Guy George Gabrielson issued the announcement that "sexual perverts who have infiltrated our government in recent years [were] perhaps as dangerous as the actual Communists." As the HUAC hearings proceeded, the State Department fired 425 employees on the basis of their "homosexual proclivities." To Senator McCarthy, a subversive was a subversive. "If you want to be against McCarthy, boys, you've got to be a Communist or a cocksucker," said the senator.

To be a rebel or to be a conformist took zealous dedication, and Henry Willson pursued the latter avocation with patriotic pride. For someone of his ambitions, it made the most sense. As social out-casts, homosexuals found themselves to the left of Jews, many of whom were also expert at obscuring their identity in Hollywood. It didn't matter that some of them controlled the town. David O. Selznick, for one, explained his dance of assimilation to a Jewish fund-raiser. "I am not interested in Jewish political problems," he said. "I'm an American and not a Jew . . . it would be silly of me to pretend suddenly that I'm a Jew, with some sort of full-blown Jewish psychology." Jack Warner and Louis B. Mayer hosted Easter-egg hunts and Christmas parties for their daughters but left it to Harry Cohn to explain how they really felt. "Relief for the Jews?" cried the Columbia Pictures chief. "What we need is relief from the Jews!" Toeing the conservative line, Hollywood's most powerful Jews caved in to HUAC's demands for a blacklist. The result: an infamous roll call, published and updated every week, of reported Communists, pinkos, homos, and lefties in the film and TV industry. Entitled *Red Channels,* the report had an early supporter in Henry's close friend and major informer, Mike Connolly. The two men had so much in common.

As Gore Vidal described the *Hollywood Reporter* columnist, "He was your average drunk Irish Catholic queen who was pretty ven-omous when in his cups and good company outside them."

In 1954, *Newsweek* took a less personal, more positive view of the scribe, who rivaled Hedda Hopper and Louella Parsons for reporting Hollywood news and secrets: "It is the forty-year-old, sleepy-eyed Connolly who gets the pick of the trade items, the industry rumors, the policy and casting switches. He has been described as Hollywood's unofficial arbiter, prosecutor, jury talent scout, trend spotter, and social register."

The newsweekly left out "red baiter." The epithet was synony-mous with "gossip columnist." In 1948, when the politically leftist Dore Schary went to M-G-M, Hopper wrote that "the studio will be known as Metro-Goldwyn-Moscow." As a homosexual, Connolly lived in a glass house, and knew how to dodge as well as throw back the stones lobbed his way. On the set of *The Robe,* Richard Burton informed Connolly that SPQR stood not for *Senatus Populusque Romanus* but the "Society for Prevention of Queer Relatives." Hedda Hopper was more blunt; she called Connolly "that drunken faggot."

Gay men like Connolly and Willson were often the most vilified object of gossip in Hollywood, which often made them its most effective disseminators. Connolly wrote the following piece of "news" in his *Hollywood Reporter* column of December 21, 1951: "Do producers bidding for *Top Banana* know that author Hy Kraft was named as a commie in the recent House hearings?"

One month later, Connolly went after Paul Robeson, who hadn't made a film in ten years. "Beware of a new Red front, 'The Provisional Committee to Restore Paul Robeson's Passport.' This warning is just in case there are any suckers left who think Robeson should be permitted to carry his anti-American ravings abroad."

Beyond his own right-wing bent, Connolly had two very good reasons to present an ultrapatriotic front. His boss at *The Hollywood Reporter* was the same Billy Wilkerson who welcomed Henry Willson at his Sunset Strip clubs, and in addition to his entrepreneurial flair, the editor in chief was HUAC's unofficial cheerleader on the West Coast. "My father hated communism," said his son W. R. Wilkerson III. "He was the founding father of the blacklist."

Politically conservative conformity served another purpose for Connolly, as it did Henry Willson: it effectively served to mask their homosexuality. Sometime in the 1950s, the journalist began delivering anonymous insider gossip to *Confidential* magazine. The tabloid had threatened to expose him as a homosexual, and to protect his own reputation, Connolly fed its editors stories on the sexual peccadilloes of the stars, in effect, keeping his own erotic exploits safely under wraps. The tradeoff was an open secret in the Hollywood community: *Time* magazine's Hollywood correspondent, Ezra Goodman, exposed the Connolly/*Confidential* connection in a blind item included in his book *The Fifty-Year Decline and*

Fall of Hollywood, published in 1961. Describing the tabloid's inside contacts, Goodman wrote, "Some of the tipsters were even among the press. One of the leading 'male' gossipists in Hollywood was a source for *Confidential*—the magazine used an unpublished story about this columnist's amorous activities as a journalistic sword over his head." Goodman had his own source in the offices of Henry Willson. His fiancée, and later wife, Bernice Cantor, worked as a secretary in the Willson firm in the 1950s.

Referring to Connolly as a "male" gossipist, Goodman made no mistake when he put quotes around the word "male." It said everything about the subject's sexual orientation. If Connolly's homosexuality ever led him to sympathize with the politically persecuted, he never allowed that sentiment to cloud his reports on goings-on in tinseltown. In a 1956 column, Connolly strongly defended the industry's attempts to blacklist anyone suspected of leftist leanings. "Our more stable citizenry call it an economic freezeout of 326 people who raised $2 million to overthrow the U.S. Government. They are not entitled to work here," he wrote.

Connolly's ultraconservative streak went back to his days at the University of Illinois when, as student reporter for the *Daily Illini,* he tried to use the newspaper to rid Champaign, Illinois, of its brothels. Two decades later, he wasn't quite so righteous when Henry's boys slept with Connolly in exchange for a one- or two-sentence mention in his *Hollywood Reporter* column. It was his most effective method for getting laid, even though a few Willson clients rated the laconic Connolly as "the worst sex of my life."

His lovemaking talents aside, Connolly showed true generosity in using his reporter job to keep his best friends well informed, not only about the status of various movie projects but their own fluctuating reputations in the industry.

"You know, Hugh O'Brian is calling you a homosexual," Connolly told Henry.

As the fractures in his hetero façade widened into chasms, Henry scrambled to repair the damage, sometimes with questionable results.

Connolly let the O'Brian bomblet drop at one of Henry's Saturday-afternoon pool parties. "And he says most of your clients are, too," added Connolly, relishing the moment as only a professional "male" gossipist could.

Henry's friend Nan Morris remembered the day of reckoning. Henry had invited a dozen boys to his house for a Saturday-afternoon pool party, and as the accused, they functioned as Greek chorus to Henry's hero defender. "Henry always wanted to get to the basis of a rumor," Nan offered. Never one to let an insult go unpunished, Henry picked up the phone to have it out with his accuser.

"I hear the things you've been saying," he told O'Brian. "I'd welcome you to come over here and meet ten of my clients, and they'd like to clear things up. The phone clicked in Henry's ear to much poolside applause.

O'Brian denied ever receiving such a phone call from the offended host on Stone Canyon Road. "I never made those accusations," said O'Brian. "And if I had, which I did not, Henry would have been much too smart to ever have called me on it."

If the gay-baiting gossip frightened Henry—and close friends said that it did—he usually defused the fear in public with a lethal mix of humor and bravado. Like the time he heard that his client James DeCloss had called him the "nelly Alfred Hitchcock." Henry lost no time in finding the actor, grabbing him by the lapel, and demanded to know, "Did you call me that?"

"Hell, no," replied DeCloss. During such moments of confrontation, Henry never displayed a trace of effeminacy. Friends said, "He was all pit bull and no poodle."

Henry finally let go of DeCloss's jacket, then broke out laughing. One of Henry's many heterosexual clients, DeCloss remarked on the laughter. "He must have carried on for close to an hour," said DeCloss.

Other people, however, claimed that such effusive laughter marked a nearly hysterical fear. It was the difference between the public Henry and the private Henry.

"He bought a pistol," said his assistant Pat Colby. "Henry kept it loaded and locked in the top drawer of his office desk." According to those who knew of the weapon, Henry wasn't interested in using it to protect himself. He felt harassed by spies, real or imagined, and he complained that his phone line crackled with static. He feared for Rock and hired private investigators and off-duty LAPD goons to take care of blackmailers. But Henry had other uses for the pistol he kept locked in his office desk.

"If it ever gets too bad, I don't have to worry," he used to say, his words punctuated with the same self-deprecating laughter that had astonished James DeCloss. "I can always shoot myself."

BHPD Interrogation

"Everyone knew Henry Willson was gay and no one gave a damn," said Robert Stack.

A decade before the actor achieved his greatest fame, playing Eliot Ness in the television series *The Untouchables,* Stack received the occasional invite to small dinner parties at Henry's Beverly Hills home. He and Henry were mere acquaintances, said Stack, but they shared a close friend in Gail Shikles Jr., the man Henry renamed Craig Stevens and took much credit for marrying off to Alexis Smith. The news of those nuptial negotiations apparently failed to reach Stack, who claimed Henry Willson as "the only gay man I knew" in 1940s Hollywood. Either very tolerant or completely blind, Stack did manage to recall one afternoon gathering that forced all eyes, including his own, to be pulled open. He and Henry had been invited to a pool party at a producer's home in Hancock Park. It was predictably uneventful until, indulging in the usual chitchat and cocktails, Stack's only gay friend in Hollywood got bored or drunk or turned on, and said something untoward to one of his agent colleagues at Famous Artists.

"Henry made a pass, or this other agent misinterpreted it as such," said Stack. "And he pushed Henry through a second-story window and into the pool below. Henry made quite a splash."

After the startled crowd collectively took another sip of their martinis, a few guests managed to put aside their shock and amazement to inquire into Henry's safety after his plunge. Spitting chlorinated water, he assured everyone that he was all right. Then, pulling himself out of the water, Henry patted his trousers and sports coat with a towel, pasted his few strands of hair back in place, straightened his tie, and promptly left the gathering. His silence said everything. An entertaining raconteur, Henry made a point never to add his tale of defenestration to his wide repertory of amusing anecdotes.

Stack may not have cared about Henry's sexual orientation, but there were others who did, and Henry gave a damn about those other people. He had good reason to. It was a time when the topic of homosexuality could not be raised in public except as an accusation.

Several of Henry's friends and business associates remember his being a terribly paranoid man. Most of these people were Henry's heterosexual friends.

Others who knew him said he wasn't paranoid: His fears were justified, they claimed. Most of those people were Henry's homosexual friends. In the 1940s, Henry had no choice but to tolerate the whispered gossip. However, when the rumors threatened to find their way onto the printed page in the 1950s, he exercised the option to fight back.

The overnight success of *Confidential* magazine in 1953 gave birth to a litter of tabloid imitators: *Dynamite, Exposed, Fame, Hush-Hush, Inside Story, The Lowdown, On the Q.T., Private Lives, Tip Off, Top Secret, Uncensored,* and *Whisper.* Even before those scandal sheets threatened his clientele, Henry had begun to suspect that private detectives trailed his every move and bugged his phone lines, not only at the office but in the restaurants where he entertained clients. A bad phone connection caused him to hang up in panic and redial from another outlet. Tom Hatcher, for one, thought Henry had good reason to be very afraid.

The twenty-two-year-old blond wanted to be a movie star, and because he fit the matinee-idol mold and drove a beer truck, Hatcher believed he could be the next Rock, Tab, or Touch—with the help of Henry Willson. Like a thousand other young men, he had read and memorized the fan-magazine stories about truck-driver Roy Fitzgerald and how his agent had transformed him into a movie star. *Photoplay* readers who had never heard the names Lew Wasserman or Charlie Feldman knew all about Henry Willson.

One day in 1953, Tom Hatcher drove his truck to Henry Willson's newly opened agency at 1046 Carol Drive to meet the starmaker he knew from the magazines. "With no appointment," said Hatcher, "I just walked into Henry's offices." With his blond hair, emerald eyes, pinned-back ears, perfect teeth, and eager smile, Hatcher needed no doctoring. Flawless on the outside, he decided not to change anything and go the blue-collar route with Henry.

"I left on my truck-driver outfit," said Hatcher. "I was pretty sure Henry Willson would like that." In the pantheon of 1950s machismo, delivering Pabst's Blue Ribbon was an improvement on Budget Pack Frozen Foods.

The future Mrs. Rock Hudson, Phyllis Gates, sat behind the desk in the outer office of Willson's Carol Drive agency. "She was a knockout," said Hatcher. "Phyllis was absolutely great, made you feel very much at home."

She looked up at Hatcher and knew after one glance. "I'm sure Henry would like to meet you," Gates said.

Shortly after Hatcher signed with Henry Willson Management, the owner of the agency invited him to a party at his home in Bel Air. As partygoers were prone to do in those predesignated-driver days, they got smashingly drunk and, on their way home, tried to negotiate the city's many hills and canyons without turning anybody into road kill. Despite his driving a truck professionally during the day, Hatcher was not so expert when under the influence at night and kept weaving his car into and out of the right lane. He made it home safely, but when Hatcher pulled into his driveway, a police car followed right behind him. Not one but two cops approached his vehicle.

"They wanted to know where I was going and where I'd been," Hatcher recalled. When Hatcher mentioned coming from a party in

Bel Air, they asked him for the address. Trying not to slur his words and otherwise act drunk, he mentioned Henry Willson. "At the mention of his name, their eyes just lit up," said Hatcher, who soon found himself sitting in the Beverly Hills police station.

The cops demanded to know who attended the party. Were there any famous people? Were there any women at Willson's or was it all guys? "They wanted to know everything," Hatcher remembered. Obviously, there had been a lot of alcohol consumed. But were drugs taken? Was there any sex going on? Had there been an orgy?

Mentioning Henry Willson's name to a Beverly Hills police officer was a mistake Hatcher learned never to repeat. "The next day, I phoned Henry to tell him about the two cops and what had happened," said Hatcher. "He was very, very upset and concerned."

Whether paranoia or justified fear, Henry's dread of public exposure soon manifested itself in a bizarre fetish. "Henry started wearing these black leather gloves whenever he drove a car," said his client John Carlyle. "I asked him about it. He said the gloves were to protect himself from getting a cold or the flu. He wore them driving even on the hottest of days."

Henry also carried packs of Wash 'n' Dry in his pockets. When the black leather gloves came off, he used the disposable alcohol-saturated paper towels to wipe his hands. Then he would break open another one to give a quick wipe to the doorknob, phone receiver or ballpoint pen. After shaking hands, he made a habit of excusing himself to go to the rest room. People thought Henry had a weak bladder. On the contrary, he wanted to give his hands a thorough washing with soap and hot water. Visitors to his home were sometimes overpowered by the odor of Lysol and Mr. Clean. Henry put so much chlorine in his pool that swimmers complained of getting bloodshot eyes. And despite his parade of sex partners, few of them ever spent the night in the master bedroom. Post-coitus, Henry directed them to the downstairs guest room, so that he could shower and change the sheets on his bed. Henry drew a hard line between the casual sex encounter, which he pursued with near-religious zeal, and the committed relationship between two men, which he forbade on professional grounds. The marked division defined the parameters of many homosexual lives in the 1950s. A man could cruise another man with brazen impunity at a Hollywood Hills party or driving on Sunset Boulevard. It often didn't take more than a prolonged stare or cock of the head to signal the desire for an assignation. Most straight men were still a decade away from picking up on the more subtle signals of the all-male mating dance that allowed Rock Hudson or Cary Grant or Cesar Romero to offer a silent invitation to an afternoon dalliance around the pool. With less fear of public exposure, straight men were more easily seduced, if only to receive oral sex in exchange for professional favors or personal release. It was an alternate universe of great sexual fluidity, and one which Rock often referred to as a "secret society" with its own language and code of behavior. "It was a club back then," Rock said of gay Hollywood. He could have been speaking of his college fraternity—if he had gone to college.

If anyone dared to ask, the chance gay encounter was easily explained away in ways the committed gay relationship could never be.

Henry Willson had no professional use for effeminate homosexuals, since they had no value in the movie marketplace. Personally, he avoided being seen with "the fairies and sissies," as he called them, because they exposed his own sexual orientation. "Henry was actually homophobic," said his assistant Pat Colby. "He had sex with men, but he couldn't stand girly men. And he certainly did not tolerate two men living together."

Along with his grooming tips and restaurant etiquette, Henry drew up a checklist of survival techniques for any homosexual actor living in Hollywood. They were rules as de rigueur as ordering red wine with filet mignon and putting white patent loafers in the closet after Labor Day.

"Don't ever let a man park his car in your driveway overnight," he instructed. "Never sit down at a restaurant with another man without a young lady being present. And never ever live with another man."

Those were the three mortal sins of his queer-in-the-closet catechism. If two male clients moved into the same house, Henry saw it as an act of career suicide and worthy of immediate expulsion from his representation. "You're no good to me as a client, advertising your private life," he said.

The notice of his displeasure rarely took the form of a simple dismissal. He preferred games of a tortuous psychology that sacrificed one partner but kept the other, more compliant actor safely ensconced in his professional care. For example, Henry launched into war mode when John Carlyle and another Willson client fell in love and decided to take the next step. "He said our living together would ruin our careers," said Carlyle. By the late 1940s, Henry had instituted the practice of spying on his clients, and he spent many nights taking tally of whose car was parked in whose driveway. After a late-night party or a premiere, it was not unusual for his black Cadillac to reconnoiter the Hollywood Hills to keep watch on his boys. Later, when Pat Colby came under his employ, it fell to him to make the evening rounds. "I don't ever remember being asked to check on a female client," said Colby.

Many chafed at the gross intrusion. "Henry tried to control the personal lives of his clients," Rock complained. "He spied on you."

Others took an oddly warm comfort in the agent's close scrutiny of their lives. "Henry was a mother hen, he wanted to protect you, and I suppose he was right about my boyfriend and me living together," said Carlyle.

In an attempt to talk his client out of openly living with another man, Henry invited Carlyle to the 1953 Las Vegas nightclub debut of Jeanette MacDonald, whom the agent then represented. Although Henry built his reputation obsessing over a large stable of good-looking male actors, much less noticed was his affectionate hand-holding of dowager clients. In addition to Margaret Dumont, these included Broadway's wisecracking sidekick Patsy Kelly, the terribly French Fifi D'Orsay (who had never stepped foot outside North America), 1930s child star Jane Withers (who had a major

comeback with *Giant*), and Hollywood's own coloratura soprano
Jeanette MacDonald. They all became Willson clients long after
their prime had deserted them and made them prime only for camp
status. Henry, who appreciated their illustrious past, offered them a
road back or, at the very least, a few welcome paychecks. His boys
called these near-forgotten beldams "Henry's fag hags." But Henry
didn't see them that way.

Long after Hollywood had stopped laughing at the operetta formula that made Nelson Eddy and Jeanette MacDonald top movie
attractions in the 1930s, Henry advised the fifty-year-old songbird
to expose her high notes to the dry, hot air and cold desert cash of
Las Vegas. It had worked for Marlene Dietrich and Noel Coward,
who trashed the audiences there as the "Nescafé society." Although
Nelson Eddy's former costar had performed solo in various concert
halls around the country, MacDonald was skeptical of singing in
front of a bunch of drunken gamblers. But it was the fad, and profitable, too.

"Longhair talent," *Newsweek* claimed, had emerged as the new
"gimmick" in Las Vegas nightclubs, which paid out an awesome
$5 million to top-line entertainers. Henry had the idea: if opera
stars like Lauritz Melchior, Ezio Pinza, and Robert Merrill could
bark for big bucks, why not Jeanette MacDonald?

When Henry invited John Carlyle to her Vegas opening, the
twenty-two-year-old actor thought it would prove to be a relaxing car
trip to the desert. "But Henry spent the entire weekend trying to talk
me out of moving in with my boyfriend," he recalled. "Henry was
adamant, and when that happened he came at you like a bulldozer."

He repeatedly told Carlyle, "No two men can live together and
have a career in Hollywood. It is not allowed. You'll ruin it all if you
live with this other man," Henry predicted.

A paradigm of his own advice, Henry lived the life he told others
to keep. "He wasn't just talking about actors," said Carlyle.

Henry's concern was born decades ago, before his own birth in
1911. As he drove Carlyle through the desert to Las Vegas, he

retreated into history-book mode and brought up the *fin de siècle* trial of Oscar Wilde and the ultimate disgrace and demise it brought the playwright. And there were other more recent examples, he said, pointing to a number of homosexual stars whom M-G-M released from their contracts in the early 1930s, a repressive era that neatly coincided with Henry's arrival in Hollywood. As he presented their individual portraits to John Carlyle, the victims of Louis B. Mayer's wrath ran the gamut from adventure to romance to comedy.

Star of the original *Ben-Hur,* Ramon Navarro owned the Latin-lover mantle after Valentino's death. Denmark's debonair Nils Asther romanced everyone from Greta Garbo to Joan Crawford on-screen. And the all-American William Haines romped through many college comedies with numbing repetition.

On his drive to Las Vegas, Henry gunned the gas pedal for needed emphasis, telling his liberal and equally naive passenger a few facts of gay life and career suicide in Hollywood. What Henry failed to mention is that the transition from silent to sound films derailed the careers of several heterosexuals, too. As for the gay stars, Henry chose to overlook their obvious flaws, such as Nils Asther's weird accent and William Haines's expanding waistline and Ramon Novarro's androgynous beauty, which didn't play well in the more conservative Depression years.

Unconvinced, Carlyle made the mistake of mentioning his need for the love and companionship of another man. "So get a dog!" Henry barked back. "You can live with your mother but not your lover." The remark was a pointed reference to perennial bachelor Clifton Webb, who played everything from an effete columnist (*Laura*) to a fertile father (*Cheaper by the Dozen*), all the while living with his beloved mother, Mabelle. According to Henry, the epicene Webb may have had no girlfriends, but he retained his position in Hollywood by also entertaining no boyfriends.

Carlyle and Willson spent their Las Vegas weekend alternately arguing with each other and hiding from a distraught Jeanette

MacDonald, whose voice was now in tatters. "I've never seen such fear," said Carlyle. "But the Vegas audiences adored her." On March 10, 1953, the movies' former songbird made her debut at the Hotel Sahara's Congo Room, opening with "Beyond the Blue Horizon" and continuing with thirty minutes of semiclassical ditties, which did nothing to uphold MacDonald's contention that "good music will appeal."

When he returned to Los Angeles, Carlyle ignored Henry's interdict and set up house with his new boyfriend in the busy Norma Triangle section of West Hollywood. They didn't have to wait long to feel the effects of their agent's ex-cathedra pronouncement. Within the month, Henry began touting Robert Wagner over Carlyle's lover, who, in the early 1950s also enjoyed a promising career at 20th Century–Fox. "He and R. J. were up for a number of the same parts, and Henry kept telling them at Fox that R. J. was the better actor and deserved the role," said Carlyle. "It happened time and again."

It could have happened to Rock Hudson, too, but he proved to be the more obedient client when it came to dumping old boyfriends on orders from Henry. Jack Navaar was a Korean War vet who met and fell in love with Rock and so found his way into Henry Willson's ever-expanding stable of male starlets. Henry baptized him Rand Saxon, but instead of finding work as a film actor Navaar ended up on the night shift at Hughes Aircraft. When he moved into Rock's house on Avenida del Sol, Navaar gave up the blue-collar job to be supported full-time by his boyfriend—that, is until Rock Hudson the contract player graduated to Rock Hudson the movie star.

Navaar signed his own divorce papers when he pulled a hissy fit at the premiere of Douglas Sirk's *Magnificent Obsession* on May 11, 1954. He considered himself one of the A-list guests, and wanted to be seated next to his lover. Instead, Navaar found himself relegated to a less conspicuous section of the theater, where he sat next to producer Ross Hunter's lover, Jacques Mapes, and their respective female escorts for the night.

"You said we'd be sitting together," Navaar complained to Rock after the premiere. "I felt like a fool. Like, you're the star and I'm the jerk!" Playing the injured lover, he chose the theater's parking lot as the unfortunate stage upon which to air his grievances. (Mapes and Hunter handled their living arrangements with somewhat less drama. When anyone dared ask, they referred to each other as "stepbrothers.")

Navaar believed that it was Henry who ended his blissful rent-free nidification among the bougainvillea, jasmine, and Rock on Avenida del Sol. He wasn't wrong there. Shortly after the release of *Magnificent Obsession*, Rock went to Ireland to film *Captain Lightfoot*, again for Douglas Sirk, and became incensed when he heard that Navaar had sullied his reputation back in Hollywood with wild all-night parties.

Navaar could only wonder how Rock had heard such stories and considered it a closed case when he got a phone call from his lover's agent. "The studio is capable of taking extreme measures to protect a property, said Henry, who wasn't talking about the house on Avenida del Sol.

According to Navaar, Rock's friends deserted him. "Everyone treated me like I was dead meat. I felt like dead meat, and I didn't want to live like that," he said. "So I did exactly what they wanted me to do." Navaar gave Henry the keys to Rock's house and moved out, an overnight banishment.

29

Around the World at Universal

One week, he was playing a Native American in brown makeup and black wig. The next week, Universal-International cast Rock Hudson in what would be its most successful film of 1954. In one respect, the career-defining *Magnificent Obsession* became a curse in disguise for Rock Hudson. Propelling him from contract player to major star, the film made Rock an immediate target for the burgeoning tabloid press. Without some gainful employment from director Douglas Sirk, the actor may have lived out his life never having known the thrill of super-size celebrity fraught with big-time blackmail.

The *Magnificent Obsession* director had also gambled on Rock two years earlier when he gave him his first comic role in *Has Anybody Seen My Gal?* Sirk had seen Hudson's work in the Jeff Chandler feature *Iron Man* the year before and been impressed with Rock the potential movie star, if not Rock the potential actor.

"Rock was far inferior to Chandler, but I thought I saw something," said Sirk. "So I arranged to meet him, and he seemed to be not too much to the eye, except very handsome." Sirk then said something that could have come from the mouth of Henry Willson, and often did. "But the camera sees with its own eye," said Sirk. "It sees things the human eye does not detect. And ultimately you learn to trust your camera. And it was not wrong about Hudson."

Sirk distrusted his own eyes so much that before awarding Rock the role in their first film together, he planned an extensive test, which required him to enact every scene his soda jerk character played in *Has Anybody Seen My Gal?* Much to Sirk's delighted surprise, Rock managed to show an early, if faint, flair for comedy, especially when the script called for him to play the raccoon coat–wearing, ukulele-plucking fool. When rubbed against his tall, granite edifice, Rock's self-deprecation created genuine comic sparks, and it didn't hurt that he towered over his petite love interest, Piper Laurie, by at least a foot.

After two Sirk pictures, Henry thought it a good idea for Rock to work with the director a third time, even if it meant his portraying (in a better-fitting wig) another Native American, the title role of *Taza, Son of Cochise.* Once again, Rock kept his voice low, his pecs high. The studio usually resisted such peculiar typecasting, but Henry considered Sirk one of Universal's best directors, and a connection well worth developing for his client. "They thought it might spoil his image," Sirk said of the Universal execs' hesitancy to cast Rock in another Western. "You know these problems about actors doing Indians too often."

Rock saw in Sirk the kind of father figure he found in Henry Willson and earlier, Ken Hodges—minus the sexual component. "He was like ol' Dad to me, and I was like a son to him, I think," said the actor. "When you're scared and new and you're trying to figure out this thing, and suddenly an older man will reach out and say, 'There, there, it's okay.' That was Douglas Sirk."

Despite the ludicrous *Taza* assignment, Henry bet that it would lead to Rock's starring in Sirk's next picture, *Magnificent Obsession,* and he was right. The original 1935 adaptation of Lloyd C. Douglas's novel featured Irene Dunne and made Robert Taylor a star. In Hollywood, where the perpetual lack of imagination creates the vacuum necessary for lightning to strike twice, Henry believed the remake could do the same for his client.

Indeed, Rock did full justice, and then some, to the role of the egomaniacal playboy Bob Merrick. If the actor knew his one-dimensional character was mere grist for a ridiculous plot, he never let on. In *Magnificent Obsession,* Merrick inadvertently causes the death of Jane Wyman's husband and accidentally injures the new widow in a freak automobile accident that leaves her blind but otherwise unscarred, all of which inspires him to complete his long-abandoned medical studies and ultimately restore her sight. *Magnificent Obsession* was magnificent junk, and one of 1954's top-grossing films.

Henry and the film's producer, Ross Hunter, shared a kindred love-laugh attitude toward Hollywood hokum and hyperbole. They knelt at the altar of heterosexual romance, worshipped it, promoted it, and made a buck off it—which didn't mean they practiced it for a minute. "I'm the world's champion crier. Maybe that's why I'm so good at producing this kind of junk," said Hunter, the self-proclaimed sultan of soap operas on the Universal lot. In addition to *Magnificent Obsession,* he went on to produce *All That Heaven Allows. Battle Hymn* and *Written on the Wind,* all made with Douglas Sirk and Rock Hudson. His formula was as pure as it was absurd: beautiful actors, beautiful costumes, beautiful sins. As he put it, "You might just as well have a murder take place on an Oriental rug as on someone's dirty linoleum."

Sirk confirmed the long-held rumor in Hollywood that Rock Hudson sexually serviced the producer to secure the career-turning male lead in *Magnificent Obsession.* Like many heterosexuals of the period, Sirk held to the dubious proposition that many homosexuals were seduced into their sexual orientation. The director placed the young Hudson "near the middle of the sexual spectrum," but after his meeting Ross Hunter, "that was it" for Rock. According to Sirk, Rock's encounter with the producer pushed him off the bisexual fence and into the pit of homosexuality.

Others disagreed with Sirk's assessment. Rock's friend and secretary, Mark Miller, insisted that Hunter and his *Magnificent Obsession* star enjoyed a strictly platonic business relationship. Rock never mentioned such an affair, and since his propensity had always been to brag to George Nader and Mark Miller about every conquest—good, bad or indifferent—the two men assumed that the *Magnificent Obsession* project was never consummated with sex. "Preposterous," said Miller. Otherwise, Rock's voracious sexual appetite remained a joke among the three buddies, if not a point of pride for the star. "You don't have to screw something just because it wiggles," Miller scolded him.

"Oh, but I do!" Rock replied.

His reputation for promiscuity eventually made itself known even in the hallowed, sweaty walls of the Beverly Hills Hotel steam room. "Rock walked in one day and dropped his towel and there was this Band-Aid on his penis," recalled a publicist. His bandaged appendage immediately drew attention from the assembled crowd.

"It's not how you think," Rock offered. "I caught it on a zipper."

The obvious question volleyed back, "Whose zipper?"

When it came to the quantity of sex Rock Hudson had in his private life, he ranked right up there with America's reigning sex symbol on the distaff side. Marilyn Monroe also came to her job of love goddess with a long résumé of on-the-job experience, as well as a laissez-faire attitude toward the physical act itself. Both stars used sex to broker business deals and saw sexual intercourse as little more than a handshake, a gesture that was more a casual greeting than a sign of emotional commitment. In Elia Kazan's autobiography *A Life*, he wrote of one such night with Marilyn when the two of them made love, or some facsimile therefore, to celebrate her just-announced engagement to Joe DiMaggio.

Although Mark Miller discounted the Hudson/Hunter coupling, he revealed another affair, one that had a truly profound effect on the actor's career. In 1953, shortly before *Magnificent Obsession* went into production, Universal-International promoted its studio general manager, Edward Muhl, to the position of vice president in charge of production. Known as a rather colorless number-cruncher, Muhl was also an extremely well-liked, even-tempered executive, one who had spent his entire career at the studio, having risen through the ranks from a lowly $50-a-week accounting job, in

1927, to replace the legendary William Goetz as Universal's top film VP. At age forty-five, Muhl arrived at his career pinnacle at the precise moment Rock most needed a highly placed guardian angel. It helped, too, that Muhl had fallen in love with the actor.

One week before shooting began on *Magnificent Obsession*, Rock suffered an injury that seriously jeopardized his chances for securing the crucial assignment. "Without Muhl, Rock would have been dropped from *Magnificent Obsession*," said Miller.

The accident happened during Rock's well-deserved vacation at Laguna Beach. He had gone swimming with George Nader and Miller when an errant wave sent Rock crashing against some rocks, and he broke his collarbone.

The pain was so extreme that Rock passed out and had to be carried to the shore by his two friends. The real agony hit when he opened his eyes again. Rock knew instinctively what the injury might cost him. "The studio wanted to replace Rock, but Muhl got the start date pushed back six weeks," said Miller.

Their affair had to be conducted with the utmost discretion. Obvious is sometimes best. The Universal vice president, who was well on his way to siring six children, chose his executive suite at the studio as the safest place for their sporadic meetings. Muhl would close the office door, tell his secretary to hold all calls, and then crawl on his hands and knees across the floor to Rock.

For Rock, it was sex in exchange for preferential treatment on the Universal lot. For Muhl, it had been something more. In 1983, Universal Pictures invited Rock Hudson back to the studio lot for a party. Although he hadn't been under contract with Universal for nearly two decades, he continued to be identified as one of the company's most illustrious stars. At the party, Rock smiled for photographers and fielded interviews. Among those waiting his turn was Ed Muhl, who finally got to take Rock aside for a brief moment and whisper to him, "I still love you."

Later, Rock told Mark Miller the story of their reunion. "Can you believe Ed Muhl?" he said, amazed. "After all these years!"

If Henry Willson ever knew of the two men's clandestine relationship, it's doubtful he objected. On the contrary, he encouraged mixing sex with business and often advised his clients to sleep with an executive or influential director. "It will take you longer if you don't," he believed. When one heterosexual actor told Henry that he couldn't respond sexually to another man, Henry had to laugh. "You're an actor, so act!" he said.

30

Confidential Reports

No sooner did *Magnificent Obsession* turn Rock Hudson into a bona fide star than Warner Bros. took extreme interest. Again, it was the smitten Ed Muhl who came to the rescue a second time. Warner Bros. wanted Rock to headline its most prestigious upcoming project, George Stevens's film adaptation of Edna Ferber's novel *Giant*. Muhl received the script on October 23, 1954, and took a mere seven days to approve it, marshaling the agreement through the Universal hierarchy in record time.

Only a month earlier, William Holden had been considered the front-runner to star in *Giant*. A publicity release from Stevens's office played up the surprise factor of the Hudson pick: "The prize acting plum of the year, and one which has often been reported in the grasp of a number of Hollywood's top male stars, goes to a dark horse who has never once been mentioned in the spirited competition."

Holden may have been more swaggering, but Stevens wanted the humorous and hulking intellectual dimness that Rock ultimately brought to the role. With a nod to the success of *Magnificent Obsession,* Stevens's statement to the press let it be known that he had found "the best-suited star for the role of Benedict." The film required Rock to age thirty years, and Stevens had seen how effectively the actor had achieved that feat in his earlier film *The Lawless Breed*.

Rock was a little more than ecstatic in his November 4 thank-you telegram to Stevens: "Just heard the wonderful, wonderful news Am walking in clouds Will arrive in Los Angeles Monday Will call you if I may."

He had reason to be "walking in clouds." *Giant* was a prestige project at one of Hollywood's top studios, and the heterosexual George Stevens had picked Rock with no interest in sleeping with him. (Like Douglas Sirk, Rock would go on to adore Stevens, but not as a father figure. "I followed him around like a puppy," said Rock.)

In exchange for letting him make *Giant* at Warners, Universal required that Rock renew his contract with the studio for four more years. Many years later, Rock spoke figuratively, as well as literally, when he said, "That was really a piece of putting the screw into you."

On November 19, 1954, Rock displayed no such cynicism regarding his *Giant* deal. He wanted only to celebrate, and *The Hollywood Reporter*'s Mike Connolly dutifully publicized the occasion ten days later when he wrote about filmland's two favorite odd couples, "Saturday Mo-somes: Phyllis Gates & Rock Hudson, Margaret Truman & Henry Willson."

At the Mocambo, Henry ordered the club's photographer, Ernest Weaver, to shoot portraits of him and Margaret Truman. "Margaret Truman and Henry Willson were quite the couple there for a while," said Paramount producer A. C. Lyles.

After Diana Lynn tired of his dating charade and got married, Henry struck up his press-worthy friendship with the singing daughter of President Harry S. Truman. It worked both ways: she gave him class and, according to Henry, he gave her something not to be found in the White House rose garden: a ten-year contract with NBC. They celebrated by getting engaged—to each other.

Perhaps Maggie Truman was in the ladies room at Mo when Henry proposed to her. She returned the compliment by not mentioning him in her autobiography, *Souvenir*, published six years after the NBC deal, in 1951. She instead credited the TV negotiations, as well as her RCA contract, to her concert manager, James Davidson.

Regarding the phantom engagement, Margaret Truman left it to Mike Connolly to dutifully run several items trumpeting the affair in *The Hollywood Reporter.* The columnist had first announced their romance in the newspaper's March 13, 1952, issue: "New 2: Margaret T & Henry Willson." A few months later, he spotted them at LaRue's and reported, "Maggie Truman dined there too, but minus gendarmes, with Henry Willson, betimes being highly amused by the goings-on at the birthday party hosted by Edgar Bergen and attended by Benita and Ronald Colman."

Connolly also reported on the couple's appearance aboard the S. S. *President Cleveland* the following year, as well as on their 1954 double date with Rock Hudson and Phyllis Gates, to celebrate his *Giant* signing.

The spectacle of Henry dating a president's daughter, of course, did not survive his client's ensuing cover-up with *Confidential* magazine. Henry, however, remembered her fondly and forever. "He often spoke about his engagements to Margaret Truman and Diana Lynn as if they were the real thing," said his assistant Gary Crutcher. When asked why he didn't marry Maggie, Henry liked to flaunt his political conservatism. "Who wants Harry Truman for a father-in-law?" he used to laugh.

Sometime before his final date with Margaret, Henry received word that *Confidential* magazine was looking for informants to expose Rock Hudson. Two of his former clients, Jack Navaar and Bob Preble, had received offers of $10,000 each to tell their story. Both had been Rock's roommates in his pre–movie star days, and while they knew the score, the two men refused to cooperate with the tabloid out of loyalty to their ex. Preble, for his part, had difficulty deciding which was Rock's greater enemy: *Confidential* or Henry Willson.

"I wouldn't have trusted him for a minute behind my back," Preble said of his old agent. "I found him offensive."

Rumors circulated that *Confidential* learned of Hudson's homosexuality as a result of the actor's less-than-circumspect attendance at Hollywood's gay bars, clubs, and parties. More likely, *Confidential*'s editors ignored the actor in his contract-player days, then quickly took another look after *Magnificent Obsession* made him a big enough fish to fry within its pages.

The tabloids weren't the only ones investigating Rock's love life in 1955. *Life* put the actor on its cover that year with the tagline, "Hollywood's Most Handsome Bachelor." Inside, his bachelor status came under close scrutiny as current fan-rag headlines, "Scared of Marriage?" and "Don't Rush Rock," were reprinted. *Life* put out the word: "Fans are urging twenty-nine-year-old Hudson to get married—or explain why not."

Confidential magazine threatened to do *Life* one better—and *reveal* why not.

John Saxon recalled riding around town with Henry one night in 1955. His agent was more agitated than usual, and he kept mentioning his need to get to a newsstand fast. In fact, Henry was desperate to find the latest copy of *Confidential*. The tabloid may have been selling more than four million copies a month, but it was considered a disreputable publication; many newsstands banned *Confidential*, and it wasn't always easy to locate a copy. Finally, Henry pulled his Cadillac over to the curb to get out.

"We both went into this drugstore on Sunset," said Saxon. Spotting *Confidential*, Henry bought every copy off the newsstand, folded them to hide the cover, then returned to the privacy of his car. He flipped through the issue. "Henry was very sort of anxious. He told me afterwards, he wanted to check what this magazine said or was going to say," said Saxon. Fortunately, the much-feared issue of *Confidential* printed not one word about Rock Hudson. Until a new issue hit the newsstands next month, the star was safe.

Henry, however, refused to rest. Never the kind of homosexual to roll over and play the dead fairy, Henry knew how to level the playing field with extortionists, and he wasn't afraid to beat them at their game. In his efforts to protect Rock, Henry's first move was to hire Nick Duber, a Beverly Hills detective who warmed to the reflected glare of his famous clients' troubles. "Nick Duber," he used to say, "PI to the stars."

In 1955, a teenager named Don Crutchfield worked as Duber's apprentice and later inherited his firm, now called Crutchfield & Associates, in Beverly Hills. Crutchfield was a high school friend of Duber's son, and over the years, he and the private eye performed several jobs for Henry Willson. As Crutchfield put it, "When things popped up." The most spectacular case involved a blackmailer who had taken sexually explicit photographs of Rock Hudson.

Henry knew trouble when he got a whiff of it, and this smelled like the end of Rock's career if those photos were ever made public. He met with Duber and Crutchfield in their Beverly Hills office.

"We've got to do something," Henry told them. "If he exposes [Rock], we're out a lot of money: the studio, Rock and me."

Crutchfield suspected that *Confidential* had negotiated with the blackmailer to publish the photographs. "But it could have been another magazine or paper," he said.

Duber's first suggestion to Henry was that his detective firm "get a pattern," as he called it, on the man threatening to blackmail Rock. Duber wanted to know at what hour this man left his home each day and when he returned.

"That's the first thing we have to learn," said the detective.

And so, for one week, Crutchfield kept watch in front of the man's West LA apartment to track his comings and goings. When Duber was satisfied that they had an accurate pattern, he brought in an off-duty cop in robbery and homicide with the LAPD.

"Jimmy was the muscle behind Duber's operation," said Crutchfield, referring to the cop.

He took Jimmy to the blackmailer's apartment one evening, and the two men waited. Crutchfield recalled, "I'm sure Duber didn't say to Jimmy, 'Beat the shit out of this guy!' But the guy got smart." When the man returned home, Jimmy immediately set out his demands: "I want all the pictures. Don't ever call Rock Hudson again. Leave the State of California."

The man snorted. "What's in it for me?" he said. Back in the 1950s, those weren't the words an intelligent person used with an LAPD officer, whether the cop was on-duty or off.

Crutchfield claimed he didn't know beforehand what would happen. "Jimmy broke his nose and grabbed him by the hair and shoved him down. You could hear ribs crack," he said. Jimmy then collected the incriminating photographs and negatives, which, as promised, showed Rock having sex with his blackmailer. Crutchfield brushed off the beating. "You wise-off to a cop and they slapped you around in those days," he said. "It was a different time."

Oddly enough, the blackmailer had never demanded money. According to Henry, the man simply wanted to be made a star. "I'm just as good an actor as Rock Hudson. You're an agent," he told Henry. "If you don't do for me what you did for Rock Hudson, I'll ruin his career." It was a twist that would be repeated a few years later, but with one major difference. The second time around, Henry actually thought the man blackmailing Rock was "a good bet" and helped to launch his career. But not this guy. Henry deemed him "nondescript."

According to Crutchfield, one of the movie studios worked with Henry to prevent the *Confidential* exposé, or at least help pay for it. "We got a hefty bonus," he said. "The boss [Duber] got a helluva bonus, a Corvette he got."

Crutchfield remembered Henry's being a tough, risk-taking operator. "You didn't mess with Henry Willson," he said. "He was not a flamer. He had to mind his p's and q's to stay in business with his gay clientele in this town."

It could not have been an easy flock to round up and tuck into bed every night. Rock's friend George Nader recalled the major dread of homosexual celebrities at the time.

"We lived in fear of an exposé, or even one small remark, a veiled suggestion that someone was homosexual. Such a remark would have caused an earthquake at the studio," said the actor. "Every month, when *Confidential* came out, our stomachs began to turn.

Which of us would be in it? The amazing thing is that Rock, as big as he became, was never nailed. It made me speculate that Rock had an angel on his shoulder or that he'd made a pact with the devil, because he seemed under supernatural protection."

31

Sacrificial Lions

Angel or devil, Henry Willson saw to it that Rock Hudson was always protected, even if that meant sacrificing the reputation of a few ex-clients. Contrary to popular myth, George Nader was not one of them. While Nader lived with his lover, Mark Miller, *Confidential* never wrote an exposé on the handsome matinee idol of programmers and B-films.

Someone, however, did throw the tabloid a bone—maybe two bones—for not publishing an exposé on Rock Hudson's sex life in 1955. Instead, that year's May issue ran the profile, "Rory Calhoun, But for the Grace of God, Still a Convict." The star's long-suppressed prison record had finally come under open scrutiny.

"I went to the local newsstand that day and bought five copies of *Confidential*," said Mark Miller. Since Calhoun had been sacrificed to save their careers, neither Rock nor George wanted to be seen carrying the rag with Francis Durgin's prison mug shot on the cover, which left it to Miller to carry home the tabloid booty. "Jack Diamond was head of publicity at Universal, and he handled the whole trade-off with Rory Calhoun," said Miller. "Both Rock and George met with Jack afterwards to thank him."

Miller did not know if Henry was involved. But among the Willson stable of boys, it was common knowledge. "I heard Henry planted the story," said his client James DeCloss. John Carlyle remembered hearing the gossip at the agent's weekly Saturday-afternoon pool parties. "It was talked about. Rory was traded for Rock, not that Henry would ever admit to such a thing," said Carlyle. "But the *Confidential* story got Rory a lot of publicity. It didn't hurt his career, on the contrary."

There was a clear precedent for arrests furthering the career of movie bad guys. In 1948, Robert Mitchum's marijuana conviction landed him in the clink, and when the actor appeared in *Life* magazine, shown mopping the prison floor during his sixty-day sentence, it only enhanced his film career. RKO released Mitchum's *Rachel and the Stranger* postarrest with due trepidation, only to watch it rise to the top of the box office charts. "Booze, broads, it's all true," Mitchum acknowledged. "Make up more if you want."

Calhoun took a less philosophical view of having his prison record made public. "He definitely wasn't happy about it," said L. Q. Jones, Calhoun's costar on several TV and film Westerns.

But it worked. "Once Rory's story was published," *Parade* magazine reported, "Hollywood made him a minor hero. Parties were thrown in his honor. Television producers vied for his services. He received more movie offers than he could accept."

If Henry planted the exposé on Rory Calhoun's prison record, it was a derring-do act of press funambulism that served to keep Rock out of the tabloids *and* put Rory on the front page of the nation's most respected newspapers. Presaging today's TV sob-confessionals, Calhoun went into interview overdrive and talked to any reporter who could produce a byline. He openly admitted to his prison record—how could he deny it?—but slathered the details in a bathetic glow of having found God and the love of a good woman, his wife Lita Baron, who divorced him fifteen years later for having had sex with more than seventy women during the course of their twenty-two-year marriage.

The Calhoun/Hudson trade-off was not an open secret in Hollywood. "It was very hush-hush at the time," said AP reporter Bob Thomas. "Few people, even on the inside, knew about it."

Thomas's AP colleague, reporter James Bacon, heard the story from Joan Crawford. At the time, she confirmed that the Rory

Calhoun exposé served to squelch a projected story on the sex life of Rock Hudson, and that the exchange was orchestrated by Henry Willson and Universal-International, which had both actors under contract. Crawford was also making films for U-I in the mid-1950s. "And she was dating the studio's president, Milton Rackmil, who told her of the trade-off," said Bacon.

In his defense to the press, Rory failed to mention the homosexual talent scout, and later agent, who converted him from ex-con to respected Hollywood citizen. Instead, he spoke of a dedicated Irish priest, Father Don Kanaly, who taught him how to get down on his knees and pray behind bars. In 1955, the religion card could never be overplayed.

It was the time to put the fear of God in men. Joseph McCarthy may have been censured by the Senate for his unfounded claims about Communists in 1954, but that same year his politically conservative friends pressured President Eisenhower to introduce the phrase "under God" into the Pledge of Allegiance. The next year, Congress authorized all U.S. currency to carry the words "In God We Trust."

Rory Calhoun's prison record had been one of Hollywood's worst-kept secrets. Mike Connolly referred to it obliquely two years before the *Confidential* story broke: "The Rory Calhoun who flew to Korea [to entertain the troops] doesn't seem like the same guy who gave the juvenile authorities so much trouble years ago," Connolly wrote in 1953. Coincidence or not, 1953 was the same year that Calhoun failed to follow Henry Willson from Famous Artists to his new outfit on Carol Drive.

Two years later, *Confidential*'s siege on Henry Willson's ex-clients began with Rory Calhoun and continued with Tab Hunter. While Calhoun's arrests were common knowledge, Tab Hunter's run-in with the law was pure arcanum, filed away and forgotten in a police report for half a decade. Few Hollywood insiders other than Henry Willson knew of it.

"Absolutely, Henry fed them the Tab Hunter story," said the

agent's friend Fred Winston. "That was the gossip," said Henry's client John Carlyle. Van Williams agreed, "Henry never had a kind thing to say about Tab Hunter." Less sure, L. Q. Jones observed, "I doubt Henry would get involved, but everything seems to point in that direction."

Confidential's sudden disclosure of the actor's 1950 arrest, buried for five years, coincided not only with Rock Hudson's blackmail crisis but Tab Hunter's firing of Henry Willson. To further provoke Henry's ire, Tab replaced him with Dick Clayton, the same agent Henry used to call his "pencil boy," an unkind euphemism for male secretary.

When Henry opened his own boutique agency in 1953, Clayton stayed put at Charlie Feldman's firm. The journeyman agent had enjoyed only a modest career at Famous Artists, that is, until he signed a New York stage actor who had already made the movie-studio rounds without sparking much interest on the West Coast. Clayton brought him back to Hollywood, bagged a three-picture deal at Warner Bros., and then watched his own reputation soar into the tenpercentery stratosphere when the actor crashed his Porsche Spyder near Cholame, California, on September 30, 1955. In one of his more prescient career decisions, Tab Hunter fired Henry and signed with Clayton a few months before Dean's fatal car accident.

"At that time, every young actor wanted to be Jimmy Dean," said Tab. "Dick discovered Jimmy Dean, and suddenly everybody wanted to be represented by Dick, myself included. And besides, Dick Clayton was my oldest friend in the business."

**calling
all Girls**

*Whistle-bait in the beefcake brigade, Tab Hunter
and Roddy McDowall do some prowling of their own!*

Neither Tab nor Roddy really
need the help of the little black book
for getting dates. Both eligible
bachelors, they have pick of film cuties.

Tab Hunter and Roddy McDowall play the bachelor game for a 1950s fan-magazine
photo spread.

32

Jimmy Dean's Maker

Confidante, confessor, nursemaid, agent, Dick Clayton enjoyed a reputation for possessing one of the most sympathetic ears in the business. His hand-holding technique wasn't bad either when it came to actors. After all, he had been one himself throughout most of the 1940s, specializing in the kind of Joe College roles that Henry had secured years ago for so many of the Puppets gang. Clayton's acting career never amounted to much. Blond, boyish, and rather nondescript, he put in so little screen time in such prewar films as *Knute Rockne, All American,* and *Those Were the Days* that the name Dick Clayton didn't warrant a credit in either of them, nor in the twenty-three other films in which he appeared. Constant rejection ultimately taught him that he had no business being an actor, but the lessons learned helped to turn him into a first-rate agent.

After toiling as Henry's "pencil boy," Clayton took care to distance himself from Hollywood's most "notorious" agent. He never trumpeted his early history at Famous Artists. Although Clayton remembered Henry cordially as a "good friend and generous person," he always took pains to credit future producer Ray Stark as his real mentor at Famous Artists. Henry, however, did teach the tyro agent at least one lesson Clayton practiced like a second religion: never share billing in Hollywood when you can take full credit. Both men claimed to have discovered Tab Hunter. In a way, they both did.

Although Clayton first encouraged Gelien to become an actor, he could hardly have launched his career in 1949. Working as Henry's secretary at Famous Artists, Clayton made the introduction that led to Gelien's signing with Henry Willson, who took matters from there. Blonder but smarter than Guy Madison, Arthur Gelien fit the Willson archetype complete with a father even more absent than either Rock's or Rory's.

Gelien came from a knockabout family that moved from New York City to San Francisco, where the mother, Gertrude Gelien, struggled to support Arthur and a younger brother, Walter, on her nurse's wages at the Matson Steamship Lines. A battered wife, Gertrude had long since left her abusive husband, Charles Kelm, and so despised him that she returned to using her maiden name, which she gave to her two sons as well. When the three of them migrated south to Long Beach, the two boys attended a number of schools, including St. John's Military Academy, and it was there that Arthur developed his lifelong interest in riding horses and ice skating. In between those hobbies, he worked odd jobs as a movie usher and soda jerk to help keep the family afloat. With college a financial impossibility, the fifteen-year-old lied about his age to join the Coast Guard, and after his stint there, Clayton introduced him to Henry Willson. Never interested in sharing credit, Clayton's boss told a different story.

Henry had gone to see his old friend Bobby Speck perform in the *Ice Capades*. On horseback or on the ice, it was nearly lust at first sight for both Henry and Clayton.

"I looked at this blond kid with the open, friendly face, and I could see him in closeup on the screen," Henry said. "I can always tell within ten minutes if the person has it or not, and with this inner sense of mine, I knew he had picture potential."

Backstage at the *Ice Capades*, Henry didn't need Bobby Speck to make introductions: "If you've ever thought of a career in the movies . . ." Henry impressed Gelien as he had dozens of other post-Guy epigonies: minutes after they were introduced, he took him to the Mocambo to talk a little business and dazzle him with a lot of Hollywood glamour. As the nightclub was owned by Henry's friend Charlie Morrison, there was never any problem when Henry brought in an underage kid like Gelien.

"Art wasn't even supposed to be in the place, since he was only eighteen," Henry said. "He ordered a Bloody Mary. Can you believe that I had never heard of a Bloody Mary?" As Henry pointed out, Gelien was an ex–Coast Guard man, and Henry always liked a uniform, even if Gelien hadn't worn one for months.

The future Tab Hunter recalled dining with Henry at not the Mocambo but the much less frothy Scandia, which struck a Viking note with plenty of hanging metal weaponry. "Henry had a way of staring through you," he said. "When he gave me that look, there was no mistaking its meaning. The little nudges under the table, the lingering hand on my arm—merely extra hints for the uninitiated."

By the time of the *Ice Capades* tryst, Clayton and Gelien were already old friends. They had met at Dubrock's Riding Academy near Griffith Park in Los Angeles six years earlier, in 1943. Clayton was twenty-six years old at the time, and he said it was Gelien's way with horses that first drew him to the twelve-year-old boy. "I had to admire the skill with which he lifted his weight from the animal at the proper moment and helped the horse jump, and the courage this kid displayed in trying it," said Clayton, who had no choice but to ride up and congratulate him. "He was just a kid, but there was a certain poised certainty about the way he moved, the way he discussed horses that made you forget how young he was." Gelien worked his same mature charms on the recruiters at the Coast Guard.

After the war, Clayton moved to Manhattan and kept an apartment there, which proved equally convenient for Gelien, now almost fifteen and in need of a place to stay in the big city. "Tab, who was in boot camp in Connecticut, became a frequent visitor, calling on me when he got leave," Clayton said. He could have been Henry talking about Guy Madison. "I took Tab to his first Broadway play," Clayton added.

In a March 1955 profile of Tab Hunter, *Modern Screen* looked back at the two men's January/May relationship and called Dick Clayton the "sage old Uncle Richard." Although fan magazines served up press-release pabulum, they were written in a sly code that breezed over the heads of naive readers yet delighted Hollywood insiders. Regarding Clayton's many Gotham weekends with the teenager, the magazine cooed, "probably not even Tab's mother knew him better."

Not printed was Tab's attempt to see his long-absent father, who continued to live in New York City. On one of his weekend visits to see Clayton, Tab took the opportunity to look up Charlie Kelm. He knocked on his apartment door, and when a woman appeared he told her, "Tell him his son came by." She slammed the door in his face.

As a father figure, Clayton presented a stark, welcome contrast. Sometime between sundaes at Schrafft's and performances of Rodgers and Hammerstein musicals, Clayton suggested a career in acting to his teenage friend. He would soon be in a position to help.

"When Tab finally left the service he came directly to Hollywood and looked me up, for by this time I'd returned to the coast and was in the midst of a transition from actor to agent," said Clayton, whose only Hollywood connection at the time was Henry Willson.

Henry had a knack for creating beginner's luck. He put Tab in *The Lawless,* a Joseph Losey film that costarred two of Henry's discoveries: Gail Russell, still married to Guy Madison (and would be for a few more months), and Johnny Sands, still a few years away from selling used cars on Sunset Strip. Tab then hit the sophomore slump and had to wait two long years for his second job in front of the movie cameras, starring opposite Linda Darnell in *Island of Desire.* Having played the Mother of God in *The Song of Bernadette,* the actress knew something about essaying a virgin and took pity on her leading man, who was eight years her junior.

"I was so scared," Tab said. "When I had to kiss her, I was shaking."

Darnell pinched him. "I'm good luck for newcomers," she said, then went in for the clinch.

So did Henry. ready to initiate yet another client, he invited Tab on a cruise from New York City to Bermuda on the *Queen of Bermuda,* a

British liner that carried the moniker "Honeymoon Ship." On the island, he reserved rooms at the Princess Hotel, which aptly described his date's behavior for the duration of their stay together. According to his autobiography, *Tab Hunter Confidential,* the actor claimed to have outfoxed one of Hollywood's preeminent wolves by striking up a friendship with two female schoolteachers.

"Using the sisters as a shield, I kept Henry at bay during our brief time in Bermuda," he wrote. "I was grateful to Henry and I felt I owed him a lot. But I didn't owe him that." Back in America, the film offers didn't exactly flood in after Tab's reportedly chaste ocean cruise with his agent. In his long interims between jobs, the male starlet honed his ice-skating skills, bought a horse named Out on Bail, and, much to Henry's consternation, got picked up for having attended a house party in Glendale in the company of twenty-six other homosexual males. Fortunately, *The Lawless* disappeared from theaters so rapidly that no tabloid hack thought to check the police files to link Tab Hunter with the arrested Arthur Andrew Gelien. And the debut of *Confidential* was still two years in the future.

Regarding the name change to Tab Hunter, the actor gave Henry full credit through most of the 1950s, then changed his story later on to credit Clayton.

In a 1958 interview with Louella Parsons, Tab told one story for an article entitled "Tab Hunter: The Girl He Will Marry": "Henry Wilson [sic], my agent, gave me 'Tab.' And I told him if I had to change my name, the name 'Hunter' would suit me because it's appropriate for my favorite hobbies, riding and hunting."

A 1970 interview with *After Dark* offered the revised version: "[Dick Clayton] was always picking up the tab for me. That's how he came up with the name Tab for me."

Publicly, Henry told the same story about "picking up the tab," with the standard caveat that it was he, and not Dick Clayton, who snatched the name out of the Hollywood ether.

Privately, Henry revealed another version, perhaps apocryphal but one he told whenever Tab Hunter was mentioned in conversation and his audience had been plied with enough liquor to fully appreciate its ripeness.

Clients came and went, but according to Henry, Tab Hunter's dismissal hit him like a son's fist in his ample solar plexus. Henry used to gloat that when he left Famous Artists in 1953 to start his own agency several clients remained faithful, and those included Rock Hudson, Natalie Wood, and Tab Hunter, who left Charlie Feldman's firm to sign with Henry Willson Management. Tab could have stayed behind to be repped by his "oldest friend in Hollywood," Dick Clayton. But in 1953, Clayton remained a very junior agent at Famous Artists, and until James Dean came along to transform his career, power topped friendship and Tab went with Henry. He secured the actor a seven-year contract at Warner Bros. in 1954. Tab started at $500 a week, a salary that escalated to $2,000 in the contract's final year. More impressive, the agreement kicked off with a featured role in Raoul Walsh's film *Battle Cry*, based on a Leon Uris best seller about World War II marines and therefore several levels up from the junk Tab had been making. In his gratitude, the actor celebrated Henry's pull with Walsh and the hard-won Warners deal by firing him. In return, Henry thanked Tab by getting Mike Connolly to publicize the upstart's abrupt departure with back-to-back items in *The Hollywood Reporter*:

"Tab Hunter scrammed Henry Willson, after 7 yrs, for Famous Artists," the columnist reported on September 6, 1955.

One week later, Connolly let go with another punch: "That deal for Tab Hunter to haul down $3,500 on Como's show was set by the Henry Willson office, whence Hunter scrams tomorrow."

Professionally, as well as privately, Henry had no problem impugning his former client's masculinity. In a letter to Warner Bros. vice president John Beck, dated October 19, 1955, Henry made the pitch: "Race Gentry, although a completely different type and far more rugged, can have the same popularity that Tab Hunter is enjoying—I guess he is enjoying it!"

33

Revenge on Tab Hunter

S uddenly, it got personal. According to several friends and associates, Henry never forgave Tab Hunter for dumping him in favor of Dick Clayton. Henry may have held the ace in Rock Hudson, now on the cusp of being the number-one box-office star in Hollywood. But the death of James Dean made Clayton a serious threat to Henry's lock on the youth market, and the two men's relationship, already strained, disintegrated as soon as they became competitors.

"They were the biggest of enemies," said actor Van Williams, who at different times in his career was repped by both men. "There was a lot of bad blood there."

It went back even further than the Tab Hunter imbroglio. Mark Miller and George Nader met Dick Clayton at a party in Studio City in 1951. Someone mentioned the colorful, flamboyant man who handled their mutual friend Rock. "I don't think much of Henry Willson as a person, but he's a good agent," Clayton told Miller.

For his part, Clayton always maintained a cordial façade when discussing Henry in public. "Henry was very successful at handling all of those wonderful looking men," Clayton said. "I guess I was never that clever." His assessment typified a circumspect, if not cagey, style of operation that defined Clayton's long, formidable career in Hollywood.

After the death of James Dean, Clayton went on to launch the careers of Burt Reynolds, Jane Fonda, and Harrison Ford, among many others. The remarkable variety of his client list effectively protected him from the "notorious" label that branded Henry's more homogenous stable. Always press-leery, Clayton granted few interviews. Always press-hungry, Henry courted reporters with dinner and wine to make sure they included his quotes in their profiles on his clients. Henry had a word for his line of work. He called it "discovering" stars. Journalists at *Life* and *Look*, however, began to use other words. They soon called it "inventing," or worse, "manufacturing."

There was also Clayton's more discreet style of providing intimate connections for his gay clients—men who, unlike Rock, found no thrill in cruising the Farmers Market at 2 A.M. For Henry, sex had always been a straightforward proposition. More the romantic, Clayton became popular in West Hollywood circles for arranging dinner dates with himself, Tab Hunter, and a lucky third party. Three men always translated as a night-out-with the boys, two men read as a date. Clayton made sure always to keep it three.

"What Clayton did wasn't all that much different from Willson," said one aspiring actor who benefited from a few dinner threesomes with the agent. "But Dick was discreet. He would disappear sometime during dessert, whereas Henry became more and more obvious. It wasn't just "three men out" with Henry; it soon turned into practically the whole football team."

Although the two men publicly professed to be friends, Henry could not resist a pointed jibe at Clayton in private, especially if he had a small audience in attendance. Rarely did Henry pass a closet door that he didn't open it to exclaim in mock surprise, "Oh, Dick Clayton's in here!"

After being fired by Tab Hunter, Henry spread an even more devastating joke about the actor, one that advertised his own sexual prowess among the boys in his stable. Whenever close friends asked how he coined the distinctive name Tab Hunter, Henry used to say he didn't need pills or medication to fall asleep after a night with the blond hunk. "He was my sleeping tab!" Henry enthused.

Hunter wasn't the only target of such remarks. As Dennis Hopper explained, "If Henry didn't have you, he would make it seem like he had."

A poolside *ad hominem* attack is one thing; squealing about a five-year-old vice-squad arrest is quite another.

For former clients of Henry Willson in the pages of *Confidential*, 1955 was a banner year. First, Rory in the May issue; then, Tab in the September issue.

The docket case no. C9848 regarding Arthur Andrew Gelien went back five long years when *Confidential* miraculously found it in 1955:

> TRANSCRIPT OF DOCKET (CRIMINAL) CASE NO. C9848. Defendant in Court having been duly arraigned for judgment and there being no legal cause why sentence should not be pronounced. Whereupon it is so ordered and adjudged by the Court this 2-6-51 that for said offense of Violation of Section 415, Penal Code, the said ARTHUR ANDREW GELIEN be imprisoned in the County Jail of the Court of Los Angeles for the term of 30 days and the said defendant be discharged at the expiration of said term. It is further ordered that the execution of sentence be suspended and that the defendant be placed on summary probation for 1 year subject to the following terms of probation. Pay $50.00 through Court. Stay granted until 2-7-51, 4 PM. Obey all laws for period of probation.

Under the banner of "Disorderly Conduct Charge Against Tab Hunter," *Confidential* obligingly translated the court-speak into the following easy-to-digest pulp:

> The real lowdown on Hunter that the buld-up boys thought was safely locked in the records of the LA vice

squad, *Confidential* file Z-84254. In it is the racy story of a night in October 1950 when the husky Hunter kid landed in jail along with some twenty-six other good-looking young men, after the cops broke up a pajama party they staged—strictly for the boys. Only a year later, Tab had zoomed to where he was being interviewed by front-rank columnists like Sidney Skolsky with whom he blushingly discussed how it feels to kiss Linda Darnell. But he was strictly an unknown on that night of October 14, 1950—just one of the cute kids who haunt the studios by day and get their kicks in an unusual fashion by night. He went by his real name, Art Gelien. And he was so far from fame then that the cops pinched him with fourteen cents in his pocket at the PJ party. The vice squad said there were two dozen guys of the gayest and a pair of women in mannish attire.

Years later, Hunter explained the incident to Andy Warhol "super-star" Brigid Polk. "A friend of mine asked me if I wanted to go to a party, and I said, 'Fine.' So we drove to the party and I walk in and I thought, Oh shit! It's a bunch of *frrruitas* doing their number. When I said doing their number I mean—they were dancing but there were more than two women dressed in mannish attire. There were guys and gals and they were dancing and you know . . . and I thought what a bore!" In Tab's version of the incident, he retreated to the kitchen to commit the innocent crime of raiding the icebox. His timing could not have been worse. Within minutes, the police raided the party.

One of the twenty-seven men who got arrested that night recalled the episode, describing it as a sedate but definitely all-male, all-gay party at 2501 Hope Street in Walnut Park, Glendale, California. *Confidential* revealed that an LAPD vice officer had gone about his usual business of "drifting in and out of Hollywood's gay bars . . . looking and listening for tips on the newest notions of the limp-wristed lads" when he overheard "a couple of lispers" lisping about the fete in Glendale.

"In fact, neighbors of the two guys who hosted the affair in their houses had supposedly gotten sick and tired of the all-boy parties at this house, and called the police," said Hunter's fellow arrestee. They wanted these guys and their parties out of the neighborhood. There was no sex, certainly. But men were dancing with each other."

In October 1950, men dancing with men in public or private was enough to violate California's Penal Code, Section 647.5, which called for the arrest of "idle, lewd, or dissolute persons or associates of known thieves." Those charges were ultimately reduced to "disturbing the peace." Mysteriously, and not by happenstance, a lawyer named Harry Weiss materialized out of the mists of the county jail to release Tab Hunter from his brief sojourn behind bars, and work his special magic with the morals arrest. Weiss was a man who would continue to play an important role in the respective lives of Tab Hunter and Henry Willson.

Confidential did its usual moralistic tisk-tisk with regard to the "swish party" and "two dozen of the gayest guys the vice squad had ever seen." They even paid Tab the compliment that he had mended his ways. "Tab seldom, if ever, goes to pajama parties anymore, but who can blame him?" the tabloid asked. "After all, he learned the hard way that you can't tell who is wearing that nightshirt next to you. It could be an understanding chap. It could also be a cop!"

Hidden away for half a decade, the Tab Hunter exposé broke into print within weeks of his giving Henry the heave-ho. If Henry did not personally contact the editors at *Confidential,* he had a useful, friendly mole in Mike Connolly to do the job.

Although never substantiated, reports have always circulated that *Confidential* was essentially an extortion operation that collected hush money from the studios. If that were the case, Warner Bros. unequivocally failed at its job to protect Tab Hunter. *Battle Cry,* his first film for the studio, went into release in the wake of the *Confidential* story. Signed to a long-term contract, Tab would make no less than six other films for the studio within the next three years, including the very A-list *Damn Yankees,* in which he played "Shoeless" Joe Hardy. Significantly, that film's story echoed Tab's own Hollywood tale: an older man makes a Faustian pact with the Devil to become a young baseball star. Tab knew all about entangled bargains. In exchange for celebrity, the homosexual Arthur Gelien became the heterosexual Tab Hunter.

Despite its success in 1958, *Damn Yankees* failed to secure Tab Hunter's place in the Hollywood firmament. Perhaps moviegoers sensed the actor brought another, unwanted dimension to the Joe Hardy role, especially when other characters said of him, "He's a strange boy." Harboring a double secret, Tab as Joe had to admit, "I don't want a really sexy lady," and he resisted Gwen Verdon's Lola with more ease than the script required.

When the *Confidential* story broke, Tab managed to keep the support of studio head Jack L. Warner. As part of the publicity machine to launch *Battle Cry,* the teen idol was named Outstanding New Personality of 1955 in an audience poll taken by the Council of Motion Pictures Organizations. The honor involved the usual press conference, but as the flashbulbs exploded, one photographer taunted him, "Smile pretty, Tab. This is for *Confidential!*"

"Oh, shit!" Tab exclaimed. He turned to leave the stage when Jack Warner stopped him to give a quick hug.

"That's OK!" Warner said. "Today's headlines, tomorrow's toilet paper."

The studio chief could have fired Tab Hunter on charges that the actor had violated his contract's morals clause. No action was taken, however, and *Battle Cry* went on to be a modest success. Decades later, *Confidential*'s influence on Hollywood careers remains a point of contention among connoisseurs of printed gossip. During the tabloid's reign of terror, Humphrey Bogart was heard to crack, "Everyone reads *Confidential.* But they deny it. They say the cook brought it into the house." But unlike the tabloid's offspring *The Star* or the *National*

Enquirer, the cook never bought *Confidential* at the supermarket. Newsstands carried it, but they weren't the most respectable newsstands. Gossip addicts had to hunt to find *Confidential.*

In fact, while *Confidential* enjoyed a circulation exceeding four million, the celebrity dirt it shoveled on a monthly basis rarely made it into the mainstream press. Editors at the *Los Angeles Examiner* and the *New York Times* considered much of the tabloid's so-called news too salacious for so-called family newspapers—and that went triple for any items regarding homosexuality.

Legends take time, and even among the gay cognoscenti, Tab Hunter's pajama-party story did not turn into folklore overnight. "At the time it appeared, *Confidential* wasn't part of the national press. It was really a local rag," said Gavin Lambert, author of *Inside Daisy Clover.* "Warner Bros. probably said the story was unfortunate, but it's not the *New York Times* or a Hearst paper. Say nothing and let it cool off."

34

Trial of the Tainted Stars

I n March 1957, Tab Hunter's single "Young Love" rose to the top of *Billboard*'s pop chart. A breathless ode to the first awakening of adolescent hormones, it failed to deliver the raucous foreplay of Elvis Presley's "All Shook Up," also released that year, but teenage girls didn't know the difference anyway. In the 1950s, they displayed a wide catholicity of taste. Pretty boys and bad boys alternated weekly on ABC's new TV rock 'n' roll show, *American Bandstand,* and were mediated by the blandest, most successful DJ in history, Dick Clark.

After the success of "Young Love," Tab's eighteen-month-old *Confidential* exposé lingered as nothing more than an errant blip in his everescalating career. However, for his old newspaper nemesis, 1957 was the year it all ended. On August 2, the *Los Angeles Times* called *Confidential*'s courtroom showdown "the spiciest trial in Hollywood."

Fred and Marjorie Meade operated Hollywood Research, Inc., which published *Confidential.* Meade was a niece of the tabloid's publisher, Robert Harrison, and theirs was a cozy setup until all three were indicted in 1957 on charges of conspiracy to commit criminal libel and print lewd literature. While Hollywood applauded the indictment, *Time* magazine reporter Ezra Goodman paused to rail against the hypocrisy that fed the mouth that trashed the stars. "Fred and Marjorie Meade lived conspicuously in a lavish Beverly Hills home and were persona grata at many a movietown gathering," wrote Goodman, who went on to imply that the Meades were on the take and, in effect, operating an extortion operation.

An all-star cast of 135 Hollywood personalities jammed Superior Judge Herbert V. Walker's courtroom for the opening day of the *Confidential* libel trial. Few were present of their own free will. The first witnesses called included Maureen O'Hara; former heavyweight boxer Buddy Baer; Josephine Dillon Gable, first wife of Clark Gable; Carol S. Hunt, author of a *Confidential* story entitled "I Was One of Father Divine's Angels"; and Tab Hunter.

Mother of a small child, O'Hara was the rare witness who relished the opportunity to discredit a *Confidential* story accusing her of making out with a Mexican boyfriend in the balcony at Grauman's Chinese Theater. For her big day in court, the Irish-born actress wore a prim, white-striped cotton dress and a straw hat to cover her most flamboyant trait: the thickest, brightest red hair this side of Dougherty County. For his part, Tab Hunter wasn't quite so eager to set the record straight in his starched seersucker suit and short blond crewcut. After all, *Confidential* had been accurate, if a bit tardy, in its report of his "disorderly conduct" arrest. Fortunately for Tab, he arrived at court under the expert guidance of "Mr. Fixit" attorney Harry Weiss, who specialized in massaging the arrests of homosexuals in the city of Los Angeles. Weiss had a way of unknotting such legal cramps and making them disappear in pretrial negotiations. Regarding *Confidential*, Tab had to sweat it out for a few days at the courthouse before Judge Walker somehow never got around to calling him to testify, then threw the entire case out on a technicality.

"I never had a *Confidential* trial," Tab Hunter claimed years later.

But an AP photo and news blurb printed on August 3, 1957, told a different story: "It's *Confidential*," the wire service declared. "Actor Tab Hunter gestures in Hollywood court where he was among many celebrities to appear at first day of *Confidential* magazine criminal libel trial. Intimate lives of many stars may be brought into the open."

There was also the *Los Angeles Times* photo that caught Tab standing next to Deputy Arne A. Knudsen at the trial: "Waiting Off Stage: Tab Hunter, one of the Hollywood stars, placed on two-hour-call status for the libel-conspiracy trial of *Confidential.*"

In one respect, the mainstream press allowed a veil of discretion to descend around Tab's unfortunate tale. One headline blared "Tab Hunter Seeks to Duck *Confidential* Trail," but in their coverage of the blond heartthrob, newspapers like the *Los Angeles Times* and the *New York Journal-American* never revealed the nature of Tab's run-in with *Confidential.* Homosexuality remained a taboo not to be mentioned in the respectable press. Other celebs weren't so lucky. Authenticated or not, hetero scandals were fair game, and the tabloid's take on these private lives found their way into the very best family newspapers: "Maureen O'Hara Cuddled in Row 35," "What Dorothy Dandridge Did in the Doods," and "Robert Mitchum—the Nude Who Came to Dinner" were just a few of the *Confidential* headlines reprinted everywhere.

Tab Hunter wasn't the only *Confidential* victim who had a story to tell but never got his day in court. The intrepid Mike Connolly alluded to the Rock/Rory cover-up in a blind item published that August in his *Hollywood Reporter* column:

> A sensational scandal may crack the *Confidential* trail wide open any minute and make the other testimony sound like tittle-tattle tossed off at a Ladies' Aid tea. To be specific: Some time ago a major studio, tipped off that the magazine had a terribly detrimental tale on tap about its top star, contacted the mag and made a deal for it to drop the story in return for a true story about another star on the lot. The mag agreed—whereupon the studio actually had one of its better scripters write the yarn! To continue: Latter star learned he had been double-crossed and immediately demanded a release from his contract. He got it. Soooo—this same star has been subpoenaed to appear in

the current hearings, and the studio execs have now made
a deal with him to keep his lip buttoned about the way
they sold him down the river—deal being the starring role
in a pic for four times his former salary!

So much drama, so little time. After a six-week trial and a hung
jury, which had deliberated for a then-record fourteen days, the
state of California dropped its charges against *Confidential* in
exchange for $10,000 and a settlement that forced the tabloid to
change its format from celeb gossip to public service. The publishers declared victory when, in fact, theirs was a clear defeat. Who
wanted to read a scandal sheet devoid of scandals? In 1958, *Confidential* publisher Robert Harrison sold the title for $25,000.

Tab Hunter escaped the trial but lost the case when he failed to
burnish his image with a dose of heterosexuality. He enjoyed a five-
year run in A-list movies, a little shorter than some careers but five
years longer than most blond, extraordinarily handsome, moder-
ately talented actors get in Hollywood. With the studio system
falling into disarray, Tab bought out his Warners contract in early
1959 with his own $100,000, then secured freelance work at
Columbia and Paramount before he went the route of most under-
employed movie stars: he put himself on the tube in 1960. Even a
recently Oscar-nominated actor like Robert Stack (*Written on the
Wind* in 1956) made a TV series, *The Untouchables*.

"The words 'TV series' were never mentioned in that contract,"
said Stack. "That would have been death for a film actor." Desi
Arnaz, whose Desilu Productions Inc. produced the show, assured
Stack, "We will make little movies, not a TV series."

Desi's show became TV history. Tab's got pulled after one season.
He wasn't the only one blindsided by the public's fickle taste. NBC
believed enough in the drawing power of the blond hunk to give him
an eponymously titled sitcom, *The Tab Hunter Show,* and cast him to
type as a playboy illustrator who creates a popular cartoon strip,
"Bachelor at Large." It first aired on September 18, 1960, and the

timing could not have been worse. A month before its network debut, UPI and AP carried the story that Tab Hunter was a dog beater! *Confidential,* if it were still being published, could have cared less. But the *New York Times,* among other major newspapers that dared not report Tab's pajama-party escapade, went to town with his latest day in court: "Tab Hunter, actor, got on the police reporter today for allegedly beating his dog with a strap for fifteen minutes and also kicking the animal while holding it by a chain leash. Sgt. W. J. Chambers said that the police had been called because 'neighbors got pretty upset about it.'"

The 1955 *Confidential* report on Tab's all-boy party remained safely tucked away in the tendrils of the gay grapevine. Headlines of "Charges Tab Hunter Beat Dog for 5 Min." were instant mainstream news reports in 1960.

Life magazine covered the trial, and Tab obliged its photographer by kissing his beloved Fritz, the ninety-pound Weimaraner that had allegedly sustained the beating. In court, there were accusations, there were even threats. One witness told of receiving a mysterious midnight phone call in which a "gruff male voice" offered $2,000 if she would keep her mouth shut. Ultimately, the jurors decided in Tab's favor. The TV-viewing public did not.

Shortly after *The Tab Hunter Show* hit the air, its star was cleared of all charges in the canine-abuse case. But the damage had been done: Tab's TV series lasted only one season, and his career went from automatic pilot into immediate nosedive. Ironically, his demise had little to do with a gay arrest, which was completely substantiated, and more to do with the dog-beating charge, which was completely unfounded.

As *The Tab Hunter Show* petered out in its one and only summer of reruns, Henry Willson experienced his own dog days that sweltering July in 1961. In typical form, he had belted down a few vodkas with friends in the outdoor patio at Frascatti's on Sunset and Crescent Heights, when someone in his expanded party thought to remember, "Hey, did you know that today is Tab Hunter's thirtieth birthday?" Tab's brother, Walter Gelien, lived in the San Fernando Valley, and word had gotten out of a big to-do there.

"You don't say?" said Henry. He repeated his "sleeping tab" story for the hundredth time and then lifted his crème de menthe chaser to the ungrateful client who got away. "Let's go to the Valley and wish him a happy birthday!" he shouted, much against his companions' better, if not more sober, judgment.

"But there was no reasoning with Henry when he was like that," said his friend Fred Winston. "He had a wild and wicked sense of humor." Since it was common knowledge among the Willson crowd that Henry had leaked the 1950 Tab Hunter arrest to *Confidential,* Winston did not look forward to his friend's trip to the Valley that evening. Then again, he wouldn't have missed a replay of the tabloid Armageddon.

When Henry walked into Walter Gelien's house, "You could have cut the air with a knife," said Winston. Tab handled the awkward moment with considerable aplomb. He appeared cordial to his old agent and shook his hands. The two men managed a long chat about nothing much in particular, while everyone else at the party shot them the occasional, apprehensive glance.

The next day, Tab's friend and agent phoned Fred Winston to express his outrage. "Dick Clayton was livid," said Winston.

After the failure of *The Tab Hunter Show,* its out-of-work star did what most former movie actors do when their TV series get yanked. He signed with a new agency, Citron Parker Chasen, which worked considerably fewer miracles than either Henry Willson or Dick Clayton. When he wasn't in Europe making *La Freccia d'oro* or *La Freccia del Destino,* Tab found time back home to star in *Ride the Wild Surf* and *Operation Bikini.*

PART NINE

Rock Hudson and Elizabeth Taylor perform a Grauman's ritual, under the watchful eye of *Giant* director George Stevens (top right), September 26, 1955.

35

Giant Step

T he back-to-back *Confidential* exposés of Tab Hunter and Rory Calhoun gave Rock Hudson a breather in 1955. But Henry knew it was time to fortify the Rock. Even a good friend in the press like Mike Connolly felt the pressure to run the occasional blind item: "A big, big male star is in the hands of blackmailers because of a silly escapade," he wrote in his May 6, 1955, column.

While the tabloids could be coaxed into temporary abeyance, Rock's fans were getting restless. Or so *Life* and *Look* reported. In response, Henry staged the ultimate publicity stunt for the Burbank booboisie and beyond. If the world wanted a heterosexual Rock Hudson, then Henry Willson would deliver them the straight goods.

On November 9, 1955, Henry stepped into his role as godfather to the groom and watched as his secretary Phyllis Gates married Rock Hudson. The Reverend Nordahl B. Thorpe officiated at the Trinity Lutheran Church, which Henry had found in the Santa Barbara phone book a few days earlier. He also picked out the bridal bouquet of white carnations, white sweetheart roses, and gardenias, a floral combo that the bride later complained was not her favorite. So little of the wedding had been to Phyllis Gates's liking, and that included the wedding dress. Rock insisted it be cocoa brown, a sure sign it was no ordinary wedding. Direct off the rack at I. Magnin's, the ensemble was indeed brown, a peau de soie with a full skirt and portrait neck. That much Henry allowed her.

In a surprise move, the agent of the hour did not fill his customary role as best man. As he had arranged for the bride, he left it to the groom to choose his best man. That honor went to Rock's boyhood friend Jim Matteoni. In Henry's opinion, Matteoni gave the affair a real personal touch.

After the fifteen-minute ceremony, the matchmaker distributed three pounds of rice to the wedding party. Henry poured most of his share down the front of Phyllis's dress, much to her distress and much to the groom's amusement. The newlyweds then retired to a suite at the Biltmore Hotel, but not to be alone. Henry phoned Louella Parsons and Hedda Hopper. He even summoned a Universal Pictures photographer to record not only the two momentous long-distance conversations but his placing the calls. Henry enjoyed having his picture taken with Phyllis, even if it meant *he* had to play *her* secretary, the phone in his hand, a glass of champagne in hers. Henry nixed all shots of Rock and him together.

As reported in the *Los Angeles Examiner* the next day, Rock told Louella, "You were right saying we were going to get married. We are married and very happy."

Phyllis agreed. "I wish you could see the beautiful diamond ring Rock has just put on my finger. I think I'm the happiest girl in the world," she told Louella.

Once the gossips had been taken care of, Henry let Rock and Phyllis phone their respective families to break the news. Henry thought of everything: to make for the perfect photo op, he booked a room with twin beds in case conservative-minded newspaper editors would object to the backdrop of a more blatant display of impending conjugal bliss.

Back on the home front, Henry kept the agency running with the help of Phyllis's replacement, Carol Lee Ladd, the same girl who, at age six months, made the historic boat trip with Henry from New York to Los Angeles via the Panama Canal. If nothing else, the firm needed someone to open the daily haul of letters. In 1955, the *Los Angeles Examiner* reported that the mailman brought to the Willson office "9000 letters per year from hopefuls," every one of whom received a typewritten response that Henry personally autographed. Earlier that year, Alan Ladd's stepdaughter married one of Willson's clients, Richard Anderson, ready for his greatest career triumph as the stolid Chief Engineer Quinn in the sci-fi classic *Forbidden Planet*. What Phyllis Gates's nuptials lacked in pomp, Carol Lee's offered in truckloads. Her wedding had been one of those circus-tent affairs, held on the lawn of her parents Holmby Hills estate, a fete distinguished, among other things, for costarring Cary Grant as an usher.

None of which added much to the couple's longevity. The Ladd/Anderson union lasted about as long as the Gates/Hudson fiasco. On April 9, 1958, Carol Lee testified in Santa Monica Superior Court that true love didn't have a lot to do with Anderson's marrying her. Even though he had just appeared as Joanne Woodward's momma's-boy lover in *The Long Hot Summer,* Anderson had higher ambitions.

"He said I wasn't doing anything for his career," Carol Lee told the judge, "and that he should have married someone who could help him more than I was doing."

Anderson took his own advice and made his next wife Katherine Thalberg, daughter of Norma Shearer and the late M-G-M wunderkind Irving Thalberg.

If Anderson's motives in marrying Carol Lee were murky, Rock's interest in Phyllis Gates looked as clear-cut as a bank ledger. The Hudson/Gates union defined the term "marriage of convenience"— until it proved inconvenient for both parties. Three years into their marriage, the couple divorced. In her 1987 autobiography, *Rock Hudson, My Husband,* Gates wrote that she had no idea the marriage was a sham or that her spouse was anything but a confirmed heterosexual.

"Was Rock a homosexual?" she wondered. "I couldn't believe that. He had always been the manliest of men. Though our lovemaking had often been brief, we had also known moments of sexual passion."

Regarding the *Confidential* threat, Phyllis claimed the tabloid had secured photos taken of Rock at a gay orgy hosted by Henry. Not one to mince words, she called it a "gang bang," and although the incident left her deeply humiliated, Phyllis insisted she could have forgiven Rock such a major transgression. As for the real marriage-breaker, Rock broached it only moments later.

"But it was nothing," Rock said of his affair with her old boss. "Henry sleeps with most of his clients."

Bob Thomas, author of several film tomes, ghostwrote the Gates book. "A lot of people doubted it," said the Hollywood-based AP reporter. "I wrote down what she told me and that was it. I was moonlighting. The less I had to do with it, the less I had to think about, the better off I am."

Phyllis Gates's version of the story won her few believers among the Hollywood cognoscenti.

"That was the biggest blow to Henry's career, that mishmash with Rock and Phyllis," said Van Williams. "It put a seal of finality on it, that it was true: Henry was gay, Rock was gay, a number of his clients were gay. He had a lot of straight clients, but they got the reputation: if you're with Henry Willson, you got to be a fag."

The public accepted the marriage as the real thing. Hollywood did not. "When Rock got married—that's when the industry just laughed itself silly," said Debbie Reynolds. "Then people started talking about it," she added, referring to Rock's homosexuality.

"Everybody knew there was something odd about that marriage," said Tony Curtis. He likened the Hudson/Gates union to Sammy Davis Jr. marrying his secretary Loray White in 1958, and divorcing her one year later. (Sammy did as he was told and married White only when Columbia's Harry Cohn threatened to ruin his career if he didn't stop dating Kim Novak.) "People will go far to have a career in Hollywood," Curtis said.

Curtis recalled that summer of 1955 with special, ripe fondness. "It was all arranged, hot and heavy," he said. "You'd go to this party and hear what was going on where and when and who was sleeping with who, and Henry was an important peg in it all."

Phyllis Gates had already been working as Henry's secretary for two years before Rock, with a nudge from Henry, popped the big question. A native of Montevideo, Minnesota, Gates worked as a stewardess on Mid-Continent Airlines, but soon developed an ear problem caused by unpressurized cabins. Her wanderlust, however, didn't end when she gave up her wings. Before she moved to Los Angeles, there were quick trips to Miami and New York. Shirley Herz, a Broadway publicist, recalled meeting Phyllis Gates and Joe Carstairs at parties in New York City, and the three women became acquaintances, if not friends.

"Phyllis was gorgeous, a knockout," said Herz, echoing the words of Tom Hatcher and several other Willson clients. "I remember her as being very popular in that Jo Carstairs set."

At least she called herself Jo.

Marion Barbara Carstairs was an elegant and adventurous cross-dressing heiress who spent her millions on beautiful women, a manse on the Bahamian island of Whale Cay, and speed boats. Lots of speed boats. Racing for Britain in the 1920s, she established herself as the fastest woman on water. It was an avocation Carstairs pursued with total dedication and regard for money. In the previous century, her grandfather Jabez Abel Bostwick had hooked up with John D. Rockefeller to buy and sell petroleum, and the two men made out like rabbits thanks to their monopolistic practices.

By the early 1950s, Carstairs was no longer racing in boat competitions, but she nonetheless continued to cut an intriguing figure in long tie, trousers and tweed sports jackets at Manhattan gatherings attended by Herz and Gates.

When Gates moved to Los Angeles in 1953, Herz stayed in touch and continued to hear ecstatic reviews from the secretary about her new job at Henry Willson Management. "She enjoyed working for Henry," said Herz. "Phyllis loved show business and being at the center of all that."

Herz's own business eventually took her to the West Coast, where her client Kaye Ballard was performing at the Mocambo. (In her act, the singer-comedienne joked about Willson's taste in names, coining a few of her own, including "Grid Iron, Cuff Links, Plate Glass, and Bran Muffin.") After one performance, the two women decided to take an early-morning breakfast among the fruit-and-produce stands at the Farmer's Market on Fairfax and Third Avenue. "It must have been two o'clock in the morning, and there was Rock Hudson," said Herz. "He was cruising, looking to pick up some guy. He was very open about it."

A few days later, Herz went to a going-away party of sorts at Phyllis's apartment, on Fairfax down from Laurel Canyon. Gates wasn't leaving Los Angeles, but she would soon be saying farewell to her small, incommodious apartment on the busy thoroughfare. To commemorate her move to the Hollywood Hills, Phyllis invited Herz and a few other women to have brunch at her Fairfax place. The publicist had heard the gossip about Rock Hudson marrying Henry Willson's secretary, but she found it difficult to believe. "I knew Rock's story," Herz explained.

Much to Herz's surprise, Phyllis confirmed the wedding rumors when she invited her publicist friend to see Rock's house at 9151 Warbler Place. (In *My Husband, Rock Hudson,* however, Gates refers to the address as Sparrow Lane, which does not exist.) A tortuous drive north of Sunset Boulevard, Warbler is one of many so-called "bird streets" in Los Angeles that are squeezed between West Hollywood to the south and the pricier confines of Beverly Hills to the west. Rock bought the house prior to making *Magnificent Obsession,* and had he anticipated the film's success, he might have purchased a grander, more suitably palatial manse to the west. Only four rooms, the single-story ranch house on Warbler showcased none of the usual gauche extravagance of a movie star's home and instead reflected Rock's hypermasculine taste: wood-beamed ceilings, a picture window, an exposed brick wall, peg-and-groove floors, and, if that weren't butch enough, Rock made a rugged ensemble of redwood lawn chairs the centerpiece of his living room. Herz found it a relaxed, cozy place for her New York émigré friend, who never looked more content. As the two women drank coffee under the pine trees, their conversation took its natural turn to the owner of the hillside house. Herz kept referring to what a great "setup" and "arrangement" her friend had living with Rock Hudson: There would be no rent to pay, no bills. And despite its rather Spartan décor, the ranch house on the hill easily outclassed Gates's apartment on noisy Fairfax Avenue.

Finally, as the pine cones fell and the squirrels scampered, Phyllis let it be known. "I'm going to marry Rock," she said.

"Why would you do that?" Herz blurted out in disbelief.

"I think it would be fun," she replied.

As Herz put it, "Phyllis couldn't tell me she was *in love* with Rock. She knew I would have laughed in her face."

The stories about Phyllis and Rock's impending marriage had already made it back to her old party circuit in Gotham where two of her friends, Bill Hemmer and Gilbert Parker, followed the saga in near-disbelief. Before Phyllis moved to the West Coast, the three of them spent many hours over dinner gossiping about their mutual interest: show business. Hemmer worked at the Theater Guild, a prestigious producing organization that brought the plays of Maxwell Anderson and Philip Barry to Broadway. Parker was a junior agent at MCA, where he sold the foreign rights to plays and novels. (Later, he would become a William Morris agent and represent such playwrights as Terrence McNally, Beth Henley, and A. R. Gurney, until his retirement in 2001.)

According to Parker, Phyllis knew that he and Hemmer were gay. "We were open and gossipy with her," he said. A few of their stories focused on Rock Hudson, Tab Hunter, and other gay clients of the "notorious" agent Henry Willson. "In gay circles, everyone knew that Rock was homosexual. We figured she had to know. Phyllis was too smart not to know what she was getting into," said Parker.

When Phyllis told Hemmer she was marrying the matinee idol, their conversations moved to the next level. "Bill talked to her about

Rock's being gay," said Parker. "He quizzed her, 'What are you doing? Do you know what you're getting into by marrying this man?' "

Coincidence or not, her response replicated what Shirley Herz heard. "Yes, why not?" Phyllis Gates reportedly told Hemmer. "Rock and I have a lot of fun together."

Many observers wrote off the Gates/Hudson marriage as strictly business. There were some friends, however, who saw it as something more. "Phyllis and Rock did have a sexual relationship," said Willson's client John Carlyle. He and his boyfriend took trips to Palm Springs with Rock and Phyllis prior to their marriage. "Although Rock was gay, he very much liked the company of women. He shared that quality with Henry," said Carlyle. Rock loved to laugh, and any little remark could trigger uncontrolled spasms of giggles from him and Phyllis. "You wouldn't know what they were laughing about," said Carlyle. "But they laughed so much it became annoying. You felt excluded from their company."

Whatever Rock and Phyllis lacked in a big formal wedding, Henry supplied a year later with a black-tie party in his own backyard. The official purpose was to celebrate Rock and Phyllis's first anniversary; in reality, the November event capped an intense whirlwind publicity campaign to promote *Giant*. It would be a dizzy, numbing schedule.

On September 26, 1956, director George Stevens watched over Rock Hudson and Elizabeth Taylor as the two stars enshrined their shoe and hand prints in the refined cement of Grauman's Chinese Theater. Two weeks later, they all flew to New York City for the film's East Coast premiere at the Roxy Theater in Times Square. Taylor had made the film while married to Michael Wilding (a Warners press release cruelly identified the unemployed actor as her "chauffeur" for the Texas stint of the shoot), but she attended the October 10 opening with her soon-to-be husband number three, Mike Todd. The event was telecast, and from the red carpet Jack Warner insulted the TV emcee by asking, "Who are you?" When Jayne Meadows identified herself, the studio chief told one of his typical, unforgivable jokes—"I knew you when you were just a field"—and then promised, "Now that I know who you are I'll remember you."

Wearing a glistening tiara over her shellacked, bouffant hairdo, Meadows didn't have much better luck chatting up Rock, who arrived with Phyllis in a satin halter top and mink stole. "I've never heard such screams than when you got out of the car," Meadows gushed into the hand-held mike. "I don't know, Jayne," replied Rock, his banter not much improved from Halloween night 1949 when he dressed up as an Oscar and Louella Parsons first inter- viewed him. In New York, Henry's date for the *Giant* premiere was an especially giddy Natalie Wood, who, sporting a new pixie cut, did her best to look like Audrey Hepburn. With his usual bluster, Henry was unusually magnanimous. "Let's get off and let the *Giant* stars on!" he told Meadows, who proceeded to misidentify Joanne Woodward as Dennis Hopper's wife.

Inside the Roxy Theater, Rock wanted to leave when the audience took to booing and hissing his performance. "It was terrifying," he said. Only later did he realize that people were reacting viscerally to the char- acter's sexism and racism. "Not to me, but to Bick!" Rock realized.

A week later, the Los Angeles premiere on October 17 dwarfed the East Coast affair. Despite reports that Natalie Wood would attend again, this time with Elvis Presley, the eighteen-year-old actress instead sported Dennis Hopper on her arm and blond highlights in her hair. Going solo for the night, Henry played third wheel to Rock and Phyllis (same stole, different dress), who looked mildly peeved that her old boss had been seated next to her in Grauman's Chinese Theater. At least the air inside didn't induce nausea. In its first of many attempted rehabilitations, Hollywood Boulevard had been newly resurfaced with asphalt in honor of the *Giant* premiere, and the stench of tar nearly KO'd festivities on the red carpet, where Art Linkletter gamely tried to conduct interviews with Groucho Marx, Jerry Lewis, and a humbled Clark Gable, who had lobbied, and been rejected, for the role of Bick Benedict.

The premiere boasted the "longest red carpet in premiere history," all 192 feet of it, and seventy red, white, and blue searchlights. At the postpremiere party, Natalie Wood broke away from Dennis Hopper long enough to chat up Tab Hunter and his new boyfriend, Anthony Perkins, who shared a table with their respective female dates. Throughout the evening, Rock and Henry did their best to shut up and smile whenever anyone praised James Dean's performance. They both hated the dead actor. On the set of *Giant,* Dean had made fun of Rock's phony movie-star name and often joked about it with the crew. "Just call me Rack!" Dean had insisted.

Worse, it was Dean who had made the *Giant* company aware of Rock Hudson's homosexuality. "Jimmy told me that Rock was gay," said Dennis Hopper. "We were shooting in Marfa, Texas, and I didn't believe him. I was eighteen. What did I know?"

On November 9, three weeks after the *Giant* premiere at Grauman's, Henry hosted the backyard fete that celebrated Rock and Phyllis's wedding anniversary. He knew to strike while the good reviews were still hot, and he spared no expense: the circus tent, the Bernie Richard orchestra, the Chasen's food, the dance floor over the pool, the works. Henry even instructed the couple of honor to greet guests at the house entrance. "Just like a wedding reception," Phyllis recalled.

It didn't matter if people came to congratulate them or laugh behind their backs. They were the right people. As Henry kept telling Rock and Phyllis, it wasn't just any old agent who could put together a guest list that brought out M-G-M's Dore Schary, 20th Century–Fox's Buddy Adler, Warners' Bill Orr, or the producers David O. Selznick, William Goetz, Mervyn LeRoy, and Albert Zugsmith, who was already onboard to produce Rock's next movies, *Written on the Wind* and *The Tarnished Angels*. Before any of the guests arrived, Henry counted the names on his fingers. More were to arrive. The real glitz came courtesy of old friends— stars like Ginger Rogers, who had been part of the Puppets crowd, and Barbara Stanwyck, whom Henry helped rep at the Zeppo Marx Agency, and his former beard date, Jennifer Jones. For added measure, race-car driver Stirling Moss came with Mrs. and Mrs. Gary Cooper.

Stanwyck told Rock, "I saw *Giant,* and you were the only actor who aged convincingly."

After Rock exhausted the receiving line, Henry hit him with more party favors. The evening's guest of honor may have been one of the biggest stars in the world, but at that moment he could only nod and smile as Henry introduced him to a few older, dowdily dressed women. On his first wedding anniversary, Rock Hudson took turns dancing with every available mother on the premises, which meant everything to the sons who were Henry Willson clients. "My mom was a washerwoman and Henry made sure she was treated like royalty that night," said Glen Jacobson. "She never forgot Rock's asking her to dance."

In his *Hollywood Reporter* column, Mike Connolly duly noted that everyone "from Buddy Adler to Al Zugsmith was there," and that the host took care to rope off the pool so "nobody pushed Diana Dors in, although several would have liked to." Connolly hated the blond Brit bombshell ever since she defended that "commie" Charlie Chaplin, and he took memorable aim when he wrote, "Up the Hammer and Sickle, girl, and gather ye those good old Yanqui dollars while ye may."

Connolly knew how to swing a good quip—and when to shut up. He failed to mention his going to Henry's follow-up party on Stone Canyon Drive the next day when, in typical form, Henry served the Chasen's leftovers to his B-list of boys not invited to the previous night's affair.

36

Vampira among the Ivy

Amidst the soporific whirl of the movie capital—red-carpet premieres at Grauman's, boozy dinners of chili at Chasen's, costume parties at Ciro's, unlikely couples falling in love at Willson's—there hovered that one-time-only event that nearly everyone missed seeing and nobody could stop talking about.

Shortly before the Hudson/Gates nuptials took place in November 1955, Henry found himself publicly targeted for being homosexual—and by an unlikely source. Long before Edward Gorey, Elvira, or *The Munsters* recycled Charles Addams's brand of macabre camp, Maila Nurmi (a.k.a. Vampira) gave her own unique, cinched-in-the-waist, radically-arched-eyebrow take on the undead, playing the ghoul-hostess for a late-night series of horror movies on Los Angeles local TV. She later reprised her sculpted creature of the night for a cameo in *Plan 9 from Outer Space*.

Despite such moments of fame, Nurmi never recovered from feeling unappreciated in Hollywood. "My real talent was as a comic, a rubber face," Nurmi recalled, twisting her high-cheek-boned visage into a weird contortion of moveable muscle and fat. "Like Jim Carrey," she added, her lips suddenly pressed back into shape as a human mouth.

Although Nurmi claimed to have had brief, close friendships with James Dean and Tony Perkins, she admittedly called herself a "disgrace" in Hollywood. "I was somebody you weren't seen publicly with. They used to call me 'Vampira, character about town.'"

Shortly after Dean's death, Nurmi certified her outsider status by claiming to talk with the actor's ghost. "Mostly he comes to me through the radio," she told people. The actress wasn't joking when she confessed, "I had too reckless a sense of humor, too adolescent."

In one practical joke, performed for the benefit of Tony Perkins, Nurmi took over a vacant penthouse apartment in the Rossmore (then home to Mae West) and invited the impressionable, in-the-closet actor to dinner there. According to Nurmi's orchestrations, one woman wandered around naked with eyes painted on her breasts while a male acquaintance stood on his head and masturbated. As Nurmi put it, "Anything to shock Tony! Because he was such a geeky farm boy."

At least the prank took place in the privacy of the Rossmore.

Her taunting of Henry Willson was more public, carried out in his own front yard for all his neighbors to witness. Nurmi claimed she had no problem finding a few gay friends to help carry out her prank against the agent. The Vampira persona may have been a joke, but its camp notoriety won Nurmi friends among the attendants who parked cars for the restaurants that lined La Cienega Boulevard in West Hollywood. "Those boys hated Willson," she recalled. "He promised them stardom, used them, and then threw them aside. His tires were always getting slashed up and down La Cienega."

Nurmi conceived the midnight pasquinade all by herself but had to enlist the help of a few car-jockey pranksters to haul a large bed mattress to 1536 Stone Canyon Road. There in the darkness of night, her crew placed the mattress over the well-watered ivy in Henry's front lawn, and permitting herself the coup de grâce, she pinned a Pond's cold cream advertisement to it.

"They ordered the stuff by the caseload up there," said Nurmi, referring to Henry's preferred mode of sexual lubrication. The next morning, neighbors retrieving their soggy copies of the *Times* and

Examiner had no clue why a Pond's sign had taken up residence in Henry's front yard. It was a very inside joke, but Henry wasn't laughing.

According to Nurmi, the mattress contretemps resulted in his taking out a Mob contract on her life. Which came not so cheaply, at $2,000 in 1955 dollars. Nurmi admitted she had no pressing need to incur the considerable wrath of Henry Willson. "It was just my nature," she said. And besides, he infuriated her with his "boring, bland" boy clients who were the antithesis of her rebel idol, James Dean. "Henry Willson represented the worst of 1950s conformity," she said.

After a few tense days, Henry called off his hit man, a rapprochement brokered by attorney Harry Weiss, Nurmi said. By 1955, the wiry, dwarflike, hyperkinetic lawyer had begun to rival Henry Willson as the most high-profile homosexual on the Sunset Strip. His trademark was a huge panama hat worn at any time of day. But more than his resemblance to a walking mushroom, Weiss became known as "Mr. Fixit" for getting several arrested homosexuals out of jail. Strangely enough, Weiss may have been responsible for putting some of them there.

David Mixner, a prominent human-rights activist and author of the book *Stranger Among Friends,* found Weiss to be one of the profession's more colorful, less reputable lawyers. "The rumor for years in the Los Angeles gay community was that Harry Weiss built up his law practice by alerting the LAPD to gay parties and gatherings, and then being at the station house handing out his card to the prominent group of fearful men. Weiss, in turn, got them released from jail."

Weiss always poo-pooed his "Mr. Fixit" reputation. "The top fee I ever charged a gay client was $250," he claimed. "The smallest part of our business is the gay business. It doesn't amount to 2 percent of our total volume." The attorney made his big money in other ways. In addition to Tab Hunter, his fans in trouble included a bigwig on LA's alcoholic beverage commission, who got picked up one night for frequenting a bathhouse that retained Weiss as its counsel. Weiss obligingly helped out the terrified commissioner, who consequently made the lawyer cocounsel on several liquor licenses issued by his department. Many restaurants on La Cienega Boulevard soon had to pay a hefty percentage of their bar take to Weiss.

"Harry took care of things behind the scenes, and made them disappear," said one associate. "He had relationships with many of the judges, and was kept on retainer by at least one movie studio. He was as well-connected in Los Angeles as Roy Cohn was in New York. But where Cohn was a bully, Harry was a bon vivant who helped people. In the process, he happened to enlarge his pocketbook." For the 1957 *Confidential* trial, Tab Hunter retained the lawyer as his counsel, and many observers credited Weiss for being the major reason Judge Herbert Walker never called the actor to the witness stand.

Vampira was another story. Weiss's terms for the unwritten agreement between Maila Nurmi and Henry Willson were simple: she would be allowed to continue breathing provided the late-night raids on Henry's front lawn, or any other orchestrated displays of public humiliation, ceased.

Malicious whim may not have been the only reason Nurmi chose to disturb the ivy at 1536 Stone Canyon Drive. "Maila wanted to go out with James Darren and she thought Henry was standing in the way," said Troy Donahue's girlfriend Nan Morris. "She retaliated with the mattress and cold cream."

37

Importing John Saxon

James Ercolani left his home town of Philadelphia to move West, get a new name, and become a movie star. After he came to Los Angeles in 1954, he got his new name. The other part came later.

Henry told the soulful boy with the thick Philly accent and even thicker eyebrows that "Ercolani" was too many letters, too unpronounceable, too peculiar. So he gave him the name Troy Darren, the "Troy" part recycled from Rory Calhoun's discarded name, and also the name of the New York town where "Uncle" Sam Wilson had lived and died. The Philly teenager came up with Darren all by himself. Or so he said. "I took it from Darrin's sports-car shop on Sunset," the actor recalled. But in the end he dropped the "Troy" in favor of the less exotic "James Darren." So much for Henry's original contribution.

"I never felt comfortable with the name Troy," said Darren. "I wanted to keep my first name." Henry didn't object. Maybe he didn't really care. Ercolani/Darren came to Henry via another client, Carmen Orrico, the fellow Italian-American whom Henry had Anglicized as John Saxon. Henry originally intended John to be Rand Saxon, but on the recommendation of a Screen Actors Guild representative in London, who informed him that in Britain the word "randy" meant "horny," Henry retired the moniker from his supply chest of names. Orrico claimed Saxon was his own idea, having borrowed it from the name of a Brooklyn hockey team. "It sounds strong," he told Henry.

John Saxon and James Darren knew Maila Nurmi from hanging out together at Googie's, an all-night eatery next to Schwab's drugstore on Sunset and Crescent Heights. While Jack Kerouac, Neal Cassady, and Allen Ginsberg headed up the Lost Generation in San Francisco and Greenwich Village, Googie's was as close as Los Angeles got to the Beat scene, with one important difference. Everyone at Googie's wanted to be a movie star, not a poet. The crowd would meet at Schwab's, drink coffee, then head over to Googie's to get something to eat around midnight when the drugstore closed. It was a ritual. "Schwab's was overlit and noisy," said Nan Morris. "You'd leave there and go to Googie's, which was dark, moodier. There was a long banquette and booth in the back. When he died, everybody called it the Jimmy Dean booth."

In or out of her vampire drag, Maila Nurmi liked to hold court there after making a quick tour of the crowded back patio, which was made even smaller with too many tables, chairs, and rubber plants. To give the overall clutter some focus, a palm tree struggled to find the moonlight through an opening in the cracked fiberglass roof. Before death turned James Dean into the patron saint of teenage angst, Nurmi and company contributed to the actor's bad-boy rep by inspiring newspaper reporters to tag them the "night watch" and the "crew of creeps." As one Hollywood columnist summed it up, "What gaucheries Dean doesn't think up, these sycophants do." The writer could have had in mind Vampira's mattress trick.

James Darren remembered her with more politeness. "Maila Nurmi was an interesting lady," he said. "I spent time with her. I wasn't dating her. We had fun." He didn't recall Henry's warning him off the woman known as Vampira. "If she was my gal, which she wasn't, Willson would have had no reason for us not to date."

Googie's itself left the bigger, if not more lasting, impression on the teenager from Philadelphia. "It was like Vegas during the Rat Pack era," Darren said of the *jeunesse dorée* on Harleys that gathered there. Everyone from Natalie Wood and Nick Adams to James Dean and Pier Angeli might show up on a given night, which is why all the other potential bobbysoxer heartthrobs followed. Before he had been Willsonized with a new name, Ercolani made the pilgrimage to Googie's, and it was there that he met John Saxon, who bragged about being repped by the famous Henry Willson. The two teenagers formed an Italian-American diaspora of two in their new LA digs, and Saxon soon promised to introduce his new Philly friend to the agent who invented Rock Hudson.

"We were both teenagers and Italian, and I was shy," said Darren. Saxon had made the trip west, from Brooklyn, only a few months earlier. In his typical catch-as-catch-can approach to discovering talent, Henry spotted the teenage boy's photograph in *True Story* magazine, which made the rounds that year at the *Photoplay* annual awards show. Henry fell in love with what he saw on the cover and soon found his way to Mr. and Mrs. Orrico, who had no qualms about putting their seventeen-year-old son on an airplane to Hollywood to be groomed into a movie star under the tutelage of an agent they did not know.

Saxon remembered his bicoastal transformation from Brooklyn kid to teen heartthrob. "Fools go where angels fear to tread. The next thing I knew, my mom and dad were signing agreement contracts, because I was still underage," he said. Henry's assistant Pat Colby was in the office the day the Brooklyn boy arrived in LA. "He looked like a twelve-year-old Sophia Loren," said Colby. Within three weeks, Henry's latest *objet trouvé* received optimum exposure: a meeting with Rock Hudson's savior at Universal, Ed Muhl, followed by a studio contract, and a supporting role as a juvenile delinquent in the film *Running Wild*.

Fresh from the mean asphalt of New York, John Saxon marked a new make on the assembly line of male starlets. He wasn't one of the wholesome pretty boys. He brought to Henry's oeuvre a street-edge that made Marlon Brando look vulnerable and turned James Dean's defiance into soulful mush. No sooner did Universal put him under contract than Twentieth Century–Fox expressed interest and planned a major screen test. "But Universal, which was always rather economically minded, had me just do a scene for them," said Saxon. At $150 a week for forty weeks, John Saxon now took home more money than his father.

James Ercolani's father would have to wait another year to experience the same economic indignity. After Saxon introduced Henry to his new friend from Googie's, the newly renamed James Darren made several visits to the agent, whom he remembered as the one generous fountainhead in an otherwise uncaring land of strangers.

"Henry Willson was the guy who had the corner bar or grocery store. You'd go in and talk with him and he'd give you advice and help you out, if you were in a bad way," said Darren. Henry paid bills that needed being paid, he made loans that he never expected to get back. "That's the kind of guy I remember Henry to be," said Darren.

But the two men didn't click, at least not the way the seventeen-year-old Carmen Orrico clicked for Henry. "Evidently, Henry was never, 'Jesus! You're going to be a movie star!' That never happened," said Darren. "I'm sure that's why I wasn't a client."

In addition to making the VP rounds at studios, Henry liked to throw prospective clients into a social pool to see how they swam, especially on a full stomach. "I went to the Universal commissary one day with Willson," said Darren. "He knew how to work the field. People were discovered on looks in those days. Executives or producers would then call his office and ask him who he was with at lunch that day."

After one lunchtime tour, Henry told Darren, "Now let's wait and see what happens." Sometimes it happened, sometimes it didn't.

Darren remembered meeting Henry's favorite teen date material, Natalie Wood and Margaret O'Brien, at the Warners commissary. The two girls were smitten, but unfortunately, the studio executives never picked up on their hormonal rush. Four months later, his dormant career unofficially dead in Hollywood, James Darren returned to the East Coast, where he signed with the agent Joyce Selznick, who had launched Tony Curtis's career. In a very Henry Willson turn of events, she insisted that Columbia Pictures sign Darren to a contract without so much as a screen test. "You look at him and you buy him," she told the East Coast talent rep.

"That's the way it was done in those days," said Darren. "Joyce Selznick loved me and that's what it took."

People joked that Henry Willson fell in love with a different man every day of the week. For his considerable expenditure on a client's upkeep, Henry more often than not demanded interest on the loan. When sober, he might expect sex as a matter of course for his professional services. After a few drinks, the demands could acquire a theatrical flair that often outshone his clients' gift for the thespian art. On one such evening, Henry's representation of Tom Hatcher ended when the beautiful blond, green-eyed actor refused his sexual advances. (L. Q. Jones and Paul Nesbitt claimed that similar events led to their departure from the Willson firm.) Henry invited Hatcher to his bedroom. Gone were the days when he needed his lawn's sprinkler system to get a young man out of his clothes.

"You can give me a blowjob," Henry told Hatcher. "Or I can fuck you."

Hatcher didn't think much of either offer.

Rejected, Henry did not shrug his shoulders and call it a night, as he was reported to do with Jones and Nesbitt. ("He apologized profusely," said Nesbitt.) His thinking fortified by a pint of vodka, Henry took Hatcher's rejection as an act of sedition and he launched a reprisal worthy of a scene from Tennessee Williams. Henry may not have been an actor, but he knew how to create a scene better than most he repped.

"You think you're so good-looking," he told Hatcher. "I'll show you somebody who is much better looking than you are."

Henry then ordered Hatcher to get in his black Cadillac, and he drove the recalcitrant client to an apartment building in Hollywood where, as Hatcher recalled, Henry barged his way into one of the apartments. He pushed aside a bewildered roommate and did not bother to knock on the bedroom door.

"Get in here!" Henry shouted. There slept a dark-haired seventeen-year-old boy, and for the benefit of Henry's newest ex-client, he tore the sheets off the bed.

"Now, that's good-looking!" Henry said, pointing to the bed's rudely awakened occupant. Hatcher knew the boy as John Saxon.

"Yes, he is very good-looking," Hatcher agreed.

Saxon somehow avoided Henry's advances. But mission accomplished, Henry disappeared in his car, leaving Hatcher to find his own way to home and fame. In time, he found both in author Arthur Laurents. In the late 1950s, Laurents was working as a scriptwriter at M-G-M along with Gore Vidal, who had quickly developed a love-hate relationship with Hollywood. He hated the business, loved the boys. "One must admit at least the hustlers out here are good," Vidal told Laurents. "All clean-cut young athletes. Straight, of course, but the boys will do whatever you want for twenty-five dollars an hour."

Vidal, more the sexual adventurer, knew that Laurents, more the romantic, was looking for a husband, and so suggested a trip to the William B. Riley men's store, which boasted a new manager who came with emerald eyes, open smile, and a perfect 40R jacket. Having graduated from beer trucks and Henry Willson, Tom Hatcher now operated the Beverly Hills boutique. Small world. When Henry couldn't find what he wanted at Carroll's Men's Store, he sent his boys over to Riley's to complete their physical makeover, all courtesy of the agent's pocketbook. If waiting on Henry's new boys chafed at Hatcher's dignity, he didn't have to suffer it long. Shortly after their semi-impromptu meeting at Riley's, Laurents whisked Hatcher off to New York City, where the two men have lived happily ever after.

As for John Saxon, he went on to busy himself with several TV gigs before he made the big-screen comedy *This Happy Feeling*, which starred Debbie Reynolds and one of Henry's other, newer boys. If Saxon couldn't miss as the "next Marlon Brando," in Henry's opinion, then his male costar was the "next Tab Hunter"— also known as Troy Donahue.

38

Troy Donahue, Again

While Mrs. Phyllis Gates Hudson professed total ignorance, Merle Johnson Jr. knew the real story behind Rock
Hudson's marriage to Henry Willson's secretary. Little
did it matter that Johnson lived three thousand miles away on the
campus of Columbia University, where he was a journalism major.

"I didn't sign with Henry until I had gotten my own contract
with Universal," said Merle Johnson, whom Henry rechristened
Troy Donahue after dusting off the name for a third and final go-
round. "Henry was still very well-connected in Hollywood, but I
didn't want to be indebted to him. He had this reputation."

The Hudson/Gates marriage gave *Life* and *Look* the opportunity
to advertise the star's reported heterosexuality. It also certified
Henry Willson's status as a notorious homosexual in Hollywood's
inner circles. Which is why Merle Johnson Jr. decided it best to
secure his own contract at Universal Pictures in 1957—as if that
would stop the incipient rumors later that year when he joined the
Willson agency as Troy Donahue.

"Troy Donahue was a bright fixture on the Meat Rack via Henry
Willson, and everyone who knew, knew," claimed James Dean's friend
John Gilmore. There were the usual stories. After Troy and Rock
appeared in *The Tarnished Angels*, Mark Miller and George Nader
asked their friend about the new blond in Henry Willson's stable.

"Great cocksucker, tiny dick," Rock reported.

Troy heard the gay rumors but brushed them aside. "People confused me with Tab Hunter," he said. "His being gay created problems for me and that's where the stories started." That pair of names, Tab and Troy, made them so interchangeable in the public consciousness that the two men eventually played along, and signed each other's name when fans asked for autographs. Rarely did anyone ever ask them to correct the error.

Despite their parallel careers, Tab and Troy did not meet face to face until 1996 when *Vanity Fair* brought them together on the sands of Malibu for a photo session with Annette Funicello, Frankie Avalon and other stars of the surf-and-turf school of filmmaking. Photographer David LaChapelle shot Tab as he struck a surfer pose atop a lifeguard stand. Troy didn't get off so easily. LaChapelle directed him to leap through the air holding a pineapple over his head. Although *Vanity Fair* called the shoot "Beach Party Kids," Troy always took pride that, unlike all the other over-the-hill celebs present that day, his movie resumé remained unblemished in at least one respect. "I never made a beach-party movie," said Troy Donahue.

The group portrait wound up in the magazine's annual spring Hollywood issue, which is pretty much where it ended career-wise for Troy, who died of a heart attack in 2001 after taking the arthritis painkiller Vioxx. He had finished touring in a stage production of *Bye, Bye Birdie*. (Too old to play Birdie, the show's parodic stand-in for Elvis Presley, Donahue essayed the Paul Lynde role of the put-upon father, Harry McAfee.) Troy Donahue had come full circle. Malibu was also where it all began.

In 1956, the nineteen-year-old Merle Johnson Jr. and his eleven-year-old sister, Eve, drove cross-country from New York in the family's Chevrolet Bel Air and were excited to begin a new life in California. Merle had two goals: to swim every day in the Pacific and be a movie star. He and Eve started the trip with their mother, Edith, but she had to leave them halfway in Chattanooga, Tennessee. When her phlebitis flared up, the widow Johnson couldn't ride another mile and needed to rest a few days before making the emergency switch from car to TWA.

The Johnson family's transmigration took place at about the time that Jerry Lee Lewis married his thirteen-year-old cousin-niece, Myra Gale Brown. According to Eve Johnson, she and her brother got the peculiar impression that as soon as their mother left them, America's motel keepers eyed the older brother and younger sister warily at every stop after Chattanooga. Their first day in California, Merle and Eve went straight to Malibu, dove into the Pacific, and spent the night in a motel overlooking the ocean.

From there, it just sort of happened. One afternoon, the director William Asher spotted the Columbia U. dropout in a beachside diner just up the road from the Colony. Asher had already directed a few episodes of *I Love Lucy*, but he must have been thinking ahead to his future film projects like *Beach Party, Bikini Beach, Muscle Beach Party, Beach Blanket Bingo,* and *How to Stuff a Wild Bikini* when he spotted the six-foot-three sun-bleached blond chomping on a cheeseburger, the waves of the Pacific Ocean crashing for effect in the background. Before the lambent Merle could finish the day's quotient of fried food, Asher offered him a screen test at Universal.

By now, the ailing Mrs. Johnson had recovered enough to finish the trip to LA, and, eager to celebrate her son's new destiny, she bought him a red MG. Merle Jr. also celebrated by going off on one of his soon-to-be-notorious benders, and, tanked on too much gin, he drove Mom's birthday present off the road and into the Malibu canyon below. The next day, when he should have been making love to a camera lens, Merle sat in a hospital bed watching his right leg mend under a hunk of white plaster.

Merle's Hollywood ambitions might have ended there if not for his new Malibu girlfriend, Fran Bennett, who had recently joined the Henry Willson roster of talent. She had just come off her first significant film role, and as it happened, her very last one. *Giant* provided work for a whole trove of Willson clients, including Jane Withers and Nick Adams, all of whom rode in on the coattails of Rock Hudson. Fran Bennett, at age twenty, played Judy Benedict, the screen daughter of Rock and the twenty-five-year-old Elizabeth Taylor. It was pure typecasting: Born Fran Benedum, the actress was a Texas-oil heiress, whom Henry thought of as the next Debbie Reynolds.

Fran and Henry shared a deep belief in career reincarnation. "My friend Merle could be the next James Dean," she told her agent. Like a few thousand other teenagers, Fran's friend Merle had taken to wearing a red jacket in homage to James Dean. A year after the release of *Rebel without a Cause,* young men couldn't break that red-jacket habit any more than kids gave up *Davey Crockett* coonskin caps. James Dean may have been dead, but that didn't stop Henry from holding him personally responsible for the unfortunate success of Dick Clayton.

"The red jacket was a mistake," Troy recalled. But if Henry blanched at the sight of Fran's new boyfriend wearing a dead man's costume to the Luaia restaurant for his big interview, he kept it to himself. Fran held Merle's trembling knee under the table with one hand as she twirled the tiny paper umbrella in her fruit drink with the other. Henry did most of the talking as he waited for the two kids to relax. He envisioned the young lovers together in a *Photoplay* layout with photos shot at the beach and in a convertible and sipping malts at the soda fountain. With those images floating in their two blond heads, he also entertained the couple with Hollywood war stories: how Judy Turner came to his office one day twenty years ago, how he renamed her Lana, and how she had bought the Luaia so that her then-husband, Steve Crane, would have something to do.

"I was so impressed with Henry taking me to the Luaia," said Troy, "but not as impressed as a year later when Crane's daughter, Cheryl, stabbed Johnny Stompanato in her mother's bedroom."

"The Luaia was one of Troy's favorite places," said his sister, Eve, who fondly recalled double dates in the Beverly Hills restaurant with her brother's *77 Sunset Strip* costar Edd "Kookie" Byrnes, and his kid sister, Jo-Ann. (Byrnes later signed with the Henry Willson Agency, but like many other male clients, he denied the association.)

Merle resisted Henry's immediate overtures to sign with him. "It wasn't easy," he explained. The agent exuded his easy, avuncular charm and asked a dozen questions as if he expected to hear a dozen cogent answers. "Henry appeared genuinely interested, which was rare, if not unique, in Hollywood." The powerful agent asked about the Johnson family and expressed his condolences that Merle Johnson Sr., head of the motion-pictures department at General Motors, had passed away five years earlier. "My father was also in show business," Henry offered. It was then that a second hand joined Fran's atop her friend's bony knee, which had stopped trembling long ago.

Henry wanted to sign the blond orphan, and he tapped the swizzle stick against his glass of crème de menthe. "It's just that easy," he said of landing Merle a studio contract. But Fran Bennett's boyfriend had other ideas.

"Henry could not have been nicer. He wanted to take me on this round of interviews at the studios. But I wanted to make my own way," said Troy, who had his concerns. "Henry was powerful, but he had this reputation . . ."

With some help from Fran, Merle Johnson Jr. managed to secure his own six-month contract at Universal, a feat that only whetted Henry's appetite. A few days later the starmaker phoned the studio to ask about the well-being of their new contract player.

"Merle Johnson's not picking up her line," said the receptionist.

Her?! Henry knew. "That name has got to go!"

No sooner had he signed Universal's newest contractee than Henry arranged a meeting with the studio executives to come up with a new name for Merle Johnson. "I was off in this corner while Henry and a few men tossed out suggestions. At first they had Paris, the lover of Helen of Troy, in mind," he said. "But I guess they thought they couldn't name me Paris Donahue because there was already a Paris, France and Paris, Illinois."

Finally, Henry turned to him and, thinking back to his first meeting with the ex-con Frank Durgin, he exclaimed, "You're Troy, Troy Donahue!"

Let everybody else joke about the Henry Willson names. For Merle Johnson Jr., being called Troy Donahue meant he had been blessed and delivered to the Goober's masses. Or as he explained, "Troy Donahue was a star's name. Merle sounded like I ought to go out in the farmyard and do the chores. My mother and sister loved my new name from the start and never call me anything but Troy."

That name: Troy Donahue. It was one of Henry's more inspired creations, even if the charm took three times to stick. Rock, Tab, and Rory may have graced other more or less talented men, but as names they conjure up images of movie stars followed by, possibly, pet dogs. As names, they would expire along with the careers that inspired them. "Troy" somehow stuck. When this Troy invaded the fantasies of pubescent girls, it would be the sweet, laconic sound of his name they whispered into their wombs and later bestowed upon a first-born male child when life otherwise disappointed them. Troy Donahue always took special pride that he bred so many fantasies turned flesh. It all happened when he pushed Susan Kohner into the gutter on the Universal lot.

Once again, it was the ubiquitous Douglas Sirk who helped shape the newest Willson client, but not as the clean-cut sweater-boy impregnator that Troy would embody in a series of films. Sirk instead cast him as the sullen thug who beats up his mulatto girl-friend Sarah Jane, played by Kohner, in *Imitation of Life*. The 1959 remake of the Fannie Hurst novel starred Henry's old discovery Lana Turner, as well as a newer one, John Gavin, who was known around town as "the next Rock Hudson."

At first, Henry resisted Troy's taking the role of a racist brute. He feared that it might ruin his bobbysoxer image of sexy-but-safe. "Henry thought that my character's racism might actually prejudice people against me," Troy recalled. Over the years, the actor pondered "how different my career might have been" if he'd continued to play con artists and creeps instead of segueing into "the boy who did as he was told."

One thing was for sure. He didn't have to worry about being

labeled a bigot for trashing some white actress playing a mulatto who passed for white in Lana Turner's new picture. "After that film came out, black people would come up to me and thank me for treating Susan Kohner like that," Troy said. The proof was in the name-calling. "Twenty years later, the NFL had a lot of black players named Troy," he claimed.

39

Pick-up on Sunset

Before he beat up Susan Kohner, Troy took time to appear in another Douglas Sirk film, *The Tarnished Angels*, which established his early bad-boy rep. This time he played an unscrupulous daredevil aviator, Frank Burnham. As with so many feeder films for Henry's boys, the 1958 feature starred Rock Hudson.

Troy shared only two short scenes with the star, but that didn't stop Rock from putting into action one of the lessons he'd learned from his Pygmalion agent: he expected payment for his services as career doorman. "He saw me as a score," Troy recalled, refuting claims that he submitted to Rock's advances.

Being Rock's costar on *The Tarnished Angels*, Robert Stack got to know a more generous, less demanding side of the man. "Rock Hudson was one of the most respected, well-liked actors in Hollywood," said Stack. As king of the Universal lot, Rock could have reduced Stack's screen time to bolster his own role in the Sirk film. "I was a loan-out actor," said Stack, "but Rock never threw his weight around." The future Eliot Ness thought so much of his colleague—they had costarred a year earlier in Sirk's *Written on the Wind*—that Stack took Rock home to meet his mother. After the dinner dishes were cleared, Mrs. Stack took her son aside to say, "That is the most polite young man you've ever brought to this house."

Rock also charmed the press, who could be counted on not to write the truth about his love life. "He was extremely well liked," said

AP's Hollywood reporter James Bacon. "No one in the Hollywood press corps was going to expose Rock Hudson for being gay."

But he was gay—and didn't mind sharing that fact with Henry's boys regardless of their sexual orientation. From *Magnificent Obsession* onward, the agent's new clients tended to overpopulate Rock's pictures. "Rock Hudson probably thought it was his due to make it with whatever young man Henry put in the film. Henry signed a number of young actors that way," Troy Donahue explained. "Henry could just pick up the phone and get them a role in Rock's next movie."

Actor Van Williams called such assignments the "Rock trap," a career pitfall that he avoided when Henry instead steered him into a TV career with the Warner Bros. series *Bourbon Street Beat* and *Surfside 6*. Williams may have been an ex-football player from Texas, but even he had heard reports of Henry's "packaging" technique on various Rock Hudson film projects. "Henry would bring Rock bait, these young kids, and Rock would run through them like crazy," said Williams. "It was a turnstile, a swinging door. Rock's sex drive was enormous."

Glen Jacobson was another one of Henry's "good bets" who initially got the seal of approval from Rock Hudson. In 1957, the sailor was on shore leave with two navy buddies when they wandered off the Strip and into the Mocambo. They didn't know Los Angeles, but they knew their uniforms would guarantee them gratis alcohol for the night if they got drunk at one of Hollywood's better nightclubs. The sailors' second round of Mocambo highballs arrived with a card inviting Jacobson—but not his two friends—to dine with Rock Hudson. The sailor didn't know the name embossed on the card, Henry Willson, but he had heard of Rock Hudson. "Who could refuse that invitation?" said Jacobson.

Three filet mignons and a few more rounds of drinks later, Rock turned to Henry. "I think you've just found another client," he said. Henry agreed and quickly found work typecasting first seaman Glen Jacobson in such submarine fare as *Up Periscope*, with James Garner, and *Operation Petticoat*, which starred Cary Grant and

Tony Curtis and Robert Wagner climb the "bobbysockers" ladder with Rock, *Life* magazine, 1954. *Photo courtesy of Sharland / Getty Images.*

Natalie Wood
does date-duty
with another
Henry Willson
client, Tab
Hunter.

*Photo courtesy
of Photofest*

Natalie chats up
Tab and his
new boyfriend
Tony Perkins
at the Hollywood
premiere of
Giant, 1956.

*Photo courtesy of
Photofest.*

Henry entertains
the press corps
with Thanksgiving
turkey, Pocahontas
Crowfoot, and a
legally renamed
John Smith, 1957.

*Photo courtesy of
UCLA / Special
Collections.*

(TOP LEFT) Henry escorts Natalie to the New York premiere of *Giant* at the Roxy Theater, 1956. (TOP RIGHT) Henry takes a boat ride with the Paper-Mate Boy, Tom Irish. (BOTTOM) Tab Hunter visits James Dean on the set of *Rebel without a Cause* in 1955, the year the blond heartthrob fires Henry. Tab quickly signs with Dean's agent, Dick Clayton, who had been Henry's secretary at the Famous Artists Agency in the late 1940s.

All photos courtesy of Photofest.

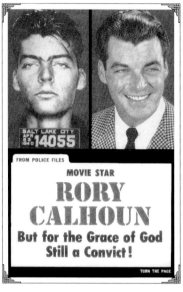

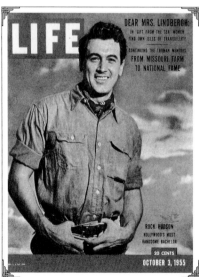

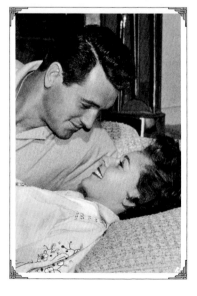

(TOP LEFT) Rory Calhoun's *Confidential* exposé, May 1955. (TOP RIGHT) Tab Hunter's *Confidential* exposé, September 1955. (BOTTOM LEFT) Rock Hudson's *Life* cover, October 1955. (BOTTOM RIGHT) Rock marries Phyllis Gates in Santa Barbara, November 9, 1955.

All photos courtesy of Photofest.

(TOP) Deputy Arne A. Knudsen watches over Tab at the *Confidential* trial, August 1957. (BOTTOM) Rock engages in a photo op aboard his sailboat, *The Khairuzan,* with fellow Willson client John Gavin. *Photos courtesy of Academy of Motion Picture Arts & Sciences.*

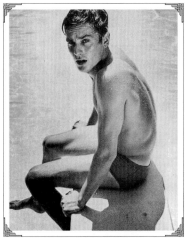

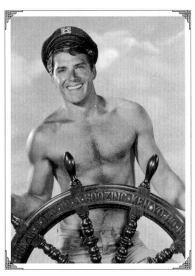

(TOP FROM LEFT TO RIGHT) Cannes discovery Alain Delon; Cal Bolder as Igor.
(BOTTOM FROM LEFT TO RIGHT) Noël Coward's Adonis, Paul Nesbitt; TV skipper Van Williams.

All photos courtesy of Photofest.

(TOP LEFT) Gena Rowlands and John Cassavetes take the high road and the money.
(TOP RIGHT) Pat Colby chats up Clark Gable on the set of *Run Silent, Run Deep*, 1958.
(BOTTOM) Troy Donahue weds Suzanne Pleshette, Beverly Hills Hotel, January 4, 1964.

All photos courtesy of Photofest.

1847-P8

Troy and Rock share a moment off-camera, *The Tarnished Angels*, 1958. *Photo courtesy of Photofest.*

Tony Curtis. Henry highly approved when Jacobson later married Janice Pennington. Prefiguring Vanna White by at least two decades, the statuesque blonde pushed back the red curtain thousands of times for Bob Barker on *The Price Is Right*. After the Jacobson/Pennington nuptials, Henry predicted: the fan magazines would pay attention to *The Price Is Right* girl's new husband and write about him, too. Henry liked girlfriends, and he liked wives even better. But Rock didn't like Henry's boys being faithful to women regardless of their status and wasted no time punishing Jacobson. Despite having an associate producer credit on *Come September*, Henry claimed he couldn't secure even the smallest role for Jacobson in Rock's new film, which was being filmed in Italy. Henry didn't lie about the reason. "Rock wants someone he can play with in Rome," he told Jacobson.

Rock's droit du seigneur also affected the career of Robert Aiken. After renaming him Ford Dunhill, Henry secured Aiken the role of Rock Hudson's younger brother in the 1959 film *This Earth Is Mine*. A somewhat less epic film than *Giant*, it failed to do for grapes what George Stevens's film did for cattle. However, before that verdict befell the project, Aiken was thrilled to be costarring in a major motion picture with Rock Hudson. Some of his scenes were to be shot in the Napa Valley wine region, which meant that San Francisco loomed as the nearest Sodom, a fact not lost on Henry Willson. He warned Aiken, "Stay away from Rock. And whatever you do, you're not to go away with him to Frisco for the weekend."

There could be no doubt. "Henry was very controlling of Rock," said Aiken.

First day of shooting in the Napa Valley, Rock asked the movie's debutant if he would join him for lunch. The questions didn't stop there, and five or ten minutes later, Rock finally got around to asking Aiken, "Would you like to go to San Francisco to spend the weekend?"

"What's to do in San Francisco?" Aiken asked.

Rock laughed. "We could have a lot of fun," he replied.

It was not until they had finished work on *This Earth Is Mine* that Aiken worked up the courage to tell Rock why, in addition to his being heterosexual, that he had resisted the invitation to San Francisco. He waited for the appropriate moment to unload the bombshell, and their sweating it out together in the steam room at the Beverly Hills Health Club somehow seemed the right place and time. Even so, "The news obviously infuriated Rock," said Aiken.

Later that morning, Henry phoned Aiken and invited him to dinner to discuss the direction of his career. Instead, the two men spoke of other things. "Henry practically threatened to have me killed," said Aiken. "He couldn't believe I had told Rock what he had said to me."

Alain Delon on the Tarmac

Henry reserved the right to pass inspection on everyone in Rock's life. After flying to Rome to visit his client on the set of the ill-fated *A Farewell to Arms*, Henry made a detour to the Cannes Film Festival in spring 1957. As usual, Henry did his talent-scouting not in the screening rooms and theaters but at the beaches, the sidewalk cafes, the night clubs. It was there, at the Whisky à Go-Go, that he saw the twenty-two-year-old Alain Delon, who had attended the festival to help promote his first film, *Quand la femme s'en mêle*, directed by his friend Yves Allégret.

"I did it to please him, I had no interest in the cinema," Delon recalled with an excess of insouciance.

His mother never thought to suggest that her son become a movie star. At her fond encouragement, he instead enlisted in the French army, where, in 1954, he arrived in Indochina just after Dien Bien Phu. Comparing the experience to his life with Maman, Delon called it "the happiest time" of his life. "You felt anything could happen, and you could play at being a man. You even had a gun."

During his military training near Toulon, Delon met a bar owner, Charles Marcantoni, who in turn introduced him to his brother, François, a man known in France as "the boss." Fortunately for the young Delon, the Marcantonis laundered money by investing in European films, and one of those became the vehicle of Delon's debut, *Quand la femme s'en mêle*.

At the Whisky à Go-Go, Henry did his usual "If you've ever thought of a career in the movies. . . ." It is not known if he delivered the words in English or had them translated into French or inscribed it on a card. When Henry first saw him, Delon was wearing a smoking jacket borrowed from Jean-Claude Brialy, his costar in *Quand la femme* . . . The former French soldier fit the Henry Willson mold: besides the military connection, he was startlingly good-looking, socially unformed (Delon had recently given up his night job hauling vegetables at Les Halles), and his Papa had long departed the family picture. Guardians who let him play football near the prison yard at Fresnes had raised the young Delon. For Henry, the hard-knocks tale gave Delon a tantalizing background that recalled the rough Francis Durgin in his pre–Rory Calhoun days.

It didn't escape Henry's attention that Delon came to the Whisky with the epicene Brialy, who was not to Henry's taste. Delon, however, intrigued him, especially when he mentioned his girlfriend, the actress Brigitte Auber. Years later, Delon may have professed to have no interest in a film career, but in the spring of 1957 at Cannes he was interested enough to accept Henry's invitation to meet with David O. Selznick in Rome. Henry made sure that Delon's arrival in the Eternal City coincided with a day Rock Hudson would not be needed on the set of *A Farewell to Arms* at Cinecittà. To pay for Delon's round-trip ticket, Henry had piqued Selznick's interest by comparing the Frenchman to Louis Jourdan, whom the producer had put under contract a decade earlier to make *The Paradine Case*. Alfred Hitchcock had balked at the choice: He wanted someone with "dirt under his fingernails," he said, to play the rough stableboy who carries on an affair with his wealthy mistress (Alida Valli). Jourdan's physical perfection removed him from the world of ordinary mortals. Delon, on the other hand, was more accessible; his beauty came with a healthy patina of sweat and grime.

Henry talked to Selznick about the novice actor's good looks and nearly flawless English. To his client, Henry spoke of other things, not the least of which was Delon's friendship with Brialy. Impressed, Rock met the Frenchman at the Rome airport to give him a royal Hollywood welcome on the tarmac. Later that evening, the three men dined with Jennifer Jones and Selznick, who liked Henry's latest catch so much he ordered a screen test for Delon at Cinecittà.

On one level, it was a success. Selznick offered and Delon accepted a seven-year contract. Henry made sure that his dutiful chronicler Mike Connolly broke the news in *The Hollywood Reporter*: "Henry Willson signed to agent Brigitte Auber's husband, . . . Jimmy Dean-type named Alain Delon."

While Connolly was prompt, he wasn't always accurate in his delivery of news. Delon never married Auber. Nor did he cross the Pacific Ocean to visit Hollywood. Nor did David O. Selznick ever make another film after *A Farewell to Arms*. Nor did Rock Hudson ever forgive Henry for putting him into such a misguided project. Rock's casting had surprised many, including Selznick's son. "He was like the fourteenth choice for the film," said Daniel Selznick. He asked his father, "Rock Hudson, do you think he can act it?"

David O. Selznick did. "Look at those Douglas Sirk pictures," he replied. "He gives subtle performances." Publicly, he was even more enthusiastic. "Rock Hudson is the first romantic idol since Gary Cooper and Clark Gable," said Selznick. "He's got it—the thing that is indescribable . . ." There were other more describable reasons for choosing him to play opposite Selznick's wife, Jennifer Jones. Just as the producer felt confident that Henry Willson would not lust after the actress in his former capacity as an escort and talent scout, Selznick liked the idea that Jennifer's newest leading man was also a homosexual and therefore no threat to his marriage. As he put it, "Jennifer and Rock have met socially and they have a rapport."

Oddly enough, their chemistry never permeated the screen. "Later they said it was because Rock was gay," said Daniel Selznick. "But Jennifer was so nervous and my father had so much riding on the film. I don't think she could relax in any sense."

It was a doomed project. Selznick confessed that John Huston was the only director of stature who would work with him. But he overestimated. One day into production, Huston walked off the set of *A Farewell to Arms,* and Selznick had to bring in Charles Vidor, whose most significant previous success had been directing Rita Hayworth in *Gilda,* a decade earlier.

Henry did make one shrewd move regarding *A Farewell to Arms.* Wanting to secure Rock top billing over Jennifer Jones, he made Selznick a bet. "If Rock gets a best actor Oscar nomination for *Giant,"* he said, "then he should have his name first."

Although *A Farewell to Arms* eventually made a small profit, the project left its producer insolvent. Again. "I take credit for my pictures when they are good," said Selznick, "so I must take the blame when they are disappointing. *A Farewell to Arms* is a job of which I am not especially proud."

Rock more than survived the film. With the previous back-to-back hits of *Giant* and *Written on the Wind,* he emerged in 1957 as the number-one box office star in the world, according to the *Motion Picture Herald*'s annual list. The disappointment of Selznick's last production, however, stymied Alain Delon's chances for a Hollywood career. With no films to offer the actor, the producer tore up their contract—at Delon's request.

"I wasn't given a chance to digest the idea," Delon said. "It was thrust on me. There was no decision for me to make. I had already paid a big price to obtain my freedom," he said of leaving military service, "and I was not going to suddenly lose it."

Henry tried to convince Delon to reconsider and make the trip to Los Angeles. He wanted to introduce him to Bill Orr, show him off at Ciro's, put him in *Photoplay,* make him a big star. But Delon had no interest being typecast as the Continental lover à la Louis Jourdan. In France, he played a cop and a hit man, respectively, in *Quand la femme s'en mêle* and *Sois belle et tais-toi,* which cast him opposite newcomer Jean-Paul Belmondo. And there were other reasons for him to remain in Europe, as he quickly went from Brigitte Auber to his new love, the German beauty Romy Schneider.

Disappointed, Henry called Alain Delon one of those "good bets" who got away. For Rock, Delon was no great loss. He told friends, "He doesn't have a big dick."

41

John Gavin Plays Rock Jr.

After five years as an independent agent, Henry closed shop to work for his old boss Charlie Feldman. In May 1956, the Famous Artists Agency welcomed him back into the fold, but not in his former capacity as a journeyman agent. Henry Willson returned to be a senior vice president at the august tenpercentary. He had ties there: according to his contract dated May 22, 1956, Henry continued to receive his 10 percent from the accounts of Tab Hunter and Rory Calhoun, both of whom he originally signed to FAA: "With respect to Tab Hunter and Rory Calhoun, we will continue to pay you the commission as we have in the past, irrespective of anything in the employment contract between us, as foresaid."

Otherwise, there was no doubt why Feldman wanted Henry. He wanted a piece of the Rock, America's biggest star, and there were other notable Willson clients to contribute their 10 percent. When his old friend Sue Carol Ladd closed her agency, Henry inherited singer Julie London, who was eager to restart her film career after getting rid of husband Jack (*Dragnet*) Webb, in 1955. Grant Williams benefited from Henry's plugging him into a supporting role in *Written on the Wind*, in 1956, which led to his headlining the sci-fi classic *The Incredible Shrinking Man* the following year. There were also Natalie Wood, Nick Adams, Troy Donahue, *Laramie*'s John Smith, *Cheyenne*'s Clint Walker, *Zorro*'s Guy Williams, and *Peyton Place*'s Barry Coe.

Most of them had strong teen appeal, and according to an AP report on Rock's box office appeal, "The bulk of the moviegoing public today comprises teenagers." With Rock in the top spot, Pat Boone and Elvis Presley followed as numbers three and four with John Wayne in between at number two. (The complete list: Hudson, Wayne, Boone, Presley, Frank Sinatra, Gary Cooper, William Holden, James Stewart, Jerry Lewis, and Yul Brynner.) Henry's propensity for signing beautiful male talent corresponded with his sexual orientation, but it also made strong economic sense. In 1957, not one actress made the Top Ten, with Marilyn Monroe and Kim Novak no longer on the list, though they placed numbers eight and nine the previous year.

If Rock was Number One, there was room in Hollywood for his clone. Born John Golenor, John Gavin came to Henry's notice via an old family friend, Bryan Foy. A B-level film producer, Foy had made nearly two hundred movies, a few of which went back to Henry's earliest days in Hollywood when the tyro agent sprinkled his Puppets clients throughout such Foy classics as *Freshman Love* and *High School Girl*. Cut from the same tall, dark, and dense mold as Rock, Golenor had never acted—a minor detraction that did not stop Foy from thinking his friend could carve a career from all the movies Rock didn't have time to make. And who knew? Universal might need an upstart contender to keep Rock in line—as if Rock Hudson ever got out of line.

Golenor may have been a total novice in Hollywood, but having grown up in Santa Barbara, he felt those questionable reverberations emanating northward from Los Angeles. Like Merle Johnson Jr., he harbored hetero concerns about Henry Willson.

"I can't help you there," Foy said of the Rock/Tab/Touch syndrome. Golenor took care of that problem by insisting he keep his first name and exchange Golenor for Gavin, his own choice of new names.

Regarding Henry's casting couch, Foy told him, "You can take care of yourself."

The newly christened John Gavin apparently did. Then again, Henry sometimes knew to leave well enough alone. Unlike most of the male actors Henry repped, Gavin came from old money, his father very much alive and still running the family ranch up the coast. "Henry was savvy," said his assistant Pat Colby. "He knew not to hit on John Gavin."

Despite the obvious comparison, Rock showed no animosity toward his agent's newest lookalike client and even agreed to a joint publicity photo session aboard his sailing boat, *The Krairuzan*, at New Beach. Rock loved his Newporter and had named it after Piper Laurie's character in their film *The Golden Blade*. On the weekend, he took the boat on sails to Catalina, but after several years of ownership, it had to be sold. Vandals kept spray-painting the bow with epithets of "faggot" and "queer."

Like so many of his peers, Gavin remembered Rock as being one of the nicest, least competitive people in Hollywood. Their photo session led to a dinner invitation from Mr. and Mrs. Gavin. Over cocktails, the newly renamed Gavin asked Rock what his mother called him.

"She calls me Roy."

From then on, the former John Golenor called him Roy.

Gavin signed with the Willson agency on the cusp of Henry's move back to Famous Artists. If the actor was leery of his agent, many employees of Famous Artists were outraged that the now-infamous Henry Willson would return to the respected firm in any capacity, much less as a senior vice president.

Ray Powers remembered the furor at Famous Artists. In 1957, he worked in the New York office and represented clients on the East Coast. "When Charlie Feldman brought Willson back, there were a lot of agents who were upset, because of Henry's reputation," said Powers. "There was real concern about Henry Willson. Whether they were true or not, the rumors were that Henry required his clients to sleep with him and he had orgies at his house."

Although the tales of wild sex parties did not include any mention of pimping, it was one chore to which Powers almost became an unwitting accomplice.

By far the most prestigious film of 1957, David Lean's *The Bridge on the River Kwai* had just gone into release when Henry, newly reinstalled at Famous Artists, made a trip to New York City to introduce himself to the firm's East Coast staff. He also wanted to meet some of the Gotham-based talent, and at the top of his list was a twenty-four-year-old actor who starred in Lean's World War II classic. Geoffrey Horne played the role of the exceedingly blond Lieutenant Joyce opposite the more grizzled William Holden and the even more grizzly Jack Hawkins.

"*The Bridge on the River Kwai* was such a hit, and overnight Geoffrey was one the hottest actors in New York City," said Powers.

Louella Parsons got on the bandwagon with one report from her syndicated column. "Horne's favored to get *Ben-Hur*," she wrote. "[Producer] Sam Zimbalist saw him in *Bridge* and sees in him the Ben-Hur for whom he and M-G-M have long been searching. Seems pretty certain Geoffrey will get it."

It was only natural that Henry wanted to scope out the competition. On his next trip to New York, he told Powers he wanted to meet Horne. "There was nothing wrong or extraordinary with that," said Powers, who arranged the meeting. More extraordinary were Henry's explicit instructions for Horne to come to his hotel room. Business interviews usually took place at the office or a restaurant. But Powers obeyed.

As requested, Horne went to the Waldorf-Astoria on Park Avenue to see the agent. It turned out to be a brief meeting. "Henry Willson was very brusque," said Horne. As soon as the actor walked in the door, Henry put it on the line. "I can get you a Hollywood contract," he said.

"I don't know that I want a Hollywood contract," replied Horne.

"They don't go for that Jimmy Dean bullshit anymore in Hollywood!" Henry shot back. Horne recalled the tense, awkward moment. "Coming from the Actors Studio, I'm sure Willson thought

I was being arrogant, that I thought Hollywood was trash. But it seemed unkind: James Dean had just been killed in this car crash."

But Henry did not mourn, and he often warned his clients to avoid emulating Dean. "He would not have lasted in Hollywood," Henry believed. "Jimmy Dean was not well liked, and to last in this town you have to be well liked."

When the hotel phone rang, Henry answered it. "Yeah, Roy, come on up," he said.

An elevator ride later, Rock Hudson materialized to walk through the door. Henry made the introductions, Rock shook Horne's hand, then preceded to ignore him. "He seemed uninterested, then started talking about his laundry problems at the hotel," said Horne, who felt the two men were speaking in some kind of code. Did "laundry" translate as "forget it"?

"When I left shortly thereafter, it occurred to me that Willson was trying to set me up as a date for Rock Hudson. I was really offended," said Horne.

42

Hollywood Leg Breaker

Geoffrey Horne and Alain Delon escaped, but Rock did not return to Hollywood empty-handed. His affair with another man during the filming of *A Farewell to Arms* led to a case of stateside blackmail, as well as an expensive divorce.

According to Phyllis Gates, "The Italian had followed Rock to California but now Rock wouldn't see him."

Rock's jilted lover was frightened and told his plight to a friend of Gates's: Henry had made threats, told him to leave Rock Hudson, or else. "His agent called and told me to leave town," the Italian man cried. "Can you believe that? We were lovers for five months and now [Rock] won't see me."

Henry had his own reasons to be afraid and feared that Rock's Italian boyfriend might go to one of the tabloids with his story. "So he's trying to convince the guy to leave town," the friend told Gates. "If that fails, there's no telling what Henry might do." What Henry did was make a call to Fred Otash, who put the Italian on a fast plane back to Rome.

According to crime novelist James Ellroy, author of *L.A. Confidential* and *Hollywood Nocturnes*, Otash was a "leg breaker for the LAPD from 1945 to 1955." As Ellroy described him, Otash sounds a lot like Don Crutchfield's "Jimmy," the off-duty LAPD cop who roughed up Rock's previous blackmailer. Then again, there were a number of LAPD cops who could have fit the description of Jimmy or Otash in the 1950s.

"When William Wharton took over stewardship of the LAPD," said Ellroy, "he formed a goon squad of ex-marines to take care of organized crime figures: take 'em off the bus, airplane, train, beat the shit out of 'em, and put 'em back on. Otash was one of those guys."

After Otash left the force in 1955, he worked as a private eye for *Confidential*. More often than not, the lurid stories the tabloid printed were true—and it was Otash's job at *Confidential* to verify the details. He made even more money with his moonlighting ventures. "Freddie was the guy you went to if you wanted a picture of Rock Hudson with a dick in his mouth," said Ellroy.

Ironically, it was Otash whom Henry and Rock approached when the movie star's Italian boyfriend refused to return to Rome of his own volition. "The kid was making demands and Freddie roughed him up," said Ellroy. "He had his green card revoked and [Otash] put him back on the airplane. Those are the kinds of favors Freddie did people in Hollywood."

Otash's favors, however, were never done free of charge. His only allegiance was money, and an employer one week could turn into his target the next. For his 1976 memoir, *Investigation Hollywood!*, Otash wrote a revealing chapter, "Homosexuals Are Also Movie Stars," in which he detailed his January 21, 1958, taping of a conversation between "one of Hollywood's most handsome of handsome leading men, a superstar par excellence," and the actor's distraught spouse, who suspected her famous husband of having several homosexual liaisons in the course of their brief marriage.

"I was hired by his wife to get the goods on him to enhance her pending divorce negotiations," Otash reported. For legal reasons, he referred to them as Mr. and Mrs. Star who lived on Singer Drive. The address is a possible pseudonym for Warbler Drive, one of the "bird streets" above Sunset Boulevard, where Rock lived with Phyllis Gates. If the dialogue between the "Star" and "Wife" in Otash's book recalls some of Phyllis Gates's more purple prose in her memoirs *Rock Hudson, My Husband*, the points of reference are identical: a potential exposé in *Confidential*, his premature ejaculation, her sexual frustration, his refusing to go into therapy, her hatred of his agent.

According to the Gates account, Rock saw her psychiatrist a few times before abruptly discontinuing the sessions. In a nearly identical story, the "Wife" on the Otash tapes makes a similar complaint about her "Star" husband, whom she had hoped would convert to heterosexuality via therapy. A Rorschach test has revealed the Star's homosexuality, and the discovery leads him to break with the Wife's shrink.

"You told me you saw thousands of butterflies and also snakes," says the Wife, who offers a unique interpretation of the ink blots: "butterflies mean femininity, and snakes represent the male penis."

The "Star" shares another trait with Rock: loyalty. Despite the protestations of the "Wife," he refuses to fire his longtime agent.

WIFE: "You told me you had an affair with your agent. How long did that last?"

STAR: "No time at all. Do you think I would enjoy having an affair with him?"

WIFE: "But you did it. Why?"

STAR: "Because of naivete, I guess."

WIFE: "That's no excuse. You must have wanted to do it. Did you do it for your career?"

STAR: "I don't know. Maybe." . . .

WIFE: "Do you know how they refer to him in Palm Springs? As a bitch in heat."

STAR (laughing): I was only in Palm Springs with him one weekend, and he had a date."

WIFE: "With a boy?"

STAR: "Sure. I feel a sense of loyalty towards him but I don't approve of his activities."

WIFE: "Do you think he doesn't talk about you? . . . I've even heard that he has told people that he procures for you."

STAR: "I know he talks about other people, but I never thought he would talk about me that way.

WIFE: "What hold does he have on you? Afraid he will talk if you leave him?"

STAR: "I don't know. Maybe."

Phyllis Gates reported that she sought the legal aid of Jerry Geisler, the same attorney who handled the Lana Turner/Johnny Stompanato/Cheryl Crane murder case. However, she makes no mention of Fred Otash or the taping of any conversations with Rock.

Unlike Otash's account of Mr. Star and Wife, Gates did broach the possible reason for her marriage. Rock, however, denied the obvious: "No, of course not! I didn't marry you because of the *Confidential* story. We got it fixed. We hired a gangst—"

According to Gates, Rock Hudson then felt the call of nature and suddenly retired to the bathroom for the rest of the evening.

Phyllis Gates obtained her divorce on August 13, 1958, in the Santa Monica Superior Court. Henry Willson accompanied his soon-to-be-single client to the courthouse where Gates recalled their being less than confident of the outcome. "They had good reason to be scared," she reported. "In the next few minutes I could destroy Rock's multimillion-dollar career with what I knew."

Always adept at delivering the less explosive side of the truth, Gates gave the judge, Edward R. Brand, the following portrait of her husband: "He was terribly moody and wouldn't talk to me for days, sometimes weeks. He is never home, and he has hit me twice and he tried to choke me once."

Instead of pronouncing Rock guilty of physical cruelty, Judge Brand pounded his gavel and pronounced, "Divorce granted on grounds of mental cruelty." Alimony came to $250 a week for ten years. Gates got to keep her car, most of the wedding presents, and the house on Warbler Place, for which Rock had paid $32,000 in 1954. There was also a cash settlement of $130,000, which represented her 5-percent interest in his company, the 7 Pictures Corporation, later renamed Gibraltar Productions.

Rock told friends that it was an "arranged marriage. It was never love or romance." She vehemently denied those rumors. "No. You're hearing from the wrong people. That was part of the Henry Willson slander campaign. He started all that."

Gates always claimed she married for love. In 1986, she told Rock Hudson's official biographer, Sara Davidson, that she had been duped. "I was set up. I believe that 100 percent. Henry Willson was so evil, he may have set it up. Rock's reputation was getting out of hand. I wish I could find out who did it."

Her story has its skeptics. "I don't know how that's possible," said Lucille Ryman Carroll, the M-G-M head of talent who rejected Rock Hudson years earlier, in part, for appearing too gay. "I knew people who knew Rock very well during the time he was married to Phyllis, and he was in and out of every gay singles' bar in town. He was notorious." So was his starmaker. "I know of no one in town who wasn't aware that Henry was gay," said Carroll.

Over the years, Gates never varied from her story. As recently as March 2004, she told Larry King on CNN, "To my knowledge the marriage was not arranged." Others disagreed. According to Rock's friend and secretary Mark Miller, the union unraveled due to the wife's "double standard."

Gates said she first met Rock Hudson at the offices of Henry

Willson Management in 1953. Miller agrees on the year, but not much else. He said the unlikely couple first met at the house he shared with his lover, George Nader, in Studio City. Miller and Nader were having a party of three with Rock. He and Nader launched into the "Hallelujah" chorus as Miller accompanied them on the piano, when into this merry group walked Phyllis Gates with her date for the evening, Jack Navaar, who was then Hudson's live-in boyfriend. Rock and Phyllis were introduced. He was pliant. She was strong. They liked each other immediately.

"Phyllis knew Rock and Jack were lovers and didn't care," Miller said. "But because he was Rock Hudson, Phyllis thought he couldn't fool around." As the concerned wife of a movie star, she worried that Rock's homosexuality might be made public and ruin his career.

"She would come down to Palm Springs, but Rock couldn't have anyone," said Miller. "There was a double standard."

According to Miller, Phyllis strapped a virtual chastity belt on her gay husband to keep his libido under control and out of the tabloids. For a few months, it worked. Rock attempted to be the heterosexual husband that his wife, Hollywood, and the moviegoing public expected. But after one year of homosexual chastity, the sexually frustrated groom put in a call to his two best friends in Studio City. "I'm alone again. She's gone off to Palm Springs again," Rock told Miller. "I've had it. I'm leaving. I want to have a boy once in a while."

In fact, he wanted a boy all the time. Many of them.

After his divorce, Rock moved into a new house, located at 9402 Beverly Crest Drive. This time, he made sure the place was a mansion, and he aptly named it the "Castle." If the two-bedroom Warbler house was too modest for a movie star, the Castle was fit for the movies' reigning king. Universal Pictures bought the house for $167,000 from Sam Jaffe, an agent and producer, and made a gift of it to Rock. Some gift. The deal locked him into another long-term contract with the studio, not that Rock gave it much thought. Happy to be single again, he decorated the place in Early Macho:

zebra skins, African masks, huge standing pewter candlesticks, and a nine-foot davenport that came from the set of *Pillow Talk*. Overhead, exposed tree trunks loomed as the ceiling. There was one article of furniture, however, that looked lost among the oversized, he-man décor. Rock would sometimes point to the small threadbare couch in the corner and laugh without much humor. "This couch is the only thing I have from that marriage," he said.

Their union was born of the best calculations and the worst intentions. Henry spent many nights with actor Van Williams and his wife, Vicky, commiserating over the disaster of the Hudson-Gates marriage. At the time, Williams was starring in his first TV series, *Bourbon Street Beat*. "We caught the tail-end of it," Williams recalled. "Henry said [the marriage] was entirely an arrangement. Phyllis didn't want to do it and I don't think Rock wanted it, but Henry brought enough pressure that they did get married. It ended up to be a big joke." The more he drank, the more sentimental Henry grew in his dinner reminiscences, admitting to Van and Vicky that he had trusted his faithful secretary, but she had morphed into the termagant of the typing pool as soon as she became a movie star's wife. Henry wondered aloud, "Why couldn't Rock and Phyllis get along like Craig Stevens and Alexis Smith?"

If the Hudson-Gates marriage represented a bald business decision on the wife's part, she did not walk away from it emotionally unscathed. "The party was over," Gates admitted. No more premieres, limousines, four-star restaurants, luxury hotels. Post-divorce, she returned to the company of an all-female circle of friends who helped Phyllis take up the social slack of not attending premieres at Grauman's and dining at Chasen's. Instead of living the life of Mrs. Rock Hudson, she returned to calling herself Phyllis Gates and started playing poker each week at the home of Nancy Kulp. The lantern-jawed character actress was then playing the hang-dog secretary on *The Bob Cummings Show*, with her *Beverly Hillbillies* heyday as the distressed Miss Hathaway yet to come.

"We met Wednesday nights," said Peggy Hadley, a blonde, perky comedienne with a pixie haircut who later became a talent agent in New York City. At Kulp's house, the women played for stakes of $100. "Phyllis really went crazy after she broke up with Rock," said Hadley. "She was quite distraught and very distracted after that marriage ended. She thoroughly enjoyed being Mrs. Rock Hudson. And she was a lousy poker player," said Hadley.

At least Rock no longer had to worry about threats from *Confidential*, which had gone belly-up. Unfortunately, knock-off publications followed in its wake to take up the slack in gossip. An article in the December 1957 issue of *TV Scandals* claimed that Rock Hudson married Phyllis Gates "on explicit orders from his studio." The tabloid went on to explain, "It was when the gossip columns started calling him 'pretty boy Rock Hudson' that his studio, Universal-International, began to be uneasy."

Five months before the divorce was made official, no less a publication than *Look*—with its 3.4 million readership—put the blame not on Universal but on Henry Willson himself. "Rock Hudson is completely an invention of his agent," the magazine claimed. "His name, his voice, his personality were all made up for him." As for his marriage to Phyllis Gates, *Look* wondered, "Did Willson have a part in this too?"

The readers of *Look* also learned that, after Henry Willson introduced Rock and Phyllis, the agent arranged "every detail of the wedding, including a Jamaica honeymoon. Despite Willson's blessing, the marriage remained stable for only two years." In conclusion, *Look* questioned Rock Hudson's sexual prowess and asked Henry to defend it. "Willson has no doubt about his client's power to enthrall the ladies, whatever the domestic value of the Hudson charm," the cover profile proffered.

Publicly, Rock and Henry were a unit. Privately, it was now difficult for Rock to decide which had been Henry's bigger blunder: his recommending he marry Phyllis Gates or that he make that turkey, *A Farewell to Arms*. There was also Henry's rejection of *Ben-Hur*, which won Charlton Heston an Oscar for best actor in 1959. Rock blamed Henry, but in truth it's doubtful that Henry had the clout to force Universal into accepting M-G-M's one-million-dollar offer for his services. It also didn't help that by the time *Ben-Hur* went before the cameras, Universal's head of production was no longer servicing Rock in his office at the studio. Ed Muhl offered a public explanation. "We rejected the possibility of lending [Hudson] at all for that picture," he said. "Rock was obviously very well established by that time, but it was more important to us to have him for our own pictures."

Whatever influence he might have brought to the situation, Henry never apologized for nixing the chariot epic. To his death, Henry insisted, "I don't want Rock in costumes—he'll look foolish."

He was right, of course. But being an actor, Rock never quite saw it that way. With somewhat more justification, Rock also complained that Henry failed to follow his success in *Giant* with the male lead in *Bus Stop*. Rock and Marilyn Monroe had talked about what fun they'd have acting together. But it was only talk. In the end, director Joshua Logan cast an unknown, Don Murray. When Rock also missed out on *Ben-Hur*, he began to doubt the unerring wisdom of his mentor-agent. "Rock had always thought Henry knew best," said Robert Osborne. "Suddenly, he wasn't so sure."

There were also problems at Famous Artists. Charlie Feldman had greatly expanded its operations since Henry had started there in the late 1940s. Never a team player, Henry found himself inept at negotiating the new corporate politics aboard Charlie Feldman's leviathan. Worse, the Hudson-Gates fiasco solidified Henry's "notorious" reputation at the agency, and it hurt, too, that his old protégé-rival Dick Clayton had emerged as "the class act" at Famous Artists. It chafed at Henry's ego, as well as his pocketbook, that he now had to share the youth market with Clayton, who was once his junior in the business.

Yet, Henry had no rival in one area. He repped Rock Hudson, the number-one box office star for three years running. Other A-list clients, however, decided to stay put at Famous Artists when Henry departed the agency to open his second boutique office, the Henry Willson Agency. Instead of following their longtime agent to his new digs on Sunset Boulevard and Sunset Plaza, Natalie Wood and Nick Adams remained behind at Famous Artists, where they were transferred to Dick Clayton. (Henry could take some satisfaction when Natalie bolted Famous Artists six months later to sign with William Morris's Norman Brokaw, who lured her with the cherished title role in *Marjorie Morningstar*.)

John Gavin also preferred to stay put at Famous Artists. "Quite frankly, this may sound prejudiced," he said, "but you got a lot of eyebrow-raising if you said Henry Willson represented you."

43

Suddenly, Last Saturday

Although never quoted as saying so, Henry Willson must have said, "Hollywood isn't what it used to be." As his reputation grew and darkened, he missed the good old days of the Depression and war years when everyone famous socialized with everyone not so famous in just a handful of ritzy nightclubs that were a short limo ride from each other. In the 1930s, he could walk into the Trocadero with a starlet on his arm and introduce her to all the big shots who in the morning would call to ask, "Who's that girl?" Photos were shot, egos pumped, careers launched.

In the 1940s, no one thought Lana Turner an old fart when she called Ciro's her favorite haunt, because it was "designed for dramatic entrances and exits." As Henry explained, "It was different in those days. People used to meet people easily."

The stars, however, were much less likely to venture out in the 1950s. Big acts like Kay Thompson and Lena Horne still played the Mocambo and Ciro's, but they were the exception, not the rule. More money was to be made in Las Vegas, and nightclubs on Sunset Strip invariably suffered. Photographers didn't help the cause, as many stopped being friendly sycophants and morphed into hounds on the hunt for candid, unattractive images. Some celebrities gave up going out in public altogether, and a casual, plebian pall descended over the clubs of Sunset Boulevard.

"There was a feeling of death on the Strip," said singer Andy Williams. "Its shining moment was over."

In the late 1950s, Henry began to spend more evening time at Villa Frascatti's, Scandia, and the Cock 'n' Bull. They were familiar, cozy places that didn't offer much glamour. Henry preferred glamour, but cozy had its uses too. "I liked to interview young people away from the office, more in private where I could get a real sense of their personality," he explained.

Rarely was it a simple talk. His one-on-one interviews had a tendency to grow in size. A prospective client might be invited to meet him at Frascatti's patio, and when he got there, Henry would already be working two or three tables, each filled with clients and friends who might have friends who'd like to be clients. Henry's penchant for mass dates proved a bizarre variation on earlier attempts to mask his homosexuality with faux engagements.

"If Henry had a group of men around him, he thought it read like he was having a night out with the boys," said the agent Richard Segel. "You know, just being pals and kicking back a few. To be seen with one other man, however, was verboten. In Henry's mind, that read as a date."

Acting coach Estelle Harmon defended Henry's extravagant approach to dating more than one man at a time. "Henry cared a great deal about his young attractive male clients," she said. "I'm not saying they were his lovers; he just cared about them a lot. He was totally devoted to being an agent. Day and night was related to them. When he finished his day, he'd either have a group over to his house for a party or take them out somewhere."

In addition to Henry's favorite restaurants on the Strip in West Hollywood, there was also a homey, new eatery farther east, on La Brea and Fountain Avenues. John Cassavetes immortalized it in his 1971 film *Minnie and Moskowitz*, but long before his cameras rolled, the restaurant with the improbable name of Panza's Lazy Susan took on cult status in the gay community as the place to meet Henry Willson and his all-male entourage. One of those boys, Steve Drexel, owned and operated Panza's with his parents, Mr. and Mrs. Carigni. The surname Drexel was Henry's touch after he banished

Carigni—"The name is impossible to pronounce"—to the Latin limbo into which Pipero, Orrico, and Ercolani had been consigned. In the 1950s, Italians, Greeks and Jews were only beginning to be fully recognized on the big screen. Television still belonged to the Nelsons and the Cleavers, and if anyone was going to pave new routes through the ethnic forest, it would never be the politically and socially conservative Henry Willson.

When Panza's first opened its doors, in 1958, Drexel had no problem finding the time between his infrequent acting assignments that year, in *The Tarnished Angels* and *Hot Rod Gang,* to operate a restaurant fulltime. He remained grateful to his agent, however. If Henry had not delivered him a brilliant acting career, he did bring Drexel's restaurant the much-needed star caché of his many famous dinner guests.

Drexel owed Henry. "If ever you're broke, Henry," the restaurateur used to joke, "I'll always feed you." It was a promise that Henry never forgot, much to Drexel's regret. Before that IOU was cashed many times over, the agent spent freely at Panza's Lazy Susan, its tables filled almost every night of the week with Henry's guests whether they were invited or not. Henry and Lucille Ball became good friends over dinners at Panza's. Robert Osborne and other Willson clients took classes at the acting school that the screwball comedienne set up at Desilu, and she and Henry used to swap predictions on which of his boys would become stars and who would go back to their day jobs. ("Yes, Johnny Sands is selling used cars on the Strip now," Henry often lamented.) Then there was Mickey Cohen, another Panza's regular, who shared a few plates of spaghetti with Henry, prompting rumors that the LA gangster was one of Henry's more productive Mob connections.

Lucy and Mickey may have dined at Panza's, but most people knew it as Henry's place. The star-struck put out the word: "If you want to meet Henry, go to Panza's after seven."

The Gargantua in residence, Henry made it his routine to reserve half a dozen tables every night of the week. "The restaurant became like a second office to him," reported actor Ray Stricklyn, "except here he could cruise the handsome young men at the bar, many of whom had come in expressly hoping to meet him."

"That's where all Henry's money went," said the agent Richard Segel. Men paraded in off the street, and throwing his dollars like confetti overhead, Henry treated them like war heroes (and he expected to be treated like their commander in chief in return).

"Going out with Henry was the loneliest thing in the world," said Troy Donahue, who swore his restive agent laced his crème de menthe with amphetamines. An early victim of attention deficit disorder, Henry kicked off the evening with one dinner guest, then as others arrived, he felt obliged to let everybody bask in his munificence for a few blessed moments. Even the unwanted at Panza's Lazy Susan found themselves worthy of Henry's brief attention, if only for him to tell them to go to hell.

Ray Stricklyn made the mistake of checking out Steve Drexel's new restaurant shortly after it opened. The timing could not have been worse. The Hudson-Gates divorce had just gone to court, and Stricklyn was Phyllis's good friend, which put him squarely in the enemy camp. On his way to the men's room, Henry took a detour past Stricklyn's table to warn, "I wouldn't testify for that bitch Phyllis, if I were you. If you do, it won't be good for your career."

Henry failed to pick up Stricklyn's check, but there were few others that escaped his pocketbook over the next ten years. Understandably, a few men who never saw the inside of Panza's wanted to get in on the action, real or imagined.

Nan Morris recalled one night at Panza's when a middle-aged man introduced his teenage companion to her friend Henry. "You're not Henry Willson!" the boy shot back.

Surprised, if not insulted, Henry replied with his usual hauteur, "Why, then, I'd like to know who I am!"

Everyone laughed—except for the boy, who, undeterred, reached into his coat pocket to produce a business card that he handled like it was his dead mother's picture. "This is Henry Willson," he claimed, handing the card to Henry. "I met him a month ago in Denver, Colorado, and he told me he could get me a job in the movies."

Henry looked at his name embossed on the bogus business card. Underneath the name "Henry Willson," it read: "Talent scout."

"I haven't been a talent scout for years!" Henry railed, his mind thick with alcohol but ready to snap. "I'm an agent, the best in Hollywood, and you're a fucking nobody!"

A Colorado panhandler had been bedding boys with promises of stardom, and using Henry Willson's name to lure them. The farce finally made Henry explode with laughter. "His hands were high above his head, waving," Nan Morris recalled. "He was just wild by the end of that evening. He was amused but in shock that people had been dining out on his name."

It happened all the time: A handsome man who had never heard of Henry Willson stumbled into Panza's, and Nan Morris—a stunning blonde who kept having to tell autograph hounds at the door that she was neither Carol Lynley nor Yvette Mimieux nor Hope Lange—often attracted his attention. "She was kind of like Elizabeth Taylor in *Suddenly, Last Summer*," said Fred Winston, a mutual friend of Nan and Henry's. "Nan was bait for a lot of straight guys who didn't know Henry Willson."

Nan saw it from another perspective. "The opposite was true," she said. "Guys came on to me all the time, hoping I'd introduce them to Henry."

If she helped with the straight side of Henry's talent acquisition, Pat Colby took care of everything else. For nearly two decades, Colby watched over the various Willson offices as their virtual gatekeeper. "You had to go through Pat to get to Henry," said Troy Donahue.

An aspiring actor, the young Texan came to work for Henry shortly after Phyllis Gates left the agency to play the part of Mrs. Rock Hudson. After her departure, Colby was the first person most prospective clients saw when they climbed the single flight of stairs at Henry's second office, on Sunset Boulevard. If Colby deemed them a "good bet," they got to meet the legendary agent, who might agree to meet them later for drinks or lunch. If truly impressed, Henry mentioned a visit to his Bel Air home "to look at my scrapbook collection." Otherwise, it was a quick descent back to Sunset Boulevard and anonymity.

At twenty-two, Pat Colby resembled Russ Tamblyn before Hollywood knew they needed another one. With Henry as his agent, he secured speaking roles in *Run Silent, Run Deep* and *PT 109*, among others, and found more success in front of the camera than most young Texans in Hollywood. Somehow, the acting jobs stood little chance in his life plans after he met Henry Willson: the warm reality of being the famous agent's praetor soon proved far hotter than any illusive promise of his own stardom. "It was so glamorous working for Henry, it was like being a star," said Colby. "After a while, I just didn't care so much about the acting."

He harbored few illusions about his boss but found him undeserving of a few myths. "Ninety percent of the guys knew what they were doing with Henry," said Colby. "I saw it happen. The most beautiful men in the world literally threw themselves at Henry." He also nixed reports of the all-gay client list. "Henry had gay clients who did not sleep with him and heterosexual clients who did," Colby said.

Apocryphal or not, lurid tales of Bel Air orgies emanated from his Saturday-afternoon pool parties. Part free lunch and part weekend goof, the Saturday ritual in Henry's backyard afforded his boys any number of diversions: It's how they got to meet each other, check out the hot new competition in the stable, meet Harry "Mr. Fixit" Weiss, chat up the *Hollywood Reporter*'s Mike Connolly, and, if nothing else, waste the hours until the night delivered more fruitful promises.

A new client might make a mistake and bring a girlfriend. Henry would be more than polite. "Henry wanted his boys to have girlfriends," said Nan Morris, who occasionally broke the all-male guest code at Stone Canyon Drive. "He treated girlfriends like royalty."

At least one woman showed up at every pool party, and she was

Henry's devoted new maid. Sometime in the early 1950s, his housekeeper Ella Mae Fuque retired and was replaced by a white woman who called herself True Delight. A strict disciple of Father Devine, the ever-buoyant True Delight believed the popular black evangelist's warnings that social welfare would one day be the ruination of America. Devine despised Franklin Delano Roosevelt, and it can be assumed that, being an evangelist, he also had few good things to say about homosexuals. Whatever she felt about her boss's sexual orientation, True Delight kept it to herself on Saturdays as she served up a basic "nothing-fancy" barbecue of hot dogs, hamburgers, and corn on the cob.

"You almost landed on your ass with laughter when Henry introduced True Delight," said Trent Dolan, a Willson client. "She came on like Little Miss Mary Sunshine, serving up cocktails with a halo to the pretty boys and the dirty old men."

According to Dolan, "Those parties were all about the dirty old men and the beauties." Firmly placed in the former group were Mike Connolly, Harry Weiss, and Henry's other lawyer friend, Lud Gerber, who rarely missed a Saturday afternoon around the pool. The boys considered the *Hollywood Reporter* columnist a good sport and, as these matters often played out, a notoriously bad lay. Although a virtual runt, Weiss was more the dynamo, and it was known around Henry's pool that a homosexual in trouble with the law had no better, or more connected, friend than Harry Weiss.

The panjandrum of the pool set, Gerber invariably received all thumbs-down. Vodka in one hand, cigar in the other, he never failed to introduce himself with the line, "Hello, I'm Ludwig H. Gerber, the lawyer." It was often pointed out that Gerber "looked like a pig" and acted like one, too. He and Connolly were cordial to each other when they weren't talking politics. While the columnist predated the Log Cabin Republicans by about fifty years, Gerber, on the other hand, was the true political liberal among Henry's peer group around the pool. He even ran for a seat in Congress a couple of times on the Democratic ticket—the second time in 1998, at the age of eighty-seven in Orange County, four years before his death in a nursing home there. He lost both elections.

At one point during the late 1950s, an ad man and an over-the-counter drug manufacturer joined the Saturday-afternoon parties at Stone Canyon Drive. The former, Lester Persky, was not yet forty, but his gap-toothed resemblance to "a smiling frog" landed him squarely in the dirty-old-man category. He and Marty Himmel, the drug manufacturer, were marketing a new cologne, Zizanie de Fragonard, that Henry used to excess and gave as gifts to his boys in hopes it would start a trend in West Hollywood's better bars and tearooms.

"Boy, did that stuff stink up the place," said Gary Crutcher. In time, Persky used the showbiz acumen he acquired from Henry's pool parties to produce a play on Broadway, Tennessee Williams's short-lived *Slapstick Tragedy*, and a few movies, including *Hair*, *Yanks*, and *Equus*.

Business aside, the older men did not come to Henry's house to chat up each other or eat his barbecue. They came to gawk at the backyard Hesperides, many of whom were prone not to be touched. Rock Hudson and Troy Donahue made occasional appearances. Gerber and company could only hope that others on Henry's roster might show up—clients like Trax Colton, Rad Fulton, Dial Roberts, and Cal Bolder. A few Saturday regulars had no business ties to their host, but had high regard for his bonhomie: muscle-man Steve Reeves of spaghetti Hercules fame sometimes joined the party, as did the Prince of Wails, otherwise known as Johnnie Ray, who belted out "Cry" before two morals arrests derailed his career. No client was required to attend—or, for that matter, become intimate with any other guest. Most showed up to please "Henny" or "the old man," as Henry was now known behind his back.

From the Puppets club to Selznick's *SYWA* gang to the Adonis factory, the party scene at Henry's house evolved but never stopped. Inevitably, the host had gotten older, gained weight, and lost his hair, but he maintained the same nubile guest list of yore, even if it had grown a lot less heterogeneous over the years. Occasionally, one of the boys would recoil at the intense camaraderie.

"John Saxon would do his macho thing and bring a girlfriend," said Fred Winston. "He'd grumble about there being nothing but a bunch of men and then leave."

Most guests considered the pool parties a benign, if not tedious, way to waste a Saturday afternoon. Henry no longer asked his guests to play charades to hone their acting skill, as he had done with such *Since You Went Away* alums as Shirley Temple and Dare Harris. But he remained an attentive audience-of-one, and delighted in watching his boys replay their big moments from a recent film success. A lawn chair sufficed as his first-row orchestra seat.

"Hey, Pat!" he yelled at his assistant. "Do your periscope scene from *Run Silent, Run Deep*." And on cue, Pat Colby mimicked his own performance as the helmsman, steering the submarine through enemy waters for costar Clark Gable. "How do you like that, Chief, we've been drilling for a bow shot all the time!" he yelled for Henry's amusement. Decades later, Colby could still repeat the line on request.

"C'mon, Troy!" Henry called from the smoking grill, a drink in one hand, a greasy spatula in the other. "Give it to Susan Kohner one more time!"

And so Troy played his one scene from *Imitation of Life*: "Just tell me one thing," he repeated. "Is your mother a nigger? Tell me, tell me! All the kids are talking behind my back. You're lying. You're lying." And then he might push a Cal, a Clint, or a Chance into the pool to replicate Kohner's infamous fall into the back-lot gutter.

For actors who hadn't eaten much all week, Saturday afternoon was chow-down time at Henry's. But only if their abdomen could handle the extra hamburger and potato salad. While Henry's girth never stopped expanding, he made sure to keep a watchful eye on everybody else's waistline. "Don't you have a scene on the beach with Sandra Dee coming up next week?" he asked Troy, who had been ready to help himself to another drumstick, which Henry quickly confiscated. It didn't matter how much Henry had consumed; he tore into Troy's drumstick with renewed appetite, sucking the barbecue sauce from his fingers. "I can eat," he told Troy. "You have to look good in those swim trunks."

"Henry could be a pain," Troy acknowledged. "Henry could also be a tremendous support." For boys who'd grown up without a father, he provided the big-city refuge where their every material whim was indulged. Like father, like son: Horace Willson gave Henry everything he ever wanted, and on some level of paternal commitment, Henry felt obliged to do the same for hundreds of other young men.

"He was very concerned about your comfort at those parties," said his client James DeCloss. In a cabana off the pool, guests found trunks, robes, flip-flop sandals, everything they needed if they'd arrived unprepared for a swim. Guests showed up in shorts and T-shirts, though Henry kept it more formal in dress slacks and a long-sleeve shirt, which looked right in step with the strains of Guy Lombardo emanating from a record player in the living room. Pat Colby got the host to expand his stereo's repertoire to include Elvis Presley. Henry liked the older, more subdued, postarmy Elvis with the short hair and cleaned-up sideburns and a new crooner-style in music. "And Elvis smiles more now," Henry said. "Not scowling all the time." Later, when the Beatles and their "I Wanna Hold Your Hand" bombarded the airwaves, Henry refused to let their records sully his turntable. He thought they looked and sounded like "a bunch of fairies."

As Henry was, in most ways, an ultraconservative man, skinny-dipping at his parties would have been deemed as gauche as a poolside statue of Michelangelo's David or a marble boy peeing into the water (which is how Rock Hudson enhanced his backyard when he moved into the Castle). And to share industry gossip was one thing, but when it came to discussing news of a more personal nature, everyone knew to deliver it in discreet whispers on a short walk up the steep hill in Henry's backyard. By late afternoon, the pine grove there threw shade across the pool, forcing sunbathers to jockey their chairs to catch another hour of light. In one such tête-a-tête stroll up the hill, a reportedly heterosexual veteran of Henry's Saturday parties assured a more recent hetero inductee that swinging both ways, to his surprise, no longer offended him very much. "Sucking cock isn't so much different from sucking on a woman's nipple," he said.

Henry returned such favors. "He preferred straight men," said Pat Colby. Persky and Himmel (married with a wife and kids in New Jersey) weren't quite so picky. The movie-star veneer of Henry's parties was novelty enough for them. Back east, they were more accustomed to "pimp parties" and prostitutes hired by Roy Cohn's procurer, who could attract the best New York City had to offer. A minor model, the pimp claimed a major fashion photographer as his lover.

A gentle man, Persky possessed at least a modicum of Henry's need to nurture. At the barbecues, Persky made a habit of taking boys aside and asking them with all due concern, "Do you like to fuck or do you like to get fucked?" Regardless of their response, the future film producer nodded and smiled wide enough to expose the split in his two front teeth. "Fine, just don't get fucked before you do a scene," he allowed. "It shows on camera."

The truth of Henry's legendary "orgies" reflects off more surfaces than there were ripples in his kidney-shaped pool after a match of water polo. Pat Colby insisted the Saturday fetes did not progress into group sex. At least not of classic proportions. "That's the other big myth about Henry," he said.

Phyllis Gates's actor-friend Ray Stricklyn, however, reported "gang bangs" at Henry's place. "I thought I was just going to a party, not knowing how the evening would evolve," Stricklyn offered. "There were dozens of the most attractive young men in Hollywood in attendance, including, to my surprise, several well-known, supposedly 'straight' movie actors . . . I was definitely not into group sex and left when I realized where the evening was headed."

Troy Donahue did admit, "I got into a pile at Henry's."

Maybe it was only a small pile. "There was the occasional three-way in the guest room," said Colby. Rock Hudson was known to participate in some of these nocturnal threesomes and did so as late as 1959, long after he needed to curry his mentor's favor. As Pat Colby put it, "Everyone wanted to sleep with Rock. No one wanted to sleep with Henry."

FBI File: Mr. Rock Hudson

In Hollywood, sex was never casual when it involved two or more men. In 1959, two FBI agents received orders from Washington, D.C. to pay a visit to the second-floor offices at 8075 Sunset Boulevard. With no interest in collecting stars' autographs, they followed Henry Willson and Pat Colby into work one day, displayed their badges, then made it clear: Willson and Colby were part of a gay-mafia probe being conducted by the FBI.

They asked the question, "Are you a homosexual?"

"No, of course not" Henry replied, lowering his voice but already shaken.

The FBI agents then turned to the young man sitting next to Henry. "Are you a homosexual?"

"No, I am not," said Colby, who practically expired on the spot. He had recently appeared in *Run Silent, Run Deep*. Now, he sat trembling in Henry Willson's office, the subject of an investigation into his sex life. "Both Henry and I were sputtering a lot that day," Colby said. "I doubt the FBI agents believed us. We were so rattled I don't think either of us were very convincing."

Neither Colby nor his boss had any doubt why they were being interrogated. "We have from good authority that Rock Hudson is a homosexual," said one agent. He had done his homework and described in detail the gay scene in Los Angeles and environs. He mentioned bars, boyfriends' homes, motels, even the addresses of houses where Rock had participated in sex parties. Colby was astonished at the accuracy of the names they provided regarding Rock Hudson's various sex partners. *Confidential* magazine, apparently, had nothing over the FBI when it came to conducting an investigation into a famous person's private life.

Shaking his jowls, Henry denied everything. "Oh, no, never. Why, Rock Hudson was married not long ago," Henry told them.

The FBI agents looked unimpressed. "Didn't that marriage end in divorce recently?" one of them asked.

"Most marriages here in Hollywood end in divorce. Nothing unusual there," said Henry.

"What were the grounds for divorce?"

Henry told them, "Mental cruelty, I think."

The FBI inquired into the whereabouts of Phyllis Gates, which was information the bureau already had in its possession. Inquiries were also made into the phone numbers and home addresses of Rock Hudson's reported sex partners. "I'm sure most of these men don't even know Rock," Henry assured. But the FBI men were not to be dissuaded, and it wasn't until Henry scribbled down a few numbers that they left his office.

"We were coughing and spitting, just total nervous wrecks, by the time those two men said good-bye," said Colby. Not knowing how to respond, he and his boss did what they always did whenever life's hurly-burly threatened to overwhelm them. They went to the Cock 'n' Bull to get inebriated. Hours later they were drunk but still shaking.

To Pat Colby's knowledge, nothing ever came of the sixty-minute interrogation. The FBI did not open files on either man. Rock Hudson, however, wasn't so lucky. The FBI's dossier on the actor began in 1959, the year of Henry's impromptu interrogation, and remained active until 1972. In an undated section, the report reads, "In view of the information that Hudson has homosexual tendencies, interview will be conducted by two mature experienced Special Agents." In the file dated February 16, 1960, three quarters of the page has been blacked out. Only two sentences are legible: "The files of guests' names were confiscated during the raid and as a result, many prominent individuals have reportedly been revealed as apparently participants in these orgies. Among these, according to (blacked out) are the name of movie actors . . . ROCK HUDSON." A two-inch list of names is blacked out. The explanation for the deletion is handwritten in the report's margin: "Not concerning the subject of your request."

A file dated October 28, 1966, reads: "On another occasion, information was received by the Los Angeles office of the FBI that it was common knowledge in the motion picture industry that Rock Hudson was suspected of having homosexual tendencies. It is to be noted in May 1961, a confidential source in New York also stated that Hudson definitely was a homosexual."

The files appear to have been kept for two reasons: Rock Hudson received the occasional film offer to play the role of an FBI agent, which required the agency to vet the script. But more important, public condemnation of homosexuals in the HUAC era continued well into the 1960s. Little did it matter that J. Edgar Hoover was a homosexual. Rock Hudson's sex life made him a subversive in the eyes of the agency, and therefore a possible threat to national security.

The Hudson file, released under the Freedom of Information Act, did not refer to Pat Colby. Several sentences and paragraphs in the report are censored under Title 5, United States Code, Section 525 (b)(1), which reads: "specifically authorized under criteria established by an Executive order to be kept secret in the interest of national defense or foreign policy . . ."

It is not known if any FBI official met with or spoke to Henry Willson after the 1959 encounter. However, shortly after that first bureau interview, several of Henry's closest associates were startled by a new retort he used to level any and all threats of blackmail. "Oh no, they won't!" Henry would say, his arms high above his head, as if to clear the steam there. "If they try anything, I'll tell J. Edgar Hoover on them."

Although the name Henry Willson appears only once in the

FBI's Rock Hudson file, as the actor's "agent," the thirty-page report does refer to an undisclosed "informant." In a memo dated December 22, 1961, and addressed to the "Director, FBI" and "Assistant Director, C.D. De Loach," an unidentified FBI agent gives high marks to an "informant" who is a "close associate" of Rock Hudson.

The file goes on to state:

> He was contacted on a regular basis since that date and has cooperated willing and enthusiastically on assignments given to him. This informant appears to have great respect for the Bureau, and has readily agreed to furnish any information of value which might come to his attention on a strictly confidential basis. Based on his past performance, it appears that this informant can be trusted to keep his contact with Bureau Agents confidential and has treated his relationship with the Bureau in a very discreet manner.

Henry's prophylactic measures intensified over the years, and in the early 1960s his associates noticed the sudden appearance of a small metal filing cabinet in the den of his Bel Air home. Guests often remarked on what an ill-fitting addition it made to the room's otherwise well-appointed décor of fine antiques and overstuffed furniture. "I tried to open it whenever Henry left the room," said his assistant Gary Crutcher. "But I never succeeded. He kept it locked up." Crutcher knew the cabinet contained secret documents that Henry considered too sensitive to keep at his office. It always happened: when faced with the threat of blackmail, Henry now invoked the name of the FBI's top man. "I'll get J. Edgar Hoover on them," he used to say. And in the privacy of his home, he often pointed to the corner of his den and said, "Not with that filing cabinet they won't!"

Increasingly, real muscle was needed. One year after Mr. and Mrs. Rock Hudson divorced, two men contacted Henry with threats to go public with their story: they had performed threeways with the star, and were ready to tell everything about their sexual exploits. Henry knew whom to call. "He phoned a Mob connection he had in Las Vegas," said his client Paul Nesbitt, the former Chance Nesbitt.

The contact was made late one afternoon, when Henry had invited Nesbitt to have drinks with him at Frascatti's patio. Nesbitt could see that Henry was agitated, distracted, and in addition to discussing other business matters, Henry brought up the matter of the twin blackmailers, who he referred to as "those two faggots I have to get rid of." The waiter didn't have to ask: he brought a phone to Henry's table the instant he sat down. Highly sensitive phone conversations were never held in his home or office, since Henry preferred the anonymity of a restaurant line, which would make the call harder to trace, he said. Even at Frascatti's, he complained of the static on one line and asked the waiter for another phone. And then another. Finally, convinced he was not being bugged, Henry let go with a heavy sigh and phoned his contact in Vegas.

For such a gregarious, blowsy talker, Henry could be succinct when business demanded. As Nesbitt remembered, Henry said very little during that phone conversation. He repeated the two men's names and the address where they were staying in Palm Springs. "I want those two faggots taken care of," he repeated, then put down the receiver. "They'll take care of it for me," Henry told Nesbitt. He could have been talking about problems on the movie set with some client's wig or corset.

The two men finished their drinks, then got into Henry's Cadillac to drive to Panza's Lazy Susan. Henry said hello to the usual gathering of clients and hangers-on at the restaurant, but being preoccupied with the latest Rock contretemps, he kept the greetings and chit-chat to a minimum, and focused instead on his spaghetti dinner. Before he could order dessert, the courtesy phone on his table rang. It gave him the news he wanted to hear. Henry nodded. "Good." The men in Vegas had done their job. "They owed me," Henry sighed as he finally let his great weight settle into the chair. He motioned for the waiter. "We're ready for dessert," he said.

Nesbitt knew the two men, vaguely. "They weren't just roughed up. They were either tortured or rubbed out," he said. "To this day, I've never heard of them again."

As Henry put it, the Mob "owed" him due to his celebrity connections. Nesbitt explained, "He was always getting stars to show up at the Las Vegas clubs for their big openings there. The Mob owed Henry a lot."

So did the Rock. Beyond the usual contract negotiations, pimp assignments, and hit jobs, Henry provided other services for his number-one client. As Rock's fame grew, Henry noticed that the IRS audited the star with increasing regularity. In his typical nothing-left-to-chance approach, Henry insisted on meeting with the auditor, even though Rock had a business manager.

"Henry would look for some weakness or desire and then play on that," said Gary Crutcher. He sometimes set up dates with a male or female prostitute, depending on the auditor's sexual orientation. Other times, a handsome out-of-work client handled the entertaining. If the tax man got a kick out of meeting movie stars, Henry arranged it. "He took them out on the town to show them a good time. It always worked," said Crutcher. "There was never a pay-off."

Often audited but never fined, Rock continued to escape the blackmailers, the FBI, and the IRS.

PART TEN

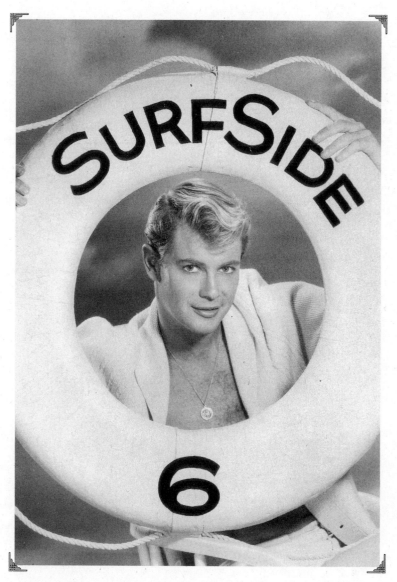

An overnight teen sensation in 1959's *A Summer Place*, Troy Donahue finds himself farmed out to a TV series, *Surfside 6*, one year later.

45

The Trouble with Warren Beatty

Every so often, Hollywood reverts to its basic instincts and goes completely nuts. The late 1950s was just such a time. Weekly box office attendance had fallen from ninety million to forty million in 1959. Two Henry Willson–friendly studios were particularly hard hit: 20th Century–Fox sold off most of its back lot, to become a new development called Century City. And over at Universal, the film division continued to post annual losses of $2 million. In December 1958, Lew Wasserman's MCA purchased Universal's 367–acre lot for $11.25 million, then turned around and leased the production facilities back to the studio for $1 million a year. It was a most curious kickback deal, so curious that it jumpstarted the Justice Department's inquiry into the agency's monopolistic practices in the entertainment business.

Despite the turmoil, Henry was one agent who felt no pain for the moment. The *Ben-Hur* mistake aside, Henry made the priceless decision to put Rock Hudson into his first major comedy, *Pillow Talk,* in which the actor performed the improbable task of playing a heterosexual impersonating a homosexual to get Doris Day into bed. ("There are some men who are devoted to their mothers," says Rock's character, Brad Allen.) The film turned into one of the biggest moneymakers of the year and showed Rock's heretofore untapped skill at comic timing, an asset that immediately established him as heir apparent to the aging Cary Grant, now fifty-five.

The miracle was all Henry's. He had replaced the movies' greatest romantic leading man with a former truck driver from Winnetka, Illinois. But then, who was Cary Grant but a former carny performer named Archie Leach who worked the piers of Bristol, England, by doing somersaults and backflips? Ever the miracle worker, Henry followed his Roy-to-Rock transformation by turning Merle Johnson Jr. into a movie star named Troy Donahue.

As the newest boy in the stable, Troy credited Henry with paying to get his teeth straightened and giving him a new name; otherwise, the makeover pretty much ended there. "I already knew which fork to use," Troy claimed.

Compared to handling the Rock, Troy was a blessed relief in at least one important aspect. There were no telltale boyfriends to worry about. He was dating Fran Bennett and then Nan Morris, who remembered Henry's being ecstatic that Troy always had a girlfriend. In fact, Troy had many, many girlfriends. Even before the release of the make-out masterpiece *A Summer Place*, Troy enjoyed a reputation for cruising up and down Sunset Boulevard in his new red Porsche, the ragtop rolled down, which made it easier for the girls to spot him, jump in his car, and take the two-minute drive up the hill to his place. Troy's New England–style house was a block north of the Strip, on Wetherly Drive, where only two plaster lions, a white picket fence, a Yorkshire terrier named Missy, and not much else guarded the premises. Henry appreciated Troy's East Coast good taste, as well as his blatant hetero behavior, even if the latter nearly caused him to blow his screen test for *A Summer Place*.

So what if Troy couldn't act? Troy Donahue was to Hollywood what big fins were to his dead father's car company. Henry just knew it. "You are Johnny Hunter," he told his client, as if to say Troy didn't have to act. "Just be yourself," advised Henry. Troy's character Johnny Hunter was the clean-cut boy who somehow impregnates Sandra Dee on an island off the East Coast that in the movie looks an awful lot like Big Sur. Pulling some well-worn strings over at Warner Bros., Henry asked the film's director, Delmer Daves, to helm Troy's screen test for *A Summer Place*. Daves, a director who was as gently paternalistic as his hair was flaming red, had been around Hollywood nearly as long as Henry. He helped pen the original 1939 *Love Affair* screenplay, as well as its 1957 remake, *An Affair to Remember*.

Daves tested Henry's latest model with a five-minute love scene. Surprisingly, despite ten movies to his credit, the twenty-two-year-old had never before engaged in an act of on-screen osculation. It was different from real life, he soon learned, and he kept getting the lips and teeth all wrong. "No, no, no!" Daves told Troy after the first attempt, as well as the second, third, and fourth. "You can't kiss like that. Your mouth is open." Troy's tongue had an instinct for finding its way out from between his lips and into Sandra Dee's mouth whenever their two heads bumped together. "Think of your lips as glued together," Daves instructed.

Troy tried pressing his mouth against hers and not inhaling for a few seconds. When he couldn't hold his breath any longer, someone yelled cut, and it was over. The crew applauded as Troy gazed down at Sandra Dee. "Does that feel like kissing to you?" he asked.

"No," she replied, "but that's the way we do it in the movies."

On July 28, 1959, Troy saw *A Summer Place* for the first time at the Academy Theatre in Pasadena. The preview audience included Jack Warner and his head of production, Steve Trilling. No one paid much attention to the six-foot-three blond when he entered the theater. Then the lights went down, the music played, the credits rolled.

Delmer Daves treated Troy's entrance in *A Summer Place* the way directors had introduced hundreds of moist ingenues over the years. Playing the benignly potent Johnny Hunter, Troy first appears on-screen with his back to the camera, and as it dollies toward him, he turns to receive the closeup that sold a million V-neck sweaters and became every girl's fantasy of perfect first love without pain, penetration, or acne. *A Summer Place* is grade-A Hollywood soap opera with so many deliciously overwrought performances (Constance Ford's frigid mother, Arthur Kennedy's drunk father, Sandra

Dee's impregnated teen) that Troy's emotional vacancy registers as poetic understatement by comparison.

Teenage girls didn't know actors from astronauts. As a heartthrob, Troy presented a blank page on which any virgin could project her ecstatic, if rather vague, notions of sex. What did it matter that his face remained devoid of emotion for the next two hours of screen time? *A Summer Place* marked the beginning of the end for Merle Johnson Jr. "I looked around the theater. I heard the music," Troy said of Max Steiner's lilting love theme, a tune that would go to the top of the pop charts and launch a thousand real-life teen pregnancies. "And I thought: We might have something here."

What Warners had here was a teen idol whom any parent could love despite his having knocked up Sandra Dee (and, two years later, Connie Stevens in *Parrish*). From the on-screen evidence, one always had the suspicion that Troy didn't quite know how he got girls pregnant, which helped to soften the blow of his virility. Not that it really mattered if adults liked Troy Donahue. By 1959, teenagers reigned at the movies. As attendance dropped precipitously among older moviegoers, *A Summer Place* filled an important niche in the market: no fewer than four thousand drive-in movie theaters ponied up to splash it across their oversized screens.

It was already a hoary movie cliché when David O. Selznick made the first *A Star Is Born* twenty-two years earlier, and yet, overnight success stories still happened if an actor waited long enough. Troy Donahue walked into Pasadena's Academy Theater a nobody but came out smelling like buttered popcorn that hot July evening in smog-filled Pasadena. He couldn't see the San Gabriel Mountains a few blocks away, but Troy did catch a glimpse of his future. Having just watched *A Summer Place* unspool for the first time, he left the screening to be greeted by a mob of well-wishers, among them, Rock Hudson's erstwhile guardian angel, Ed Muhl.

No longer rendezvousing with Rock Hudson in his Universal office, the studio vice president saw real potential in Henry's new boy. Muhl phoned Henry the day after the screening. "Let's sign him!" he exclaimed, psyched by what he had seen on-screen in Pasadena.

"Sorry," Henry replied. "You dropped him and he's been signed by Warners."

The rival studio had big plans for its newest teen idol. Unfortunately, soon after *A Summer Place* became a huge success and Troy acquired three hundred sweaters, the honeymoon at Warner Bros. quickly devolved into a marriage of servitude and drudgery. Delmer Daves would shepherd Henry's blondest star through three more films at Warners—*Parrish, Susan Slade,* and *Rome Adventure.* But Troy soon discovered that, regardless of his $400-a-week salary, the studio didn't like him to be idle between pictures for more than a weekend. When he wasn't in front of the cameras, Troy took orders to go on publicity tours to promote his movies—or worse, to perform episode work on some other star's TV series.

"That's when his drinking really started," said his girlfriend Nan Morris. "Warner Bros. had him running on a nonstop treadmill."

Actually, his alcoholism had started with his film career, if not earlier when he looked at himself in the mirror at age nine, highball in hand, and tried to imitate his screen idol, Cary Grant. "I never went before the cameras without having a buzz on," said Troy. "I was just too scared to do it without at least one drink."

Ironically, one of Troy's first film roles was as a skid row drunk, in 1958's *Voice in the Mirror,* the story of Alcoholics Anonymous and its founders Bill W. and Dr. Bob. "I remember getting drunk on martinis with Julie London on the way to the studio," said Troy. "I fell out of her limo and crawled to my dressing room, where I tried desperately to sober up to play a drunk." The martinis soon progressed to half a pint of vodka mixed with codeine, and later, four lines of cocaine got added to the mix.

The TV gigs perturbed Troy. "I was a movie star," he said. "Movie stars weren't supposed to be doing television." After the buoyant glow of *A Summer Place,* Troy fell back to reality when he was told to report to the set of Warners' new TV series *The Alaskans,* which top-lined an Englishman who, unlike Troy, had no hit movies to his credit.

On his first day on the set, Troy shook hands with the Brit, Roger Moore. Then the director asked the star of *A Summer Place* to stick his head in a snowdrift made out of white plastic flakes. Two takes later, a Warners executive came up and greeted Troy with a slap on the butt. "Oh, kid, I've got great news for you!" said the VP. "We've got you your own TV series."

Before Troy could dust off the pellets of plastic, he put in an angry phone call to his agent. "But there's nothing I can do," Henry replied. He wasn't lying. For every feature the studios made in 1962, they spat out two television series. Film production continued to plummet all over town as most of the movie money was consolidated into a handful of big-budget films. In the wake of such epic successes as *Ben-Hur* ($12.5 million) and *Spartacus* ($12 million), the studios were betting even more money on sagas like *Mutiny on the Bounty* ($30 million) and *Cleopatra* ($40 million) to rescue them from possible bankruptcy and certain obsolescence. Fewer films meant fewer contract players, which had always been the life blood of Henry's agency. Those actors lucky enough to have a renewed contract found themselves farmed out to television.

"Besides, TV is where it's at," Henry told Troy. "Look at Lucille Ball and Robert Stack. This will be good for your career. You can do the TV series *and* make films." As Henry pointed out, Delmer Daves had already expressed interest in using Troy for *Parrish,* and paying him all of $3,000 for his services. "Henry told me *Surfside 6* was a good idea," said Troy. "I knew he didn't believe it."

It was a new series but Troy would be reprising an old role, private detective Sandy Winfield, which he had already played in two episodes of *77 Sunset Strip*. Henry kept telling Troy to look forward to *Parrish* and another new film that Warners had on the fast track. Elia Kazan was directing an original script by William Inge, author of *Bus Stop* and *Picnic*. Best of all, it would star his old client Natalie Wood, and Henry promised to get Troy the top spot opposite her. Warners was calling it *Splendor in the Grass,* a real classy project, something to do with "a girl going nuts over her boyfriend and William Wordsworth," Henry told Troy. "I'll talk to Natalie. She owes me."

Whatever she owed Henry for *Rebel without a Cause,* the word did not find its way to her new East Coast director. "Elia Kazan wouldn't even meet with me," said Troy. Instead, Warners handed him yet another series, *Hawaiian Eye,* which Troy dismissed as a weekly beach-blanket-bingo movie on TV. It starred his *Parrish* lust-interest Connie Stevens and was well into its third season. *Surfside 6* had been canceled, and with it Troy's movie career. "Kazan was looking for a new face, someone from the East Coast," he said. Someone not represented by Henry Willson.

It left Troy profoundly bummed that Kazan rejected him without so much as the obligatory hello-and-goodbye drinks at the Polo Lounge. "Kazan went with this actor whose biggest credit until then had been in *The Many Loves of Dobie Gillis!*" he complained. The new actor's name: Warren Beatty.

Henry did not give up. With the election of John F. Kennedy in 1960, Warners dredged up the new president's old bestseller, the autobiography *PT 109,* and thought it would make a swell movie. "You can play Kennedy! Who needs Kazan?" Henry told Troy.

And so it wounded Troy when a newspaper reporter asked John F. Kennedy which actor he'd like to star in his biopic and the president of the United States replied, "Warren Beatty." (Beatty rejected the role, which eventually went to Cliff Robertson.)

Meanwhile, Henry did continue to meet with success in keeping Rock's latest orgy out of the tabloids. However, he failed utterly when the mainstream press picked up on Troy's 1961 fistfight with fiancée Lili Kardell, best known in Hollywood for making a Nazi-spy comedy, *Looking for Danger,* and dating James Dean a couple of times. Kardell charged Troy with assault and battery and filed suit for $60,450. Jack Warner had looked the other way when *Confidential* passed judgment on Tab Hunter's old arrest, but he quickly made an out-of-court settlement to cover up Troy's more publicized run-in with the law.

Ironically, since the love affair between Roberto Rossellini and Ingrid Bergman, heterosexual scandals had been fair game. While *Life* and *Look* only hinted at the real reasons for Rock Hudson's new bachelor status, staid old *McCall's* took off the white kid gloves to put a few holes in the aggressively hetero lifestyle of Troy Donahue. "His home was always an open house and the worst people in Hollywood and along Sunset Strip took advantage of his hospitality," the magazine reported. "Some of these people were real creeps. There were times that some of his friends avoided visiting him for fear of a police raid."

McCall's titled the profile "The Night They Invented Troy Donahue," which mirrored the "How to Create a Movie Star" slug that *Look* used to profile Rock Hudson a decade earlier. The slide in vocabulary from "create" to "invented," however, left no doubt of the general decline. Troy finally decided to put on the brakes. First off, he said no to Warners' latest project for him.

"*Palm Springs Weekend* was just this beach-blanket-bingo movie set in the desert," complained Troy. "They had a bunch of contract players sitting around the studio with nothing to do, so they concocted this movie, no script, about a weekend in the desert. I said no."

But Henry said yes and sent his recalcitrant star packing to Palm Springs, where Troy loaded up with alcohol and codeine before every take. Otherwise, he did as he was told and left it to his costar to be the wench in the ointment. Even though *Palm Springs Weekend* was a short twenty-one-day shoot, Connie Stevens provided the cast and crew with an unscheduled twenty-four-hour hiatus, which she blamed on Jack Warner.

Two weeks into shooting on *Palm Springs Weekend*, the studio boss announced that Audrey Hepburn would headline Warner's most spectacular new project. Jack Warner could forget about Julie Andrews's disappointment over not starring in *My Fair Lady* onscreen. Connie Stevens claimed that he had promised *her* the coveted role of Eliza Doolittle! Stuck in the desert on a low-budget teen movie, the actress walked off the set of *Palm Springs Weekend* and took an unauthorized day off to dry out her swimsuit. Only later did Connie Stevens realize that she and Troy Donahue were the lucky ones in a film populated with such soon-to-be-former Warners contract players as Ty Hardin, Stephanie Powers, and Robert Conrad. In 1960, Warners boasted a contract list of 140 actors. Four years later, Connie and Troy were the only two left in the studio's stable. At least they were employed and working.

Henry never got rich on the 10 percent he received from Troy's $400 a week at Warners. His big money came from Rock Hudson's 7 Pictures Corporation, a partnership that gave him the promise, if not the reality, of a comfortable retirement. "Take care of the money you're making from 7 Pictures and you'll be set for life," Rock told Henry. The problem was, Henry thought that the money would go on forever. He had ambitions to be a producer like his mentor Charlie Feldman, and he rightfully blamed Doris Day's husband, Marty Melcher, who later absconded with all her money, for not getting a producer credit on *Pillow Talk*.

"Farty Belcher," Henry called him.

Against considerable odds, he didn't let Doris Day's husband stand in his way a second time. Henry secured a waiver from the Screen Actors Guild to take a producer credit on Rock's next films, *Come September*, with Gina Lollobrigida, and *Lover, Come Back*, again with Doris Day. Those SAG waivers were not easy to secure, and for good reason. The actors' union saw a conflict of interest whenever an agent tried to double as producer. Regardless, MCA had grown into a bloated octopus with its waivers from SAG, and over at Famous Artists, Charlie Feldman had been producing movies packaged with talent from his own agency ever since *The Lady Is Willing* in 1942.

Unfortunately for his bank account, Henry came late to the agent-producer game, and his hopes of making more Rock Hudson pictures ended in the summer of 1962. The Justice Department filed suit against MCA, SAG, and the Writers Guild of America West to declare their waivers in violation of antitrust laws. On July 13, it was official: MCA had to divest itself of its talent agency to avoid antitrust prosecution. Within twenty-four hours, the agency known as MCA was history.

For Henry, who got in at the tail end of the agent-producer phenomenon, it had been profitable while it lasted. When he returned to agenting full time, others of his profession took the more lucrative route. Lew Wasserman segued to running Universal Pictures. Feldman sold Famous Artists to Ted Ashley (who renamed it Ashley Famous) and went on to make movies, with wildly divergent results: *The Group, What's New, Pussycat?* and finally *Casino Royale* in 1967. The next year, Feldman married his thirty-four-year-old girlfriend, Clotilde Barot, then died of cancer two weeks later at age sixty-four.

"Charlie was brilliant, and a born wheeler-dealer," Henry eulogized. "He was the first of the agents to break into the producing end of the business and, had he not died in 1968, he would probably have become head of a studio like others of our ilk—Freddie Fields, Ted Ashley, Ray Stark, and David Begelman." Henry made special note: "It was Darryl F. Zanuck who always predicted that one day agents would end up owning the business. And during his lifetime he's seen it happen."

Henry ended up owning not much of anything. His cash flow from 7 Pictures ended with the very profitable *Lover, Come Back* and *Come September,* released back to back in 1961. For Rock, the enterprise became the foundation of his fortune. For Henry, it covered the never-ending tab at Panza's Lazy Susan and other watering holes. Rock could only shake his head. "You know Henry and money," he said.

46

Jock-Turned-Extortionist

Rock Hudson and Henry Willson were business partners. They also shared the same bed, but not always at the same time.

Pat Colby lived at the Cahuenga Garden Apartments, a courtyard building that was painted Jayne Mansfield pink and rests on Cahuenga Boulevard across from where the 101 Freeway blasts its way through the Hollywood neighborhood. Even in bad traffic, it's less than five minutes from the Universal Pictures lot on the other side of the hills. Not the quietest dwelling in the city, its location made 2026 Cahuenga a convenient rest spot for Henry and Rock, who shared a studio apartment only a flight down from Colby's one-bedroom. Colby kept the place clean and well-vacuumed, he changed the bed sheets, and made sure the refrigerator never ran out of their favorite snacks and the liquor cabinet always remained well-stocked.

But most important, "Henry and Rock used the place as a sex pad," said Colby. In addition to Henry's pimping, Colby also provided the star with a wide variety of chance encounters. "My friends all wanted to sleep with Rock," said Colby. "Henry had his standards, but Rock would sleep with anybody."

In March 1962, Henry and Rock booked a suite at the Fairmont Hotel on Russian Hill in San Francisco. Pat Colby came along, but as usual, stayed at one of the bed-and-breakfasts at the foot of the hill, on Van Ness Avenue, a more suitable address for the hired help. Colby didn't complain. Courtesy of Henry, he managed his fill of steak dinners at Ernie's, the historic, red-flocked restaurant that Hitchcock had incorporated so memorably four years earlier in *Vertigo,* his masterpiece of sexual obsession and impotence.

On that extended weekend trip, Henry introduced Rock to an acquaintance who was a sports entrepreneur. Clearly infatuated with the movie star, the businessman invited Rock to his estate on the East Coast.

"Rock didn't want to go," said Colby, "but Henry talked him into it."

Henry said it would be a needed break from the Hollywood routine, and as he explained the setup to Rock, "You can only imagine what kind of men a guy who promotes and brokers athletes might have roaming around his house!"

On that score, Rock was not disappointed. While being feted by the businessman, Rock met a professional athlete, which led to their having a memorable weekend together. Forty-eight hours later, it was over, they said their good-byes, and when Rock returned to Hollywood, he never expected, or much wanted, to see his ballplayer again.

"Rock and Henry were alike in that way," said Henry's assistant Gary Crutcher. "They each had these sexual adventures. But when the adventure was over, it was over."

Having not been groomed in the ways of Hollywood, the jock saw it differently. He made a surprise visit to Rock's doorstep at the Castle and let it be known: he wanted to move in with Rock so that the two of them could continue their love affair. And there was something else.

"He wanted to be a movie star," said Colby.

Rock avoided emotional commitments, or anything else that got in the way of making a quick sexual conquest. In response, the jock threatened blackmail.

"I got a phone call from him one day," said Henry's secretary Betty Butler. "He said he wanted to talk to Henry. I asked him why, thinking he was just another actor who wanted to sign with the agency. Instead, he told me that he had proof that Rock Hudson was a homosexual."

Henry took the threat seriously enough to post Gary Crutcher at the Cahuenga Boulevard studio. Crutcher was also instructed to check out the Las Palmas newsstand for any mention of the star. Coincidently, this new crisis in the continuing drama of Rock Hudson's sex life came on top of one that threatened to blow up the world in October 1962.

"The latest Rock bombshell hit during the Cuban Missile Crisis," said Crutcher, "Henry had real paranoia, always, but in this particular incident he was genuinely worried about Rock."

On the hour, Crutcher made his trip to the newsstand, then dashed back to the apartment to phone his newspaper report to Henry. Due to the United States government's Cuban standoff with the USSR, several papers put out new editions on an hourly basis. "The newsstand guy thought I was interested in what was happening with Cuba; but in fact, Henry had feared that one of the papers was going to break a story on Rock's being gay," said Crutcher.

Henry could have called in detective Nick Duber or the Mob to take care of the jock, but in the end he adopted a more radically conciliatory approach with this new blackmailer. Unlike the "nondescript" George who wanted to exchange sexually explicit photos for a major Hollywood career, Henry considered the athlete "a good bet" and had no problem securing him a small, uncredited role in a B-film. Friends of Rock even recall his saying that Henry got the athlete a TV series. To keep his distance, Henry never officially signed the inexperienced actor, and so the commission went to another agent.

"That wasn't unusual," said Nan Morris. "Henry wasn't always so good with business."

For the moment, it didn't matter. Henry protected the Rock, and the former jock now had his own career to protect from the whispers of a homosexual affair.

Married to Suzanne Pleshette

Heterosexuality has its advantages. After squelching yet another exposé on Rock, Henry took comfort in planning Troy Donahue's first wedding, a fete that cast him in his new role as stepfather to the groom.

After the battered-girlfriend fallout from Lili Kardell, Troy took it as a sign of faith that Warners was willing to foot the five-figure bill for his wedding to Suzanne Pleshette, the sultry, deep-voiced actress he'd met on the set of *Rome Adventure*. Warners liked the blond-and-brunette combo so much that the studio paired them again in *A Distant Trumpet*. It wasn't much of a movie, but its release did coincide nicely with their wedding. The Warners press release called the affair an "internationally heralded Hollywood wedding."

On January 4, 1964, Henry produced the same smile that he beamed for Sue & Nick and Alexis & Craig and Guy & Gail and Rory & Lita and Phyllis & Rock when Suzanne & Troy tied the knot. Like some modern-day Hymen, Henry took full credit for getting Jack Warner to pick up the tab for the blow-out affair. He even selected the venue: the gold and glittering Rodeo Room at the Beverly Hills Hotel. As a reward, Troy chose Henry for his groomsman. Top honors went to one of Troy's oldest friends, Owen Orr. The two boys had attended military academy together in the East, and after Troy established himself in Hollywood, Owen came to visit and soon found himself on Henry's roster with a new name: Greg Benedict. This time, Henry's inspiration for an actor's name had been drawn from the intensely macho, intellectually dense Bick Benedict, the character Rock played in *Giant*.

Betty Butler considered the name Greg Benedict one of Henry's least winning concoctions. "It always sounded like eggs benedict to me," said the secretary.

Troy invited Betty to his wedding, but she politely declined. "No, but I'll make it to the next one," she told him.

Gary Crutcher was no less judgmental. "So is the divorce going to be this big an affair?" he asked the groom at his wedding.

Troy and Suzanne exchanged vows, the music played, the caterers uncorked the champagne, and since it was a Henry Willson affair, Rock Hudson got to dance with everybody's mother. The star even gave Troy's kid sister, Eve, her moment on the dance floor. "I always thought Rock was handsome in the movies," said Eve Johnson, "but I underestimated him. Rock was absolutely gorgeous!"

Three hundred people attended, and since it was only January 4, Henry didn't have to lie when he crowed, "The wedding of the year!"

Jack Warner, Steve Trilling, William T. Orr, and other studio honchos put in their appearance at the reception but did not stay long enough to witness the effects of too much alcohol: A few of Henry's boys abandoned their female dates to start twisting with each other. Appropriately horrified, Henry loosened his bow tie, wiped his brow, then went to work as den mother. More than one set of broad, padded shoulders had to endure his pointed jab. "The lovely young lady you came with has inquired about you," he whispered with fierce intensity.

"Henry was like the mother of the bride, taking care of all the details," said Troy. "I think after the Rock Hudson disaster with Phyllis Gates, he was happy to have planned a real wedding."

Six months later, on June 30, 1964, Suzanne Pleshette filed for a divorce on grounds of mental cruelty. As she explained in court, her new husband had climbed through the bathroom window at 5 A.M., then accused her of locking him out. Troy was also reported to abuse her dinner guests after failing to eat a bite of the food she'd spent hours preparing.

Suzanne dumped Troy, but Troy remained faithful to Henry. He was one of the few who did. Most of his other clients joined the mass exodus from his agency. The actor Trent Dolan sought new representation when Henry devised one too many cockamamie gimmicks. "You should write your name Trent and follow it with a dollar sign," Henry told him. Instead, Dolan returned to New York to study with Uta Hagen, who had recently achieved her greatest success as the original Martha in *Who's Afraid of Virginia Woolf?* "Henry was Henry," said Dolan, who continued to use his real name, Trent Dolan, sans the dollar sign. Even Ford Dunhill tired of his fancy Henry Willson name and returned to calling himself Robert Aiken. "The name sounded like a car and I had more serious aspirations," he said. The turning point for Aiken came in 1964 when the ubiquitous Delmer Daves cast him as the glamorous best-selling novelist Howard Fain, James Franciscus's major competition in the literary potboiler *Youngblood Hawke*. In his one big closeup, Aiken kept forgetting his lines—all three sentences. "I blanked out on several takes and they had to walk me around," he recalled. "This had never happened before."

Finally, the script girl wondered out loud. "Who is your agent?" she asked Aiken.

"Henry Willson," he replied.

She sniffed, then went back to reading her script. "I thought so."

"I knew then it was time to get another agent," said Aiken, who eventually followed his more serious aspirations by starring in the Russ Meyer classic *Cherry, Harry, & Raquel*.

Another client, Rad Fulton, signed with a new agent after a nasty altercation with Henry at Panza's Lazy Susan. Insulted over some real or imagined infraction, Henry delivered his ultimate obloquy. "And I want that name back! Rad Fulton! It's mine!" he screamed.

"You can have your lousy name back," said the actor, who returned to using the one his parents gave him, James Westmoreland.

For a brief moment in the 1960s, George Nader became a client. He and his lover, Mark Miller, never cared much for Henry. "But we had been out of the Hollywood scene for a while," said Miller. Nader said, "Let's give Henry a try." By 1967, Nader had already enjoyed a long run playing the CIA agent Jerry Cotton in the West German spy franchise. When Henry got him the role of Joan Crawford's leading man in the C-level thriller *Berzerk!*, Nader showed his gratitude by committing to yet another Jerry Cotton movie.

"Tell the Germans to fuck themselves!" screamed Henry.

"Fuck yourself!" replied Nader.

Henry remained a colorful pasha on the scene. Too colorful for many people. Always outrageously funny, often outrageously cruel, he sometimes managed to be both at the same time. Like the night he threw darts at Dirk and Dack Rambo and Troy Donahue's sister, Eve. One of his more daring creations, the twin acting team (birth names: Orman and Norman Rambeau) played brothers on the short-lived *The New Loretta Young Show* in 1963. Prior to its quick cancellation, Henry had dreams the twins could be the next teen singing sensation, like the Everly Brothers or Jan and Dean. Because Nan Morris agreed with that assessment, she came up with the name Dack. Henry thought up Dirk. They even put together a label, Swing, to issue the twins' records. But the newly renamed Rambo brothers also had other aspirations and dumped Henry for the William Morris Agency. (Dirk died in a fiery car crash in 1967; Dack achieved greater TV fame on *Dallas* before dying of AIDS in 1994.) Their leaving him was understandable. Like any good father, Henry demanded respect. When he didn't get it, he threw things. In the case of Dirk and Dack, it was darts.

"We were at some party, and Dirk and Dack weren't paying enough attention to Henry," said Eve. In fact, they were chatting up Troy Donahue's sister instead of talking to Henry about their new record deal. Angered by their lack of attention, Henry, grabbed some darts the three teenagers had been playing with and started tossing them at his competition, the seventeen-year-old Eve. "Thank God he was drunk!" she said.

Henry's clients were used to such things, if anyone ever gets used to having sharp objects thrown at a kid sister. If it was around midnight and a parking-lot attendant or waiter crossed him, Henry liked to use the word "fag" a lot. Often in public. Other favorites were "mick, "wop," "cunt," and combinations thereof. Such incendiary language got him banished from the restaurant Scandia, but surprisingly few other respected establishments on the Strip gave him the brush. Henry made his apologies to the management the next day. He sent flowers, too. An expensive piece of silver from David Orgell's might arrive if he had really lost his temper the night before.

"Henry didn't mean anything by those slurs," said his client Paul Nesbitt. "But they got him in trouble."

PART ELEVEN

After once claiming "more stars than there are in heaven," M-G-M has only one actor, Chad Everett, under contract in 1968.

48

Bazooka and Brillcreem

I t was the tale of 10,000 men. Climbing the stairs at 8075
Sunset Boulevard, the tall, dark-haired Adonis would make it
10,001.

Multitudes of biblical proportions had preceded the young man
in his pilgrimage to the corner of Sunset Plaza and the Strip. Like
all the others, he knew by heart the stories of beautiful boys who
drove their Buicks from Pasadena, rode the Greyhound from
Kansas, hitchhiked all the way from Tampa to meet and impress the
starmaker of first choice: Henry Willson. "The fairy godfather of
Hollywood," they called him.

A few dressed for the occasion. They showed up in Ivy League
jackets, trousers meticulously pressed, neckties rolled into the perfect knot with a dimple. Many more made do with their tightest
T-shirts and jeans. Arms crossed, biceps flexed, they lined up outside the two-story building like so many flesh-and-blood telamons
pressed against the white Georgian façade.

David Jones Flowers, "florist to the stars," occupied the ground
floor. But who among these acolytes of Bazooka and Brillcreem
came to buy the long-stem roses or sniff the potted gardenias? These
guys came to smell success, taste fame, live forever on the big screen.

And so they ascended the narrow stairs at 8075 Sunset Boulevard to await their own pop apotheosis among a thousand other
head shots and résumés in the cramped second-floor office. Many

were called and—this being the house of no ordinary Hollywood shaman—many were chosen.

Fresh from the boulevard below, the new beauty-in-waiting looked around the office. "So this is the Henry Willson Agency," he announced.

Betty Butler looked up from her Smith-Corona. "May I help you?" she asked. As office secretary, Betty had been on the job less than a year, but the sculpted faces and physiques had already begun to merge, refract, fade. She had seen this one before. She just couldn't remember where or when.

As for the young man, he barely noticed the beehive adjutant in horn-rims. Nothing more than a smoky glass wall separated her from the keeper of the flame, his fiery hyperbole ready to anoint the next subscriber to *Photoplay*. "No, I just wanted to see the place," he said. "I'd always heard so much about it."

His curiosity sated, Warren Beatty turned to leave. His departure signaled the end of an era.

Splendor in the Grass had been in release only a few months. It was the film Troy Donahue so desperately wanted to make, and for good reason: thanks to Elia Kazan's direction, the movie made Beatty an overnight star. It helped, too, that he had the talent, good looks, and blatant heterosexual reputation courtesy of his affair with Robert Wagner's wife, Natalie Wood. Beatty personified a whole new breed of edgy, brooding actors with East Coast stage credentials who had begun to eclipse the pretty male pinups known as, disparagingly, "Henry's boys."

Henry always took pride in the fact that hopeful, eager "kids" never stopped flocking to his Sunset Boulevard office. He was known to be honest with them. "He was good to his word," said one client. "If you slept with him, Henry got you work."

The callow hopefuls continued to seek him out, and Henry obliged by never abandoning his open-door policy. Nick Nolte's mother brought her seventeen-year-old son to the Henry Willson Agency for an interview. The boy had done some acting at the

Pasadena Playhouse, and Henry signed him. A young woman who claimed to have been a model in New York City was less lucky. Henry told the aspiring actress Sherry Lansing to get a nose job. She later became president of 20th Century–Fox and Paramount Pictures.

More intriguing was Henry's refusal to represent a nightclub entertainer whose appearances at the Red Velvet in the mid-1960s prefigured the following decade's glittering, ambisexual glam rockers. He called himself Monti Rock III. In Johnny Carson's 1970–1971 season alone, *The Tonight Show*'s producers booked the self-proclaimed long-haired, mascared, velvet-robed singer "who could not sing" no fewer than thirteen times. In 1966, however, Henry was less impressed; outrage and shock were never his scene, especially when it threatened homosexual exposure. He took in a few performances at the Red Velvet; afterwards, he told Monti Rock a few innocuous stories about his most famous client, "Roy," but no contracts were ever signed.

"Henry told me I was born in the wrong era, that I should never be heard, that my face didn't match my voice," said Monti Rock, who knew he was being let down easily. He nonetheless appreciated the gracious gesture, especially when Henry added, "You would have been a star in the 1930s," or better yet, "silent films."

"Henry was very kind, very old-school, and always wore a suit and tie. But he was unkempt, a drunk," Monti Rock recalled. "You couldn't help but be fascinated. Henry Willson *was* the decline of fabulous, old Hollywood."

People said Henry had lost it, that he had lowered his standards and his taste in men had changed. In fact, Henry suffered the opposite problem. While the public fashion in hunks and heartthrobs continued to evolve, his eye for male beauty remained fixed, locked in the time capsule of post–World War II heroics that lionized clean-cut, do-or-die soldiers and sailors. By the 1950s, those he-men continued to score with teenage girls, but more and more they were being called "pretty boys" when compared to the edgier, more dangerous James Dean and Marlon Brando. In the 1960s, with Vietnam and the escalation of the

Cold War, "pretty" continued its slide downward in the public consciousness where it kept company with "passé," "weak," "frivolous," and, of course, "gay." The hypermasculinization Henry brought to the screen in the 1940s never went out of fashion. Rather, it continued to transmogrify to develop dark, sinister undertones.

In the mid-1960s, Clint Eastwood in *The Good, the Bad, and the Ugly* and *A Fistful of Dollars* brought an antiheroic dimension to Henry's uncomplicated Marlboro Men of a hundred TV Westerns from the previous decade. Sean Connery in *Goldfinger* and *Thunderball* wore a tuxedo as well as Rock Hudson (or Cary Grant) but he carried a license to kill, and could be counted on to use it postcoitus on his sex partners. Unlike the Rock, Connery was anything but safe in bed.

Public taste was one problem, studio policy another. In danger of becoming the Norma Desmond of agents, Henry now watched as the old power structure crumbled and gave rise to the independent producer. He could no longer phone Ed Muhl at Universal, Bill Orr at Warners, or Darryl F. Zanuck at Fox to put some kid under contract. The times had changed in ways that Henry not only refused to acknowledge but couldn't begin to fathom. And it wasn't just the meal ticket of his leading men.

In August 1965, Henry sat with Gary Crutcher on the patio at Frascatti's. It was shortly before sunset, and the California sky bled a deeper, more menacing red than what the smog usually allowed to filter through a summer sky at twilight. The day before, a routine traffic stop in South Central Los Angeles provided the spark that lit a thousand fires in Watts. Those riots lasted six days, leaving thirty-four dead, more than a thousand people injured, nearly four thousand arrested, and hundreds of buildings destroyed.

"We could smell the smoke in the air that evening," Crutcher remembered. He and Henry were drinking a concoction of champagne and fruit juice on the patio. Crutcher remarked on their syrupy drinks as the sweet taste mingled unpleasantly with the acrid stench from South Central on that fiery August evening. He told Henry, "It's so strange, us sitting here with drinks while a riot is going on."

"Tomorrow is another day!" exclaimed Henry.

Crutcher couldn't believe his boss's attitude. "It was like something out of Marie Antoinette," he said. "Henry had no idea of the immense irony."

Henry's wealth and social position in Hollywood protected him from having to identify with anyone farther to the south in Los Angeles, their homes suddenly destroyed by riots and fire. Four years earlier, in the great brushfires of August 1961, Henry nearly lost his own house on Stone Canyon Drive. Dennis Hopper had phoned him the news: "I just escaped from the canyon. I was driving by and I saw your house go up in flames."

But the actor had confused it with another manse nearby. Miraculously, Henry's Bel Air home never burst into flames, unlike the 460 others that amounted to $25 million in property damage. In typical fashion, Mike Connolly obliged Henry by playing up the drama in his next column.

"Henry Willson managed to save 3 suits, his passport & an armful of presoaks from the holocaust that exterminated his Stone Canyon home," he wrote. Despite the report, the house required little more than a new coat of paint. But it was a scare. The items mentioned in Connolly's column—the suits, passport, and Henry's beloved books of press clips—were the things Henry managed to cart away as the flames encircled his black Cadillac.

If the Watts riots reminded him of the Bel Air holocaust, Henry didn't mention the flashback to Gary Crutcher. Instead, Henry sprawled back in his wire chair, kicked off a wing-tipped shoe, and wondered aloud about Rock's latest movie, "Do you think *Strange Bedfellows* will outgross *Pillow Talk?* I think it could be our most popular one yet," he said as the smoke wafted over the patio walls.

Joan Didion described the urban catastrophe in her novel *Slouching Towards Bethlehem.*

> At the time of the 1965 Watts riots what struck the imagination most indelibly were the fires. For days one could

drive the Harbor Freeway and see the city on fire, just as we had always known it would be in the end. Los Angeles weather is the weather of catastrophe, of apocalypse . . .

For people in show business, words like "catastrophe" and "apocalypse" get tossed around but are generally reserved for Monday morning when the latest box office results hit the front page of *Variety*, and careers rise or tumble depending on the number of zeroes delivered. Now, the real fires were burning and Henry could not have cared less.

Henry's Last Chance

In 1965, Rock Hudson made three films—*Blindfold, Strange Bedfellows* and *A Very Special Favor*. None of them hits, none of them flops, all of them not very good. After seven enviable years at the top, his star got nudged to the number-two spot as the movies' box office draw. In 1967, Rock would watch as his name slid off the Top 10 list all together.

In public, he continued to be seen with his good friend, the actress Marilyn Maxwell. "She loved him," said the publicist Jerry Pam. "She wanted to marry him and make him straight, but she said it was impossible."

In private, Rock had fallen under the influence of an M-G-M flack named Tom Clark, who waited long enough to eventually became his lover. It would be a most gradual shift in power from Henry to Tom. As father-protector, Henry kept Rock's name out of the scandal sheets, but he was much less effective as the agent who had once delivered him *Giant* and *Pillow Talk*. It was now Henry who depended on Rock for his prestige and power base in Hollywood. The two men would always share the bond of their sexual orientation. There weren't many straight agents who could find it in their job description to pimp for Rock. And then there was the booze. Since Rock was the younger man, his alcoholism hadn't yet affected him acutely. He could drink to excess and still look like Rock Hudson the next day. But it was different for Henry, and by the

1960s his problem was in full, fatal bloom. Never one to accept anything less than star treatment, he now bristled and took extreme umbrage at the slightest infraction, whether it be a waiter's lack of attention or a long wait for a free phone line.

Richard Segel worked as an agent in Henry's office and remembered the scenes around midnight. "It would be late at night at some restaurant, and Henry would be carrying on, creating a ruckus. He would take great offense at any inattentiveness from a waiter. Rock would be with him, and you could tell he was embarrassed. It wasn't his scene at all," said Segel.

Henry's thinking may have been dulled and aggravated by alcohol, but he remained savvy in at least one respect. In 1953, he had orchestrated the expulsion of Jack Navaar from Rock's life. In 1964, he knew not to tangle with Tom Clark.

Clark did not return the favor. Sometime between his becoming friends and falling in love with Rock, the M-G-M publicist instigated a one-man campaign to "get rid of Henry Willson," whom he thought to be nothing less than "diabolical." He accused Henry of mendacity, laziness, and, worst of all, taking sides with Universal against his own client. Clark had a point there.

After making the lackluster thriller *Blindfold*, Rock felt he had reached an impasse with the studio, and asked Lew Wasserman to release him from his contract. Wasserman agreed, but not before Rock learned why the superagent-turned-movie mogul was the best dealmaker in Hollywood. "Rock received notice from Universal that he owed them for the Beverly Crest house, which the studio had bought him," said Mark Miller. Rock had failed to read the fine print in his contract, which Henry renewed in 1958. The Castle, purchased by Universal for $167,000, had been a major reason Rock reupped. Now that he wanted out of the contract, he discovered that he owed Universal for the house. "He was furious that Henry hadn't protected him. Rock had to borrow the money to pay for the house," said Miller.

Released from any obligation to Universal, Rock was free to

make John Frankenheimer's sci-fi movie *Seconds*. It was a gritty, black-and-white drama in which the hero undergoes extensive plastic surgery to be reborn with a completely new identity. Rock responded to the theme of rebirth, as well as the acting challenge, and considered it his best role since *Giant*. Henry, however, hated the project. "He was back in those Doris Day movies," said his secretary Betty Butler. "I doubt Henry ever saw *Seconds*."

And there were other problems, according to Rock. Due to mad love or some less complicated state of mind, Henry had begun to lavish undue attention on yet another protégé, who required the usual lengthy makeover. It was time and attention that Rock felt should have been spent resurrecting his career, not gambled away on some unknown.

Henry, as always, preferred to busy himself on the launch of a new career. Of course, the young man's plebian name, Dick Scholler, would have to go despite its priapic connotations. Henry tossed the leftover Race Gentry and Chance Nesbitt into his mental blender and spit out Chance Gentry. No matter that Tennessee Williams had forever linked the name Chance to a less-than-prime hustler in his 1959 drama *Sweet Bird of Youth*. Henry failed to make the connection that his once-catchy names now belonged to hustlers and porn actors, not movie stars. Something about Chance Gentry spoke to Henry, and what he heard drowned out the cries of resentment coming from his peeved dauphin.

"Chance! Chance! Chance! All Henry ever talks about is Chance Gentry!" complained Rock.

It was a given that Chance could not act, but that small limitation had never before deterred Henry. He saw Chance's ineptitude in front of the camera as nothing more than another challenge to overcome, like getting him to use the right fork or show up on time for interviews. To soften Chance's fears of failure, Henry repeated the story about Rock's "bligger backboard" goof.

But Henry failed to perceive the obvious truth: Unlike the young Rock Hudson, Chance Gentry would never get the opportunity to blow a line on a movie set. Despite Henry's Herculean efforts on his behalf, Chance appeared in front of the cameras only once, and it was a bit role in the Troy Donahue film *Come Spy with Me*. Released in 1967 by Hollywood's most budget-conscious studio, American International, *Spy* came late to the James Bond craze but wasted little time receding at the box office. For better or worse, it provided no opportunity for Chance Gentry to prove himself as an actor. In *Come Spy with Me*, Chance played a guy named Chance.

Henry never understood why Hollywood rejected Chance Gentry. The apparatchiks in his agency, however, knew the answer.

"He was dull as dishwater," said the secretary Betty Butler.

"He had absolutely no charisma," said the agent Richard Segel.

Henry's assistant Pat Colby gave him only slightly more credit. "Chance had a certain cowboy charm," he said.

The three of them shared a special joke about the would-be actor. Whenever he phoned the agency, they put him on hold and shared a good laugh. "It's Henry's last chance," they used to say.

It was near the truth.

50

Losing the Rock

As Henry put it, "One day I was in control, the next day I was not."

Under the implacable macho façade, Rock once again found a stronger man to take control of both his career and personal life. "First Henry, then Tom Clark," said Pat Colby. "Tom helped Rock get rid of a lot of people in his life."

"Tom took control of Rock," said the actor's former roommate Bob Preble. "And also he got him to drinking heavily."

No sooner did the two men meet, in 1964, than Tom Clark did what any new friend with ulterior motives would do: He nixed the sex pad that Rock and Henry shared at 2026 Cahuenga Boulevard. They weren't kids, Rock and Tom. Both men were in their forties, and in addition to their respective six-foot-plus frames, Rock and Tom had much in common: they liked to play bridge and drink, they liked to throw a football and drink, they liked to travel and drink, they liked to listen to Joan Sutherland and drink, and they also liked to trash Henry and drink. In fact, Rock engaged in more talk about Henry (all of it negative) than he did talking with Henry (little of it productive).

"Henry got lazy," said Clark.

Henry responded by refusing to believe the rumors. His carapace of booze, drugs, and sycophants left him oblivious to the reality of his decline, and up to the very last day he insisted that what was happening could not be happening. "Rock will never leave me. I made him a star. Rock owes me everything," said Henry, who then took another drink. From his perspective, he had spent half a decade making Rock a star and the other half protecting him from tabloid exposure. Even Henry's father was less myopic. Despite Henry's occasional invitation to the Castle, it troubled Horace Willson that the secretary Betty Butler increasingly played go-between for Rock and his son. Horace's own career in show business may have been but a memory three thousand miles away, but he remained a dogged negotiator, a pragmatist who knew that loyalty had no currency with a performer whose career lifespan could be counted in months, not years.

"Horace had a sharp business mind," said Gary Crutcher, "and he could see where Henry's business would end up without Rock." As communication between client and agent disintegrated, Horace took it upon himself to stop the collapse of Henry's firm. Risking his son's alienation, he scheduled a private talk with Rock.

"Rock was ready to leave Henry," said Betty Butler. "But Horace Willson begged him to stay for another year, until Henry could get back on his feet. Rock agreed, which was very generous of him and loving."

But not especially good business for an actor caught in career free fall.

Proud of his work in *Seconds,* Rock scheduled several private screenings at his home to show friends the film, which he considered a departure, a new beginning. Betty Butler attended one of those screenings shortly before the film's release in October 1966. "It was there that I met Rock's new agent, John Foreman of CMA," said Butler.

With an impressive dramatic performance to his credit, Rock believed he could rejuvenate his career with another agent, and he took necessary action. He had kept his promise to Horace Willson, but now his long year of waiting was over. After the screening, Rock told Betty Butler in precise detail how he wanted the termination handled: A letter severing his business relationship with Henry Willson would be sent to the Sunset Boulevard office. However, before she gave the missive to Henry, Rock wanted Betty to phone him. He could not handle firing Henry in person, face to face. Few men in Hollywood had that much guts, much less decency. But Rock did have enough respect and regard for the man who discovered him twenty years earlier to give the matter a degree of finesse beyond the harsh black-and-white of the printed word. He also knew that on some deluded, drug-induced level, Henry would not know it was over unless Rock Hudson told him.

Expected or not, the day arrived for Henry. The messenger delivered the letter, and as she had been instructed, Betty placed the call to Rock. Like most firings, it did not go well. Henry never discussed what happened that day. But later, Rock told Tom Clark (and the lover who replaced him, Marc Christian) that Henry became belligerent and lashed out in a truculent fit that was worse than any living nightmare Rock could ever have imagined.

"All you have going for you is your face. You don't have the talent!" Henry threatened Rock over the phone. "I have a jar of acid and I'm going to throw it in your face!"

Betty Butler did not witness the screaming match, but she found the acid story plausible. "Henry was pretty upset that day," she said.

When Henry finally slammed down the phone, Betty heard him in his office as he paced furiously and yelled obscenities. Henry did not mention anything to her about throwing acid in Rock's face, but he did put forth a few other threats. "I'm going to call Jaik Rosenstein and give him the story that Rock is a fag!" Henry bellowed. "I've been protecting Rock for all these years. Now Rosenstein can have his story!"

By 1966, Jaik Rosenstein's career as a journalist had been reduced to a four-page vanity rag, *Hollywood Cover-Up*, which he wrote, printed, and distributed from his garage in Los Angeles. The monthly scandal sheet was a real act of love for the town he hated most and all the people in it.

Twenty years earlier, Rosenstein's major calling had been his gig as Hedda Hopper's leg man. He even codified his status by writing a book, called *Hollywood Leg Man*. Hedda wore the crazy hats and did the puffy interviews with the celebrities; Jaik wandered the studio alleys and made the nosy phone calls to dig for the real scoops that made the gossip hag's column worth reading. Never one to withdraw from a good fight, Rosenstein had a reputation for throwing a few fists, like the time he busted the agent Irving "Swifty" Lazar in the face. Rosenstein landed the first punch and got the last laugh when he wrote: "Swifty had a great target, my nose, but couldn't reach it, even with his lifts on!"

That was 1959. Seven years later, his power base diminished, Rosenstein maintained whatever was left of his bad-guy reputation by publishing *Cover-Up*. He tended to limit his muckraking to the misguided business decisions of tinseltown execs ("Bluhdorn's Blow Job") and Mafia-connected stars ("The Sinatra Smell") but threw in the occasional sexual peccadillo as a blind item in his "Now I'll Tell You One" column. "*Cover-Up* was not a major operation," said Betty Butler. Indeed, the newspaper's permanently posted front-page reward for $5,000 said it all: "For information leading to the arrest and conviction of the person or persons responsible for the tire bombing of *Cover-Up* on April 26, 1960."

Butler remembered Rosenstein's many phone calls to Henry over the years—none of them laced with any love, all of them devoted to Rock's sex life. But Henry knew how to handle the press. If a reporter wanted dirt, Henry obliged by giving him unsavory reports on somebody else's client. It took even less to shut up Rosenstein. "Henry had many subscriptions to Jaik's magazine," said Butler. "I think if Jaik threatened anything, Henry just took out a few more subscriptions." As a result, no reports on Rock Hudson's sex life ever surfaced in *Cover-Up*.

Likewise, Henry never followed through on his promise to deface Rock, either literally or figuratively. The day he fired Henry, Rock was scheduled to tape an episode of *The Carol Burnett Show*. Afraid his former agent suddenly might appear, the star asked Tom Clark to be present in the audience—just in case Henry arrived with his aforementioned jar of acid.

Butler attended the taping and did not recall seeing Henry there.

In Tom Clark's version, Henry showed up as promised. "But the object of fear was as cheerful and friendly as a puppy," Clark reported. "Not only was there no acid, not even an unkind word was spoken."

Rock shared the acid story with another lover, a bartender named Marc Christian, who, in the early 1980s, came to replace Clark in Rock's affections. "We were watching John Waters's film *Female Trouble*," said Christian. The scene unspooled in which Edith Massey as Aunt Ida disfigures the face of Dawn Davenport, played by the three-hundred-pound transvestite Divine. "Here's some acid in your face, motherfucker!" screams Massey.

According to Christian, the scene's violence upset his famous lover. "Rock flinched, he became visibly upset," said Christian. "I asked what the matter was, and he told me the story about Henry threatening to throw acid in his face the day Rock fired him."

With or without the threats of facial disfigurement, it was a difficult break for both men. "I think on some level Rock loved Henry," said Pat Colby. "He didn't have a father. Henry became his father."

At least that's the way Henry saw their twenty-year relationship, and he took his firing as nothing less than an act of patricide. Back in the 1950s, *Life, Look, The Saturday Evening Post,* and *Parade* gave Henry full credit for making Rock a star. But as every parent and child comes to realize near the end, Henry needed Rock much more than Rock needed him. By 1966, Rock not only had no further use for Henry. Henry had turned into a major liability.

"Every time Henry Willson sucks some cock, I get blamed for it," Rock complained to Mark Miller.

As Tom Clark pointed out, Henry's very representation branded Rock as a homosexual not only to the Hollywood community but to the cognizant world beyond. Their association also recalled humble, if not disreputable, beginnings that could best be laid to rest with new representation. "Rock wanted to separate himself from Henry Willson's reputation," said the actor's friend Bob

Preble. "Everyone in Hollywood knew about Henry Willson. That was no secret, and being connected with that did not help Rock's career."

For Henry, it was the end. "When a big star like that leaves his agent," said AP's Hollywood reporter James Bacon, "it can be the death of an agency."

As Henry Willson predicted, *Seconds* bombed at the box office. No one who wanted to see a serious drama wanted to see Rock Hudson in it, and vice versa. If Henry took pleasure in being right, he enjoyed his moment alone. For the movies, 1966 marked a watershed change in public taste: At age sixty-two, Cary Grant called it quits with his final film, *Walk, Don't Run*. Twenty-one years younger, Hollywood's other major playboy figure now had to fight off premature retirement. Henry Willson's taste in leading men was suddenly worse than notorious in Hollywood. It was obsolete.

51

Bel Air Breakdown

Shortly after being fired by Rock, Henry attended a movie premiere—he still got invited to movie premieres—and on his way home from the party, he ran a red light. Too much booze, too many pills, Henry confounded his friends' concerns by driving under the influence with death-defying dexterity. On this particular night, however, he got himself arrested. No sooner did the police officer glance at Henry's driver's license than he laughed in his face.

"So you're the famous starmaker Henry Willson!" the cop began.

There is such a thing as bad luck. And then there is titanic misfortune. Henry knew the cop. Vaguely. The guy was a silly, OK-looking, star-struck kid Henry had seen at the Mocambo or Ciro's years ago, another one of those just-off-the-Greyhound bumpkins who fell for his line "If you've ever considered a career in the movies . . ." Henry neither signed him as a client nor blessed him with one of his fancy names. Most of these losers found their way back to Dubuque or Omaha. This guy, unfortunately, ended up as a Beverly Hills cop.

Henry's injured dignity did not allow him to be taunted by some "napkin actor," he called them, whom he'd tossed aside years ago. His grand impulse was to resist arrest, which was the wrong impulse, and led to Henry's being handcuffed and loaded into the back of the squad car. The cop called him a "drunken old queen," then slammed the car door shut. He would let Henry sleep off his humiliation overnight in the Beverly Hills jail.

But Henry Willson never closed his eyes that night. The jail sojourn instead triggered an emotional spiral downward that did not hit bottom until Henry had been hospitalized. "Henry absolutely freaked," said Pat Colby. "There he was—arrested by this old trick, in jail, wearing his best tuxedo. Henry had just come from a big premiere. It all just blew his mind."

After his release from jail, Henry continued to unravel emotionally and physically. When his DUI made the papers, in the smallest print reserved for such arrests, Henry believed the whole town was talking and refused to leave his Bel Air home. He had long been plagued by paranoia, saying that his phone lines were bugged and that the FBI was out to get him. But now his feelings of persecution pushed him to accuse his housekeeper, True Delight, of stealing his socks and underwear. Three days into his Bel Air siege, Henry refused to get out of bed, much less leave his house, and from between the sheets he guarded his chest of drawers as if it contained his last hit of codeine.

Finally, Pat Colby contacted one of Willson's actors, Clint Ritchie, to help him admit Henry into St. John's Hospital in Santa Monica. The two men spent hours pleading with Henry to sign his own admittance papers to the psych ward. Under state law, the hospital could keep him against his will for only twenty-four hours. With just one hour to go before Henry's mandatory release from St. John's, Colby screamed at his boss, "Sign the goddamn papers! You're sick!" For the first time in his life, Henry did exactly as he was told.

His paranoia, however, found no immediate relief. "Here was this successful agent, accusing the nurses and other patients of stealing his underwear," said Colby.

When sedation did not calm him, the doctors at St. John's saw no other remedy and ordered Henry to undergo a series of electroshock treatments. Colby agreed with the doctors on their diagnosis— "What did I know?" he said—but Henry's friend Nan Morris thought the doctors overreacted. "There was nothing mentally wrong with Henry," she claimed. "Yes, the thing with the cop did freak him out. But Henry had gone without a drink for a few days, and as an alcoholic he was suffering from the DTs."

The doctors told Horace Willson that the shock treatments would cause Henry to suffer temporary amnesia, and his short-term memory could be adversely affected for up to six months. Upon hearing the news, Horace took immediate control of the agency. With his son getting juiced every day at St. John's, only Horace Willson knew what he was doing, and even when he didn't know, at least he had experience running a business. It was more than Henry would ever be capable of again.

After his son's release from the hospital, Horace Willson recommended Henry go on a long ocean cruise. Still dazed from the shock treatments, he asked his father what ocean he might suggest. "That's your choice," replied Horace. Henry thought a moment, but had trouble making a decision. Finally, his father said, "How about the Caribbean?" Henry's face lit up. "Yes, the Caribbean," he said. "I've always liked the Caribbean."

As Horace explained the situation to Pat Colby, "It's best if we keep Henry out of town until he has completely recovered." Horace asked his son's assistant if he might want to make the trip with Henry, but Colby knew that time spent with Henry never qualified as a vacation, and he recommended Chance Gentry for the tour of duty in the Caribbean.

Ever since his historic cruise through the Panama Canal in 1933, Henry had been fond of the sea. He found visits there especially soothing, and a trip to the Caribbean held the nostalgia of an earlier, hope-filled voyage. In the coming months, Henry sent Colby postcards from Trinidad and the Virgin Islands. "I feel like I could sleep 25 hrs a day," he wrote, and signed the cards, "Henry & Dick."

Over the past two difficult years, Horace Willson had loaned Henry much of his life savings to keep the agency afloat. Now, to protect his investment, Horace hired the agent Richard Segel to help run his son's business. Shortly after Henry and Chance Gentry set sail, Horace asked Segel to meet with the lawyer Lud Gerber. "It was a peculiar meeting," said Segel. Exuding the charm of a Prussian general, Gerber let him know, "Henry is not feeling well. He has had some health problem. He'll be going on a long cruise until he recovers."

Segel had never formally met Henry, and he didn't much want to work for him after witnessing his rowdy, late-night behavior at various Sunset Boulevard restaurants. There was also Henry's reputation, now solidified as legend in the Hollywood community, and Segel worried that his own homosexuality would be disclosed if he worked for the notorious Henry Willson. "Gay agents in the 1950s and 1960s always kept it under their hat. We knew each other, of course, but it was best for business that the studios didn't know," said Segel. He had been an agent at several small firms but was now unemployed. As much as he resisted working for Hollywood's most infamous agent, there were the inevitable bills to be paid, so he accepted the offer.

Horace left it to the new agent to chart the agency's new course: Segel recommended that he meet with each client before any news of Henry's mysterious ailment broke out in the press. At least, Mike Connolly could be counted on to manufacture some charade, massaging the facts in his usual style, for *The Hollywood Reporter*. One by one, Segel made the phone calls to set up the individual interviews. Most clients took a minute or two to express their regrets, then proceeded to wonder aloud how Henry's health might impact their careers. They came to the agency to meet with Segel. Only two clients took the grand route and refused to make the trip to the agency's humble second-floor digs on Sunset Boulevard.

Segel drove the half mile to Troy Donahue's house at 1234 Wetherly Drive. It was the Cape Cod structure that he would soon lose when a business manager absconded with all his money. Until that fateful day arrived, Troy continued to host his midday drug orgies there. At least, that's the way it looked to Segel, who discovered the front door wide open and his new client nowhere to be found. He inquired as to the whereabouts of the house's famous owner, but no one knew or bothered to offer a response.

"Finally, Troy Donahue himself appeared. He was completely zonked out of his mind," said Segel. "There were another dozen degenerates hanging about. I was the only sober person on the premises." Segel didn't remain to talk business with Troy. "He wasn't in any condition to carry on a conversation about his career, which was already in shambles," said the agent.

Troy never remembered meeting Richard Segel or any other agent in Henry Willson's employ. "During all those years, I never dealt with anyone but Henry," said Troy.

Gena Rowlands presented a more sedate and only slightly less ungrateful portrait of Hollywood celebrity. "Unlike Troy, Gena met me in the living room of her home," said Segel. "She was terribly grand. John Cassavetes was the fair-haired boy over at Universal in those days. Rowlands wasn't considered much of an actress then, but she obviously knew she had some clout because of her husband."

Over the years, Henry handled female clients who had breakthroughs and became stars, notably Lana Turner, Joan Fontaine, and Natalie Wood, and a few others who achieved a degree of fame, such as Anne Shirley, Marie Wilson, Julie London, and Diane Baker. By the 1960s, however, his knack for picking winners among the female sex had diminished to such feeble attempts at star-making as Anna Capri, whose romantically overwrought name even Henry refused to take credit for. No less an authority than *TV Guide* reported that Henry "complained bitterly that the name was artless, the product of typical Warner Brothers thinking." Another of Henry's hoydens, Anna Capri was best remembered among the Willson yeomen for answering her apartment door stark naked whenever they stopped by to deliver scripts. Henry proclaimed her "Part Turner, part Monroe" and occasionally adjusted her name to read Ahna Capri.

Detractors claimed that Henry stole credit for many of his more sparkling trademark monikers, from Lana Turner to Rock Hudson. Now, such questionable excursions into marquee taste as Ty Hardin and Rip Torn were falsely blamed on the agent. Not that Henry's twilight attempts at nomenclature were any less passé in the groovy decade of play-it-as-it-lays and let-it-all-hang-out.

Henry gave the name Cal Bolder to a highway patrolman who came to him on the recommendation of his agent-friend Robert Raison, who had been stopped for speeding by the cop. Raison took one look at Patrolman E. G. Craver and said, "I know an agent who could get you into the movies." According to the cop-turned-actor, Henry told him that "Cal" was short for "California" and "Bolder" meant "big rock" or "fearless," depending on which way you spelled it. Forty years later, Craver had perfect recall when it came to describing his most impressive attributes. At six foot four and 260 pounds, "I had a 32–inch waist, a 52–inch chest, and 22–inch arms," said the actor. Which made him the perfect Igor in 1966's *Jesse James Meets Frankenstein's Daughter*. Bolder remembered being introduced to Rock Hudson as soon as he signed with the Henry Willson Agency. "We talked about the movie business," he said. Too bad for the oversized Bolder: He arrived a decade before Arnold Schwarzenegger turned the pumped-up action hero into a movie staple.

Darlene Lucht was another 1960s client who benefited from Henry's expertise by snagging bit parts in *Muscle Beach Party, Bikini Beach,* and *Beach Blanket Bingo*. On those occasions when Henry broke away from his all-male claque at Panza's Lazy Susan, Darlene and he made a May-December couple on the Bel Air and bar mitzvah circuit. On one such night, Henry told Darlene the problem with her career. She needed a new sobriquet.

"Nobody will be able to pronounce Lucht correctly," he said. Producing pen and bar napkin, Henry began to scrawl. "I've been saving this one up for you," he let her know.

"He made a very big deal out of it," said Darlene Lucht.

Henry liked the way the name sounded, rolling off his liberally liquored tongue. "Tara Ashton," he whispered dramatically. Darlene could almost hear the paint peeling off the plantation pillars. Her agent proclaimed her new name a winner. "One of my best ever," he said, oblivious to the fact that it would see the light of only one credit roll, for *Five Bloody Graves.*

Henry's only significant female client of the 1960s was, in fact, the recalcitrant Gena Rowlands. She came to him on suggestion of Ray Powers, who had left Famous Artists in the early 1960s to be the actress's manager. He recalled the inspired logic that briefly wedded Gena to Henry. "She was looking for an agent who had few female clients," said Powers. He didn't have to think long to remember the name Henry Willson and his nearly all-male stable. "Gena didn't want any competition within the agency." No problem there from the likes of Tara Ashton or Anna Capri.

Henry and Gena had met in 1962 on the set of the Rock Hudson picture *The Spiral Road.* "And Henry just adored her," said Powers. "She and Cassavetes went to his Bel Air house for dinner one night. They were both very impressed. They found his house elegant, and Henry was quite classy, Gena told me."

Henry secured the actress several TV roles. No longer content making the standard studio movies, she and Cassavetes were looking to finance one of their own films, something defiantly new and challenging, not the usual Hollywood glamour crud. Under Henry's representation, Gena Rowlands made only one movie, the Judy Garland vehicle called *A Child Is Waiting,* which her husband directed. It did not go well. Playing against type, Judy behaved, but Gena did not.

"She got in a fight with her husband and walked off the set," said Betty Butler, who took the irate phone calls from the very concerned execs at Hecht-Lancaster, the film's producers. Rowlands had made the dramatic choice to fly off to Paris, and when Cassavetes followed her, the reconciliation went so well that they quickly returned to Los Angeles to finish *A Child Is Waiting,* give birth to a son, Nicholas, and fire Henry Willson, although not necessarily in that order. Henry's love of the movies was strictly old-school, but in one respect he helped spawn a new wave of filmmaking. By securing her several TV gigs, Henry provided

Gena Rowlands with the income to help finance the seminal Cassavetes film, one that is often credited as the genesis of the American independent-film movement. Rowlands played an aging call girl named Jeannie Rapp in *Faces*.

52

Camelot Before Dying

Shortly after he returned from his Caribbean cruise, a radically subdued Henry Willson followed Rock Hudson to Creative Management Associates. CMA's Freddie Fields and David Begelman offered Henry a one-year contract, with one caveat: he had to sever all business ties to his former star client.

As a fitting valediction for Henry's soon-to-shutter agency, ten clients made the trek over the Hollywood Hills to the nearly deserted Warner Bros. lot. Although few films were in production at the once bustling studio, there was an air of retro expectancy as visitors approached by Mustang or Peugeot from the west. *Camelot* was being filmed, and it would be Jack Warner's last major production as titular head of the company. A few months earlier, on November 14, 1966, Warner had sold his 1.6 million shares, fully one third of all Warner Bros. stock, to 7 Arts Productions for $20 a share. The final price tag came to $32 million, but even that lofty sum wasn't enough for a man of Jack Warner's pride and ego. He wanted to go out in grand style, which meant that he would personally produce the Lerner-Lowe musical at a then-astronomical cost of $14.5 million. And that wasn't all. For King Arthur's mythical castle, he built a replica of Spain's famed Castle of Coca and turned it into the largest set ever erected on his hallowed lot. Like some overstuffed Christmas tree ornament, it burst forth from the fabled studio walls to rise up nearly a hundred feet in the San Fernando Valley, a gaudy reminder of what had once been and would never be again. (Alas, instead of being his grand, final masterpiece, *Camelot* turned into a monumental flop, one that inspired Jack Warner to paraphrase King Arthur, "Uneasy lies the head that wears the toilet seat.")

There in the shadow of King Arthur's plaster-and-plywood castle, Henry met his clients as ten of them made their way through the legendary Warners gate that once welcomed Bette Davis and Errol Flynn. His boys had come to audition for director Joshua Logan, and Henry insisted that both Betty Butler and Richard Segel be there to greet them all. He should have known better, but Henry somehow got it into everyone's head that Logan was auditioning for significant speaking roles that day. "Why else would Josh Logan be here in person if this were just some open call?" he told them. As each client waited his turn, Henry did his usual fussing to comb hair, check teeth, and ask, "How's your mother doing?"

Henry's eyes continued to provide a mirror to his boys, but he no longer knew how to watch over himself. Once an immaculate dresser, he now looked rumpled, askew, disheveled. His tie never stayed knotted, his own hair needed combing, perspiration dotted his shirt collar. Since the shock treatments, Henry let go with fewer witty zingers and instead indulged in sentimental stories from the past. But Henry always said he felt most at home on the Warners lot, and it was no lie. There was his close friendship with Jack Warner's son-in-law, Bill Orr, and Henry kept telling his boys how he had discovered the vice president on his eighteenth birthday three decades ago at the Trocadero. "I can always get my actors a role in a Warner Bros. TV series," he bragged, momentarily forgetting that *Camelot* was a Warner Bros. film and Orr now worked off the lot as an independent producer.

Richard Segel recoiled at the downscale spectacle of Henry Willson and his gaggle. "This was the man who got Rock Hudson *Giant* and Natalie Wood *Rebel without a Cause* at Warners," said the agent. "Henry acted as though these new boys were up for equally significant roles in *Camelot,* which just wasn't the case."

Segel may have been a junior agent, but he knew the scene better than his befuddled boss. Despite Henry's promises to the contrary, Josh Logan cast only small nonspeaking roles that day, and there were literally hundreds of others waiting in line for what was every actor's nightmare: a cattle call. It surprised Segel that Logan bothered to show up for such a minor moviemaking ritual. What Segel did not know is that Logan and Henry shared a similar appreciation of the male anatomy, especially if it were large enough to warrant their attention.

Betty Butler noticed something odd about many of the actors' trousers. "They stuffed their pants," she recalled. "Probably Henry told them to. Josh Logan supposedly liked it."

"That was obscene," said Segel. He swore one of Henry's clients had "put a beach towel down his pants."

For all their sartorial preparations, Henry's boys walked away from the experience empty-handed. Not one of them was awarded even a bit part in *Camelot*. No romping on horseback alongside Franco Nero. No gawking at Vanessa Redgrave's pumpkin-seed wedding dress. Josh and he may have gone "way back," as Henry liked to point out—he had been very successful at placing several well-endowed clients in Logan's sailor comedy *Ensign Pulver* three years earlier—but their future together ended that day on the *Camelot* set.

With his duties done at Warners, Henry closed his Sunset Boulevard agency on April 10, 1967, and moved a few blocks west to Creative Management Associates. Located at 9100 Sunset Boulevard, the tall, recently erected black tower cast a long shadow into neighboring Beverly Hills. Always the fabricator, Henry told the press, "Actually, the deal made with Fields was predicated not on what people I brought over but simply to handle the top talent they already have at CMA, i.e., Rock Hudson and Natalie Wood, whom I started in the business."

Skeptics wondered about the arrangement. Close associates said the powers at CMA feared Henry might carry out his threat to blackmail Rock. According to them, the deal constituted so much hush money—a cash infusion that provided Henry much-needed income while CMA financially weaned him away from the star.

CMA's president, however, expressed a less jaundiced view. "Rock asked if I could do something for Henry," said Freddie Fields. "Rock felt genuinely sorry for him. Henry had been his agent for so many years. Henry was at a point in his career where he couldn't find work. It was done as a favor to Rock." The two men arranged that Fields, not Rock, would make the call to offer Henry a position at CMA. "I liked Henry. And when I made him the offer, he was very grateful," said Fields.

Two weeks after Henry closed his agency, Horace Willson died at age eighty-eight. Henry was now fifty-seven, not a good age to be broke and supporting one's mother. Margaret Willson had recently retired to a nursing home, and bills had to be paid to keep her there. Horace had pampered her as much as he did his son, and the money was now running out. From Long Island, New York, Henry's brother, Arthur, made rumblings about their father's will and came to Los Angeles to collect his share of what remained. "There should be a lot more of it," he told Henry when they divided their father's estate, and he accused his brother of tricking Horace into investing in his money-losing agency. Guilt-stricken, Henry told Arthur not to worry and insisted he pay the nursing home bills for their mother. Before returning to the East Coast, Arthur asked to meet with Henry's assistant Pat Colby.

The visit was as unpleasant as it was memorable. Colby went to Arthur's hotel room where he found Henry's brother in his underwear, seated on the bed, his head in one hand, a highball in the other. It was not his first drink of the morning. Arthur felt that Henry's homosexual lifestyle made him untrustworthy, and he called his younger brother "an alcoholic and a sexual deviant." Arthur did not understand: *he* was the son who got married, raised two kids, and lived a decent life near his parents' home in Forest Hills. But it wasn't enough. Horace and Henry loved show business, and Arthur never cared for the bond that his father and brother shared.

Before Colby left the hotel room, Arthur mentioned suing his brother but never took legal action. One thing about Henry's brother, however, deeply unsettled Colby. "Both Henry and his father had this very proper New England way of speaking. Their grammar was impeccable," he said. "But Arthur spoke with the lowest Bronx-sounding accent imaginable. He just destroyed the English language."

Henry's move to CMA was only seven blocks on Sunset Boulevard from his old office, but it represented a generational change in the way Hollywood made deals and created stars. The dozens of mom-and-pop boutique agencies that once dotted the Strip had gradually given way to a few huge publicly traded corporations like CMA—its shares available on the American Stock Exchange, its annual revenues at $11 million, its consolidated power in Hollywood enormous.

With his pretty boys and their silly names, Henry Willson represented the old, louche Hollywood of yesteryear, a place where one man's fancy got a film made and a nobody could be turned into a star overnight on a whim. To the new number-crunchers at CMA, Henry was nothing more than an atavistic press whore who reeked of minorleague publicity stunts that ran the gamut from foolhardy to embarrassing. Not that the new breed at CMA offered much in the way of distinguished taste and style. Decked out in white Gucci loafers, gold chains, and black safari shirts opened to the navel, agents who had spent little or no time behind the gates of a motion-picture studio now ran the business—and according to Henry, they ran it without care, flair, or regard for the personal well-being of the talent.

Freddie Fields and David Begelman formed CMA shortly after they lost their jobs in the MCA break-up. Unlike Charlie Feldman or Henry in their heyday, they spent little time scouting and developing new stars. CMA wasn't a greenhouse where talent was nurtured and agents waited years for that investment in a performer to pay off. Their business objective for an actor was to make as much as possible as soon as possible, and even if the company's initials earned it the nickname Can't Make a Deal, clients who didn't bring in at least $100,000 a year in commissions found themselves looking for other representation.

Henry took a dozen clients with him to CMA, but few lasted there for more than a month or two. Whenever any of them showed up at the office, they were treated to unguarded sneers and giggles. The CMA agents couldn't resist whispering, "He's Henry Willson's boy," and roll their eyes whenever one of them walked by.

After Troy Donahue's star faded with *Come Spy with Me*, Chad Everett was the only actor on Henry's roster who held any real currency at CMA. In 1966, he and Richard Chamberlain were the sole remaining actors under contract to M-G-M, a studio which once claimed to have "more stars than there are in heaven." By the time Henry arrived at CMA, Chad held the dubious distinction of being M-G-M's very last contract player. But there was hope. The studio was eyeing the dark-haired hunk for its new TV series *Medical Center*, which Henry considered a huge mistake for an actor with such immense movie star potential. "He could be the next Clark Gable," Henry insisted. "Why would he want to do television?" In the end, Chad Everett settled for being the next Vince Edwards.

The man whom Henry named Chad Everett was originally represented by the New York-based agent Bret Adams, who felt his client Ray Crampton needed some West Coast representation to make the big jump to movies. It was 1962.

Henry being Henry, he did what came naturally and suggested a name change. The circuitous route from Ray Crampton to Chad Everett invoked such Henry-rejected names as Geoff Yorke, Chad Colter, Chad Colton, Chad Barton, Chad Everett, and Chad York before Henry went back to Chad Everett. "It was the era of Rock and Tab," said the actor. "At the time, there weren't any other Chads in town. Now there must be five." In time, he regretted not using his real name. "People didn't take me seriously because of that name, Chad. I don't blame them."

Before Everett experienced that epiphany, he put his career in the capable hands of Henry, who said there would be no problem getting the twenty-five-year-old actor under contract at M-G-M. But he warned Bret Adams, "It will take three years to make this kid a star."

"That was 1962," Adams recalled, "and Henry was right to the day." Give or take a couple years.

In the meantime, Henry thought it would be a good idea if he and his newest charge went sailing with Lester Persky on the Long Island Sound. As Henry put it, "To get to know each other better."

"I was very petrified for Chad," said Adams. "This young guy was from Michigan, so square." And very religious. The actor's phone conversation invariably ended with "And God be with you." On Monday morning, Adams asked Chad about his weekend sailing expedition. "It was fun, great weather," said the actor. "But you know, Mr. Adams, I don't know about Mr. Willson."

"What do you mean?" asked Adams.

Chad Everett wondered, "I think Mr. Willson is a homosexual."

"It was sort of like, Chad wasn't quite sure," said Adams.

Henry signed Chad Everett, not to M-G-M but to Warners Bros., where his connections to Bill Orr once again paid off. One-shot appearances on Troy Donahue's TV series *Hawaiian Eye* and *Surfside 6* materialized, and Henry secured Chad a role in Troy's film *Rome Adventure*. Chad would also suffer the indignities of *Get Yourself a College Girl* and *The Singing Nun* before *Medical Center* happened. Perhaps it was psychological that Henry could not be found when it was time to close the TV deal. He always considered a TV-doctor series beneath Chad's talent. "*Ben Casey? Dr. Kildare?* Are they still making those?" he asked in 1968. Henry chose the least opportune time to demand originality of the entertainment business.

With his agent totally missing in action, Chad grew frantic. "Henry was off on one of his trips and could not be reached," said Betty Butler, "and finally Chad had to go with another agent at CMA to close the deal." As a result, Henry lost what turned out to be a lucrative 10 percent of Chad's earnings in the series for the next seven years.

The powers at CMA never had any intention to renew Henry's one-year contract. When it expired in 1969, the agency no longer had much interest in Rock Hudson either. Despite the criticism Tom Clark heaped on Henry, CMA proved far less effectual at handling the actor's career. In his twelve months with the mega-agency, Rock endured the longest period of inactivity in his career and made not a single film. It wasn't until 1971, when he signed with another agency, Citroen Citron, that he enjoyed a true career rebirth with a successful TV series. When Henry heard that news, he could only shake his head and pity what had become of his chef d'oeuvre. Under his representation, he never would have allowed Rock Hudson to make "a piece of TV junk" called *McMillan and Wife*, Henry told friends.

Rock revived his career with the TV series. Henry, however, had exhausted all his options. At age sixty, he opened his last firm, Henry Willson Worldwide Management, in 1969. "But it was a joke," said Betty Butler. After nine years as his secretary, she had no choice but to leave her longtime boss. "I told Henry he couldn't afford me. There was no business. It wasn't fair to take his money."

Deeply in debt, Henry found it difficult to close shop and retire, even when Betty Butler left him and returned to working as an office temp at other agencies. Months after leaving his employ, she went in for a routine check-up with Dr. Maynard Brandsma, the doctor Henry recommended to all his clients and friends. When Butler tried to pay the bill, Brandsma's receptionist waved her away. "Oh, I'll just put it on Henry's account," she said. "That's what we do with all his clients."

Butler insisted otherwise. "No wonder Henry was broke," she said. "He didn't really have any clients, and yet everybody was still dining out on his generosity. The poor man."

53

Mannix for Lunch

By 1972, only the housekeeper True Delight remained in Henry Willson's employ. Instead of giving her a weekly salary, he spent his days bartering with her to cook and clean in exchange for pieces of his valuable antiques and silverware. She turned out to be a much better negotiator than her agent boss.

"I'll give you this lamp if you stay another week," said Henry.

True Delight smiled her angel smile, then shook her head. "I'll work another week for the lamp *and* the end table," she said.

Henry looked everywhere for money and a job. Chance Gentry and John Saxon made loans. So did Henry's old Lazy Susan pal Lucille Ball. There were even vain attempts to salvage his agent career, and Henry tried to call in a few distant favors from actors he once represented. "I remember Henry calling Natalie and me," said Robert Wagner. "He said he was ready to lose his house, and asked if we would lend him some money." The couple expressed their collective regrets but declined a gift or loan.

The man Henry once called "Touch" Connors also heard the Bel Air *cri de coeur* of financial destitution. "We went to lunch. Henry asked if I could get him a job on *Mannix,*" said Mike Connors, who was starring on the popular TV detective series. "Henry said he would do anything." The actor promised to check with his producers at Paramount Pictures, but the studio wanted nothing to do with the formerly respected, now lubricious agent.

Once a stylish dresser, Henry wore a frayed shirt to his meeting with Connors and did not protest when the TV star offered to pay for lunch, even though it had been arranged at Henry's invitation. Henry ordered his favorite drink, white crème de menthe, and proceeded to spend much of his meal complaining to Connors that Rock Hudson had forgotten him. "Henry was not the man I knew from twenty years before. It was sad. All his big clients who he made stars had nothing to do with him," said Connors.

Like any desperate man, Henry did not tell Connors the whole truth. Rock, in fact, had recently lent his former agent $20,000, but the money disappeared within the month. What Rock did not know is that the Stone Canyon house carried multiple mortgages. He felt betrayed, but in one sense, Rock said the $20,000 was money well spent. It freed him from the past. "I don't owe Henry any more," he said.

Henry lost the house to the bank, and after all his bartering with True Delight, there wasn't much left in the way of furniture for his new one-bedroom apartment at 1314 Hayworth Avenue in West Hollywood. The art deco apartment offered a spectacular view of the Hollywood Hills and beyond to Beverly Hills, and Henry spent hours gazing at the cityscape. The view, though, gave him no joy. Most days, it was a painful reminder of the world he had loved and lost. Other times, he felt it had all disappeared: Ciro's had morphed into the Comedy Store. Grungy rock stars now inhabited the Chateau Marmont where Greta Garbo once lived. When Henry left his Hayworth apartment, he tended to avoid the Strip and instead could be seen a block south in his espadrilles, flip-flopping to and from the corner liquor store on Fountain Avenue. It had a simple name: Liquor. Once the connoisseur of such libations, Henry now purchased bottles of wine with screw-on tops and no cork.

In the evening, he carried his mantle of desuetude one block farther south to a bar, the Garden District, on Crescent Heights and Santa Monica Boulevard. Henry luxuriated in these brief nighttime respites from his otherwise plunging fortunes. Among the gay clientele of the Garden District, he continued to invoke the noblesse oblige that once came naturally to him. If the heterosexual establishment of Hollywood thought of him as a pariah—if they thought of him at all—young homosexuals still afforded him the respect due an eminence grise.

For many gay men, Henry Willson was their Hugh Hefner, a flamboyant playboy whose status came wrapped in an intoxicating concoction of money, celebrity, and sexual freedom overlaid with just a twinge of exploitation. He made beautiful boys into stars the way the *Playboy* publisher turned beautiful girls into Bunnies. Patrons at the Garden District thought Henry could still work his bubblegum thaumaturgy on them, and it was a myth he never tried to dispel as his huge frame fought to find balance on a bar stool. After buying thousands of drinks for sailors and soldiers, Henry found the favor returned at the Garden District. He always accepted the firm handshakes of struggling actors who asked him if they possessed star quality and whether the name Clint had been overused. Henry nodded and listened and told them what they wanted to hear and drank his crème de menthe until their cash ran out.

Lack of money took its toll on Henry's fabled sense of humor, but not his bite. At the Garden District, men who bought him drinks wanted to know if it was possible in the new, liberated Hollywood for an openly gay man to be a movie star. On that one point, Henry never bullshitted them. He shook his head and said, "No, absolutely not. It will never happen." The movies were make-believe, and no woman fantasized about making love to a man who made love to men. All of which made Henry laugh. It didn't make sense, as if Hollywood ever did. "There's more homosexuals in the Polo Lounge," he used to say, "than there are in this bar."

Through his old lawyer connections, Henry managed to find "acting" employment for some patrons of the Garden District. Always friendly rivals, Lud Gerber and Harry Weiss became even friendlier business partners in the late 1960s when they started a multifaceted gay business. They called it Huge. "Gerber and Weiss owned bars, clubs, steam baths, an escort service," said Monti Rock III. "They were top of the line in the gay underworld. They were kings."

In 1973, they expanded the Huge franchise to include porno-graphic films geared to the homosexual market. It was the year that the Supreme Court struck down most "community standard" pornog-raphy laws in its ruling, *Miller v. California,* and the two lawyers had the foresight to kick off what would soon become the San Fernando Valley's biggest business: porn films and, later, videos. Gerber and Weiss made a small fortune. Henry, on the other hand, took no money for making the occasional talent recommendation to his old friends at Huge. It was more than a job—scouting talent is what he did. Weiss always said, "Henry Willson has the best eye in the business."

Henry left the Garden District each day when the cocktail hour slid into dinner time and made the trip farther east to Panza's Lazy Susan. Steve Drexel remained true to his original word, but with sincere regrets. "I promised Henry I'd feed him if he ever went broke," said Henry's old client, "and now I'll go broke feeding him."

Drexel never went broke, but he did stop feeding Henry.

In 1974, the former agent left West Hollywood to move into the Motion Picture Country Home in Woodland Hills, the first of his profession ever to be accepted there. "Henry didn't have to be mus-cled in," said his assistant Gary Crutcher. "He had gotten his stars to do so many charity events for the home, they were happy to accept him." William Campbell, husband of John F. Kennedy's old Mafia mistress Judith Exxner, ran the place and "treated Henry like visiting royalty," said Crutcher.

Retired members of the film community entered the home through a variety of programs. Some residents paid a monthly fee that pro-vided board and lodging, as well as medical insurance at the home's hospital. Henry came to the home under a different policy which made him one of its many charity cases.

"Henry hated taking charity," said Betty Butler. It didn't come free: The home required him to sell nearly everything he still owned, including his black Cadillac. Once in residence, he considered the home his Gethsemane, stuck away in the San Fernando Valley and miles away from the cooler slopes of Bel Air and Beverly Hills where he used to live in style and throw the year's most lavish A-list parties. He considered it cruel humiliation to live at the home. How could he know that, in years to come, several of his closest friends and business associates would follow him there? Future residents included agent Richard K. Polimer, Henry's first boss; his agent-friend Robert Raison; casting director Ruth Burch, who had worked as his Selznick secretary; his junior agent Richard Segel; and actor Tom Brown, who offered Henry his first invitation to Hollywood, in 1933.

As a charity case, Henry received an allowance of one dollar a day from the Motion Picture Home. He got it first thing in the morning and immediately converted it into dimes to make phone calls. Fortunately, there was a phone booth in front of his studio apartment, No. 32. Henry would call collect and then wait by the booth for the phone to ring. By early afternoon, after placing his many calls, he would head back to his studio apartment to sit on the bed and watch *The Edge of Night* and *Search for Tomorrow,* always on the lookout for the next handsome unknown he could groom to be a movie star. What he did not live to see was how, in the 1980s, photographers Bruce Weber, Herb Ritts, and Matthew Rolston resurrected his aesthetic of idealized male beauty and used it to sell everything from celebrities to underwear. It was a paradox. Henry hated the gay liberationists "who wear their sexuality on their sleeve," he said, "and tell secrets." And yet, it was their influence in the 1970s that popularized his ethos of man as sex object. Before then, it remained little more than a dirty, gay joke to many heterosexuals.

At the home, life slowed down for Henry Willson, but it was no less hassled. He still feared that the phone had been bugged and the gardener was stealing his socks. Occasionally, Betty Butler would come to visit and drive him into West Hollywood for dinner at the Cock 'n' Bull. "It was one of his favorite places, and when we went there, he would always see people he knew," she said. His former secretary took care of the bill before they entered the restaurant, and she was careful to hand Henry the money in the parking lot.

Over the years, Henry had picked up countless tabs at the restaurant, and he used to energize the room at the Cock 'n' Bull with his delicious gossip and constant table-hopping. Now, old business associates kept the conversation brief out of embarrassment—or worse, they pretended not to notice him when, entering the room, he cast the gloom of his failure. A few even denied that Henry had ever represented them.

Others remembered. Rhonda Fleming was one who paid regular visits to the Motion Picture Home. "She always gives me full credit for discovering her," Henry claimed.

During one visit, the actress asked him, "How did you ever came up with the name Rhonda Fleming?"

Henry thought for a long time, then shrugged. "I have no idea," he told her.

Some chance encounters at the home were less pleasant. Robert Wagner was scheduled to perform at a charity event there one evening when he heard raised voices outside his dressing-room door. "Let me in there!" someone bellowed. Wagner opened the door to find an attendant being chewed out by Henry, as if he were still holding court at Frascatti's patio. Launching into his major-domo act, Henry let Wagner's assistant know, "This character doesn't know that the two of us go way back."

Not yet sixty-five, Henry looked a wreck—bloated, rutilant, disheveled, wheezing, his abdomen swollen several inches beyond his belt. Henry's appearance left Wagner shaken. "He had this huge, really extended stomach," he said. "It must have been his alcoholism."

Ray Powers attended one benefit at the home in the company of a few other agents and managers who had been at Famous Artists during Henry's tenure there. From across the auditorium, Henry managed a curt wave at the powerbrokers. He was alone and seated apart from the home's other residents, as if Henry didn't want to be seen in such company. "Afterwards, we all commented on his being there," said Powers. "It devastated us. Henry Willson at the home! It really made you think about your life."

In 1976, Henry went to see Rock Hudson and Carol Burnett in *I Do! I Do!* The stage musical was playing a limited engagement at the

Huntington Hartford Theater in Los Angeles, and it marked Rock's stage debut after six seasons on the highly successful *McMillan and Wife*. After the performance, Henry offered his congratulations backstage. "And, as we shook hands, we suddenly both realized how far he had come in the last thirty years!" Henry told a reporter.

Privately, it tormented him that his greatest creation never returned the favor with a trip to Woodland Hills, and Henry spoke about Rock as if he were a "disowned child." Henry had reason to get sentimental seeing Rock in *I Do! I Do!* He had taken Roy Fitzgerald to see his first stage show, *Annie Get Your Gun,* on one of their many trips together to New York. Sometime between Ethel Merman's singing "Doin' What Comes Naturally" and "There's No Business Like Show Business," Henry noticed that his date for the night kept squinting at the stage. "Afterwards I got him a pair of horn-rimmed glasses. He became a regular theatergoer."

Whatever Henry meant to him, Rock kept his distance, but only in a physical sense. Just as sons grow to resemble their fathers, Rock could not escape inheriting some of Henry's defining traits: the drunken bouts of depression and violent mood swings, the flair for pool-party bacchanals, and a penchant for youth and beauty, which in middle age bordered on the pathological. "The little uglies have taken over the business!" Rock ranted when Dustin Hoffman and Al Pacino eclipsed his stardom in the 1970s. Henry Willson couldn't have said it any better.

In the company of handsome men half his age, Rock had a tendency to wax on about the good old pre–gay lib days when there was an all-male "secret society." Like his mentor, he took an overly positive view of the past that housed his prime. "Being gay was more fun then," Rock said. "As long as the publicists and press and the studios stood behind you, you could do what you wanted in private." The star forgot how one man, now stuck away in the San Fernando Valley, had watched over him to hire the thugs and make the payoffs that kept the name Rock Hudson in lights on movie marquees and out of the tabloids.

Among his Hollywood colleagues, Rock Hudson continued to

be thought of as the nicest man. Geoffrey Horne met him a second time, years after Henry's misguided introduction of the two men at the Waldorf-Astoria. "Rock could not have been nicer," said Horne. "I did not remind him that we'd met before."

Henry Willson was best left unmentioned. "No, I wasn't discovered," Rock believed. "Nobody is discovered. Ever. Publicity departments loved to say that." He even resented the name Rock. "I hated it. But the agent insisted," he said. "I think I took bad advice."

Near the end, Henry Willson's reputation in Hollywood rested on his having reportedly slept with much of the phenomenally attractive talent he once managed. "Don't do a Henry Willson," young agents were warned. Henry, however, gave somewhat different advice to a young agent, David Del Valle, who came to visit him at the home. "Never fall in love with your clients," Henry advised.

Biographers approached him to write his life story, but Henry resisted telling the tales that publishers wanted, the ones that would engender lawsuits, and, more important, destroy the very fantasies he had worked his whole life to create. Always good with names, Henry did get as far as a title for his autobiography. He wanted to call it *Fooled by Faces, or the Asses I Have Known.*

Henry Willson was not entirely forgotten in Hollywood. Shortly before he died in 1978, Henry's old agent rival Warner Toub was in the process of making Mae West's last and unquestionably worst film, *Sextette.* To complete the spectacle of having an 85-year-old woman romanced by a 32-year-old Timothy Dalton, Toub cast a back-up crew of Regis Philbin, Alice Cooper, Keith Moon, George Hamilton, and Harry Weiss, who played the Don. According to the man known as Mr. Fixit, there was never a good day at Paramount Pictures during the filming of *Sextette.* Chief among the problems was the bevy of male beauties assigned to populate Mae's boudoir. They weren't closeup worthy, in the lawyer's expert opinion, and thinking back to Saturday afternoons around the pool at 1536 Stone Canyon Drive, Weiss was heard to murmur between takes, "Where's Henry Willson when we need him?"

54

Finally, No Name

It was an autumn day in 1978 when Troy Donahue heard the news. The man who made him a star was dying. "Henry at the home? I couldn't believe it!" said Troy.

The actor had recently been immortalized on Broadway by the hit musical *A Chorus Line*. Audiences there laughed along with the line: "If Troy Donahue can be a movie star, then I can be a movie star . . ."

Unlike most days over the past fifteen years, Troy was making a film in the Valley. Years later, he couldn't remember the title, what it was about, or if it ever got released. As he described it, "Just another piece of crap to make rent." A crew member mentioned Henry's illness, and Troy learned that his old agent had been living at the Motion Picture Home for four years. They hadn't seen or talked to each other since Henry closed up his last, short-lived management shop in 1971. "There's nothing else I can do for you," Henry had told him.

Fortified with a few hits of cocaine, Troy decided to make the trip to the retirement community in the Valley. By the time he arrived there, however, Henry had already passed into a coma. There was nothing to do but sit down beside him in his hospital room and hold Henry's hand for a few minutes. "I owed him everything. A lot of people in Hollywood did," said Troy.

On November 2, 1978, Henry Willson died of cirrhosis of the liver. During visitation rites at the Pierce Brothers Hollywood

Chapel, Henry's lawyer Lud Gerber walked into the funeral home and nearly passed out. There in front of him was his old friend, laid out in a black business suit and a white Styrofoam coffin lined with blue nylon. The Motion Picture Home made a practice of keeping burial expenses to a minimum with its charity cases. Before the funeral on November 7, Gerber replaced the Styrofoam coffin with a more appropriate mahogany model.

Obituaries in *Variety* and *The Hollywood Reporter* accurately credited the agent with discovering Rock Hudson, Tab Hunter, Troy Donahue, and Chad Everett but embellished Henry's earliest days in Hollywood: "His career dated back to the early 1930s, when David O. Selznick brought him to the Coast, and he became Selznick's closest associate." The misinformation appeared in both trade papers, and it is likely that Henry wrote the words before his death.

At the funeral, Rory Calhoun, John Smith, and Pat Colby were among the pallbearers. Bill Orr came with his former girlfriend Nan Morris, who had recently lost her husband, Edgar G. Robinson Jr. Rock Hudson sent flowers. Tab Hunter and Troy Donahue did not. Gary Crutcher remembered it being a "very nice turnout of maybe thirty or forty people." Few mourners, however, made the short trip from the Pierce Brothers funeral parlor to Valhalla Memorial Park in North Hollywood. It was there that Henry Willson was buried in the cemetery's far north block of plots called Restland. A peculiar choice of names, Restland lies just beyond the end of a runway at the Burbank Airport where jets zoom a few hundred yards overhead on their way in and out of the San Fernando Valley.

Henry Willson's final resting place held an even greater irony, although one not discovered until a year after his death.

"Henry was big into names," said Pat Colby. And not just the crazy, snappy marquee names he invented. There were also the birthday cakes and the gifts of silver bowls and plates from David Orgell's on Rodeo Drive. Henry always had everything engraved with names and initials. "Henry left a big unpaid bill at Orgell's," said Colby.

At the height of his power in Hollywood, Henry Willson gave *Parade* magazine his line about being a Salvation Army worker at heart. As he explained, "I earn anywhere from $50,000 to $75,000 a year, but I don't have a buck to show for it. Why? Because I'm always spending it on the youngsters."

Considering his reputation, Hollywood insiders must have laughed at the remark when they read it.

But Henry was right. In the end, he didn't have a buck to show for it.

Pat Colby returned to Valhalla cemetery a year after Henry Willson's death to commemorate his passing and to offer another good-bye to his old boss. It surprised Colby that he could not find the grave. Finally, he asked the cemetery's caretaker to look up the name Henry Willson in the mortuary's directory and give him exact directions to the plot. Valhalla is a huge cemetery, and Colby thought he might have confused Restland with another section. After a brief search, the caretaker wrote several numbers on a piece of paper and handed it to him. The note read: lot 3, section 215, curb number 673 in Restland B.

Pat Colby had made no mistake. There under a withered fir tree—three plots in from the cement curb and six feet under—rested Henry Willson, the man best known in Hollywood as the maker of stars and star names. But the plot remained bare except for a few tufts of crab grass.

"There was no money left to buy Henry a headstone," said Pat Colby. "There is no name on his grave."

EPILOGUE
BEST OF FRIENDS

On August 5, 1987, Rock Hudson became the first major celebrity to die of AIDS. He was fifty-nine.

Ross Hunter visited him shortly before his death. Later, when the body of Rock Hudson was carted out of the Castle and into a hearse, the producer of *Pillow Talk* told reporters the star's final words. "Hi, buddy," Rock said, and then he died. Ross Hunter also took the opportunity to tell the reporters assembled in the Castle driveway about Rock's greatest love, Marilyn Maxwell.

"He was devoted to her," said Hunter. "He was very much in love. She was a terrific gal. She adored him dearly." The next day, the *New York Post* summed up the surprising news in its headline: "Pal Bares Rock's Love for Blonde Bombshell."

Tom Clark offered his own defense of his ex-lover's death. "I will go to my grave convinced that Rock got AIDS from contaminated blood during a transfusion," reported Clark.

Even though he had been dead ten years, Henry Willson didn't get off so easily, and the virulent homophobia that surrounded the star's death quickly found its way to him. "I'm so glad Henry didn't live to see that," said Betty Butler. "It would have killed him."

Henry Willson, of course, was already dead. But that fact didn't stop the tabloids from resurrecting him for one last crucifixion. According to their reports, here was the man who had seduced the twenty-one-year-old Roy Fitzgerald into a life of homosexual depravity that ultimately led to the star's death by the gay plague known as AIDS. The walls of one West Hollywood men's room envisioned a perdition worse than any imagined by either the *National Enquirer* or the *Star*: "Why did the notorious homosexual 'agent' Henry Willson lead Rock Hudson 'down the gardenpath'? Inquiring minds want to know. Ludwig Gerber, the gay Bev Hills attny. knows all about it and celebrates it," scrawled the anonymous informant.

The revelation that Rock Hudson had AIDS brought forth an even more notable display of public condemnation. The deceased man's former lover Marc Christian sued the Hudson estate for wrongful endangerment on the grounds that the defendant had carried on a long-term sexual liaison with the actor and had not been notified of Hudson's health status. Even though Christian tested negative for the HIV virus, a Los Angeles jury awarded the twenty-seven-year-old bartender $21.75 million in a landmark legal case. There were those who reviled the decision and some who applauded it. (Superior Court Judge Bruce Geernaert later reduced the award to $5.5 million.) The latter group included Phyllis Gates, who sent a letter of congratulation to the new multimillionaire. According to Christian, he and the former Mrs. Rock Hudson met as a result of that letter and they became friends.

For her part, Phyllis Gates recalled meeting Marc Christian for lunch at a restaurant overlooking the Pacific Ocean. He later called to set up another date, but she politely refused the invitation. "I was worried about the public," she said. "I shouldn't have been. But I was."

NOTES AND REFERENCES

Chapter 1

p. 3   Nicknamed "Henry's boys, . . .": *Academy Players Directory, 1950–1968*; Henry Willson client lists; Selznick Productions client lists, David O. Selznick Archives, University of Texas at Austin.

p. 4   "I use names . . ." Joe Finnigan; "Willson Tags Are Unique," UPI, July 22, 1964.

p. 4   "When you start . . .": Robert Stack to author.

p. 4   He found Robert . . . : Lloyd Shearer, *Parade,* June 29, 1958.

p. 4–5   "The next thing . . .": "John Saxon, *Dramalogue,* March 12–18, 1987, 4.

p. 5   "The acting can . . .": Lloyd Shearer, "He Made Rock Hudson a Star," *Parade,* June 29, 1958.

p. 6   "It's like discovering . . .": Troy Donahue to author.

p. 6   "He smells of milk": Eleanor Harris; "Rock Hudson: Why He Is No. 1," *Look,* March 18, 1958, 48.

p. 6   Frank Rich's obit . . . : Frank Rich, "The Lives They Lived: Pretty Boys," *Sunday New York Times Magazine,* December 30, 2001.

p. 6   "a disgusting person . . .": *Rock Hudson, E!*

p. 6   "a notorious homosexual . . .": Hudson and Davidson, *Rock Hudson,* 45.

p. 6   "He was like the slime . . .": Roddy McDowall to author.

p. 7   "Anyone today who . . .": Robert Osborne to author.

p. 7   "Hollywood's first manager": Dale Olson to author.

p. 7   Lana Turner and Joan Fontaine . . . : Henry Willson client list, David O. Selznick Archives, University of Texas at Austin.

p. 7   Natalie Wood: *Academy Players Directory, 1953–1956.*

p. 7   Gena Rowlands: Ray Powers to author; *Academy Players Directory, 1964–1966.*

p. 7   "Everybody wants to . . .": Nan Morris Robinson to author.

Chapter 2

p. 9   Budget-Pack a frozen-foods . . . : Cecelia Ager, "Rip, Rock, Race," *New York Times,* February 2, 1958.

p. 9   Rock Hudson chose to alter . . . : Eleanor Harris; "Rock Hudson: Why He's No. 1," *Look,* March 18, 1958, 51.

p. 10   "I'd never owned . . .": Oppenheimer and Vitek, *Idol*, 18.

p. 10   Herbert Millspaugh, a retired . . . : Hudson and Davidson, *Rock Hudson*, 44.

p. 10   Tall enough to . . ." Eleanor Harris, "Rock Hudson: Why He's No. 1," *Look*, March 18, 1958, 51.

p. 11   "Ken wanted a . . .": *Rock Hudson, E!*

p. 12   It was endorsed . . . : Hudson and Davidson, *Rock Hudson*, 45.

p. 12   "Henry Willson named . . .": Mark Miller to author.

p. 12   "You can't do . . .": Ibid.

p. 13   "I also saw . . .": Harris, *Look*, March 18, 1958, 54.

p. 13   "Only twice in my . . .": Oppenheimer and Vitek, *Idol*, 22–3.

p. 13   "Henry liked men . . .": Gary Crutcher to author.

p. 14   Rory Calhoun (born . . . : *The Times* (London), May 4, 1999.

p. 14   "As soon as . . .": Unidentified newspaper clip, New York Library for the Performing Arts.

p. 14   "An agent often . . .": Stine, *Stars & Star Handlers*, 209.

p. 15   "You don't know . . .": Richard G. Hubler, *Look*, 1952.

p. 16   Roy accepted . . . : Anonymous sources.

p. 16   "Be older than . . .": Harris, *Look*, March 18, 1958, 54.

Chapter 3

p. 17   As the studio's . . . : Richard Natale, *People*, November 2, 1987.

p. 17   "I had a very . . . .": Lucille Ryman Carroll to author.

p. 17   "He stumbled and . . .": Natale, *People*, November 2, 1987.

p. 18   "Although he cared . . .": John Carlyle to author.

p. 18   "Henry stalked the . . .": Natale, *People*, November 2, 1987.

p. 18   "Henry couldn't believe . . .": Lucille Ryman Carroll to author.

p. 19   "Henry never wasted . . .": Ibid.

p. 19   "Rock had a . . .": John Carlyle to author.

p. 19   "For heaven's sake . . .": Ibid.

p. 20   To help lower . . . : Hudson and Davidson, *Rock Hudson*, 47.

p. 20   "You're a movie . . .": Mark Miller to author.

p. 21   "You don't want Hedda . . .": Joe LeGrasso to author.

p. 21   "You don't drag . . .": Craig Hill to author.

p. 21   "you will soon be . . .": Joe LeGrasso to author.

Chapter 4

p. 25   Born July 31 . . . : Willson funeral program, November 7, 1978.

p. 25   The obit read . . . : *New York Times*, April 25, 1967.

p. 25   Horace L. Willson became . . . : *New York Times*, March 7, 1922; March 9, 1922.

p. 26   In that endeavor . . . .: Sherman, *Note the Notes*, 20.

p. 26   His great-great uncle . . . : Internet, "Uncle Sam's Home Page Project."

p. 26   "His grade-A . . .": John Carlyle to author.

p. 27   Long Island estates . . . : *Variety*, January 23, 1935.

p. 27–28   savvy businessmen who . . . : *New York Times*, July 1, 1936.

p. 28   "He is my favorite . . .": *Variety*, January 23, 1935.

p. 28   "I rode in . . .": Pat Colby to author.

p. 28   "Our home was . . .": *New York World-Telegram,* September 1, 1951.

p. 28   first movie role . . . : *New York Herald-Tribune,* February 3, 1936.

p. 29   "made my father . . ."/"my vacation in . . .": Pat Colby and John Carlyle to author.

p. 29   Asheville School . . . : *Asheville School Yearbook, 1930–1931.*

p. 30   The little cupids . . . : *Variety,* November 9, 1988.

p. 30   William Janney, whose father . . . : *New York Times,* February 5, 1933.

p. 30   Buster Brown Shoes boy Tom Brown . . . : Tom Brown bio, Hal Roach Studios.

p. 30   "I can always . . .": Stine, *Stars & Star Handlers,* 202.

p. 31   out-of-town penance at Wesleyan . . . : Henry Willson bio, Selznick Productions.

p. 31   "Will Rogers never was . . .": *Variety,* February 2, 1932.

p. 31   "Walter Winchell was about . . .": *Variety,* October 27, 1931.

p. 31   Queens-bred touch singer . . . : *Variety,* February 9, 1932.

p. 31–32   Hopkins sisters, Ruby . . . : *Variety,* February 11, 1932.

p. 32   "Another cordial shop . . .": *Variety,* October 30, 1931.

p. 33   The mighty Shuberts . . . : McNamara, *The Shuberts of Broadway,* 163

p. 33   Flo Ziegfeld begged . . . : Higham, Charles, *Ziegfeld,* 211.

p. 33   director Alexander Leftwich . . . : *New York Times,* May 31, 1932; Patricia Ellis bio, Paramount, 1935; Garland, Robert; "Smug Theatre Blamed for Dearth of Talent," uncredited clip from the New York Library for the Performing Arts.

p. 33   "The transition period . . .": Selznick, *A Private View,* 116.

p. 34   Seduced by the . . . : Willson, Henry; "Tom Brown's Buddy," *New Movie Magazine,* September 1933, 42.

p. 34   "Just a few days . . .": Gary Crutcher to author.

p. 34   When Tom Brown . . . : Willson, *New Movie Magazine,* September 1933, 42.

Chapter 5

p. 37   Most studios—M-G-M . . . : Mosley, *Zanuck,* 123–4.

p. 37   "What else was . . .": John Carlyle to author.

p. 38   "He was an . . .": Carol Lee Ladd Veitch to author.

p. 38   Dixie Lee (born . . . : *Citizen News,* November 1, 1952.

p. 38   Cecil B. DeMille wanted . . . : Smith, Frederick; "An Overnight Hit," *Liberty,* June 30, 1928.

p. 39   Fox Film even . . . : McNaught Syndicate.

p. 39   "Miss Carol divorced . . .": Ibid.

p. 39   "And since I'd . . .": *Los Angeles Times,* August 25, 1934.

p. 39   "They were outspoken . . .": Anonymous source.

p. 40   Shortly after the . . .": Pat Colby to author.

p. 40   singer Reine Davies . . . : *Variety,* March 10, 1976.

p. 40   Entitled "Baby Talk" . . . : Henry Willson, "Baby Talk," *Photoplay,* May 1934.

p. 41   No sooner did Sue . . . : *Los Angeles Times,* October 31, 1936.

p. 41   "It was a natural . . .": Linet, *Ladd,* 36.

p. 41   In "Tom Brown's . . .": Willson, *New Movie Magazine,* September 1933, 42, 84.

p. 42   "Lupy's Lousy Lot" . . . : Henry Willson, "Junior Hollywood," *New Movie Magazine,* July 1934.

p. 42   days at the races . . . : *Photoplay,* December 1936.

p. 42   Ginger Rogers's benefit . . . : AP, January 26, 1936.

p. 42   Even more fun . . . : Henry Willson, "Junior Hollywood," *New Movie Magazine,* August 1935.

p. 42   ". . . which sent us . . .": Henry Willson, "Junior Hollywood," *New Movie Magazine,* September 1934.

p. 43   The Puppets included . . .": Henry Willson, "Meet the Puppets," *New Movie Magazine,* 78, January 1934.

p. 43   "Walking to the . . .": Ibid.

p. 44   "Notice how many . . .": Jack Jamison, "Hard Times in Hollywood," *Modern Screen,* January 33, 31.

p. 44   "If I go . . .": Molly Marsh, "She's a Star at 16," *News-Telegram,* 1934.

p. 44   High school attendance . . . : Thomas Hine, *The Rise and Fall of the American Teenager,* 198.

p. 45   "Henry Willson's chauffeur . . .": *Hollywood Reporter,* August 7, 1936.

p. 45   "In Beverly Hills . . ."/"Connecticut house . . .": John Carlyle to author.

p. 45   "My mother and . . .": Pat Colby to author.

p. 46   Ella Mae Fuque . . . : Ibid.

p. 46   "Don't ever live . . .": John Carlyle to author.

Chapter 6

p. 49   Legendary gossip columnist Hedda . . . : *Hollywood Reporter,* June 26, 1935.

p. 50   "The agent profession . . .": Budd Schulberg to author.

p. 50   "Agents . . . were just . . .": Schulberg, *Moving Pictures,* 446.

p. 51   "In order to combat . . . .": *Hollywood Reporter,* April 1934.

p. 52   "There are more agents . . .": Wilkerson, *Hollywood Reporter,* December 1934.

p. 52   "Fade Out for Agents" . . . : *Variety,* January 15, 1932.

p. 52   When the movies . . . : Schulberg, *Moving Pictures,* 446-7.

p. 52   The William Morris . . . : Petrikin, Chris; "Comings and Goings," *Variety,* October 1998, 18.

p. 52   Music Corporation of . . . : Bruck, *When Hollywood Had a King,* 70.

p. 52   astonishing 95 percent . . . : Ezra Goodman, "Feldman's People," *Pageant,* January 1950, 156.

p. 53 $100 licensing fee . . . : Rose, *The Agency,* 70.

p. 53   "When I became . . .": McDougal, *The Last Mogul,* 135.

p. 54   In the 1930s . . . : *Los Angeles Times,* June 13, 1984; *Variety,* June 12, 1984.

p. 54   "It was well known . . . .": Budd Schulberg to author.

p. 54   "Frank Orsatti had . . .": McDougal, *The Last Mogul,* 80.

p. 54   "Who do I . . .": Skolsky, *Don't Get Me Wrong,* 155.

p. 54   "A lot of these producers . . .": *Bette Davis: Benevolent Volcano,* TCM.

p. 54   Two decades later . . . : McDougal, *The Last Mogul,* 257.

p. 54   Columbia Pictures's Harry . . . : Thomas, *King Cohn,* 105.

p. 55   20th Century–Fox's . . . : Mosley, *Zanuck,* 219–20.

p. 55   "The Neck" . . . : Sara Hamilton, "What Is a Strip?", *Photoplay,* November 1933, 24.

p. 55   "When I got . . .": John Carlyle to author.
p. 56   "you can eat . . .": Hamilton, *Photoplay*, November 1933, 24.
p. 56   Coconut Grove, and . . . : Heimann, *Out With the Stars*, 35–6.
p. 56   "They can relax . . .": Pat Colby to author.
p. 56   High-drama negotiations . . . : *Photoplay*, November 1933, 24.
p. 57   Larded Tenderloin of . . . : Heimann, *Out With the Stars*, 105.
p. 57   Darrin's, a redo . . . : Hamilton, *Photoplay*, November 1933, 24.
p. 57   Mrs. Lewis J. Selznick . . . : Thomson, *Showman*, 167.
p. 57   A failed eatery . . . : *Variety*, October 1, 1935.
p. 57   "Now it's a . . .": *Variety*, August 1, 1933.
p. 58   "If Zeppo had . . .": Richard Segel to author.
p: 58   Like the Brass . . . : Petrikin, *Variety*, October 1998, 18.
p. 58   June 1936, as a vice president . . . : *Hollywood Reporter*, July 2, 1936, 8.
p. 58   "It's not right . . .": Ibid., undated.
p. 58   The great Margaret . . . : *Hollywood Reporter*, November 19, 1935.

Chapter 7

p. 59   Junior refused . . . : Junior Durkin bio, Warner Bros.
p. 59   "personal supervision . . .": *Hollywood Reporter*, March 10, 1934.
p. 60   O'Neill's *Ah, Wilderness* . . . : *Hollywood Reporter*, January 31, 1935.
p. 60   "my first and . . ."/"Probably sex . . .": Anonymous source.
p. 60   "late-bloomer . . .": Nan Morris Robinson to author.
p. 60   Together with Coogan's . . . : *Variety*, May 8, 1935.
p. 60   Henry's client Patricia . . . : AP, May 5, 1935.
p. 61   "It came fast . . .": AP, May 5, 1935.
p. 61   Mrs. Coogan grieved . . . : Skolsky, *Don't Get Me Wrong*, 159.
p. 61   "Death always seems . . .": Henry Willson, "Younger Hollywood," *New Movie Magazine*, August 1935, 42.

Chapter 8

p. 65   "Here we are . . .": Gerald Clarke, "Cary Grant and Randolph Scott," *Architectural Digest*, April 1996, 280.
p. 65   1223 North Sweetzer: Paramount photos, *Architectural Digest*, April 1996, 280–3.
p. 65   drag entertainers like . . . : Mann, *Behind the Screen*, 144–5.
p. 66   "floor show in . . .": Heimann, *Out With the Stars*, 73.
p. 66   On July 1, 1934 . . . : Mann, *Behind the Screen*, 141.
p. 66   "long-haired town . . .": Mann, *Behind the Screen*, 154.
p. 66–67 "Cary Grant, Randy . . .": *Hollywood Reporter*, March 1936.
p. 67   "Still he seems . . .": Mark Hughes, "Bachelors By Choice," *Photoplay*, November 1935.
p. 67   "Not even a . . .": Esther Meade, "Still Pals," *Photoplay*, September 1934.
p. 67   "The revulsion against . . .": Chauncey, *Gay New York*.
p. 68   "Margaret Dumont got . . .": *Hollywood Reporter*, November 19, 1935.
p. 68   the Orsattis nabbed . . . : *Photoplay*, May 1937.

p. 68   "Vic Orsatti's idea. . . .": *Hollywood Reporter,* November 8, 1935.

p. 69   "He was safe . . . .": Epstein, *Portrait of Jennifer,* 10.

p. 69   "Her sister, Olivia . . .": Stine, *Stars & Star Handlers,* 212.

p. 69   "I didn't get . . ."/"I traveled east . . .": Marge Champion to author.

p. 70   "There wasn't really . . .": Harry Hay to author.

Chapter 9

p. 73   A dashing, inveterate . . . : Weller, *Dancing at Ciro's,* 86–7.

p. 74 $7.50-a-plate for dinner . . . : Heimann, *Out With the Stars,* 105.

p. 75   "This can all be . . .": John Carlyle to author.

p. 75   Bar and Grill . . . : Heimann, *Out With the Stars,* 105.

p. 75   Out on a date . . . : Charles Champlin, *Los Angeles Times,* June 20, 1966.

p. 75   Every Warner Bros. TV . . . : *Variety,* December 27, 2002.

p. 76   "He was from . . .": Nan Morris Robinson to author.

p. 76   George Sidney was . . . : Willson, *New Movie Magazine,* August 1935, 42.

p. 76   attack of appendicitis . . . : Champlin, *Los Angeles Times,* June 20, 1966.

p. 76   Undaunted, Henry regrouped . . . : William T. Orr bio, Warner Bros., August 25, 1961.

p. 77   "It's got to . . .": Stack, *Straight Shooting,* 119.

p. 77   Billy Wilkerson was . . . : Morella and Epstein, *Lana,* 4.

p. 77   Like most powerful . . . : *Hollywood Reporter,* March 29, 2000.

p. 77   Top Hat Malt . . . : Skolsky, *Don't Get Me Wrong,* 194.

p. 78   "She brought her . . .": Paul Nesbitt to author.

p. 78   "open up": Pat Colby to author.

p. 78   "I think she . . .": Morella and Epstein, *Lana,* 21.

p. 79   "I didn't say . . .": Ibid.

p. 79   "I was looking . . .": LeRoy, *Take One,* 130–1.

p. 80   "I hope I don't . . .": Morella and Epstein, *Lana,* 21.

p. 80   "It's all right": Cal York, *Photoplay,* January 1938, 49.

p. 80   "I was just cute . . .": Marge Champion to author.

p. 80   "Lana Turner's sketches . . .": *Hollywood Reporter,* June 16, 1938.

p. 81   "Lana Turner is . . .": Ibid., December 1, 1937.

p. 81   In 1937, Roy Fitzgerald . . . : *Rock Hudson, E!*

Chapter 10

p. 85   "Dear Mr. O'Shea . . .": Henry Willson letter, Selznick Archives, University of Texas of Austin.

p. 86   "There is absolutely . . .": Daniel T. O'Shea letter, Selznick Archives, University of Texas of Austin.

p. 86   In 1940, the . . . : *New York World-Telegram,* June 23, 1965.

p. 86   "What movie can . . ."/"They were valuable . . .": Selznick, *A Private View,* 239.

p. 86   "Selznick was a flesh . . .": Stine, *Stars & Star Handlers,* 202.

p. 87   "I thought I'd . . .": Shirley Temple Black to author.

p. 87   "We're leaving [Shirley] . . .": Black, *Child Star,* 350.

p. 87   "I couldn't understand . . .": Selznick, *A Private View,* 239.

p. 87	He adapted *Since* . . . : Thomson, *Showman*, 194.
p. 88	"Regardless of what . . .": Selznick, *A Private View*, 217.
p. 88	Selznick introduced the . . . : John Carlyle to author.
p. 88	opium pills.: Pat Colby to author.
p. 88	"Less brains are . . .": Thomas, *Selznick*, 22.
p. 89	"Spend it all.": Ibid., 15.
p. 90	"Veronica Lake is . . .": Behlmer, *Memo*, 307.
p. 90	"the girl standing . . .": DOS memo to HW, November 5, 1947.
p. 90	"Please look her . . .": DOS memo to HW, November 22, 1947.
p. 90	Selznick and Henry . . . : DOS memos to HW; January 13, 1947; March 23, 1945.
p. 91	"There is no expense . . .": HW memo to DOS, October 15, 1947.
p. 91	Selznick expanded on . . ./"Quite seriously . . .": DOS memo to HW, July 14, 1943.
p. 91	"I suggest you . . . : DOS memo to HW, October 26, 1943.
p. 92	"If you walked . . .": Shirley Temple Black to author.
p. 92	"David was, to . . .": Epstein, *Portrait of Jennifer*, 12.
p. 92	"Selznick was a . . .": Rhonda Fleming to author.
p. 92	"I'll punch that . . .": Craig Hill to author.
p. 93	"Some guys just . . .": Troy Donahue to author.
p. 93	The instructors he . . . : Stine, Stars & *Star Handlers*, 207.
p. 93	And there were . . . : HW memos to DOS, December 2, 1943; July 5, 1943.
p. 93	Ingrid Bergman's tour . . . : HW memo to DOS, December, 2, 1943.
p. 93	"My pride and . . .": Shirley Temple Black to author.
p. 93	"Gregory Peck's ears . . .": DOS memo to HW, July 7, 1943.
p. 94	"What is happening . . ."/"sex-appeal favorites . . .": DOS memo to HW, July 6, 1943.
p. 94	month-long engagement . . . : Hine, *The Rise and Fall of the American Teenager*, 231.
p. 94	"I didn't think . . .": Gary Crutcher to author.
p. 94	"Although Ladd is . . .": DOS memo to HW, July 6, 1943.
p. 95	studio's "greatest miss": DOS memo to to HW, August 10, 1943.

Chapter 11

p. 97	"some young director . . .": DOS memo to HW, July 21, 1943.
p. 98	Henry drew up . . . : DOS memo to HW, August 17, 1943.
p. 98	"I frankly want . . .": DOS memo to HW, August 17, 1943.
p. 99	"You take 90 . . .": Thomas, *Selznick*, 198.
p. 99	"I am in . . .": DOS memo to HW, August 17, 1943.
p. 99	"I am pretty . . .": DOS memo to HW, August 19, 1943.
p. 99	"innate dignity . . .": Haver, *David O. Selznick's Hollywood*, 338.
p. 100	"Cromwell was not . . .": Shirley Temple Black to author.
p. 100	"Every studio in . . ."/"I think Clift . . .": HW memo to DOS, October 31, 1944.
p. 100	Indeed, when the . . . : Bosworth, *Montgomery Clift*, 82–3.
p. 100	"Monty wasn't arrogant . . .": Roddy McDowall to author.
p. 101	Myron Selznick had . . ./"I hope that . . .": DOS memo to HW, December 27, 1944.
p. 101	Pat Kirkland, on . . . : Pat Kirkland bio, IMDB.

Chapter 12

p. 103	"I wish you . . . .": DOS memo to HW, October 14, 1943.
p. 103	$100 an hour: *New York Times*, March 28, 1992.
p. 103	$250 a week: *Time*, January 8, 1945, 42.; HW contract, June 28, 1943.
p. 103	"It is a fascinating . . .": Daniel Selznick to author.
p. 103	"Colby is his . . .": *Time*, January 8, 1945, 44.
p. 104	"She was in charge . . .": Jinx Falkenburg, *The Herald Tribune*, January 4, 1950.
p. 104	"You cannot overpower . . .": *Time*, January 8, 1945, 44.
p. 104	Clark Gable and Jimmy Stewart . . . : *New York Times*, March 28, 1992.
p. 104	"Henry would have . . .": Robert Osborne to author.
p. 105	Selznick had loaned . . . : Thomson, *Showman*, 166–9.
p. 105	"My father certainly wasn't . . .": Daniel Selznick to author.
p. 107	Other reporters weren't . . . : Leo Mishkin, *Morning Telegraph New York;* March 18, 1969.
p. 107	"Selznick would ask . . .": Thomson, *Showman*, 168.
p. 107	Zanuck . . . Linda Darnell . . . : Mosley, *Zanuck*, 220.
p. 107	One attempt to . . . : Thomson, *Showman*, 194.
p. 107–8	"I would really . . .": Black, *Child Star*, 356.
p. 108	"If you hold . . .": Shirley Temple Black to author.
p. 108	"David kept expanding . . .": Ibid.
p. 108	"He might have . . ." Thomson, *Showman*, 194.

Chapter 13

p. 109	"really attractive girls": DOS memo to HW, October 18, 1943.
p. 109	Queen of Technicolor . . . : Haver, *David O. Selznick's Hollywood*, 372.
p. 109	named Dare Harris . . . : Anthony Cassa, "John Derek," *Hollywood Studio Magazine*, October 1981.
p. 110	"Some of us . . ."/ : Shirley Temple Black to author.
p. 110	"With a real . . .": DOS memo to HW, July 14, 1943.
p. 111	At Selznick's insistence . . . : DOS memo to HW, June 26, 1945.
p. 111	Janet Gaynor: Stine, *Stars & Star Handlers*, 215.
p. 111	Claudette Colbert/*So Proudly We Hail:* Billips and Pierce, *Lux Presents Hollywood*, 299.
p. 111	Judy Garland/*A Star Is Born:* Ibid., 283
p. 111	Robert Moseley took . . ./"My name is . . ."/ Henry planned to . . . : Arthur Mann, *Collier's,* April 6, 1946.
p. 111	"Guy was Tom . . .": David Del Valle to author.
p. 112	"a place in Hollywood . . .": Heimann, *Out With the Stars*, 202.
p. 112	"You could be . . ."/"Are any of . . . : John Carlyle to author.
p. 113	Henry's old client . . . : "Hollywood's Strangest Love," *Modern Screen*, December 1948, 95; Helen Louise Walker, "What a Guy!," *Photoplay*, May 1944, 37.
p. 113	"If you've got . . .": *Modern Screen*, December 1945, 94.
p. 114	"Chew gum . . .": Ibid.
p. 114	"Guy Dunhill . . .": Robert Aiken to author.
p. 114	"There was the bakery . . .": Stine, *Stars & Star Handlers*, 202.

Chapter 14

p. 115   commissary at 20th . . . : Golden Globes press release, undated.

p. 115–16   Since its inception . . . : Holden, *Behind the Oscar,* 168.

p. 116   A few seats . . . : Selznick, *A Private View,* 221–2.

p. 117   "I always thought . . .": Epstein, *Portrait of Jennifer,* 185.

p. 117   "The biggest Oscar . . .": Wiley and Bona, *Inside Oscar,* 138.

p. 117   "I knew then . . .": John Carlyle to author.

p. 118   "Look at Jennifer's . . .": Epstein, *Portrait of Jennifer,* 12.

p. 118   "I apologize, Ingrid . . .": Ibid., 14.

p. 118   "No, Jennifer, your . . .": Holden, *Behind the Oscar,* 169.

p. 118   "Jennifer Jones has . . .": Thomson, *Showman,* 196.

p. 120   the word "beefcake" . . . : Haver, *David O. Selznick's Hollywood,* 372.

p. 120   In one memorable . . ./"Nowadays, when Guy's . . .": Walker, *Photoplay,* May 1944, 37.

p. 120   Later that afternoon . . . : Gilmore, *Laid Bare,* 34.

p. 120   of Perry Como's . . . : Haver, *David O. Selznick's Hollywood,* 372.

p. 121   "I can't even . . .": Walker, *Photoplay,* May 1944, 37.

p. 121   "sissy"/"grease": John Carlyle to author.

p. 121   "I hope you . . .": DOS to HW, April 26, 1946.

p. 121   Selznick, however, hated . . . : DOS memos to to HW, April 26, 1945; September 19, 1945.

p. 121   He felt Henry . . . : DOS memo to HW, June 21, 1946.

p. 122   "The reaction has . . .": HW memo to DOS, February 5, 1946.

              "His success in . . .": DOS memo to HW, November 24, 1946.

p. 123   "I know that . . .": HW memo to DOS, December, 3, 1946.

p. 123   "I have a . . .": DOS memo to HW, June 26, 1945.

Chapter 15

p. 125   "It will be . . .": HW memo to DOS, July 25, 1946.

p. 125   "My daughter is . . .": Shirley Temple Black to author.

p. 126   Selznick flew into . . . : DOS memo to HW, July 21, 1946.

p. 126   "Bankers' hours . . .": Stine, *Stars & Starmakers,* 204.

p. 126   "I have to . . .": HW memo to DOS, July 25, 1946.

p. 127   "a rather frightening . . .": DOS memo to HW, July 26, 1946.

p. 127   "Henry's engagement? That's an . . .": Keith Andes to author.

p. 127   "It was like . . .": Richard Lamparski radio interview with Diana Lynn, 1971.

p. 127   Born Dolly Loehr . . . : Lamparski, *Whatever Became Of . . . ?* Eighth Series, 186–7.

p. 128   "It sounds like . . .": Richard Lamparski radio interview with Diana Lynn, 1971.

p. 128   Diana and Henry . . . : Dorothy Manners, King Features Syndicate, 1946.

p. 128   Despite his I–A . . . : Selective Service System report.

p. 128   The scarlet category . . . : Kaiser, *The Gay Metropolis,* 28.

p. 129   "Di is my . . .": Gail Russell, "My Kind of Guy!" *Photoplay,* August 1946.

p. 129   In 1949, Guy . . . : *New York Herald Tribune,* August 28, 1961.

p. 129   *Photoplay* played along . . . : Helen Pine, *Photoplay*, undated clip, New York Library for the Performing Arts,

p. 130   "If you have . . .": HW letter to *Hollywood Reporter*, March 29, 1946.

p. 131   "The figures are . . .": DOS memo to HW, December 3, 1946.

Chapter 16

p. 135   "You simply must . . .": DOS memo to HW, November 24, 1946.

p. 135   "vast experience" . . . : HW memo to DOS, November 23, 1946.

p. 136   "You're good-looking . . .": Anonymous source.

p. 136   "strictly one to . . .": DOS memo to HW, April 10, 1947.

p. 136   "broader appeal" . . . : Ibid.

p. 136   "most exciting man": Pat Colby to author.

p. 137   Francis Durgin's hard-core . . . : Rory Calhoun, "My Dark Years, Part One," *The American Weekly*, August 21, 1955.

p. 137   "We went into . . .": Ibid.

p. 137   Then, one day . . . : "Rory Calhoun," *Photoplay*, August 1952.

p. 137   Sue Carol Ladd's . . . : Rory Calhoun, "My Dark Years, Part Two," *The American Weekly*, August 28, 1955.

p. 138   "I was deciding . . .": Helen Louise Walker, "The Life of Rory," *Photoplay*, February 1948.

p. 138   "You don't even . . .": John Carlyle to author.

p. 138   Henry called him . . ." Troy Donahue to author.

p. 139   identical "cookie dusters" . . . : Lauren Tracy, *Modern Screen*, February 1948.

p. 139   "Cary Grant . . .": John Carlyle to author.

p. 139   "He is moody . . .": Walker, *Photoplay*, February 1948.

p. 139   "Henry was well bred . . .": Gary Crutcher to author.

Chapter 17

p. 141   "Rory Calhoun had . . .": Lauren Tracy, *Modern Screen*, February 1948.

p. 141   (As late as . . . : Anonymous source.

p. 142   "Those photographs of . . .": Frank Liberman to author.

p. 143   "You're finished," Cohn . . ./"A virgin!": Calvet, *Has Corinne Been a Good Girl?* 9, 2, 11, 13, 221.

p. 145   "Henry gave Rory . . .": Helen Louise Walker, "Week-End Wedding," *Photoplay*, November 1948, 91.

p. 145   "They went out on three . . .": Jane Withers to author.

p. 145–46 "I was on . . ."/"flattered": Rhonda Fleming to author.

Chapter 18

p. 147   "It was very . . .": Ed Colbert to author.

p. 148   "Henry was very . . .": Pat Colby to author.

p. 148   "He much preferred . . .": Gary Crutcher to author.

p. 149   As Henry told . . ./"The Jaguar . . ."/"Tennessee Williams . . .": Paul Nesbitt to author.

Chapter 19

p. 151   "It is urgent . . . .": HW memo to DOS, December 22, 1947.
p. 152   "David concentrated . . .": Shirley Temple Black to author.
p. 152   The blonde jazz . . . : HW memo to DOS, April 6, 1948.
p. 152   signed Tod Andrews . . . : DOS memo to HW, April 8, 1948.
p. 153   "I think [William . . .": DOS memo to HW, April 10, 1947.
p. 153   "After giving it . . .": HW memo to DOS, April 6, 1948.
p. 153   "I am candidly . . .": DOS memo to HW, July 26, 1948.
p. 154   "I am informed . . .": DOS memo to HW September 24, 1948.
p. 154   "Selznick always needed . . ." Stine, *Stars & Star Handlers*, 212.
p. 154   *Portrait of Jennie . . .*": Haver, *David O. Selznick's Hollywood*, 386.

Chapter 20

p. 159   "Coming from the Selznick . . .": Roddy McDowall to author.
p. 159   "Henry didn't wait . . .": Jack Larson to author.
p. 160   "It is clear . . .": Friedrich, *City of Nets*, 351.
p. 160   "Henry had a . . .": Van Williams to author.
p. 160   "teenagers": Hine, *The Rise and Fall of the American Teenager*, 225.
p. 160   *Seventeen* . . . : Ibid., 232.
p. 160   *American Bandstand* . . . : Ibid, 246.
p. 161   drive-in theaters . . . : Ibid., 235–6.
p. 161   "It was the time . . .": Robert Osborne to author.
p. 161   Whereas Feldman drew . . . : Cameron Shipp, "Portrait of a Hollywood Agent," *Esquire,* March 1947, 124.
p. 161   "Salvation Army worker . . .": Shearer, *Parade,* June 29, 1958.
p. 162   "Rock Hudson was a cross . . .": David Del Valle to author.
p. 162   "smart, feminine, and refined": *Time,* January 8, 1945, 44.
p. 162   On movie sets . . . : *New York Times,* January 3, 1981.
p. 162   He even played . . . : *New York Times,* January 3, 1981.
p. 162   "Raoul was tough . . .": L. Q. Jones to author.
p. 163   "Green but ripe . . .": Oppenheimer and Vitek, *Idol,* 24.
p. 163   Henry and Walsh . . . : Harris, *Look,* March 18, 1958, 54.
p. 163   "Jack Warner had . . ."/"Walsh had him . . .": Jack Larson to author.
p. 164   "He just stood . . .": Robert Stack to author.
p. 164   "I did a screen . . .": Jack Larson to author.
p. 164 $75/$9,000 . . . : Hudson and Davidson, *Rock Hudson,* 47.
p. 165   "One day, Rock . . .": Joseph Pevney to author.

Chapter 21

p. 167   "no-name no-talents": Mike Connolly, *Hollywood Reporter,* March 6, 1958.
p. 167–68 "His handsome features . . .": Willard Wiener, "Charmer for a Nice Fee," *Collier's,* August 6, 1949, 50.
p. 168   By the time Henry . . . : *Pageant,* January 1950, 154.
p. 168   "package deal": Goodman, *The Fifty-Year Decline and Fall of Hollywood,* 152.

p. 168   "I didn't go . . .": *New York Times,* May 26, 1968.

p. 168   In a master stroke . . . : Peter Biskind, "The Superagent," *Vanity Fair,* April 2003, 212.

p. 169   Wasserman's MCA . . . : Bruck, *When Hollywood Had a King,* 185.

p. 169   In 1949, the year . . . : Shipp, *Esquire,* March 1947, 124.

p. 169   Henry landed in . . . : DOS memo to O'Shea and Hungate, February 7, 1950.

p. 169   Valued at $1,800,000 . . . : Wiener, *Collier's,* August 6, 1949, 50.

p. 169   "Warner Brothers needed . . .": Shipp, *Esquire,* March 1947.

p. 169   Bayonne, New Jersey . . . : Biskind, *Vanity Fair,* April 2003, 217.

p. 170   the English-style paneled . . . : Wiener, *Collier's,* August 6, 1949, 50.

p. 170   reading Henry James . . . : Shipp, *Esquire,* March 1947, 47.

Chapter 22

p. 171   One morning, Henry . . . : Stine, *Stars & Star Handlers,* 214.

p. 172   "We gave personal . . .": Ibid.

p. 173   Bo Peep . . . : Ed Colbert to author.

p. 173   "That convict . . .": Soren, *Vera-Ellen,* 134.

p. 173   "He's queeeeeeeer.": Ibid., 135.

p. 174   the Toni Twins . . . : Robert Osborne to author.

p. 174   "Henry was brilliant . . .": Frank Liberman to author.

p. 174   "I couldn't believe . . .": Soren, *Vera-Ellen,* 111.

p. 174   photographers' fete . . . : *Photoplay,* January 1950, 60.

p. 175   sick in bed . . . : Robert Osborne to author.

p. 175   "For years after . . .": A. C. Lyles to author.

p. 175   "The best thing . . .": Soren, *Vera-Ellen,* 135.

p. 175   Ciro's stripper act, a 1951 . . . : *Los Angeles Mirror,* October 22, 1951, 3.

p. 175   "Sex is currency . . . .": *New York Times,* February 6, 1999.

p. 175   her attempted suicide . . . : *Los Angeles Times,* November 1, 1958.

p. 176   "You're the tops!": David Del Valle to author.

p. 176–7 a man of the law . . ./"God, I love . . .": *Los Angeles Times,* November 27, 1957.

p. 176   "Gary Cooper type": Warners archives, Willson letter, October 11, 1955.

p. 177   parade of Marlboro Men . . . : Academy Players Directory, 1954–1964.

p. 177   "I need my . . .": Clint Walker to author.

p. 177   "That's our business.": L. Q. Jones to author.

p. 177   "I just got . . .": Oppenheimer and Vitek, *Idol,* 21.

Chapter 23

p. 179   "Henry came into . . ."/"I never had . . .": John Pipero to author.

p. 180   "Must be the . . .": Ager, *New York Times,* February 16, 1958.

p. 180   "Newman told someone . . .": Mike Connors to author.

p. 182   Born to Armenian . . . : "Mike Connors," *Dramalogue,* July 26–August 1, 1984, 16.

p. 183   . . . he was studying . . . : Mike Connors bio, Warner Bros., June 13, 1962.

p. 183   "You're the young . . .": Ibid.

p. 183   "Against my better . . .": Ibid.

p. 184   "There were days . . .": Quirk and Schoell, *Joan Crawford,* 163.
p. 184   "That Touch Connors . . .": Mike Connolly, *Hollywood Reporter,* November 17, 1952.

Chapter 24

p. 185–7   "Henry had represented . . .": Tony Curtis to author.
p. 186   "Rock and I . . .": Hugh O'Brien to author.
p. 187   "Hollywood forgets who . . .": Stine, *Stars & Star Handlers,* 210.
p. 187   "These kids who . . .": Kendis Rochlen, *Mirror-News,* April 11, 1956.
p. 188   "We used to do . . .": Richard Hubler, *Look,* 1952.
p. 188–9   Robert Aiken was . . . : Robert Aiken to author.
p. 189   Dungg Heep . . . : Goodman, *The Fifty-Year Decline and Fall of Hollywood,* 201.
p. 189   "Wyatt Trash": Connolly, *Hollywood Reporter,* May 11, 1956.
p. 189   "Ben Dover . . .": Tony Curtis to author.
p. 189   "He had an aura": Jack Larson to author.
p. 189   "I often think . . .": Roddy McDowall to author.
p. 189   "I met Henry . . .": Elaine Stritch to author.
p. 189   "It was awful . . .": Farley Granger to author.
p. 190   "Feldman was the . . .": Biskind, *Vanity Fair,* April 2003, 212.
p. 190   "Henry made no . . .": Joseph Pevney to author.
p. 190   "At a time when . . .": Oppenheimer and Vitek, *Idol,* 19.
p. 190   "Henry was obvious . . .": James DeCloss to author.
p. 190   "Henry would come . . .": Dennis Hopper to author.
p. 191   . . . "always denied that . . .": Kaiser, *The Gay Metropolis,* 76.
p. 191   "Anybody who knows . . .": Ibid.
p. 191   "Henry did speak . . .": Gary Crutcher to author.
p. 191   "Hey, Guy Madison!": Author interviews with Pat Colby, Nan Morris Robinson.
p. 191   "Henry Willson had no idea . . .": Betty Butler to author.
p. 192   "Henry had no . . .": Richard Segel to author.
p. 192   "Henry was not campy . . .": Pat Colby to author.
p. 192   "He came off tough . . .": John Gilmore to author.
p. 192   "He had the silhouette . . .": John Pipero to author.
p. 193   "It all begins . . .": McCourt, *Queer Street,* 14.
p. 193   "Big Bill" Tilden: Kaiser, *The Gay Metropolis,* 52.
p. 194   "Rock Hudson and . . ." Mark Miller to author.
p. 194   Kinsey himself . . . : Halberstam, *The Fifties,* 273.
p. 195   "quality" interviews: John Carlyle to author.
p. 195   "I would put you . . .": John Carlyle to author.
p. 195   "Henry had tremendous . . .": L. Q. Jones to author.
p. 196   "Henry aimed too . . .": Robert Fuller to author.
p. 196   fifteen TV shows . . . : *Los Angeles Examiner,* January 13, 1957, 14.
p. 197   "Whatever you do . . .": John Carlyle to author.
p. 197   "Natalie Wood could . . .": Terry Moore to author.
p. 197   Terry added lessons . . . : Dalton, *The Mutant King,* 188.
p. 197   Howard Hughes . . . : Peter Harry Brown and Pat H. Broeske, "Howard's End," *Vanity Fair,* April 1996, 295.

p. 197–8   "Rory and Guy . . .": Terry Moore to author.

p. 198   "There's nothing like . . .": Lloyd Shearer, "He Made Rock Hudson a Star," *Parade,* June 29, 1958.

Chapter 25

p. 201   "Lou loved the . . .": Robert Wagner to author.

p. 201   "The changing expressions . . .": Harris, *Natalie & R. J.,* 7.

p. 201   "At first [Wagner] used . . .": Ibid., 8.

p. 202   "Each agent at . . .": Robert Wagner to author.

p. 202   "Willson took him . . .": Robert Wagner bio, *The Mountain,* August 1955.

p. 202   Tony Curtis, Jack . . . : Author interviews with Tony Curtis, Jack Larson, and John Carlyle.

p. 202   Fox's legal counsel . . .": Contracts, 20th Century–Fox contracts, Fox Archives, UCLA.

p. 202   According to Fox . . . : Letters from Fox to Willson, April 12, 1950; April 18, 1950; March 26, 1952; March 23, 1953.

p. 202   "I was represented . . .": Robert Wagner to author.

p. 203   Clark Gable, Cary Grant . . . : Harris, *Natalie & R. J.,* 5.

p. 203   In 1946, three . . . : Famous Artists client list, 1946–1947.

p. 203   The archetypal stage . . . : Finstad, *Natasha,* 33.

p. 204   "Natalie's mother went . . .": Robert Wagner to author.

p. 204   "Natalie adored Henry . . .": Lana Wood to author.

p. 204   . . . Rock Hudson and Natalie . . . : Academy Players Directory, 1953.

p. 204   "The fan magazines . . .": Lloyd Shearer, "He Made Rock Hudson a Star," *Parade,* June 29, 1958.

p. 205   Beginning in 1953 . . . : UPI, February 23, 1954.

p. 205   "She could have . . .": Finstad, *Natasha,* 96.

p. 205   "Beverly Hills theater . . ." Nan Morris Robinson to author.

p. 205   "The most ambitious . . .": Lambert, *Natalie Wood,* 116.

p. 205   "Once the machine . . .": Mireya Navarro, "I Love You with All My Hype," *Sunday New York Times,* May 22, 2005, E7.

p. 206   "cheapening herself with . . .": Lambert, *Natalie Wood,* 116.

p. 206   "Tab Hunter . . . was . . .": Wood, *Natalie,* 101.

p. 206   "I can always . . .": Natalie Wood bio, Warner Bros., *Rebel without a Cause,* September 21, 1955.

p. 206   "it was pure . . .": Finstad, *Natasha,* 98.

p. 206   Irish claimed . . . : Ibid., 96–104.

p. 207   "I hardly knew . . ." Tom Irish to author.

p. 207   "Debby [sic] Reynolds": Warner Bros. casting file, *Rebel without a Cause,* March 2, 1953.

p. 207   "The big problem . . .": Eisenschitz, *Nicholas Ray,* 243.

p. 208   "she was knocked . . ."/"Nick was having . . .": Dennis Hopper to author.

p. 208   "I also get slapped . . .": Natalie Wood bio, Warner Bros., *Rebel without a Cause,* September 21, 1953.

Chapter 26

p. 209   Crowned Miss Burbank . . . : *Los Angeles Times,* December 28, 1960.

p. 209–10 "My mother was . . ."/"It was raining . . .": Hofler, Robert, "Reynolds Raps," *Buzz Weekly*, December 20–26, 1996, 5.

p. 210   "as a front . . .": Finstad, *Natasha*, 136.

p. 211   "It's a free . . .": Ibid.

p. 211   "Henry would have . . .": Ibid.

p. 211   "Natalie was a . . .": John Carlyle to author.

p. 211   Henry invited Gilmore . . ./ "The obvious inference . . .": Gilmore, *Laid Bare*, 33–7.

p. 212   "Jimmy Dean developed . . .": Roddy McDowall to author.

p. 213   "James Dean was . . .": Gordon Gow, "Actors Always Try," *Films and Filmmaking*, June 1976, 12.

p. 213   "I wanted more . . .": Gilmore, *Laid Bare*, 30.

p. 213   "Raison and Willson . . .": Dennis Hopper to author.

p. 214   Radio producer Rogers . . . : Holley, *James Dean*, 6.

p. 214–15 "good angle . . ."/"Why would they?": Larry Quirk to author.

p. 215   "It was amazing . . .": Fred Winston to author.

p. 215   "These young guys . . .": Nan Morris Robinson to author.

p. 215   "Gay men, straight . . .": Pat Colby to author.

p. 215   "shot at stardom . . .": John Gilmore to author.

p. 216   "He would fix . . .": Van Williams to author.

p. 216   "Your career could . . .": John Caryle to author.

Chapter 27

p. 217   A staunch conservative . . . : Gary Crutcher and others to author.

p. 217   "sexual perverts who . . .": Mann, *Behind the Screen*, 295.

p. 217   "If you want . . .": Halberstam, *The Fifties*, 54.

p. 218   "I am not . . .": Hecht, *A Child of the Century*, 539–40.

p. 218   Jack Warner and . . . : Friedrich, *City of Nets*, 357.

p. 218   "Relief for the . . .": Zierold, *The Moguls*, 190.

p. 218   "He was your . . .": Holley, *Mike Connolly*, 45.

p. 218   "Hollywood's unofficial arbiter . . .": *Newsweek*, February 2. 1954.

p. 218   "Metro-Goldwyn-Moscow . . .": Schary, *Heyday*, 206.

p. 219   "Society for the . . .": Anonymous source to author.

p. 219   "that drunken faggot . . .": Anthony Slide, "Hedda Hopper," *Stallion*, June 1986.

p. 219   "Beware of a . . .": Mike Connolly, *Hollywood Reporter*, January 7, 1952.

p. 219   "My father hated . . .": *Las Vegas Life*, October 1999.

p. 219   insider gossip to . . . : Holley, *Mike Connolly*, 27–38.

p. 220   "Some of the . . .": Goodman, *The Fifty-Year Decline and Fall of Hollywood*, 52.

p. 220   "Our more stable . . ." Connolly, *Hollywood Reporter*, July 2, 1956.

p. 220   Connolly's ultraconservative . . . : Holley, *Mike Connolly*, 60–73.

p. 221   Henry's friend Nan . . . : Nan Morris Robinson to author.

p. 221   "I never made . . .": Hugh O'Brian to author.

p. 221   "Hell, no": James DeCloss to author.

p. 222   "He bought a . . .": Pat Colby to author.

p. 222   "If it ever gets . . .": Ibid.

Chapter 28

p. 223   "Everyone knew Henry . . .": Robert Stack to author.

p. 223   Stack received the . . . : Stack, *Straight Shooting*, 119.

p. 223   "Henry made a . . .": Robert Stack to author.

p. 224   *Dynamite, Exposed, Fame* . . . : Neal Gabler, "Confidential's Reign of Terror," *Vanity Fair*, April 2003, 194.

p. 225–6   "With no appointment . . ."/"The next day . . .": Tom Hatcher to author.

p. 226   "Henry started wearing . . .": John Carlyle to author.

p. 227   "It was a club . . .": Anonymous source to author.

p. 227   "Henry was actually . . .": Pat Colby to author.

p. 227   "Don't ever let a . . .": John Carlyle, Pat Colby to author.

p. 228   "He said our . . .": John Carlyle to author.

p. 228   "I don't ever remember . . .": Pat Colby to author.

p. 228   "Henry tried to . . .": Marc Christian to author.

p. 228   "Henry was a mother . . .": John Carlyle to author.

p. 228–29   D'Orsay, Withers, Kelly, MacDonald . . . : Academy Players Directory, 1950–1960; Pat Colby to author.

p. 228   outside North America . . . : Lamparski, *Whatever Became of . . . ?* 87.

p. 229   "Longhair talent" . . . : Turk, *Hollywood Diva*, 303.

p. 229   "But Henry spent . . .": John Carlyle to author.

p. 231   On March 10 . . . : Turk, *Hollywood Diva*, 303.

p. 231   "He and R. J. . . .": John Carlyle to author.

p. 231   Henry baptized him . . . : Mann, *Behind the Screen*, 351.

p. 231   Navaar signed his . . . : Ibid., 77.

p. 232   "step-brother . . .": Mann, *Behind the Screen*, 351.

p. 232   "The studio is . . .": Hudson and Davidson, *Rock Hudson*, 77.

p. 232   "Everyone treated me . . .": Ibid., 77.

Chapter 29

p. 233   "Rock was far . . .": Halliday, *Sirk on Sirk*, 86.

p. 234   "They thought it might . . .": Ibid.

p. 234   "He was like . . .": Hudson and Davidson, *Rock Hudson*, 77.

p. 235   "I'm the world's . . .": Bill Hudson, "Ross Hunter: The Last Dream Merchant," *Show*, August 1962, 74.

p. 235   Sirk confirmed the . . . : Mann, *Behind the Screen*, 357.

p. 235   "near the middle . . .": Kashner and MacNair, *The Bad and the Beautiful*, 148.

p. 236   "Preposterous!"/"You don't have . . .": Mark Miller to author.

p. 236   "Rock walked in . . .": Anonymous source.

p. 236   In Elia Kazan's autobiography . . . : Kazan, *A Life*, 455.

p. 236   Universal-International promoted . . . : *Variety*, January 3, 1970.

p. 237   "Without Muhl, Rock . . .": Mark Miller to author.

p. 237   "Can you believe . . .": Ibid.

p. 238   "It will take . . .": Anonymous source.

p. 238   "You're an actor . . .": Anonymous source.

Notes and References

Chapter 30

p. 239   October 23, 1954: Letter, George Stevens Archives, AMPAS.
p. 239   "The prize acting . . .": George Stevens press release, *Giant*, November 6, 1954.
p. 240   "Just heard the . . .": Rock Hudson telegram, George Stevens Archives, AMPAS.
p. 240   "I followed him . . .": *Giant* DVD interview.
p. 240   "That was really . . .": Willsmer, *George Stevens' Giant*, 17.
p. 240   "Saturday Mo-somes:": Connolly, *Hollywood Reporter*, November 29, 1954.
p. 240   She instead credited . . . : Truman, *Souvenir*, 270.
p. 241   "Margaret Truman and . . .": A. C. Lyles to author.
p. 241   Mike Connolly's items on Truman and Willson . . . : *Hollywood Reporter*, March 13, 1952; September 10, 1952; March 24, 1953; November 29, 1954.
p. 241   "He often spoke . . ."/"Who wants Harry . . .": Gary Crutcher to author.
p. 241   Two of his . . . : Hudson and Davidson, *Rock Hudson*, 74.
p. 241   "I wouldn't have . . .": Rock Hudson, *E!*
p. 242   "Fans are urging . . .": *Life,* October 3, 1955, 129.
p. 242   . . . over four million . . . : Gabler, *Vanity Fair,* April 2003, 194.
p. 242   "We both went . . .": Rock Hudson, *E!*
p. 242–4   In his efforts . . . /"hefty bonus . . .": Don Crutchfield to author.
p. 244   "We lived in fear . . .": Hudson and Davidson, *Rock Hudson*, 74.

Chapter 31

p. 247   "I went to . . .": Mark Miller to author.
p. 247   "I heard Henry . . .": James DeCloss to author.
p. 247–48   "It was talked . . .": John Carlyle to author.
p. 248   In 1948, Robert . . . : Marc Santore, "Dude's Future?" *New York Times*, February 12, 2003.
p. 248   "He definitely wasn't . . .": L. Q. Jones to author.
p. 248   "Once Rory's story . . .": Shearer, *Parade*, August 5, 1956.
p. 248   "very hush-hush . . .": Bob Thomas to author.
p. 248   Joan Crawford . . .": James Bacon to author.
p. 249   Instead, he spoke . . . : Calhoun, *The American Weekly*, August 21, 1955, 6.
p. 249   "The Rory Calhoun . . .": Connolly, *Hollywood Reporter,* February 11, 1953.
p. 249–50   "Absolutely, Henry fed . . .": Fred Winston to author.
p. 250   "That was the . . .": John Carlyle to author.
p. 250   "Henry never had . . .": Van Williams to author.
p. 250   "I doubt believe . . .": L. Q. Jones to author.
p. 250   "pencil boy": Paul Nesbitt to author.
p. 250   "At that time . . .": Tab Hunter to author.

Chapter 32

p. 253   "good friend and . . .": Dick Clayton to author.
p. 253   credit future producer Ray Stark . . . : *Variety,* December 5, 1984.
p. 254   Working as Henry's . . . : Dick Clayton and Tom Ellis to author.
p. 254   Gelien came from . . . : Bernard Weinraub, "A Star's Real Life Upstages His Films," *New York Times*, September 9, 2003, E1.

p. 254   "I looked at . . .": Stine, *Stars & Star Handlers,* 202.
p. 255   "Art wasn't even . . .": Ibid., 203.
p. 255   "Henry had a way . . .": Hunter, *Tab Hunter Confidential,* 43.
p. 255   "I had to admire . . .": Dick Clayton, "And They Call Him Dreamboat," *Photoplay,* August 1954.
p. 255   "Tab, who was . . .": Ibid.
p. 255   "sage old Uncle Richard . . .": Toni Noel, "But This Kid Was Different," *Modern Screen,* March 1955, 85.
p. 256   "probably not even Tab's . . .": Ibid.
p. 256   "Tell him his . . .": Weinraub, *New York Times,* September 9, 2003, E5.
p. 256   "When Tab finally . . .": Clayton, *Photoplay,* August 1954.
p. 256   "I was so . . .": Ibid.
p. 256   "Using the sister . . .": Hunter, *Tab Hunter Confidential,* 61–2.
p. 257   "Henry Wilson [sic] . . .": Louella O. Parson, "Tab Hunter: The Girl He Will Marry," *Pictorial,* undated, 3.
p. 257   "[Dick Clayton] was always . . .": *After Dark,* March 1970.
p. 257   "I went over . . .": Stine, *Stars & Star Handlers,* 203.
p. 258   Tab started at $500 . . . : Warner Bros. contact, February 1, 1954.
p. 258   "Tab Hunter scrammed . . .": Connolly, *Hollywood Reporter,* September 6, 1955.
p. 258   "That deal for . . .": Connolly, *Hollywood Reporter,* September 13, 1955.
p. 258   Willson letter to Beck: Warners archives, letter, October 19, 1955.

Chapter 33

p. 259   "They were the . . .": Van Williams to author.
p. 259   "I don't think . . .": Mark Miller to author.
p. 259   "Henry was very . . .": Dick Clayton to author.
p. 260   "What Clayton did . . .": John Carlyle to author.
p. 260   "Oh, Dick Clayton's . . .": Pat Colby, Nan Morris Robinson to author.
p. 260   "sleeping Tab . . .": Ibid.
p. 261   "If Henry didn't . . .": Dennis Hopper to author.
p. 261   "Transcript of docket . . .": *Confidential,* September 1955, 18.
p. 262   "A friend of . . . .": Brigid Polk, "The One and Only Tab Hunter," *Interview,* vol. 4, no. 11, 1974, 26.
p. 263   "In fact, neighbors . . .": Anonymous source.
p. 264   "Smile pretty, Tab": Polk, *Interview,* vol. 4, no. 11, 1974, 26.
p. 264   "Everyone reads *Confidential* . . .": Goodman, *The Fifty-Year Decline and Fall of Hollywood,* 51.
p. 265   "At the time it appeared, *Confidential* . . .": Ehrenstein, *Open Secret,* 94.

Chapter 34

p. 267   On August 2 . . . : *Los Angeles Times,* August 3, 1957.
p. 267   "Fred and Marjorie . . .": Goodman, *The Fifty-Year Decline and Fall of Hollywood,* 52.
p. 268   An all-star cast . . . : *Los Angeles Times,* August 3, 1957.
p. 268   O'Hara was the rare . . . : Gabler, *Vanity Fair,* April 2003, 204.

p. 269   "I never had . . .": Polk, *Interview,* vol. 4, no. 11, 1974, 25.

p. 269   "Maureen O'Hara Cuddled . . . : Lee Belser, *New York Journal-American,* August 8, 1957; Florabel Muir, *Daily News,* August 10, 1957.

p. 269   "A sensational scandal . . .": *Hollywood Reporter,* August 5, 1957.

p. 270   After a six-week . . . : Gabler, *Vanity Fair,* April 2003, 204.

p. 270   "His own $100,000 . . .": Warners contract, January 24, 1959, Warners Archives, USC.

p. 270   "The words 'TV series' . . .": Robert Stack to author.

p. 270   "Tab Hunter, actor . . .": *New York Times,* July 10, 1960.

p. 271   "Charges Tab Hunter Beat . . .": *New York Post,* October 14, 1960.

p. 271   Life magazine covered . . . : Alexander, Shana, "Could This Man Beat His Dog?" *Life,* November 21, 1960.

p. 271   its star was cleared . . . : *New York Times,* October 26, 1960.

p. 271–2 "Hey, did you . . ."/"Dick Clayton was . . .": Fred Winston to author.

Chapter 35

p. 275   "A big, big . . .": Connolly, *Hollywood Reporter,* May 6, 1955.

p. 275   The Reverend Nordahl . . . : Gates and Thomas, *My Husband, Rock Hudson,* 83.

p. 276   "You were right . . .": Parsons, *Los Angeles Examiner,* November 10, 1955.

p. 276   Back on the . . . : Carol Lee Ladd Veitch to author.

p. 277   Her wedding had . . . : *Los Angeles Times,* January 23, 1955.

p. 277   "He said I wasn't . . ." *Los Angeles Times,* April 10, 1958.

p. 277   made his next wife . . . : Richard Anderson, Universal Studio bio, February 14, 1964.

p. 277   "Was Rock a homosexual?" Gates and Thomas, *My Husband, Rock Hudson,* 207–9.

p. 278   "A lot of people . . .": Bob Thomas to author.

p. 278   "That was the . . .": Van Williams to author.

p. 278   "When Rock got . . .": Hofler, Robert, "Reynolds Raps," *Buzz Weekly,* December 20–26, 1996, 5

p. 278   "Everyone knew there . . .": Tony Curtis to author.

p. 279–81 "Phyllis was gorgeous . . ."/"Phyllis couldn't tell . . .": Shirley Herz to author.

p. 279   Marion Barbara Carstairs . . . : Summerscale, *The Queen of Whale Cay,* 1–11.

p. 280   "Grid Iron, Cuff Links . . .": Connolly, *Hollywood Reporter,* February 28, 1955.

p. 280   In *Sparrow Lane* . . . : Gates and Thomas, *My Husband, Rock Hudson,* 54, 57.

p. 281   Two of her friends, Bill . . . /"We were open . . .": Gilbert Parker to author.

p. 282   "Phyllis and Rock . . .": John Carlyle to author.

p. 282–4 *Giant* premieres: Warners newsreels, photos, and press releases, Warners Archives, USC.

p. 283   "It was terrifying": Gow, Gordon, "Actors Always Try," *Films and Filmmaking,* June 1976, 4.

p. 284   "Jimmy told me . . .": Dennis Hopper to author.

p. 285   Wedding anniversary: Gates and Thomas, *My Husband, Rock Hudson,* 151.

p. 285   "My mom was . . .": Glen Jacobson to author.

p. 285   ". . . from Buddy Adler . . .": Connolly, *Hollywood Reporter,* November 12, 1956.

p. 285   *Hollywood Reporter* . . . : Holley, *Mike Connolly,* 104.

p. 285   Henry's follow-up . . . : Pat Colby and Gary Crutcher to author.

Chapter 36

p. 287   Long before Edward . . . : Lamparski, *Whatever Became Of . . . ?* 286.

p. 287   "My real talent . . ."/"1950s conformity": Maila Nurmi to author.

p. 288   "I was somebody . . .": Winecoff, *Split Image,* 104.

p. 288   "Mostly he comes . . .": Goodman, *The Fifty-Year Decline and Fall of Hollywood,* 291.

p. 288   In one practical joke . . . : Winecoff, *Split Image,* 111.

p. 288   "Those boys hated . . ." Maila Nurmi to author.

p. 288   Nurmi conceived the . . . : Ibid., and anonymous sources.

p. 289   "The rumor for . . .": David Mixner to author.

p. 289   Weiss was Tab . . . : Polk, Brigid, "The One and Only Tab Hunter," *Interview,* vol. 4, no. 11, 1974, 26.

p. 289   "The top fee . . .": "L.A. Attorney Weiss," *The Advocate,* June 21, 1972.

p. 289   "Harry took care . . .": Anonymous source.

p. 290   "Maila wanted to . . .": Nan Morris Robinson to author.

Chapter 37

p. 291   James Ercolani left . . ./"I left it . . .": James Darren to author.

p. 291   Anglicized as John Saxon . . . : "John Saxon," *Dramalogue,* March 12–18, 1987, 4.

p. 292   "It sounds strong . . .": *Coronet,* May 1960, 14.

p. 292   Googie's, an all-night . . . : Ed Colbert, James Darren, John Gilmore, Nan Morris Robinson to author.

p. 293   Henry spotted the teenage . . ./"Fools go where . . ."/"But Universal was . . .": "John Saxon," *Dramalogue,* March 12–18, 1987, 4.

p. 293   "twelve-year old Sophia . . .": Pat Colby to author.

p. 294   "Henry Willson was . . ."/"You look at . . ." James Darren to author.

p. 295   L. Q. Jones and . . . : Author interviews with L. Q. Jones, Paul Nesbitt to author.

p. 295   Henry invited Hatcher . . ./"Yes, he is . . .": Tom Hatcher to author.

p. 296   "One must admit . . ."/Vidal, more the . . . : Laurents, *Original Story By,* 339.

Chapter 38

p. 299   "I didn't sign . . .": Troy Donahue to author.

p. 299   "Troy Donahue was . . ." John Gilmore to author.

p. 299   "Great cocksucker, tiny . . .": Mark Miller to author.

p. 302–5 Luaia and Fran Bennett/"treating Susan Kohner . . .": Troy Donahue and Eve Johnson O'Neill to author.

Chapter 39

p. 307   "He saw me . . .": Troy Donahue to author.

p. 307   "Rock Hudson was . . .": Robert Stack to author.

p. 307   "He was extremely . . .": James Bacon to author.

p. 308   "Rock Hudson probably . . .": Troy Donahue to author.

p. 308   Actor Van Williams . . ./"Rock trap": Van Williams to author.

p. 309   Willson client Glen . . ./"I think you've . . ."/"Rock wants someone . . .": Glen Jacobson to author.

p. 309   Rock's droit du . . ./"He couldn't believe . . .": Robert Aiken to author.

Chapter 40

p. 311   Henry made a detour . . . : Haymann, *Alain Delon*, 32.

p. 311   "I did it to . . ." Fox, James, "The Delon Affair," *Hello!* 29.

p. 311   the Marcantonis . . . : Ibid.

p. 311   he enlisted in the French . . ./". . . happiest time . . .": Haymann, *Alain Delon*, 32.

p. 312   Delon was wearing a smoking jacket . . . : Ibid.

p. 312   Guardians who let . . . : Ibid.

p. 312   Henry made sure . . . : Walter Hogan, "Alain Delon," *Film International*, April 1975, 66.

p. 312   Delon's arrival . . . : Ibid.; Rode, *Le Fascinant Monsieur Delon*, 26.

p. 313   Later that evening . . . : Walter Hogan, "Alain Delon," *Film International*, April 1975, 66.

p. 313   "Henry Willson signed . . .": Connolly, *Hollywood Reporter*, June 24, 1957.

p. 313   "He was like . . ."/"Look at those . . .": Daniel Selznick to author.

p. 313   "Rock Hudson is the first . . .": Haver, *David O. Selznick's Hollywood*, 398.

p. 314   "If Rock gets . . .": Connolly, *Hollywood Reporter*, January 21, 1958.

p. 314   "I take credit . . .": Haver, *David O. Selznick's Hollywood*, 403.

p. 314   With the previous back-to-back . . . : Ibid.

p. 314   "I wasn't given . . .": Walter Hogan, "Alain Delon," *Film International*, April 1975, 66.

p. 315   "He doesn't have . . .": Anonymous sources to author.

Chapter 41

p. 317   Henry closed shop . . ./Actor signings including London, Smith, Fuller, etc.: Academy Players Directory, 1955–1957; also studio bios; also, Pat Colby to author.

p. 318   "The bulk of . . .": AP, December 26, 1956.

p. 318   Born John Goleanor . . ./"I can't help . . ."/"Roy": John Gavin to author.

p. 319   "Henry was savvy . . .": Pat Colby to author.

p. 319   The *Krairuzan* . . ./"faggot": Anonymous source.

p. 319   "When Charlie Feldman . . ."/"nothing wrong . . .": Ray Powers to author.

p. 320   "Horne's favored to . . .": Louella Parsons, *Los Angeles Examiner*, December 9, 1957.

p. 320   "I can get . . ."/"laundry": Geoffrey Horne to author.

p. 321   "He would not . . .": Robert Aiken to author.

Chapter 42

p. 323   "The Italian had . . .": Gates and Thomas, *My Husband, Rock Hudson*, 211.

p. 323   James Ellroy . . . leg breaker . . ."/"Freddie was the . . .": Ehrenstein, *Open Secret*, 104.

p. 324   "I was hired . . ."/"Star" and "Wife" transcript: Otash, *Investigation Hollywood*, 31–37.

p. 325   According to the Gates . . ./"No, of course . . .": Gates and Thomas, *My Husband, Rock Hudson*, 219.

p. 326   "They had good . . .": Gates and Thomas, *My Husband, Rock Hudson,* 208.

p. 327   "No. You're hearing . . .": Hudson and Davidson, *Rock Hudson, His Story,* 89.

p. 327   "I was set up . . .": Ibid., 98.p. 327   Alimony came to $250 . . . : Ibid., 218.

p. 327   "arranged marriage . . .": Ken Maley to author.

p. 327   "I don't know . . .": Natale, Richard, *People,* November 2, 1987.

p. 327–8   "double standard."/"Phyllis knew Rock . . .": Mark Miller to author.

p. 328   The deal locked . . . : Mark Miller to author.

p. 329   "This couch is . . .": Ken Maley to author.

p. 329   "We caught the . . .": Van Williams to author.

p. 329   "The party was . . .": Gates and Thomas, *My Husband, Rock Hudson,* 219.

p. 329   Postdivorce, she . . ./"And she was . . .": Peggy Hadley to author.

p. 330   "on explicit orders . . .": Ehrenstein, *Open Secret,* 16.

p. 330   Five months before . . . : Harris, *Look,* March 18, 1958.

p. 331   "We rejected the . . .": Oppenheimer and Vitek, *Idol,* 52.

p. 331   "I don't want Rock . . .": Gates and Thomas, *My Husband, Rock Hudson,* 125.

p. 331   "Rock had always . . .": Robert Osborne to author.

p. 332   Wood and Nick . . . : Academy Players Directory, 1957–1958.

p. 332   Henry could take . . . : Norman Brokaw to author.

p. 332   "Quite frankly, this . . .": John Gavin to author.

Chapter 43

p. 333   Lana Turner an old . . . : Turner, *Lana,* 84.

p. 333   "It was different . . .": Morella and Epstein, *Lana,* 23.

p. 333   "There was a . . .": Weller, *Dancing at Ciro's,* 260.

p. 334   "If Henry had . . .": Richard Segel to author.

p. 334   "Henry cared a . . .": Oppenheimer and Vitek, *Idol,* 19.

p. 335   "The name is . . .": John Pipero to author.

p. 335   "If ever you're . . .": Gary Crutcher to author.

p. 335   "If you want . . .": Richard Segel to author.

p. 336   "The restaurant became . . .": Stricklyn, *Angels & Demons,* 118.

p. 336   "That's where all . . .": Richard Segel to author.

p. 336   "Going out with . . .": Troy Donahue to author.

p. 336   "I wouldn't testify . . .": Stricklyn, *Angels & Demons,* 118.

p. 336   Nan Morris recalled . . ./"Talent scout": Nan Morris Robinson to author.

p. 337   "She was kind of . . .": Fred Winston to author.

p. 337   "The opposite was . . .": Nan Morris Robinson to author.

p. 337   "You had to . . .": Troy Donahue to author.

p. 337   An aspiring actor . . ./"Ninety percent . . .": Pat Colby to author.

p. 338   "Henry wanted his . . .": Nan Morris Robinson to author.

p. 339   "You almost landed . . .": Trent Dolan to author.

p. 339   "Hello, I'm Ludwig . . .": John Carlyle to author.

p. 339   Congress: Dennis McLellan, *Los Angeles Times,* December 19, 2001; April 27, 2002.

p. 340   Zizanie de Fragonard/"Boy, did that . . .": Gary Crutcher to author.

p. 341   "John Saxon would . . .": Fred Winston to author.

p. 341   " 'Hey, Pat!' he . . .": Nan Morris Robinson to author.

p. 341   "Don't you have . . .": Troy Donahue to author.
p. 342   "He was very . . .": James DeCloss to author.
p. 342   Guy Lombardo . . . : Pat Colby to author.
p. 342   "And Elvis smiles . . .": Troy Donahue to author.
p. 343   "Sucking cock isn't . . .": Anonymous source.
p. 343   "He preferred straight . . .": Pat Colby to author.
p. 343   "pimp parties": Helms, *Young Man from the Provinces*, 124.
p. 343   Roy Cohn's procurer . . . : Anonymous source.
p. 343   "Do you like . . . ?": Anonymous source.
p. 343   "That's the other . . .": Pat Colby to author.
p. 343   "I thought I was . . .": Stricklyn, *Angels & Demons*, 118.
p. 344   "I got into . . .": Troy Donahue to author.
p. 344   "There was the . . .": Pat Colby to author.

Chapter 44

p. 345   In 1959, two FBI . . . ./"We were coughing . . .": Pat Colby to author.
p. 346   The FBI's dossier . . .": Federal Bureau of Investigation, "Subject: Rock Hudson."
p. 347   "Oh no, they . . .": Paul Nesbitt to author.
p. 348   "I tried to . . .": Gary Crutcher to author.
p. 349   "He phoned a . . ."/"They owed me": Paul Nesbitt to author.
p. 350   "Henry would look . . .": Gary Crutcher to author.

Chapter 45

p. 353   90 million to . . . : McDougal, *The Last Mogul*, 243.
p. 353   Over at Universal . . . : Ibid., 244.
p. 353   In December 1958, Lew . . . : Ibid.
p. 354–56 "I already knew . . ."/"I looked around . . .": Troy Donahue to author.
p. 354   two plaster lions . . . : Sidney Skolsky, *Hollywood Citizens News*, July 20, 1961.
p. 355   On July 28, 1959 . . . : A Summer Place guest list, Warner Bros. Archives, USC.
p. 356–57 "Let's sign him!": Skolsky, *Hollywood Citizens News*, July 20, 1961.
p. 357   "That's when his . . .": Nan Morris Robinson to author.
p. 357   "I never went . . .": Troy Donahue to author.
p. 357   "I remember getting . . .": *Recovery*, September/October 1985.
p. 357   The martinis soon . . . : *People*, August 13, 1984, 95.
p. 357   "I was a movie . . .": Troy Donahue to author.
p. 358   On his first day on the . . . : Pat H. Broeske, *Dramalogue*, undated clip, 21.
p. 358   For every feature . . . : Rose, *The Agency*, 250.
p. 358   In the wake . . . : McDougal, *The Last Mogul*, 285.
p. 358   "Besides, TV is . . ."/"Henry told me . . .": Troy Donahue to author.
p. 358 $3,000 for his services . . . : *People*, August 13, 1984, 90.
p. 359   *Splendor in the Grass:* Troy Donahue to author.
p. 359   "You can play . . .": Ibid.
p. 359   "Warren Beatty": Byrnes, *"Kookie" No More*, 90.
p. 359   Kardell charged Troy . . . : *Los Angeles Mirror*, August 24, 1961.

p. 360   "His home was . . .": Judith Krantz, "The Night They Invented Troy Donahue," *McCall's,* September 1962, 142.
p. 360   Even though *Palm* . . . : Robert Osborne to author.
p. 361   "Take care of the . . .": Clark, *Rock Hudson, Friend of Mine,* 67.
p. 361   "Farty Belcher": Troy Donahue to author.
p. 361   The Justice Department . . .": McDougal, *The Last Mogul,* 287.
p. 362   "Charlie was brilliant . . .": Stine, *Stars & Star Handlers,* 212.
p. 362   "You know Henry . . .": Clark, *Rock Hudson, Friend of Mine,* 67.

Chapter 46

p. 363   2026 Cahuenga/"Henry and Rock . . .": Pat Colby to author.
p. 363   "Henry and Rock . . .": Gary Crutcher to author.
p. 364   "phone call . . .": Betty Butler to author.
p. 365   "The latest Rock . . .": Gary Crutcher to author.
p. 365   "That wasn't unusual . . .": Nan Morris Robinson to author.

Chapter 47

p. 367   Donahue's first wedding . . . : Troy Donahue to author.
p. 368   "eggs benedict . . .": Betty Butler to author.
p. 368   "So is the divorce . . .": Gary Crutcher to author.
p. 368   "I always thought . . .": Eve Johnson O'Neill to author.
p. 368   Jack Warner, Steve . . . : Gary Crutcher to author.
p. 368   "Henry was like . . .": Troy Donahue to author.
p. 368   June 30, 1964 . . . : *Los Angeles Herald Examiner,* September 8, 1964.
p. 369   "You should write . . .": Trent Dolan to author.
p. 369   "The name sounded . . .": Robert Aiken to author.
p. 369   "I thought so.": Ibid.
p. 369   Rad Fulton . . . : James Westmoreland to author.
p. 370   "But we had . . .": Mark Miller to author.
p. 370   Swing: Connolly, *Hollywood Reporter,* August 15, 1961; Nan Morris Robinson to author.
p. 370   "We were at . . .": Eve Johnson O'Neill to author.
p. 371   Such incendiary language . . . /"Henry didn't mean . . .": Paul Nesbitt to author.

Chapter 48

p. 375   "The fairy godfather . . .": Richard Segel to author.
p. 376   Betty Butler looked . . . /"So this is . . .": Betty Butler to author.
p. 376   "He was good . . .": Anonymous source to author.
p. 376   Nick Nolte's mother . . . /Sherry Lansing . . . : Betty Butler to author; Henry Willson client list.
p. 377   "Henry told me . . .": Monti Rock III to author.
p. 378   In August 1965 . . . /"Marie Antoinette . . .": Gary Crutcher to author.
p. 379   . . . 460 other . . . : Friedrich, *City of Nets,* 7.
p. 379   "I just escaped . . .": Gary Crutcher to author.
p. 379   "save 3 suits . . .": Connolly, *Hollywood Reporter,* November 7, 1961.

Chapter 49

p. 381   "She loved him . . .": Jerry Pam to author.

p. 382   "It would be . . .": Richard Segel to author.

p. 382   . . . less than "diabolical" . . . : Clark, *Rock Hudson, Friend of Mine*, 65.

p. 382   "Rock received notice . . .": Mark Miller to author.

p. 383   "He was back . . .": Betty Butler to author.

p. 383   . . . protégé . . . Dick Scholler: Joe Finnigan, "Willson Tags Are Unique," UPI, July 22, 1964.

p. 383   "Chance! Chance! Chance! . . .": Marc Christian to author.

p. 384   "He was dull . . .": Betty Butler to author.

p. 384   "He had absolutely . . .": Richard Segel to author.

p. 384   "Chance had a . . .": Pat Colby to author.

Chapter 50

p. 385   "One day I . . ."/"First by Henry . . ."/No sooner did . . . : Pat Colby to author.

p. 385   "Tom took control . . .": Rock Hudson, *E!*

p. 385   "Henry got lazy . . .": Clark, *Rock Hudson, Friend of Mine*, 66.

p. 386   "Rock will never . . .": Pat Colby to author.

p. 386   "Horace had a . . .": Gary Crutcher to author.

p. 386   "Rock was ready . . .": Betty Butler to author.

p. 387   But later, Rock . . . : Clark, *Rock Hudson, Friend of Mine*, 67.

p. 387   "All you have . . .": Marc Christian to author.

p. 387   "Henry was pretty . . ."/"I'm going to . . .": Betty Butler to author.

p. 387   Hopper's leg man . . . : Rosenstein, *Hollywood Leg Man*, preface.

p. 388   "Swifty had a great . . .": Connolly, *Hollywood Reporter*, April 3, 1959.

p. 388   "*Cover-Up* was . . ."/"subscription to Jaik's . . .": Betty Butler to author.

p. 388   "Bluhdorn"/"Sinatra": *Hollywood Close-Up*, January 21, 1965, 1; December 19, 1963, 1; June 3, 1971, 8.

p. 389   "But the object . . .": Clark, *Rock Hudson, Friend of Mine*, 67.

p. 389   "We were watching . . .": Marc Christian to author.

p. 389   "Rock loved Henry . . .": Pat Colby to author.

p. 389   "Every time Henry . . .": Mark Miller to author.

p. 389   "Rock wanted to . . .": Rock Hudson, *E!*

p. 390   "When a big . . .": James Bacon to author.

Chapter 51

p. 391   Shortly after being . . ./"Henry also freaked . . ."/"It's best if . . .": Pat Colby to author.

p. 392   "There was nothing . . .": Nan Morris Robinson to author.

p. 393   "I feel like . . .": Postcard, Pat Colby collection.

p. 394   "Henry is not . . ."/"Unlike Troy, Gena . . .": Richard Segel to author.

p. 395   "During all those . . .": Troy Donahue to author.

p. 395   "complained bitterly that . . .": *TV Guide*, April 18–24, 1964, 27.

p. 396   Ty Hardin and Rip Torn: Ager, *New York Times*, February 2, 1958.

p. 396   "32–inch waist . . .": E. G. Craver to author.

p. 396   Darlene Lucht/"Tara Ashton . . .": Darlene Lucht to author.
p. 397   "She was looking . . .": Ray Powers to author.
p. 397   "She got in . . .": Betty Butler to author.

Chapter 52

p. 399   November 14, 1966 . . . : Thomas, *Clown Prince*, 279.
p. 399   For King Arthur's mythical . . . : *Camelot*, Warner Bros. press release.
p. 400   "Uneasy lies the head . . .": Sperling, *Hollywood Be Thy Name*, 330.
p. 400   "Joshua Logan . . ."/"This was the man . . .": Richard Segel to author.
p. 401   "They stuffed their . . .": Betty Butler to author.
p. 401   "That was obscene . . .": Richard Segel to author.
p. 401   "Actually, the deal . . .": *Variety*, March 30, 1967.
p. 402   "Rock asked if . . .": Freddie Fields to author.
p. 402   Margaret Willson . . . : Betty Butler to author.
p. 402   "There should be . . ."/"alcoholic and degenerate": Pat Colby to author.
p. 403   American Stock Exchange/$11 million . . . : Rose, *The Agency*, 306.
p. 403   Decked out in . . ./ $100,000 a year: Ibid., 319.
p. 404   "Henry Willson's boy . . .": Betty Butler to author.
p. 404   In 1966, he . . . : Charles Champlin, *Los Angeles Times*, February 23, 1966.
p. 404   By the time Henry . . . : Ibid.
p. 404   "It was the era . . .": Skolsky, Sidney, "Tintypes: Chad Everett," *New York Post*, July 10, 1971.
p. 404   "next Clark Gable . . .": Betty Butler to author.
p. 404   Bret Adams . . ./"It will take . . .": Bret Adams to author.
p. 404   The circuitous route . . . : Champlin, Charles, *Los Angeles Times*, February 23, 1966.
p. 404   "Rock and Tab . . .": Skolsky, Sidney, "Tintypes: Chad Everett," *New York Post*, July 10, 1971, 42.
p. 405   "petrified for Chad . . ."/"It was fun . . .": Bret Adams to author.
p. 405   "Henry was off . . ."/"Henry was broke . . .": Betty Butler to author.

Chapter 53

p. 407   "I'll give you . . .": Anonymous source to author.
p. 407   Chance Gentry and . . . : Gary Crutcher, Pat Colby to author.
p. 407   "I remember Henry . . .": Robert Wagner to author.
p. 407   "We went to . . .": Mike Connors to author.
p. 408   Rock, in fact . . . : Mark Miller to author.
p. 408   "I don't owe . . .": Ken Maley to author.
p. 408   The art deco . . . : Betty Butler to author.
p. 408–9 Garden District/"There's more homosexuals . . .": Anonymous source to author.
p. 409   "bars, clubs, steam baths . . .": Monti Rock III to author.
p. 410   porn films . . . : Anonymous source to author.
p. 410   "I promised Henry . . ."/"Henry didn't have . . .": Gary Crutcher to author.
p. 410   "Henry hated taking . . .": Betty Butler to author.
p. 411   "wear their sexuality . . .": Anonymous source to author.

p. 411   They included Richard . . .": Obits of Richard K. Polimer, Ruth Burch, Richard Segel to author; Tom Brown.

p. 412   "She always gives . . .": Stine, *Stars & Star Handlers*, 215.

p. 412   "How did you . . .": Rhonda Fleming to author.

p. 412   "Let me in . . .": Robert Wagner to author.

p. 412   Ray Powers attended . . . : Ray Powers to author.

p. 413   "we shook hands . . .": Stine, *Stars & Star Handlers*, 215.

p. 413   Privately, it tormented . . . : David Del Valle to author.

p. 413   "The little uglies . . .": Hudson and Davidson, *Rock Hudson*, 138.

p. 413   "secret society" . . . : Anonymous source to author.

p. 414   "Rock could not . . .": Geoffrey Horne to author.

p. 414   "No, I wasn't . . .": Gow, Gordon, "Actors Always Try," *Films and Filmmaking*, 3.

p. 414   "Don't do a . . .": David Del Valle to author.

p. 414   *Fooled by Faces* . . . : Pat Colby to author.

p. 414   "Where's Henry . . .": Anonymous source to author.

Chapter 54

p. 415   "Henry at the . . .": Troy Donahue to author.

p. 415   "There's nothing else . . .": Ibid.

p. 415   During visitation rites . . . : Pat Colby, Gary Crutcher, and Nan Morris Robinson to author.

p. 416   His career dated . . . : *Variety*, November 6, 1978; *Hollywood Reporter*, November 12, 1978.

p. 416   "very nice turn-out . . .": Gary Crutcher to author.

p. 416   "Henry was big . . .": Pat Colby to author.

p. 417   "I earn anywhere . . .": Shearer, *Parade*, June 29, 1958.

p. 417   The note read . . . : Pierce Brothers Valhalla Memorial Park and Mortuary.

p. 417   "Pat Colby returned . . .": Pat Colby to author.

p. 417   "There was no . . .": Ibid.

Epilogue

p. 419   "Hi buddy."/"He was devoted . . .": *New York Post*, October 4, 1985, 3.

p. 419   "I will go . . .": Ehrenstein, *Open Secret*, 167.

p. 419   "I'm so glad . . .": Betty Butler to author.

p. 419   "Why did the . . .": Photographs, Pat Colby collection.

p. 420   The deceased man's former . . . : Martin Kasindorf, *Newsday*, February 18, 1989, 4.

p. 420   (Superior Court Judge Bruce . . . : AP, August 12, 1989.

p. 420   According to Christian . . . : Marc Christian to author.

p. 420   "I was worried . . .": *Larry King Live*, March 2004.

BIBLIOGRAPHY

Bach, Steven. *Dazzler: The Life and Times of Moss Hart.* New York: Alfred A. Knopf, 2001; Da Capo Press, 2002.

Behlmer, Rudy. *Memo from David O. Selznick.* New York: Viking, 1972.

Billips, Connie, and Arthur Pierce. *Lux Presents Hollywood: A Show-By-Show History of the Lux Radio Theatre and the Lux Video Theatre, 1934–1957.* Jefferson, N.C.: McFarland & Company, Inc., year.

Black, Shirley Temple. *Child Star: An Autobiography.* New York: McGraw-Hill, 1988.

Bosworth, Patricia. *Montgomery Clift: A Biography.* New York: Harcourt Brace Jovanovich, 1978.

Bruck, Connie. *When Hollywood Had a King: The Reign of Lew Wasserman.* New York: Random House, 2003.

Byrnes, Edd, with Marshall Terrill. *Edd Byrnes "Kookie" No More.* New York: Barricade Books, 1996.

Calvet, Corinne. *Has Corinne Been a Good Girl?* New York: St. Martin's Press, 1983.

Ceplair, Larry, and Steven Englund. *The Inquisition in Hollywood: Politics in the Film Community, 1930–1960.* Berkeley: University of California Press, 1979.

Clark, Tom, with Dick Kleiner. *Rock Hudson: Friend of Mine.* New York: Pharos Books, 1990.

Curtis, James. *James Whale: A New World of Gods and Monsters.* London: Faber and Faber, 1998.

Custer, George F. *Twentieth Century's Fox: Darryl F. Zanuck and the Culture of Hollywood.* New York: Basic Books, 1997.

Dalton, David. *James Dean: The Mutant King.* San Francisco: Straight Arrow Books, 1974.

Didion, Joan. *Slouching Towards Bethlehem.* New York: Farrar, Straus & Giroux, 1970.

Ehrenstein, David. *Open Secret: Gay Hollywood, 1928–1998.* New York: William Morrow, 1999.

Eliot, Marc. *Cary Grant.* New York: Harmony Books, 2004.

Eisenschitz, Bernard. *Nicholas Ray: An American Journey.* London: Faber and Faber, 1993.

Epstein, Edward Z. *Portrait of Jennifer: A Biography of Jennifer Jones.* New York: Simon & Schuster, 1995.

Finstad, Suzanne. *Natasha: The Biography of Natalie Wood.* New York: Harmony, 2001.

Fontaine, Joan. *No Bed of Roses.* New York: William Morrow, 1978.

Freedland, Michael. *All the Way: A Biography of Frank Sinatra.* London: Weidenfeld & Nicholson, 1997.

Friedrich, Otto. *City of Nets: A Portrait of Hollywood in the 1940s.* New York: Harper & Row, 1986.

Gabler, Neal. *An Empire of Their Own: How the Jews Invented Hollywood.* New York: Anchor Books, 1988.

Gates, Phyllis, and Bob Thomas. *My Husband, Rock Hudson.* New York: Doubleday, 1987.

Gilmore, John. *Laid Bare.* Los Angeles: Amok, 1997.

———. *Live Fast—Die Young: Remembering the Short Life of James Dean.* New York: Thunder's Mouth Press, 1997.

Goodman, Ezra. *The Fifty-Year Decline and Fall of Hollywood.* New York: Simon & Schuster, 1961.

Halberstam, David. *The Fifties.* New York: Random House, 1993.

Halliday, Jon. *Sirk on Sirk.* New York: Viking, 1972.

Harris, Warren G. *Natalie & R. J.: Hollywood's Star-Crossed Lovers.* New York: Doubleday, 1988.

Haver, Ronald. *David O. Selznick's Hollywood.* New York: Bonanza Books, 1980.

Haymann, Emmanuel. *Alain Delon: Splendeurs et mystères d'une superstar.* Paris: Favre, 1998.

Hecht, Ben. *A Child of the Century.* New York: Simon & Schuster, 1954.

Heimann, Jim. *Out with the Stars: Hollywood Nightlife in the Golden Era.* New York: Abbeville Press, 1985.

Helms, Alan. *Young Man from the Provinces: A Gay Life Before Stonewall.* Boston: Faber and Faber, 1995.

Higham, Charles, and Roy Moseley. *Cary Grant: The Lonely Heart.* New York: Harcourt Brace Jovanovich, 1989.

Higham, Charles. *Ziegfeld.* Chicago: Henry Regnery Company, 1972.

Hine, Thomas. *The Rise and Fall of the American Teenager.* New York: Perennial, 2000.

Holden, Anthony. *Behind the Oscars.* New York: Simon & Schuster, 1993.

Holley, Val. *James Dean: The Biography.* New York: St. Martin's Griffin, 1995.

———. *Mike Connolly and the Manly Art of Hollywood Gossip.* Jefferson, N.C.: McFarland & Co., 2003.

Hudson, Rock, and Sara Davidson. *Rock Hudson: His Story.* New York: William Morrow, 1986.

Kaiser, Charles. *The Gay Metropolis.* New York: Harcourt Brace & Co., 1997.

Kashner, Sam, and Jennifer MacNair. *The Bad & the Beautiful: Hollywood in the Fifties.* New York: W. W. Norton, 2002.

Kazan, Elia. *A Life.* New York: Alfred A. Knopf, 1988.

Lambert, Gavin. *Natalie Wood: A Life.* New York: Alfred A. Knopf, 2003.

———. *The Slide Area.* New York: Ballantine, 1959.

Lamparski, Richard. *Whatever Became of . . . ?* Eighth Series. New York: Crown, 1982.

Laurents, Arthur. *Original Story By: A Memoir of Broadway and Hollywood.* New York: Alfred A. Knopf, 2000.

LeRoy, Mervyn. *Mervyn LeRoy: Take One.* New York: Hawthorn Books, 1974.

Linet, Beverly. *Ladd: The Life, the Legend, the Legacy of Alan Ladd.* New York: Arbor House, 1979.

McCourt, James. *Queer Street: Rise and Fall of an American Culture.* New York: W. W. Norton, 2004.

McDougal, Dennis. *The Last Mogul: Lew Wasserman, MCA, and the Hidden History of Hollywood.* New York: Da Capo Press, 1998.

Mann, William J. *Behind the Screen: How Gays and Lesbians Shaped Hollywood, 1910–1969.* New York: Viking, 2001.

Maychick, Diana, and Borgo, L. Avon. *Heart to Heart with Robert Wagner.* New York: St. Martin's Press, 1986.

Morella, Joe, and Edward Z. Epstein. *Lana: The Public and Private Lives of Miss Turner.* New York: Citadel Press, 1971.

Mosley, Leonard. *Zanuck: The Rise and Fall of Hollywood's Last Tycoon.* Boston: Little, Brown, 1984.

Oppenheimer, Jerry, and Jack Vitek. *Idol: Rock Hudson.* New York: Villard, 1986.

Osborne, Robert. *Fifty Golden Years of Oscar: The Official History of the Academy of Motion Picture Arts & Sciences.* La Habra, Calif.: ESE California, 1979.

Otash, Fred. *Investigation Hollywood!* Chicago: Henry Regnery Company, 1976.

Quirk, Lawrence J., and William Schoell. *Joan Crawford: The Essential Biography.* Louisville: University Press of Kentucky, 2002.

Robinson, Ray. *American Original: A Life of Will Rogers.* New York: Oxford University Press, 1996.

Rode, Henri. *Le Fascinant Monsieur Delon*. Paris: Pac, 1974.

Rose, Frank. *The Agency: William Morris and the Hidden History of Hollywood*. New York: HarperBusiness, 1995.

Rosenstein, Jaik. *Hollywood Leg Man*. Los Angeles: The Madison Press, 1952.

Schary, Dore. *Heyday*. Boston: Little, Brown, 1979.

Schatz, Thomas. *The Genius of the System: Hollywood Filmmaking in the Studio Era*. New York: Metropolitan, 1988.

Schulberg, Budd. *Moving Pictures: Memories of a Hollywood Prince*. New York: Stein & Day, 1981.

———. *What Makes Sammy Run?* New York: Vintage, 1990.

Selznick, Irene. *A Private View*. New York: Alfred A. Knopf, 1983.

Sherman, Michael W., and R. Nauck III. *Note the Notes*. New York: Monarch Record Enterprises, 1998.

Skolsky, Sidney. *Don't Get Me Wrong—I Love Hollywood*. New York: G. P. Putnam's Sons, 1975.

Soren, David. *Vera-Ellen: The Magic and the Mystery*. New York: McGraw-Hill, 1999.

Sperling, Cass Warner, and Cork Millner. *Hollywood Be Thy Name: The Warner Brothers Story*. Rocklin, Calif.: Prima Publishing, 1994.

Stack, Robert. *Straight Shooting*. New York: Macmillan, 1980.

Stine, Whitney. *Stars & Star Handlers*. Santa Monica, Calif.: Roundtable Publishing, 1985.

Stricklyn, Ray. *Angels & Demons: One Actor's Hollywood Journey*. Los Angeles: Belle Publishing, 1996.

Summerscale, Kate. *The Queen of Whale Cay*. London: Fourth Estate, 1997.

Thomas, Bob. *Clown Prince of Hollywood: The Antic Life and Times of Jack L. Warner*. New York: McGraw-Hill, 1990.

Thomas, Bob. *Joan Crawford*. New York: Simon and Schuster, 1978.

———. *Selznick*. New York: Doubleday, 1970.

Thomson, David. *Showman: The Life of David O. Selznick.* New York: Alfred A. Knopf, 1992.

Truman, Margaret. *Souvenir: Margaret Truman's Own Story.* New York: McGraw-Hill, 1956.

Turk, Edward Baron. *Hollywood Diva: A Biography of Jeanette MacDonald.* Berkeley: University of California Press, 1998.

Turner, Lana. *Lana: The Lady, the Legend, the Truth.* New York: Dutton, 1982.

Vidal, Gore. *Myra Breckinridge.* Boston: Little, Brown, 1968.

Weller, Sheila. *Dancing at Ciro's.* New York: St. Martin's Press, 2003.

Wiley, Mason, and Damien Bona. *Inside Oscar.* New York: Ballantine, 1996.

Willsmer, Trevor. *George Stevens'* Giant. Burbank: Warner Bros., 2000.

Winecoff, Charles. *Split Image. The Life of Anthony Perkins.* New York: Dutton, 1996.

Wood, Lana. *Natalie: A Memoir by Her Sister.* New York: G. P. Putnam's Sons, 1984.
Yagoda, Ben. *Will Rogers: A Biography.* New York: Alfred A. Knopf, 1993.

Zierold, Norman. *The Moguls.* New York: Coward, McCann, 1969.

INDEX

Index

Index